THE DRAWINGS OF
ANDREA PALLADIO

EX LIBRIS

M. G.

LAVIN

MICHAEL GRAVES '87

ANDREA
PALLADIO
ARCHITEÑO
VICENTINO.
1576.

THE DRAWINGS OF
ANDREA PALLADIO

DOUGLAS LEWIS

ORGANIZED AND CIRCULATED BY THE
INTERNATIONAL EXHIBITIONS FOUNDATION
WASHINGTON, D.C.
1981–1982

This project is supported by an indemnity from the Federal Council
on the Arts and the Humanities, by a grant from the National
Endowment for the Arts, and by a grant from Fiat S.p.A./Turin,
Italy. The catalogue is underwritten in part by The Andrew W.
Mellon Foundation.

Printed for the International Exhibitions Foundation
by Schneidereith & Sons, Baltimore, Maryland
Designed at The Hollow Press by Alex and Caroline Castro
Special Consultant: Washington Corporative Arts, Inc.

Cover Illustration: Cat. No. 37

Contents

PARTICIPATING MUSEUMS

NATIONAL GALLERY OF ART
WASHINGTON, D.C.

THE ART INSTITUTE OF CHICAGO
CHICAGO, ILLINOIS

THE WILLIAM HAYES ACKLAND
MEMORIAL ART CENTER
THE UNIVERSITY OF NORTH CAROLINA
AT CHAPEL HILL
CHAPEL HILL, NORTH CAROLINA

SAN ANTONIO MUSEUM OF ART
SAN ANTONIO, TEXAS

FOGG ART MUSEUM
HARVARD UNIVERSITY
CAMBRIDGE, MASSACHUSETTS

BROOKS MEMORIAL ART GALLERY
MEMPHIS, TENNESSEE

LENDERS TO THE EXHIBITION

BIBLIOTECA CIVICA BERTOLIANA, VICENZA

BIBLIOTECA COMUNALE, TREVISO

BIBLIOTECA NAZIONALE BRAIDENSE, MILAN

CENTRO INTERNAZIONALE DI STUDI DI
ARCHITETTURA "ANDREA PALLADIO,"
VICENZA (CISA)

CORNELL UNIVERSITY LIBRARY

COLLECTION OF PHYLLIS LAMBERT, ON LOAN TO
CANADIAN CENTRE FOR ARCHITECTURE

THE LIBRARY OF CONGRESS, WASHINGTON, D.C.

MUSEO CIVICO, VICENZA

MUSEO CIVICO CORRER, VENICE

THE PIERPONT MORGAN LIBRARY, NEW YORK

ROYAL INSTITUTE OF BRITISH ARCHITECTS,
LONDON (RIBA)

THE RUSKIN SCHOOL OF DRAWING AND FINE ART,
UNIVERSITY OF OXFORD

SZÉPMÜVÉSZETI MÚZEUM, BUDAPEST

THE TRUSTEES OF THE CHATSWORTH SETTLEMENT

VICTORIA AND ALBERT MUSEUM, LONDON

THE PROVOST AND FELLOWS OF WORCESTER
COLLEGE, OXFORD

The exhibition is supplemented by
additional loans from the following:

AMERICAN INSTITUTE OF ARCHITECTS LIBRARY

VISITORS OF THE ASHMOLEAN MUSEUM, OXFORD

THE GARDEN LIBRARY, DUMBARTON OAKS

GARRETT LIBRARY, THE JOHNS HOPKINS UNIVERSITY

JOHN HARRIS

Note: The following drawings are restricted to showing
only at the National Gallery of Art: Cat. nos. 1, 5, 14, 22,
25, 26, 29, 31, 36, 37, 55, 69, 70, 101, 103, 107, 109, 111,
112, 119 and 129.

Acknowledgments

"The Drawings of Andrea Palladio" marks the culmination of more than three years of close collaboration between the International Exhibitions Foundation and Dr. Douglas Lewis, Curator of Sculpture at the National Gallery of Art. As a member of the Advisory Council of the Palladian Center in Vicenza, Dr. Lewis has devoted countless hours to the study and understanding of this Renaissance master to create for us an exhibition which, in both its scope and content, represents an important contribution to art historical scholarship, and we are deeply in his debt.

Never before has such a comprehensive selection of Palladio drawings been assembled for exhibition in America, and this could not have been achieved without the generous cooperation of many lenders. We particularly wish to thank Mr. John Harris of the Royal Institute of British Architects for agreeing to lend more than 90 drawings which comprise the main body of the exhibition, and which have been restored through the generosity of the Leche Trust. In addition, unprecedented loans from Italy have greatly enhanced the scholarly significance of this show, and we are extremely pleased to extend our most sincere thanks to the following institutions: Museo Civico (Pinacoteca) di Vicenza; Biblioteca Nazionale Braidense, Milan; Biblioteca Civica Bertoliana, Vicenza; Biblioteca Comunale, Treviso; Museo Civico Correr, Venice, and the Centro Internazionale di Studi di Architettura "Andrea Palladio," Vicenza. Finally, we gratefully acknowledge the generosity of the Trustees of the Chatsworth Settlement and other lenders in Great Britain and North America.

The approval for the Italian loans was obtained through the invaluable assistance of His Excellency Paolo Pansa Cedronio, Ambassador of Italy and the honorary patron of our tour. He and the Cultural Attaché of the Embassy, Professor Piergiuseppe Bozzetti, together with Minister Sergio Romano, Director of Cultural, Scientific and Technical Cooperation at the Ministry of Foreign Affairs in Rome, have given unstintingly of their time and expertise to aid us in our loan negotiations. Mrs. Marisa Diaz of the Cultural Attaché's office has also been most helpful. Our warm appreciation is extended to all of them.

Exhibition projects of this magnitude nearly always require financial support, and we have been fortunate to obtain it from several sources. It is a pleasure to acknowledge the grant received from the National Endowment for the Arts, and the indemnity approved by the Federal Council on the Arts and the Humanities. We are also grateful to Fiat S.p.A./Turin, Italy for its generous corporate sponsorship. Finally, we once again wish to thank The Andrew W. Mellon Foundation for funds in support of this publication.

Our colleagues at the participating museums, especially those at the National Gallery of Art, have been helpful and cooperative throughout the long months of preparation, and we are most grateful to them. We also appreciate the work of our designer and printer in the production of the catalogue, and to Alex and Caroline Castro of The Hollow Press, and Tom Phillips of Schneidereith & Sons we extend our heartfelt thanks. Our editor, Taffy Swandby, deserves very special mention for her painstaking supervision of all phases of the catalogue production. Finally, the staff of the International Exhibitions Foundation, notably Heidi von Kann and Christina Flocken, are to be commended for their fine performance in handling the myriad practical details involved in organizing and preparing this exhibition for its American tour.

Annemarie H. Pope
President
International Exhibitions Foundation

Author's Acknowledgments

To the memory of my Palladian preceptors

Rudolf Wittkower (1901–1971)
Ludwig Heinrich Heydenreich (1902–1978)

I feel myself, alas, far behind in my knowledge, but at least I know the way. Palladio has opened it to me, and the way to all art and life as well.

—Johann Wolfgang von Goethe,
Venice, 8 October 1786

This exhibition and catalogue are direct results of the generous support of Annemarie Pope and John Harris, who jointly conceived the project three years ago. Their respective staffs, headed by Heidi von Kann at the International Exhibitions Foundation in Washington, and Jane Preger at the Drawings Collection of the Royal Institute of British Architects in London, have been exceptionally kind in helping me to examine and select the majority of the drawings, and to prepare a catalogue that became far more complex than we had originally envisaged. In this latter activity I have been generously supported by the staff of the National Gallery of Art, both in my own department and especially in the department of Graphic Arts, as well as by our administrative officers, in creating the necessary time for study and writing. These activities have also been materially assisted by appointments to teach a seminar on Palladio drawings during the fall quarter of 1979 at the University of California at Berkeley, and by a decade of work at the Centro Internazionale di Studi di Architettura "Andrea Palladio" in Vicenza, where Guglielmo Cappelletti, Renato Cevese, and Maria Vittoria Pellizzari have been unfailingly helpful.

The individual colleagues whose counsel I must acknowledge most gratefully are Howard Burns and Lynda Fairbairn, who have been engaged for several years on the preparation of a catalogue raisonné of all the drawings of Palladio. The present catalogue, though frequently incorporating the results of our discussions, offers an independent approach to Palladio's graphic oeuvre; as such I hope it may possibly prove useful not only to their compilation of the eventual master catalogue, but also as the expression of an alternative viewpoint about many still open questions posed by the drawings themselves.

For consultations on the figural drawings connected with Palladio I am deeply indebted to Roger Rearick, Hugh Macandrew, Peter Cannon-Brookes, Diane DeGrazia Bohlin, and David Alan Brown; for guidance to related prints I owe a special thanks to Caroline Karpinski; and William Cross has made highly useful suggestions about the relation of the drawings to fresco decorations, especially at Malcontenta. William L. MacDonald and Wendy Stedman Sheard have offered the benefits of their wide knowledge of 16th-century attitudes toward the antique, and Ken Haltenhoff has been invaluable as an art-historical and personal consultant at every stage. The task of editing the catalogue has been rendered infinitely easier by the exceptionally careful and sensitive work of Taffy Swandby, to whom I owe a special expression of pure thanks. Many other friends in the Veneto, in England, and in America have offered loyal support during the often difficult preparation of this work: they will all recognize the two-edged truth of that great motto about the exclusive delight of learning, which was adopted as an *impresa* in Palladio's homeland by Inigo Jones: ALTRO DILETTO CHE IMPARAR NON TROVO.

D.L.

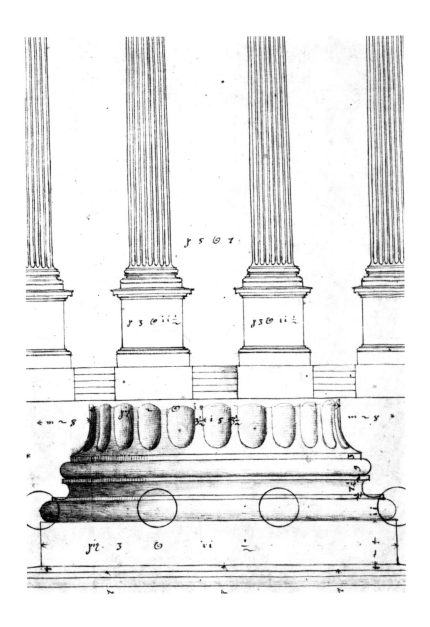

The Rediscovery of Palladio

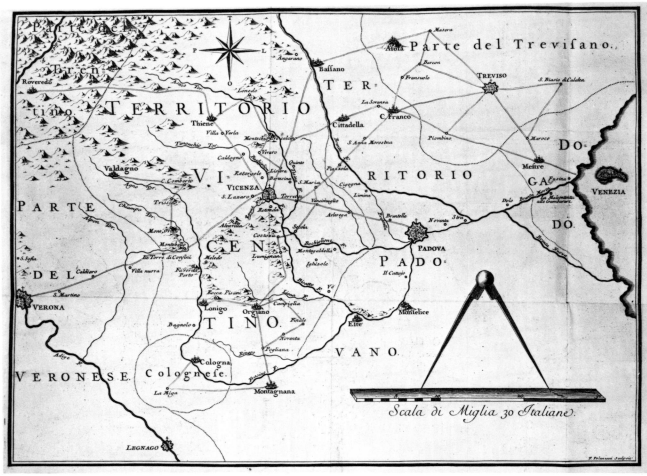

Mainland territories of the Republic of Venice ("The Veneto"): map issued with
broadside text to advertise Francesco Muttoni's *Architettura di Andrea Palladio* in 1739
(*cf.* cat. no. 129).

The Rediscovery of Palladio

Our only comprehensive information about Palladio's life is a vivid account by a contemporary, the Rev. Paolo Gualdo, Canon of the Cathedral of Padua:[1]

Palladio was born in [Padua] in the year of Our Lord 1508, on the 30th day of November, which is the Feast of Saint Andrew the Apostle: for this reason he was given the name of Andrea. Having reached the appropriate age he worked for a while as a stonemason. But he developed a very close relationship with the Vicentine humanist Gian Giorgio Trissino, one of the greatest scholars of his time in the noble disciplines of the arts and sciences. Finding Palladio to be a young man of very spirited character and with a great aptitude for science and mathematics, Trissino encouraged his natural abilities by training him in the precepts of Vitruvius, and even took him three times as far as Rome itself. There Palladio measured and made drawings of many of those sublime and beautiful buildings which are the revered relics of Roman antiquity.

The fourth time Palladio went to Rome he was called there for consultations on St. Peter's. But upon his arrival he found that His Holiness the Pope [Paul III Farnese] had died, and the whole city was disorganized. It still remained feasible, though, for him to see again, remeasure and make new drawings of the greater part of those antique buildings such as Theatres, Amphitheatres, Triumphal Arches, Temples, Tombs, and Baths, as well as others of the most famous structures within the walls and outside the city of Rome. He traveled there a fifth time with several Venetian Gentlemen who were his special friends, and again they devoted themselves to studying, measuring, and discussing the beauty and grandeur of those marvelous buildings. At the same time he published a little guidebook to the city's antiquities, which is commonly sold together with the book called *The Wonders of Rome*.

After he had most thoroughly mastered all the principles of classical architecture in that City, he returned home to Vicenza, where he very happily put into practice everything he had been studying theoretically until then. His fame began to spread, not simply throughout Italy but also abroad. Thus he was called by the Cardinal Bishop of Trent to design a palace in that city; and similarly the Duke Emanuele Filiberto of Savoy invited him to Turin for the same purpose. He was asked by the city of Bologna to design the facade for the great church of San Petronio, and also by the city of Brescia to restore or rather rebuild completely their principal civic building that had burned. In the Venetian Republic, in the same way, Palladio was employed throughout his life for the public buildings as well as the private houses built by the Lords of Venice, as one sees in that City as well as in the countryside and villages surrounding it. But especially in his own city of Vicenza and throughout its province he left a splendid record of his talent. A large number of these works are illustrated in the plates of the famous book he wrote about Architecture. This is exceptionally useful, and has been widely embraced by admirers of that art throughout the world. In it Palladio never departs from the measures and the rules of good architecture as established by the ancient Romans, and for this reason the work has been printed and reprinted many times, acquiring continually greater reputation and respect.

Palladio prepared the materials for another book, including many designs of Ancient Temples, Arches, Tombs, Baths, Bridges, Towers, and other public buildings of Roman antiquity. Just when he was ready to have it printed he was overtaken by death, and all these noble efforts remained in the hands of his most devoted friend, the Venetian nobleman Sir Giacomo Contarini—who, as a great patron of such works, had a very beautiful studio in his house at Venice that was filled with the most beautiful things. But since that Senator died in turn everything was dispersed, and there has been no means of recovering the slightest bit of it.

Beyond his interest in architecture Palladio had an unflagging appetite for the writings of the ancients, and most especially for the *Commentaries* of Julius Caesar. Through this interest he conceived the plan of making illustrations of Caesar's armies, formations, encampments, and sieges of cities, and of demonstrating the structure of that famous emperor's bridge over the Rhine. Having reproduced all these drawings as copper-plate engravings, he dedicated this work to His High Excellency Sir Giacomo Boncompagno, Duke of Sora and General of the Holy See. The work has been much praised, as one which clarifies the interpretations of many difficult passages to be found in that most elegant History.

He made as well a number of highly perfected studies of Polybius, dedicating them to the Grand Duke of Tuscany Francesco Maria de' Medici, in which he showed himself to hold them consummately dear.

In the last days of his life there was built to his design in Vicenza, for the most noble Academy of the Olympians (of which Palladio had been a founding member), a most famous and beautifully arranged theatre for the presentation of Tragedies, Comedies, and Dramatic Plays. It has been esteemed as one of the most beautiful works in all of Italy, since from the days of the ancient Romans to our own we have no other example that has been built of such a classical theatre. It is not found illustrated in Palladio's treatise, because as we said he made it only in the last years of his life, as was also the case with his projects for the Ducal Palace of the Republic of Venice, the Rialto Bridge for the same City, and others that are among his noblest inventions.

And because Palladio kept firmly in mind the image of all those wondrous creations of the ancient Romans, his genius was incapable of stooping to the design of mean or humble structures. In this manner even in his private buildings and Palaces, as also in his country houses, he could not be content until he had endowed them with elements of grandeur such as pediments, colonnades, rich cornices, and other ornaments in the grand style.

Palladio was a most extraordinary able and attractive conversationalist, so that he gave the most intense pleasure to the Gentlemen and Lords with whom he dealt. The same is true of the workmen he used, whom he kept constantly cheerful, treating them with so many pleasant attentions that they all worked with the most exceptional good cheer. He eagerly and lovingly taught them the best principles of the art, in such a way that there was not a mason, stonecutter, or carpenter who did not understand the measurements, elements, and rules of true architecture.

He left many disciples, expecially in his home town of Vicenza; they subsequently, with recollections of Palladio's style, have built both public and private buildings that are very beautiful in that city and abroad. One among them was Vincenzo Scamozzi of Vicenza, who has just died. A year ago, in 1615, he bought out through a Venetian publisher the eight books of his *Architettura Universale;* by the time of his death he had finished preparing for the press two other books of this work, dealing with public buildings.

Palladio died on the 19th of August of the year 1580 at the age of seventy-two, and was buried in the church of the Domenican fathers at Santa Corona . . . Palladio's casket was accompanied to the grave by all the Academicians of the Accademia Olimpica, which we mentioned earlier. His funeral oration was delivered by a Doctor of

Philosophy, also among the number of the Academicians, named Valerio Belli; and the very charming poet Giovanni Battista Maganza recited in praise of Palladio many poems in both Latin and Italian, his own as well as those of other most learned men. Palladio's death grieved the whole city most extremely, even to those who knew him in the slightest degree.

No epitaph of any kind was placed on Palladio's tomb, since an adequate reminder of his immortal greatness and a sufficient preservation of his memory is provided by the most noble corpus of works that he made, and by the very elegant eulogy of the most illustrious and most excellent President M. de Thou of the French Academy.

—Paolo Gualdo, 1616

Gualdo was a member of a prominent family in Vicenza (where his childhood and seminary training coincided with the last two decades of Palladio's life), and a respected humanist with a doctoral degree from the University of Padua; it was thus to Gualdo as a reliable local authority that Jacques-Auguste de Thou wrote from Paris for material with which to compose a biography of Palladio, for his projected *Clarorum virorum elogia*—of which only Gualdo's manuscript survives.[2] His description of Palladio is straightforward but appealing in a down-to-earth way, and in this sense it projects much the same image of its subject as the unique contemporary portrait of Andrea, a work by the modest painter and poet Giambattista Maganza, that was rediscovered only this year (frontispiece).[3] Gualdo's and Maganza's portraits, however, are both a bit formal and stiff; so that it may perhaps not be amiss for us to enliven their literal descriptions with a wittier and more incisive testimony about the architect's popular reputation, from a Venetian satirical rhyme of the 1560s:

Palladio does not visit prostitutes for any bad reasons
And even if now and again he does visit them,
He does it in order to urge them to build
An ancient atrium in the middle of the brothel district.[4]

Palladio emerges from these few sources, and from a host of documentary references, as one of those extraordinarily gifted people who combine radiant charm with outstanding ability. "With his many virtues," wrote the great Vasari, evidently captivated by their meeting in 1566, "he has conjoined such an amiable and gentle nature that it makes him beloved of everyone."[5]

Palladio has been extremely well studied, and important critical works in every major language attest to his status as one of the most widely discussed, as well as "the most imitated architect in history."[6] Early and sympathetic students of his work were especially plentiful in England (with Lord Burlington and his circle)[7] and America (with Thomas Jefferson and his),[8] so that the Anglo-American literature on Palladio is particularly rich. The reader need only be referred to the superb and easily available book in the *Architect and Society* series by James Ackerman, or the equally admirable essays in Howard Burns's recent work,[9] to have readily at hand two fine representatives from both sides of the Atlantic of this long art-historical tradition. There also exists an English translation of Lionello Puppi's outstanding catalogue raisonné of the master's architectural oeuvre.[10] Indeed, as Deborah Howard in her review of "Four Centuries of Literature on Palladio" has now just asked, "what, if anything, remains to be said about Palladio?"[11]

One of the answers (which Miss Howard immediately gives) is that Palladio's drawings are only beginning to receive the attention they deserve. It was recognized at about the turn of this century that they would revolutionize Palladian studies,[12] for they exist in numbers almost unparalleled for any Renaissance architect, and—in addition to their great intrinsic beauty—they contain a very large amount of information about executed as well as unexecuted works that is not available from any other source. At the mid-point of this century the dean of Venetian art historians, Giuseppe Fiocco, published an awesome list of the qualifications needed for the then still urgent task of cataloguing the Palladian drawings.[13] He was convinced that a group of expert art historians, architects, archaeologists, and paleographers would be required for their adequate elucidation, "since no one person could conceivably combine all these talents." After having attempted myself to write at least preliminary catalogue notes on only 130 of some 330 or more surviving sheets, I can heartily concur with Fiocco's cautionary view; and to his list of *desiderati* I would add, above all, an expert on the manufacture and circulation of paper; an experienced student of Renaissance inks, pencils, and crayons; a master of Vicentine dialect and philology; and a scholar of mensuration, scales, and proportion. None of these areas of expertise has yet been applied to the Palladian corpus in a comprehensive way, although important beginnings have been made in Heinz Spielmann's fine catalogue of Palladio's drawings of antiquity (1966), in Lynda Fairbairn's extensive work toward a complete technical study of all the surviving drawings (in collaboration with Howard Burns), and in a very modest way in the present work, which offers a selection of the most beautiful and most interesting sheets (see *Notes to the catalogue,* p. 11). Only after one has had the temerity to tread this strangely uncharted terrain can one recognize the full

force of Fiocco's reservations: it even seems possible that the authority of his pronouncement may have frightened scholars away from the drawings, and thus delayed our expectations of achieving a completely annotated catalogue of Palladio's graphic oeuvre, until almost a full century after its need was clearly recognized.

Or perhaps we should say almost four and a half centuries; since a series of wistful references to the need for publishing the drawings, by commentators who perceived their fundamental importance, forms a kind of Labrador current of bracing pragmatism within the expansive sea of Palladian literature. It is suggested in the present catalogue that already in 1540 Sebastiano Serlio may well have been referring to Palladio's drawings when he commented that the Roman antiquities at Pola "have been surveyed by a better draftsman, who is an expert in numbers and measures."[14] At least three other interested contemporaries—Anton Francesco Doni in 1555, Daniele Barbaro in 1556, and Giorgio Vasari in 1568—referred with glowing praise to Palladio's increasingly impressive body of drawings, which they all hoped would soon be published.[15] But it was not until 1570 that he finally brought out his long-awaited treatise, and even then it embraced only *Quattro Libri dell'Architettura di Andrea Palladio.* It nevertheless seems almost certain that Palladio had consistently been planning (on the examples of Vitruvius and Alberti) to issue a "standard sequence" of ten books, as Gualdo suggests[16]—in the same breath in which he laments, as the first of a legion of later commentators, that Palladio had not been able to publish them all.

At this point we find ourselves obliged to confront the influence of Palladio's exceedingly famous treatise, in terms of its effect on the study of his drawings. And here we come at once to the unpopular necessity of defining that influence as almost wholly negative. In fact, I would go so far as to suggest that the celebrated *Quattro Libri,* which I do immediately acknowledge to have been one of the most influential and even beneficial books of its kind in the whole history of Western culture, has still been heavily prejudicial to an accurate study of Palladio's own work, both graphic and architectural. This paradox is easily understood by glancing at the nature of the treatise itself. Palladio intended it for wide dissemination (though he could hardly have imagined its scores of editions, or especially its many translations "in states unborn, and accents yet unknown"): its four books present wonderfully succinct and superbly illustrated information about the principles of architecture, and the designs of private buildings, public buildings, and temples. Its text is a model of clarity, and its woodcuts have been universally praised for their splendid sense of design, as well as for their highly effective transmission of a maximum of graphic information with a minimum of clutter or confusion. But the problem of the *Quattro Libri* in relation to Palladio's personal architecture is that it succeeded far too well in projecting its own peculiar image. Palladio had primarily intended it as a manual through whose use other architects might be helped to create analogous works, with equal fidelity to the primary exemplars of antiquity: as a handbook, in short, for the imaginative evolution of new architectures that would combine Palladian rationality with Antique authority. In this role the *Quattro Libri* has had such a phenomenal, global, and enduring success that its deleterious effect on Palladio himself has been almost entirely overlooked.

This posthumous misfortune was engendered by the very factors that made the book so successful, for so long, at such distances from Vicenza. It began to be assumed, because of its superlative qualities in other aspects, that it could be used as a reliable guide to Palladio's own architecture: as a monograph, in other words, or a pictorial compendium which accurately represented the many inventions of his own that the author had included in its second and third books, as illustrating the design of private and public buildings. But for this purpose it is an almost total failure. That seemingly heretical judgment is severe, but completely true. Palladio himself frankly stated in the treatise that he was indeed basing his recommendations for certain residential or civic building types on models of his own that he had developed and found successful. But it remains quite clear that he interpreted this process as primarily didactic, and that he was concerning himself above all with the creation of a broadly applicable manual for the dissemination of a sober, practical, and well-proportioned architecture whose ornament could be judiciously derived from antiquity. For this purpose the simplicity and clarity that distinguish his text were applied to his illustrations as well: plans were regularized, facades were simplified, idiosyncracies were omitted, and (perhaps most crucially) the whole determining influence of the surrounding context for each building was left out—all for the purpose of rendering these design inventions easily understandable, and generically applicable to the widest range of comparable programs.

The images of Palladio's own works in the *Quattro Libri* thus became, under the very hand of their author, completely untrustworthy as a reflection of their original corporeal reality. This fundamental discrepancy in fact operates on several levels. First, the later images prepared for the treatise simply do not correspond wih the buildings in any consistently meaningful way, for the reasons we have seen. Second, they are presented in uncompromising black and white, whereas Palladio's actual structures shimmer in kaleidoscopes of color, a fact which is only just beginning to be adequately understood. Third, the *Quattro Libri* images are not only guilty of gross simplifications (which do significantly increase the effectiveness of their didactic function), but in many or even most instances they shamelessly "improve" on their respective designs, according to the hindsight of the author's advancing years. And fourth, most damaging of all to an adequate assessment of Palladio's executed architecture, they programmatically supress all evidence of the pre-existing contexts that determined his development of their designs, in favor of presenting blank expanses on which idealized facades and plans float without anchor or reference to their generating environments. Finally, in the fifth place, and most distressing to the admirer of Palladio's graphic oeuvre, the *Quattro Libri* plates are for the most part only coarsened and heavy-handed paraphrases, in the unwieldy medium of woodcuts, of the extraordinary refinement, delicacy, and sparkle of his original drawings.

Having compiled this catalogue of indictments of the *Quattro Libri* as a guide to Palladio's own architecture, it is all too evident that the apologist for his drawings will enter an immediate plea that the master's own autograph images form a far more reliable and illuminating index of his work. But it is important to keep the discussion in balance. It is after all only the second of the "Four Books" that is devoted exclusively to Palladio's own designs—in a few cases, ideal reconstructions of antique texts; in the broad majority, inventions for actual clients, many with correspondences to executed fabrics; of which again a majority survive, and can be visited today. With these last the lapses from accuracy in the published plates are often shocking. But all the remaining images in the *Quattro Libri* are either abstract inventions to illustrate some general principle of good building, or detailed renderings of ancient monuments—both of which types succeed brilliantly in their respective functions, and are often masterpieces of visual instruction, or invaluable images of perished antiquities, prized for their accuracy and completeness.

In such a context it may seem ungenerous to criticize the *Quattro Libri's* images of Palladio's own architecture as inadequate or misleading to our hope of achieving a true understanding of his style. Es-

6

pecially since original drawings of these structures are often available, to say nothing of the structures themselves (or at any rate good photographs of them), one might think that quite extensive materials for a better assessment are readily at hand. But in fact this is very far from the truth. One of the principal difficulties with the work of this most famous and most widely published of architects is that his architecture (in all its aspects) is excessively difficult to see. His drawings, as we have noticed, are not widely known; they are only published in ponderous volumes, limited to large libraries. His surviving buildings are mostly in small country towns or villages, very far from airports or even bus or train stations; and adequate maps are virtually non-existent. There is probably no Palladian scholar who would know without hesitation exactly how to reach the surviving villa of Marco Zen, or who, in any event, has visited it more than a couple of times; there is almost certainly none who has drawn it, or measured it thoroughly, or even photographed it adequately; hence its date, circumstances of patronage, and history are as completely unknown as its archaeology is untouched. And this handsome little villa at Cessalto (which, perhaps because of its "underdog" status, is one of my favorite Palladian buildings) is hardly an isolated case. Ackerman wrote in 1967 that "even today it is nearly impossible to buy any decent photographs of the villas,"[17] and the situation has not materially improved since then; photographs of the backs, sides, and interiors of the palaces are just as rare; and a project to publish measured drawings of even the most celebrated buildings has slowed to a halt through lack of funds.

Since so many and such severe difficulties confront the study of Palladio's drawings and executed buildings, it is thus hardly surprising that almost everyone, even today, succumbs to the temptation to use the *Quattro Libri* images as tools of analysis. The treatise, as we have seen, is extraordinarily widespread; almost every library in the Western world has multiple copies, in the original and local languages; an excellent reprint of the first edition is still available at a modest cost.[18] But this very ease of access has proved almost fatal to an unprejudiced awareness of Palladio's buildings. They are not black and white; they are not flat and boldly outlined; and once more, above all, they do not sit on pristine, abstract, inviolate Euclidean planes, but instead are jostled and nudged and crowded in dense urban or agrarian contexts, which almost universally have never been measured, drawn, photographed, dated, or otherwise acknowledged to exist. Paul Hofer's book on *Palladios Erstling* is a welcome exception,[19]

but even here the fact that Palladio certainly designed the garden of the Villa Godi is not made transparently clear; and it is still more unfortunate that the great monographic volumes of the new *Corpus Palladianum,* on famous individual buildings, have generally left the whole environmental context undiscussed (even when it profoundly influenced the Palladian design, as at Fanzolo). Palladio has thus been ironically, indeed almost tragically successful—even to the present day—in conditioning us, through the programmatic abstractions of the *Quattro Libri,* to regard his existing buildings as flawed reflections of the Platonic ideals he published in the treatise, rather than as the pre-existing and inescapable models, with all their contextual constraints and idiosyncracies, from which those images were later deduced.

But surely the great corpus of Palladian drawings, it will be argued, must by now have corrected most of these misconceptions about what their resulting buildings were intended to be. Alas, they have not: and indeed there are inescapable reasons for which they can never perform that role. As a general rule, the drawings for Palladio's executed buildings cannot be expected to survive, and in the overwhelming majority they have certainly perished. In most cases, they were literally consumed on the building site, through constant consultation by the workmen: in the early 18th century Muttoni found one such elevation at Quinto, in an advanced state of deterioration (*cf.* cat. no. 54); it does not survive today. The drawings that did initially outlive the building process—such as this one at Quinto—became the property of the patrons (as did those, presumably, of a substantial number of unexecuted projects), and tended to disappear in housecleanings or the periodic settlements of estates. And those few that survived in Palladio's possession, as comprehensive images of executed works, were almost all consumed in another process, that of the actual preparation of the *Quattro Libri* plates. In 1567, at the very moment that Palladio's associated craftsmen were probably beginning work on the woodcut blocks with which to print the *Quattro Libri,* his French contemporary Philibert de l'Orme gave a distressing account of their techniques: "the cutters have the habit of soaking and sometimes even of boiling slightly the paper of the [drafted] illustration, before pasting it on the block for the management of the cutting."[20] As Dinsmoor concluded, in publishing this passage, "after the drawings pasted on the wood blocks had been completely destroyed by the cutters, it is obvious that it would be hopeless to expect to find the manuscript drawings of a published book of this period."[21]

Thus it turns out, finally, that the surviving drawings by Palladio that deal with his own buildings are almost all early works (*e.g.* cat. nos. 2–4, 6–7, 41–49); or, in some few cases, very late ones (many of which are assembled here, cat. nos. 107–118, 121, 124). The *Quattro Libri*—to add one more indictment to its list of pernicious influences—was thus actually responsible for the destruction of a major part of the original drawings for its author's own inventions. Fortunately for the study of his work, however, Palladio's consistent wish to "improve" their images meant that in many cases he redrew the monuments in preparing the book, sometimes frequently enough to leave us traces of the process (cat. nos. 52, 67, 93, 96, 99, 109); and so the earlier projects were sometimes spared, and have reached us intact. An exactly analogous process, of course, has destroyed as well all of the wonderful late drawings for the Temples in the published Book IV; in partial recompense, we have some preliminary studies for them (cat. nos. 102, 105), and a good many sheets were redrawn especially for the block cutters, thus preserving the originals (*e.g.* cat. nos. 103, 104, 106).

And so, as Gualdo once more most accurately explained at the very beginning of Palladian historiography, what we presently find among roughly 330 drawings by Palladio are sheets that can be grouped in three broad classes. First, and so much the most numerous as to include almost two-thirds of all the survivors, are images of the antique structures that would apparently have made up the six remaining books of the treatise, but which (fortunately for the drawings!) remained unpublished. Second, there are a considerable number of early projects and designs for Palladio's own buildings (thus providing a record of his career that is weighted in favor of his formative years), as well as some few projects from his last decade, that is from the "safe" period after the *Quattro Libri* had been printed. Finally, there is a third miscellaneous group of individual sheets (*e.g.* Budapest, Montreal) or pairs (*e.g.* Brescia) or trios of drawings (*e.g.* Bologna), that Palladio had given or sold, usually on commission, to clients or friends. All but about a dozen of the surviving sheets (those being the ones corresponding to the third group above, which Palladio dispersed himself) are in three fortunate institutions, to which they tortuously descended from Palladio's own collection.

The drawings which we know through Gualdo to have been held by Giacomo Contarini at the moment of the architect's death are almost certainly those that have passed, as a fragmentary group of 33 sheets, to a highly appropriate repository at the Museo Civico of Vicenza, housed in Palladio's own Palazzo Chiericati. They include several of the projects from

his last fifteen years (when Palladio actually lived in Venice, often in Giacomo Contarini's house, thus confirming the provenance), and a selection of finished drawings after the antique. Apart from these links they seem to have retained what character they have as a group primarily through their status as handsome "old master" sheets, whose appeal was almost independent of their subjects; they represent a selection that any connoisseur would have been happy to cull out from the surviving drawings in the Venice studio (and as such they are unusually appropriate as graphic representatives in "the City of Palladio"). Because of their many changes of hands they are in quite poor condition, and are not usually exhibited or lent.[22]

Inigo Jones, the great founding father of English (indeed Anglo-American) classical architecture, was the first "architectural historian" to study Palladio *in situ,* by annotating a copy of the *Quattro Libri* in the presence of the buildings themselves.[23] These he studied apparently in a first Italian sojourn of c. 1597 to c. 1603 (he may have bought his copy of the treatise in 1601), but especially in a second journey of 1613–14, when he inscribed dates on several pages of the book.[24] It was evidently on this latter trip—when he was demonstrably becoming as disillusioned as the most skeptical modern historian about the reliability of the *printed* images of Palladio's designs and projects—that he took an inspired and profoundly fortunate step toward achieving their more accurate study, as his own models of good architecture: he bought what seems to have been the entire stock of drawings that had remained in Palladio's studio in Vicenza. John Harris has shown in a series of studies[25] how these have eventually come to form the major part of the Burlington-Devonshire Collection, now mostly in the Drawings Collection of the Royal Institute of British Architects in London, with some pieces still in the Devonshire Collections at Chatsworth House in Derbyshire.

Richard Boyle, Lord Burlington, is in many ways the pivotal figure in the abundant survival and splendid preservation of Palladio's graphic oeuvre. Burlington traveled to Vicenza and Venice in 1719 to study the master's work (the date symbolizes his programmatic inauguration of English Neo-Palladianism), and he had the great good fortune to be offered there a very substantial group of Palladio's drawings after the antique, including almost all the Imperial bath reconstructions. In the preface to his publication of the latter in 1730, where he announces his acquisition of these sheets, he says that he had been fortunate to find these drawings which "had been in the famous house of Monsignor Daniele

Barbaro at Maser in the Trevigiano, which Palladio designed, and where it is said that he died." But Lionello Puppi has now suggested that we can no longer entertain the romantic notion of the great English *milord* making this coup through the accident of a chance visit to Maser, though the provenance may well be accurate: Burlington may perhaps more probably have acquired the drawings in Venice itself, from the Barbaro-Trevisan descendants.[26]

By a singular stroke of fortune Burlington was also able to buy most of the Palladio drawings from Inigo Jones's collection, two years later, in 1721 (eight or ten of the remainder went to the third major repository of Palladio's drawings at Worcester College, Oxford). He was thus able to unite in his villa at Chiswick House the bath and other antique reconstructions which Palladio apparently had with him when he died at Maser, as well as the original projects and designs, plus some other drawings of antiquities, that had remained in Palladio's studio at Vicenza. When Burlington himself died his drawings all passed to his daughter, and through her marriage into the family of the Dukes of Devonshire; in 1894 the 8th

Duke made a gift in trust of the great majority of them to the RIBA, where during the 1970s they were carefully removed from their former albums and remounted in protective mats, in an elaborate restoration program. The present exhibition draws mainly on this great accumulation in England; but with additions of important sheets from almost every other collection containing drawings by Palladio, it is the first truly international gathering of his graphic work. It has provided the opportunity for a descriptive catalogue devoted exclusively to Palladio's drawings—a publication which, through its selection and analysis of a considerable number of their most attractive and most significant examples, and especially through its development of criteria for establishing a general chronology, may serve as a kind of provisional handbook to this precious legacy that has helped to shape so significant a part of the architecture of the modern world.

D.L.
Washington, D.C.
St. Andrew's Day
30 November 1980

NOTES TO THE INTRODUCTION

1. Gualdo's manuscript life of Palladio is in the Biblioteca Nazionale Marciana, Venice, Cl. Ital. X, cod. 73 (= 7097), fols. 156–157; it was published first by Montenari 1749, pp. vii–ix, and again directly from the manuscript by Zorzi 1958–59, pp. 93–94 (the version followed here), with commentary pp. 95–104 (details about Gualdo p. 98 n. 11; see also Puppi 1972, pp. xxi–xxiv). As far as I know it has never been published in any other language, so that my own translation is offered here as a further aid to the understanding of Palladio by a wider audience.

2. Montenari 1749; Zorzi 1958–59, p. 96; Vicenza 1980 p. 72 (Camerlengo).

3. Maganza (c. 1509–1586) was a contemporary, compatriot, and close friend of Palladio: for the most recent résumé of his life and work, see Sgarbi 1980, pp. 101–106. The portrait and its many derivations are discussed in Vicenza 1980, pp. 104–113 (Piva); it is reproduced here by the generous permission of Counts Angelo and Paolo di Valmarana, of Vicenza.

4. Translation by Burns, Arts Council 1975, p. 72; original in Temanza 1778, p. 395.

5. Vasari 1568, Milanesi ed., vol. VII, p. 531; translation slightly revised from DeVere 1915, vol. IX, p. 214.

6. Ackerman 1966/1977, p. 19.

7. An excellent introduction to the subject of Palladio as he was interpreted by his English admirers is provided by Wittkower 1974.

8. By far the best study of this subject is in Italian (Azzi Visentini 1976), but important essays have been contributed by Nichols 1976 and (again in Italian) Valmarana 1980, both summarizing much previous literature.

9. Arts Council 1975, esp. the brilliant biographical summary on pp. 69–72.

10. Puppi 1975 (translation by Pearl Sanders of Puppi 1973, used in this catalogue).

11. Howard 1980, p. 241; Miss Howard answers her own question, in part, by noting that "even today, Palladio's drawings are too little known." For another and more substantial answer, see the discussion below of the very typical problems that are posed by the Villa Zen (and cat. nos. 47, 65, and 88).

12. See *e.g.* Penrose 1895, Burger 1909–II, etc.

13. Fiocco 1949, p. 184.

14. Cat. no. 17. An alternative identification of the "better draftsman" would be Falconetto, as Burns suggests (Verona 1980, p. 84), in maintaining (very plausibly) that Serlio was in fact reproducing those Pola drawings by Falconetto that Vasari says were published only after the latter's death (1535). Yet Serlio specifically says that the unnamed draftsman made Pola drawings *that were better than the ones he was reproducing,* which thus cannot be both Falconetto's and better than Falconetto's at the same time. Serlio also very strongly implies that the other draftsman's images have yet to be published, whereas his own (very probably based, as I agree with Burns,

9

on drawings by Falconetto) are printed on the same pages as the reference to the better ones—evidently by a third architect—that are yet to come. Serlio's characterization of the latter as "an expert in numbers and measures" is so close to Gualdo's biographical description of the young Palladio as "highly talented in mathematics and the sciences" as to leave little doubt of the identification; indeed, and as a distinction from Falconetto as a painter, this seems to be the purpose of the phrase. The question seems to me to be resolved by Serlio's obvious intent to suggest that the "better draftsman" is alive (though perhaps not yet well enough known to give his name) and hoping to publish: in 1540 Palladio was 32 and fulfills all these requirements, whereas Falconetto had been dead for five years.

15. A masterful note on this aspect of the drawings (and their publication) is in Wittkower 1949/1971, pp. 64–65, n. 4 (although Zorzi, 1959, showed that four Vatican Library drawings mentioned here as Palladio are in fact late copies). See also Puppi 1973, pp. 443–444.

16. Gualdo lists, in his first generic reference to Palladio's drawings after antiquity, the six further subjects of *"Teatri, Anfiteatri, Archi Trionfali, Tempii* [though Temples already occupied the published Book IV], *Sepulture,* [and] *Terme"*; in his second list specifically of other books prepared for publication, he again enumerates six subjects, though in part different ones: *"Tempi Antichi* [still duplicating Book IV], *Archi, Sepolture, Therme, Ponti,* [and] *Specole."* Drawings exist for all eight of these categories except the last (literally "Observatories," a subject now unrepresented by Palladio); if we also remove the replicated "Temples," we obtain a reliable early list of six

unpublished books, for which considerable graphic material survives: Theatres, Amphitheatres, Triumphal Arches, Baths, Tombs, and Bridges. (Some elements among these are represented in the published books, *e.g.* bridges in Book III; but we know from the drawings that more could have been added.) Among all these only the Baths were published before the 20th century, in Lord Burlington's beautiful *Fabbriche Antiche disegnate da Andrea Palladio* of 1730, with 25 engraved plates reproducing a selection from Palladio's drawings now in London.

17. Ackerman 1967, p. 19.

18. Palladio, *Quattro Libri,* Venice, 1570: facsimile reproduction, Ulrico Hoepli Editore Libraio, Milan, 1968.

19. Hofer 1969.

20. De l'Orme 1567, fol. 106 *verso;* translation by Dinsmoor 1942.

21. Dinsmoor 1942, p. 83.

22. Wittkower 1949/1971, p. 64 n. 4.

23. Allsopp 1970 (for a facsimile and transcription of the surviving book, now at Worcester College, Oxford); Tait 1970 (for its commentary).

24. Summerson 1966, pp. 16–18, 35–37; Allsopp 1970.

25. Harris 1971, p. 34; Harris 1972, pp. 6–7; Harris/Tate 1979, pp. 1–3, 54–55. The number of sheets that Jones acquired was probably over 200; they were originally more numerous, for some have been pasted together since his time. Burlington acquired probably some 75 or more sheets during his own Italian sojourn (see below).

26. Puppi 1980: lecture of 30 August 1980 at Vicenza.

Notes to the Catalogue

The technical information about Palladio's drawings is surprisingly complex, and in this catalogue is organized as follows. The catalogue number refers to the side of a sheet which is exhibited (either *recto* or *verso*); if the second side is referred to, it is qualified by the appropriate descriptor, *e.g.* cat. no. 5 *verso*. All drawings not given an artist's name are in my opinion by Palladio; since I do not believe that he used assistants for drafting his basic architectural forms until the very end of his life, this means that I usually consider such sheets to be entirely autograph, even to the figures: this selection of the drawings has in fact been made partly with a view to showing Palladio's considerable interest as a figural draftsman (esp. in cat. nos. 7, 12, 13, 32, 37, 67, etc.).

The main title refers to the side of the sheet exhibited and illustrated; if the second side is also exhibited, it appears as well in the main title; otherwise it is named and described in the section on media and inscriptions. All titles represent in my opinion the most probable names or destinations of the images; many, however, are at variance with the previous literature. The date(s) are normally extrapolated from a confluence of paper type, style, documentation, and patronage. Most could fluctuate by a year or so; those still more imprecise are usually given the "*circa*" of approximation; those externally fixed are so indicated (or explained in the text). This is the first attempt at a general chronology of Palladio drawings, and it has to a striking degree emerged from details of interrelationships among both exhibited and unexhibited sheets: when the other 200 items among the extant drawings are added to produce a comprehensive chronology, the one here proposed may be expected to change in certain details, but its general structure is probably sound.

Each technical description is preceded by a collocation line giving a summary indication of the owning institution, and detailed information for the inventory number of the piece exhibited. These (as in cat. no. 1) attempt to correct previous mis-citations, and above all to function as a guide to finding the sheet on the spot. The physical description gives the metric size of the sheet with height preceding width: all the items exhibited were newly measured in 1980 with the same rule, and may be taken as more nearly correct than previously published dimensions—save that where Lynda Fairbairn's quotations of sizes (Mostra 1973, Arts Council 1975) differed from mine by only one millimeter, I have conformed to hers in deference to the published precedent. For the first time in discussing Palladio's drawings (save for random notes in Spielmann 1966), pasted sheets are so described, and all components are measured; the main reason for this increased precision of measurement is that sheet sizes provide important clues to origin (i.e. watermarks) and use (i.e. full, half, quarter, or fragmentary sheets).

The descriptions of watermarks are brief and general, although followed wherever possible by at least a comparative reference to an illustration, probable place of origin, and date: the standard compendia of Briquet, Heawood, and Mošin are described in the bibliography. Palladio's papers are essentially unstudied, for Spielmann's valiant efforts to read their marks were made when the sheets were still partly pasted down; but Fairbairn has now been working for almost ten years on a complete review of all Palladian watermarks and countermarks. These are so numerous and form so complete an index to good North Italian papers in the fifty years between 1535 and 1585, however, that they provide vastly more varieties than are indexed in the handbooks, most of them earlier than the published examples. Palladio's watermarks thus deserve a volume of their own, for their accurate placement in his chronology will provide new information about contemporary Italian papers, unavailable in this accuracy and density from almost any other source.

Descriptions of media are subjective and *ad hoc,* though each exhibited sheet was examined during 1980 with a strong glass to study crayon, pencil, and ink colors. I have used everyday terms (*e.g.* "pencil" instead of "graphite," though of course Palladio's points were not bonded into a wooden matrix), and my own descriptions of the two main color ranges into which his inks have faded: the first tending to lighter reddish colors which I have called *siena,* and the second to darker, heavier browns which I have called *umber*. These last are also the pigments held in a waxy medium that I have called "umber crayon": since the matrix in this case seems to me certainly to include wax, I have avoided the concept of chalk, which I find misleading. Apart from this rough sketching "crayon" and the lead point I have called "pencil," all of Palladio's lines are drawn in ink with a quill pen or a more specialized drafting instrument. His washes (laid on with a brush) are close to the inks in color, and may be dilutions of them; much work remains to be done in defining the components of all these substances.

Inscriptions are given in full (if unpublished), but normally they can be found expanded in the early bibliographic citations, especially in Spielmann; following his precedent labels and figures of dimensions are usually omitted from transcriptions, but mentioned for their types. Notations on the *recto* precede those on the *verso,* which are given in full if they are of interest, though arithmetic sums and other casual inscriptions have been omitted. John Talman's coded inventory marks are quoted in their numerical components only. All scale bars have been carefully measured, to reconstruct the rule Palladio was using for each drawing: these prove to be astonishingly varied, among Vicentine, Venetian, Veronese, "antique," and Roman inches, as well as one or two in Florentine *braccia* and Roman *palmi*; they demonstrate Palladio's eclecticism and skill in handling all the metrical techniques of his discipline (*cf.* cat. nos. 8, 13, etc.).

Palladio's handwriting is a special problem, for its changes can be used as an index for dating. We do not know how he learned to write; I feel that Trissino's tutelage (cat. no. 1) may have had a decisive influence. It was certainly from Trissino that Palladio acquired the humanist conceit of a handwriting using a Greek *epsilon* (ϵ) in the place of the modern *e*: I feel this to be the earliest Palladian hand that we know, and I date its standard use very restrictively, approximately to the five years between c. 1537 and c. 1542. There are rare outcroppings of epsilons

after the early 1540s, but in my view they are idiosyncratic relapses, and cannot be used as a dating device; the individual entries of the catalogue discuss this problem further (*cf.* cat. nos. 8, 16, 19, etc.). A transitional hand, occasionally using both e's, occupies part of this first decade of Palladio's earliest graphic survivals; an early mature hand occurs around 1550, which is delicate and uses exclusively modern e's; Palladio's late hand, after the mid 1550s, is rough but boldly formed. His use of dialect should also be studied for its help with dating: there are recognizable differences between Venice (here used as the capital city only) and the Veneto (here used, in adjective form as well— *Venetan* as opposed to *Venetian*—to signify the Republic's mainland territories), and even between towns on the *terraferma* such as Padua and Vicenza; enough clues may show up in Palladio's spellings to make this a useful undertaking.

The bibliography has proved unexpectedly difficult, for it exemplifies a new departure in the literature on Palladio's drawings, by attempting to cite the specific page(s) on which a given sheet is actually *discussed,* as well as the figure in which it is reproduced. It aims at a responsible summary of meaningful previous commentary, rather than completeness: passing references and even casual reproductions of exhibited sheets have been omitted, in the interests both of space and of achieving a real usefulness to the further study of an individual sheet. Expansions of references are found in the bibliography. The final element in each entry formally identifies the lender.

The vocabulary of Venetian Renaissance architecture is partly based on standard historical terms (which may still be unfamiliar to the average reader), and partly on local usage (which is almost certainly confusing enough to anyone but a fellow specialist in the field). For this reason a short list of certain of these more unusual words, with a working definition describing my own use of them, is offered here as a help to the general reader's understanding of Palladio's architecture.

Definitions of Specialized Terms

acroterion (pl. *acroteria*)—sculptural figure on the apex or outer corner of a *pediment,* originally of a Greek temple: used by Palladio there and at other points on *attics* and roof lines.

architrave—broad flat band, with two or three overlapping faces, forming the lowest element of a classical *entablature.*

attic—the uppermost half-story of a classically articulated facade.

barchessa (pl. *barchesse*)—Venetan dialect term for a long shed-like open barn, with closed rooms supporting lofts on the north side, and piers or columns supporting a common roof over an open area for agricultural implements on the south side (*cf.* cat. no. 47); regularized by Palladio into a close approximation of a classical stoa.

braccia—literally, "arms": the standard units of linear measure of many Italian centers, esp. Florence.

bucrania—bulls' skulls, used (in alternation with *paterae*) as ornaments on the *metopes* of a *frieze* of the Tuscan order: derived from the iconography of Roman sacrifices.

capital—a large round decorative sculptural element at the top of a column, supporting the *architrave* (see *echinus*).

corona—the "crown" molding of a classical cornice, one of the uppermost elements of an *entablature.*

dentils—small "tooth-like" square pegs, aligned as a three-dimensional molding band above the *frieze* of a classical *entablature.*

double-pile—conventional name for a domestic ground plan whose two main blocks of rooms, front and back, are divided by a central transverse wall or corridor.

echinus—the broadly spreading cushion-shaped element forming the principal molding of a Doric or Tuscan capital; in this order—as also joined with the curving volute in Ionic, or substituted (in place of both elements) by the bell in Corinthian—it is the component which supports the square tablet of the abacus, directly below the *architrave.*

entablature—the whole assembly of horizontal moldings above the columns and *capitals* of a classical order: composed of *architrave, frieze,* and cornice (see *corona*).

frieze—central band of a classical entablature (sometimes omitted, esp. in the Tuscan order), between *architrave* and cornice: in Doric or Tuscan composed of alternating *triglyphs* and *metopes,* but in Ionic or Corinthian a single continuous band, plain or sculptured.

impluvium—from Roman domestic architecture, a system of catch-basin in the floor, and downward-sloping roof pitches forming a rectangular aperture above, to bring rain water into an interior; projected by Palladio only at Bagnolo (cat. no. 48), but executed by Scamozzi (in the form of an oculus in an upward-curving dome) for the same patron at Rocca Pisani (*cf.* cat. no. 126).

impresa—an emblematic device, or the verbal motto from that device, adopted as a symbolic self-portrait by a humanist.

loggia (pl. *loggie*)—any roofed pedestrian area open to the weather, usually through a colonnade or arcade: by extension (when capitalized), civic ceremonial and administrative centers incorporating such open spaces below, with enclosed halls above; loggias themselves may occasionally be superimposed, though by Palladio only to the height of two stories.

metopes—the small square fields of a Doric or Tuscan *frieze,* separated by three-grooved elements called *triglyphs;* metopes can be plain or sculptured with iconographic symbols such as the alternating *bucrania* and *paterae* of Roman sacrifices.

modillions—elaborately carved small scroll-shaped brackets placed closely together as a band of sculptural ornament, supporting the upper elements of a Corinthian cornice.

order—a full classical system of columns and *entablature;* the five principal orders are Doric, Tuscan, Ionic, Composite and Corinthian.

palmi—standard units of linear measure in centers such as Rome, corresponding to the span of a palm.

passi—literally "strides": standard Venetian and Venetan units for large linear measures, corresponding to 5 local feet.

paterae—disks ornamenting alternate *metopes* of a Doric or

Tuscan *frieze:* representing ceremonial "patens" or plates, from which celebrants at Roman sacrifices poured out libations.

pediment—untraced English word, supposedly a corruption of "pyramid": a decorated triangular gable at the end or center of a roof, bounded by horizontal and raking cornices, enclosing either a plain or sculptured field, the latter often ornamented with a heraldic shield.

pertiche—standard Venetan agricultural and surveying units for large linear measures, corresponding to 6 local feet.

piano nobile—Italian term for "main floor," usually one raised above a basement.

pilaster—the columnar element of a classical *order,* flattened to a rectilinear strip and applied to a wall; as distinct from the same element applied to the wall in half-round form, referred to as an "engaged column."

pulvinated—"pillow-shaped" or bulging convex curve, usually of an Ionic or Corinthian *frieze* band, plain or sculptured.

pronaos—porch or entrance portico of a temple.

ressaut—portion of an entablature broken forward from the wall plane, over individual, paired, or grouped elements of an *order.*

rustication—the articulation of an architectural surface (usually of a wall or of the elements of an *order*) to display or simulate courses of stonework. Technically the term applies exclusively to rough-hewn masonry (real or fictive, but usually real stone) left or represented in an unsmoothed or "rustic" state, the individual blocks or bosses of which are called *bugne,* and the whole system *bugnato,* or *bugnato rustico.* But in practice the term is also loosely applied to smooth-faced courses of regular ashlar blocks (real or fictive, but usually fictive, as images of stones and mortar channels drawn on a stucco wall), which are differentiated as *bugnato liscio,* or "smooth rustication." A third variety (not used by Palladio) employs projecting blocks of geometrical shapes (*e.g. bugnato a diamante*).

serliana—an opening for a window or portal with a central arched aperture, flanked by two lower flat-headed apertures. The motif is antique, and was most importantly revived by Bramante and Raphael; Peruzzi's follower Sebastiano Serlio made it internationally popular through his writings, and it conventionally carries his name. Palladio used it widely, and his English Neo-Palladian followers made it a hallmark, so successfully that in England and America it is still called a "Palladian window."

socle—a base or pedestal, or a zone incorporating a series of them, often applied to a wall.

soler—Italian term for beamed (rather than vaulted) interior space, usually on an upper floor.

spandrel—the negative space, resembling a spherical triangle, between an arch and its rectangular frame.

stereobate—the visible substructure of a temple, usually a three-stepped platform, the topmost element of which is the *stylobate.*

stringcourse—a narrow and slightly projecting horizontal band applied to a wall, usually as a visual key to the division between stories.

stylobate—the "column platform" or topmost element of a temple structure, which in full is called the *stereobate.*

triglyph—a small rectangular plate with two vertical grooves and three projecting strips, the whole originally applied as a decorative cover (*e.g.* of terracotta) over exposed beam ends, and forming the recurrent motif in a *frieze;* since early classical times reproduced in fine materials as the major sculptural decoration of the Doric (and later the Tuscan) *order.*

villa—a country property with an administrative center, usually (but not necessarily) including a house for the owner. Palladio never applies the term to a building, and (in classical precedent and strict modern usage) it should not be so applied; the house of the owner of a villa is called in Italian (*e.g.* by Palladio) a *"casa di villa,"* in English a "country house," and in American a "plantation house" (which most accurately reflects the original meaning). For convenience, however, the term is very widely used to refer succinctly to the main dwelling house on such an estate.

CHAPTER ONE

Architectural Apprenticeship:

First travels in the Veneto, the Adriatic, and to Rome

Figure 1

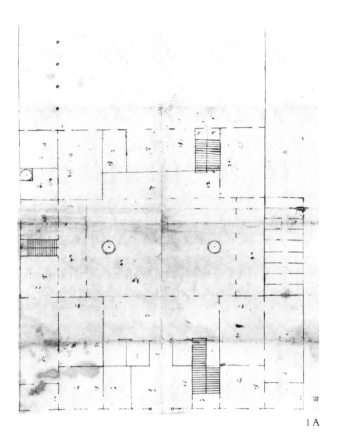

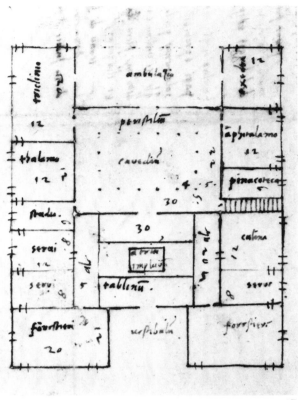

1 A

1 D

1. GIANGIORGIO TRISSINO: THREE SKETCH PLANS FOR PALAZZO TRISSINO, VICENZA; TOGETHER WITH PLAN RECONSTRUCTION OF A ROMAN HOUSE (AFTER VITRUVIUS)

c. 1535?

Biblioteca del Brera: Manoscritto Castiglione 8, volume 3 (*"Varie rime, e prose inedite di messer Giovan Giorgio Trissino dal Vello d'Oro e di altri autori al medesimo indirizzate: volume terzo,* Vicenza, MDCCXLVI . . .").

Drawing A, labeled palace plan on paper 29.4 × 38.5 cm. (single sheet, as fold-out, on fols. 37 [*recto*] and 38 [*verso*] of bound volume); watermark, small anchor in circle with star, and B beneath (*cf.* Mošin 901/902); Drawing B, second plan on paper 25.9 × 27.2 cm. (single sheet, fol. 39a), with countermark B; Drawing C, third plan on pieced paper (fol. 40) with watermarks of cardinal's hat (*cf.* Briquet 3416: Vicenza 1533); Drawing D, Vitruvian plan on paper 22.2 × 19 cm. (single sheet, as fol. 41a, with indistinct partial watermark).

Umber ink; 1-A plan labeled on *verso* "Alcune piāte đ la casa da/ Vicᵃ p Fabricarla," and Roman house plan annotated with descriptive labels from Vitruvius.

Dalla Pozza 1943, pp. 51–52, fig. 4 (Vitruvius plan); Puppi 1971, p. 83, figs. 116, 117, 118 (palace plans), and 119 (Vitruvian plan, from copy of 1754); Puppi 1973-II, pp. 79–86 (text of treatise fragment), figs. 5 (Drawing A), 6 (Drawing B), 7 (Drawing C); Burns 1975, pp. 80–81, no. 149, with fig. 149 (second palace plan).

Biblioteca Nazionale Braidense, Milan.

On the personality of the great Renaissance humanist Giangiorgio Trissino (1478–1550), the Vicentine author and statesman who "discovered" Palladio, gave him his classical name and education, and effectively launched his independent career as an architect, Rudolf Wittkower has written a famous chapter celebrating the ideal of the "universal man" (*Architectural Principles in the Age of Humanism,* 1949/1971, pp. 57–69), and Burns has provided an excellent statement of Trissino's determining influence on Palladio's artistic and intellectual formation (1975, pp. 77–82). However, the 29-year-old Andrea was already a talented stonemason and "junior partner" in a prosperous local building firm when he met his noble protector through a campaign of remodeling which in 1537–38 Trissino was bringing to completion on his manor house at Cricoli, just outside Vicenza (fig. 1). It is thus as important for us to analyze their association in the light of a pragmatic means toward the end of a consciously sought self-improvement on Palladio's part, as it is to consider more critically the too facile stereotype of his "creation" by an enthusiastic amateur of classical architecture.

Certainly these four architectural drawings which survive from Trissino's hand, in conjunction with the fragment of his unfinished treatise on building, render highly problematical (as Zorzi warned, 1965, p. 26) any thesis of his having had a serious influence on Palladio as a designer (for, apart from some interesting proportional relationships, the three "modern" plans are very haphazard) or even as a draftsman (for their execution is quite extraordinarily rudimentary). Yet the combination of Trissino's practical-minded treatise fragment (which addresses directly such problems as the siting of buildings) and ideally reconstructed Vitruvian house plan (an antiquarian exercise that was to become a lifetime preoccupation of Palladio's) accurately defines two major areas in which his influence was indeed critical to Palladio's development: namely, helping to establish his younger colleague's preoccupation with functional practicality, and engendering in Palladio a consistent reverence for the models of antiquity, particularly through the sympathetic study of Vitruvius. He introduced Andrea to "pragmatic theoreticians" of architecture such as Alvise Cornaro in Padua, and Sebastiano Serlio there and at Cricoli itself (Puppi 1971, pp. 83–86); and encouraged Palladio's metamorphosis into a well-trained and experienced critic of antique classicism by underwriting (as we assume him to have done) a series of crucially important archaeological investigations, for the purpose of which he apparently supported three of Palladio's residences in Rome.

Though in the older literature Trissino's Brera drawings were consistently related to the remodelings of his country house at Cricoli (which survives as Trissino built it), he in fact labeled them as referring instead to the site of his city palace (a project that he did not fully succeed in building) on a plot in Vicenza which Burns has carefully analyzed in relation to the plans (1975, p. 81), and where in fact Palladio is documented as an intimate of the house as early as 19 February 1538. While nothing thus links either the drawings themselves or Palladio's own architectural activity with the rebuilding of Cricoli, still Andrea's documented association with Trissino, in these very months when the latter's remodelings at his suburban manor were being completed (his housewarming parties were given three months later, in May), means at least that Palladio would have been very thoroughly acquainted with Trissino's (and Serlio's) designs that had been realized at Cricoli, which—significantly in its character as a *built* building—we shall see to have been seminal to Andrea's training and development.

These very modest sketches by a gentleman amateur, who (at about the same time as their production) was also

preeminent in Palladio's emergence as an architect, have engendered a curious congeries of critical errors in the Palladian literature. Morsolin (1878, pp. 225–226) discussed them—as relating, misleadingly, to Cricoli—without publishing images of them; the first illustration (of the Vitruvian plan only) was printed by Dalla Pozza (1943, fig. 4), who however perpetuated the idea of a Cricoli connection, to be followed on this point by Wittkower (1949/71, p. 59) and Ackerman (1967, p. 3). In helping to correct this misconception, Wolters followed Zorzi's accurate association (1965, p. 26) of the "modern" sheets with Trissino's city palace, but also announced (1968, pp. 349–350) the confusing presence of exact copies of all four drawings in the Biblioteca Marciana at Venice (Ms. Ital. Cl . IV Cod. 190 = 5159). These had been made—according to an inscription on the Vitruvian sheet—on 3 October 1754 by Bartolomeo Ziggiotti, who in 1746 had discovered the originals in the process of his reorganization, binding, and printing of title pages for five volumes of Giangiorgio's papers in the Trissino family archive (two of which had migrated to the James de Rothschild library, Paris, before 1912). Puppi, in a monograph article on Cricoli (1971, p. 83), noted the imperfect knowledge of the Brera and Marciana manuscripts (plus further reflections of them, in the Biblioteca Bertoliana at Vicenza), by virtually all previous commentators, but himself mistakenly published a Marciana copy as a Brera original (the Vitruvian plan: his fig. 119 displays the 1754 label), referred to the "Rotschild" collection (*sic*), and confused the collocations of the Brera volumes (1971, p. 86, n. 2: *Varie rime e prose* is actually Castiglione 8/3, *Lettere* is 8/2, and *Zibaldone* is 8/1, rather than in inverse order; in this he was followed by Burns, 1975, p. 80, no. 149). After such a tangled history, and in the presence of such minimally attractive drawings, we may perhaps be justified in seeing them primarily as representative illustrations of the architectural ambience out of which Palladio directly emerged, in the period just before he was to come under the much more important aesthetic influences of great artists such as Giulio Romano and Sanmicheli—on whose masterly examples of draftsmanship (such as cat. no. 5) he was immediately to model his own brilliant graphic beginnings.

2. FACADE PROJECT FOR PALAZZO DA MONTE, VICENZA (I)

c. 1538/39

RIBA: Palladio XVII/26

14.2 × 22.0 cm. (single sheet); no watermark; Talman 150 mark on *verso*. Siena ink with gold-brown wash; basic structure with ruled lines, details freehand.

Zorzi 1954, p. 109, fig. 4; Pane 1961, p. 110, fig. 137:43; Zorzi 1965, p. 31, fig. 16; Arts Council 1975, pp. 231–232, no. 409 (Fairbairn); Berger 1978, pp. 57–61.

Royal Institute of British Architects, London.

This modest sheet makes a considerable claim on our attention, for it may with some justice be identified as one of Palladio's earliest surviving drawings. It certainly represents an early stage of Palladio's graphic "handwriting," but its execution is extremely rough and amateurish: the column capitals are mere ciphers, and the awkward hatched shading of the lower story implies a light source on the right, while the brushed-in shading with wash, above, shows light coming from the left. Portions of the drawing have been reworked, and traces of Corinthian capitals that were later erased may be seen on three of the four ground-

2

floor pilasters, which were later extended into a taller Tuscan order. (Since the redrawn columns are at right, we may surmise that Palladio worked up his drawings from right to left).

Our main interest in this beginner's idea for a city palace facade lies in what the sheet reveals about the architectural prototypes that were influencing Palladio at this very early phase in his emerging independence as a designer. Ursel Berger recently noticed, as had I, that this design exactly reproduces the four widely spaced pilasters on the identically proportioned facade of the Casa Genova, begun in 1500 at Padua (probably by Lorenzo da Bologna—per Rigoni 1970, p. 164 fig. 9), of which the upper story is virtually repeated in the Paduan Loggia del Consiglio, completed in 1516–33 by Biagio del Bigoio with the help of Gian Maria Falconetto. The window frames on both Paduan prototypes, however, are old-fashioned round-headed openings set in large panels of empty wall space. Palladio's are more up-to-date, and on the lower windows the sturdy columnar tabernacles with flanking niches recall the middle story of the Torre del'Orologio of 1500 in Venice. The upper central windows with their spreading segmental pediment, while perhaps deriving in part from those on the Loggia del Consiglio of 1493 in Verona, are in fact quoted almost verbatim (as are the two flanking

tabernacles) from the Paduan house completed in 1502 by Annibale de'Maggi, the architect who had begun the Loggia del Consiglio in 1496.

Zorzi suggests that the alternating pediments and repetitive niches of this drawing are evidence of Palladio's familiarity with Raphael's facade design for the Palazzo Branconio del'Aquila of 1515–20 in Rome, of which a drawing could certainly have reached the Veneto. But such an august and distant paternity for the rather haphazard forms in Palladio's drawing is neither necessary nor even very likely, given the general currency of local versions of these motifs, especially in the work of Lorenzo da Bologna, Maggi and Falconetto in Padua (fig. 2), where Palladio was evidently learning about "modern" architecture at the time this drawing was made. The one substantial novelty in this eclectic design, by which Palladio already begins to supercede these exemplars of early 16th-century regional style, is his device of connecting the tabernacles through heavy entablature bands along the wall. This full classical motif (which occurs for example in the Pantheon interior, as in Serlio's plate III:16) might easily have reached him through Serlio's drawings, to which Palladio apparently had access, via Trissino, before the publication in Venice of Serlio's *Third Book* in 1540 (Puppi 1971, pp. 83–86).

19

3. FACADE PROJECT FOR PALAZZO DA MONTE, VICENZA (II)

c. 1538/39

RIBA: Palladio XVII/23.

18.1 × 26.2 cm. (single sheet); no watermark; Talman 150 mark on *verso*.

Umber ink with gold-brown wash.

Fiocco 1949, p. 186, fig. 186; Zorzi 1954, p. 106, fig. 2; Pane 1961, p. 110, fig. 137:42; Zorzi 1965, p. 24, fig. 1; D'Ossat 1966, p. 37, fig. 42; Ackerman 1966/77, p. 93, fig. 44; Puppi 1973, p. 249, figs. 13–14 (p. 30); Berger 1978, pp. 57–61; Verona 1980, p. 112, fig. 113 (Burns).

Royal Institute of British Architects, London.

Figure 2

Although both this and the preceding facade project were previously thought to be unspecific "study" drawings from Palladio's experimental beginnings, this design provides a link which ties the two to an early commission for Palazzo Da Monte. The door and window openings on the present sheet are drawn at the same size, to the same scale, and in the same positions as those on the following sheet (cat. no. 4), which is the model (or rather a close prototype for the lost working drawing) from which the existing Palazzo Da Monte was actually built (fig. 3). This project and the one following therefore present two different facade designs that could be superimposed over a fixed internal framework, represented by the identically placed and proportioned openings; and even though this exact congruity of measurements is lacking in the first drawing (cat. no. 2, drawn to a slightly smaller scale), that design is still such a precise prototype in style and structure to our present project as to leave no possible doubt of its role as the first conception in this three-part series. Our first two sheets in fact demonstrate an interesting progression of graphic techniques: the first sheet is a personal study drawing, mostly freehand, on which Palladio successively records various quickly sketched ideas; the second is a finished presentation drawing for the patron's approval—which in

3

20

this case was evidently not forthcoming, thus necessitating Palladio's development of a third quite different solution.

As we might expect, the present drawing stands almost equidistant in style between its associated designs. The broadly spaced single pilasters of the earlier project (cat. no. 2) are here replaced by rhythmically grouped pairs of engaged Tuscan columns, surmounted by fluted Corinthian pilasters, whose intercolumniations contain smaller and less numerous niches. (This much of the arrangement is borrowed directly from Sansovino's Roman-inspired Loggetta of 1537–40 in Venice, which suggests that Palladio must have had early access to a drawing or model of the structure—perhaps gained during Sansovino's visit to Vicenza in January/March 1538 to consult with the masters of the Pedemuro shop.)

Within this extremely up-to-date and Roman-oriented framework, however, Palladio's slightly awkward door and window frames revert to more conservative models. The Venetian architect Scarpagnino had participated in consultations on the Basilica in Vicenza in 1525 and 1532, and his presumed encounters with the Pedemuro shop would help to explain Palladio's close repetition here of the central portal and window frame of the Scuola di S. Rocco, elements constructed by Scarpagnino between about 1527 and 1535. A still closer connection with the pedimented central window frame of the Venetian Palazzo Contarini delle Figure (of an indeterminate date between 1504 and 1546) has often been noticed. While that beautiful facade has also traditionally been ascribed to Scarpagnino, Bassi (1976, pp. 382–385) has astutely pointed out Palladio's own longstanding association with the palace—through his close friendship with its mid-16th-century owner Giacomo Contarini—and the post-Scarpagnino quality of such elements as its central pediment, so similar to the one on this sheet. The latter's unusually robust proportions, however, recall the closer prototype on the Palazzo Maggi at Padua, of 1502 (*cf.* cat. no. 2).

Palladio's lateral window frames derive very precisely from such well-studied models by Falconetto as the Loggia Cornaro (1524, fig. 2) and the Monte di Pietà (1531–35), both also in Padua; while the relative flatness of his facade strongly recalls the loggia at Cricoli, which Trissino himself adapted from a design by Serlio (1537, fig. 1), and whose upper niches are here exactly copied by Palladio.

4

4. FACADE PROJECT FOR PALAZZO DA MONTE, VICENZA (III)

c. 1540–41

RIBA: Palladio XVII/19.

22.1 × 26.5 cm. (single sheet); watermark, crossed arrows with star (variant of Briquet 6292/6293), "Palladio's standard paper" of c. 1540; Talman 150 mark on *verso*.

Light siena ink with gold-brown wash; inscribed lower left with project label, A.

Zorzi 1954, pp. 108–109, fig. 3; Pane 1961, p. 111, fig. 136:41; Zorzi 1965, p. 31, fig. 17; Puppi 1973, pp. 248–250, fig. 296; Arts Council 1975, p. 232, no. 410 (Fairbairn); Berger 1978, pp. 57–61, fig. 4.

Royal Institute of British Architects, London.

There is a startling difference in quality between this beautiful design and its immediate predecessor (cat. no. 3). Despite the exact congruity of measurement governing their common widths (24.4 cm. on the base lines) and the identical dispositions of their apertures (12.4 cm. to tops of the upper windows), the amateurish borrowings from early 16th-century Venetian classicism evident in the two preceding projects have here been almost completely replaced by a much grander and more soberly monumental reflection of High Renaissance architecture in Rome. Ever since Zorzi suggested two Roman models—the Raphael-esque Palazzo Caffarelli-Vidoni and Sangallo's "Piccola Farnesina"—for aspects of this design, it has been a commonplace of Palladian criticism to agree on these "sources," even though both are relatively late, only shortly predating the 1527 Sack of Rome. In fact Palladio's handsome facade has virtually no relation to either building, although several of its motifs do refer to Raphael more specifically. The most obvious of these (which Zorzi also pointed out, though secondarily) is the dependence of the center of the composition on the papal palace depicted in Raphael's great Vatican fresco of *The Fire in the Borgo* (1514). Not only are the triple-lighted windows of Palladio's earlier projects converted into an arched *serliana* essentially identical with Raphael's, but the close juxtaposition of this window to a powerful basement story of heroic rustication, including even the detail of boldly angled keystones directly beneath its center, is evidently derived from the fresco (or rather from one of its reproductive engravings). Beyond their framing pilasters these central elements are associated in both designs with nobly scaled columnar tabernacles supporting triangular pediments (on the flanks of Palladio's same facade and around the corner at the end of Raphael's). A still more exact Raphaelesque source for the highly unusual courses of rarely jointed or even continuous rustication, in the right-hand alternative on Palladio's ground floor, as well as for the broadly proportioned pedestals of the next zone, is provided by the imposing Palazzo Jacopo da Brescia (1515–18) in the Vatican Borgo Nuovo, of which a Heemskerck drawing of c. 1534/35 survives (Frommel 1973, pls. 21–24).

The question of Palladio's access to these Roman High Renaissance models involves the uncertain date of his own project. It has been assumed that his awareness of Central Italian prototypes as reflected in this drawing would have been gained on his first trip to Rome with Trissino in 1541, and so the resulting fabric of the Palazzo Da Monte in Vicenza (fig. 3) has commonly been dated to the early 1540s (also for the reason that an accurate depiction of it, as built, appears in G. A. Fasolo's *Supplication* fresco of c. 1550 in the Villa Colleoni at Thiene). But the paper of this sheet is one that Palladio was demonstrably using before his Roman journey, and more importantly, his drafting style here is still a very early one with rather stylized capitals, though indeed beautifully refined, with its light touch and delicate hatching. As Zorzi observed, the centrally projecting entablature with flanking *ressauts* over the corner pilasters probably documents Palladio's very recent acquaintance with similar Paduan motifs of Falconetto (*cf.* fig. 2, or the Porta Savonarola of 1528); and it might be added that Palladio's central pedimented pavilion even more strongly recalls the outer (1533) and inner (1540) frontispieces of Sanmicheli's Porta Nuova in Verona. Thus we may argue that this splendidly resolved design—evidently produced with the help of Roman drawings—might in fact represent the culmination of Palladio's Venetan accomplishment, on the eve of his journey to Rome in 1541.

Figure 3

22

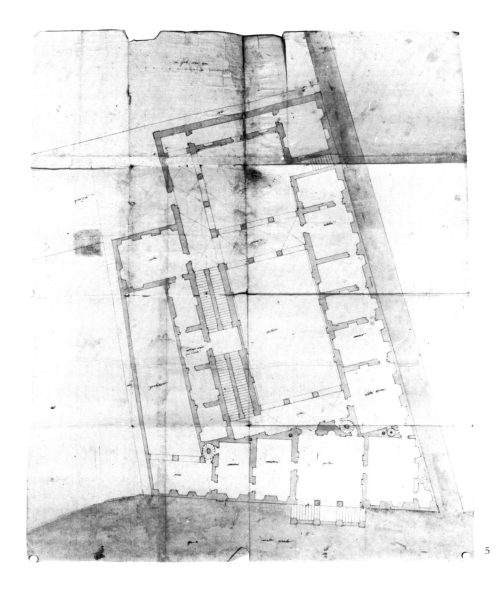

5

5. MICHELE SANMICHELI: PLAN PROJECT FOR PALAZZO GRIMANI AT S. SAMUELE, VENICE

April 1528–January 1529

Biblioteca Molmenti, Museo Correr: Disegni III/6038.

72.6 × 58.1 cm. (single sheet); watermark, an anchor (*cf.* Mošin 717).

Siena ink with gold-beige and light blue wash, pricked for transfer. *Recto* inscribed (from top left), "Tutto v[ie]ne passi X (inverted) / calle / piaza / Salotta; logia; Salotta / mezani avie[-]za (?) Scala; cortile / calle; giardino—; camera / logia; Salotta apiano / logia; camera; camera; porttico / canale grande." *Verso:* SANMICHELI (?): SKETCH OF A BASE MOLDING, very light pencil; inscribed at top in the hand of the Grimani secretary of 1597 (*cf.* ASV, Proc. de Supra, b. 36), "Desegnio dl Teren a S Samuel / Pianta p far Palazo a S Samuel."

Lewis 1972 I, pp. 7–36, figs. 1, 3–6, 14, and frontispiece; Venice 1980, p. 175, no. and fig. 174 (Olivato—as Sebastiano Serlio [?]).

Museo Civico Correr, Venice.

This drawing assumes a fundamental place in the history of Renaissance architecture in the Veneto, for it constitutes the first proposal for a great Venetian palace in a developed 16th-century style, as well as the first document for the North Italian resumption of Sanmicheli's architectural activity, after the Sack of Rome in May of 1527. Indeed it is to date the sole surviving drawing that can confidently be attributed to Sanmicheli: his authorship is effectively guaranteed, both through an alternative project of his for the same Grimani patron within the next few years, and also by Sanmicheli's immediate reuse of this unexecuted design in his plan for Palazzo Canossa, constructed at Verona from 1529/31 to 1537 (figs. 4, 5).

The sharply skewed site on the Grand Canal had been recognized as exceptionally difficult, ever since contemporary observers had described Bartolomeo Bon's preceding design of 1456–60 for an arrested Palazzo Corner (the later "Ca'del Duca"), on whose immense but irregular foundations the 1528 Grimani replacement was intended

Figure 4

Figure 5

to rise. Sanmicheli's solution to these twin problems, of an intransigent site and the colossal remains of an underlying masterwork, is itself—and at an even higher level of achievement—a masterpiece of Renaissance clarity and grandeur. The plan is resolved without the intrusion of a single non-rectilinear room, and a dominant central axis is opened from the gondola landing straight through to the back of the court. We have abundant proof of the admiration which the plan elicited: Sanmicheli's patrons in the Canossa family immediately took it over in its entirety, and their almost literal realization of it in Verona has consistently been acknowledged as a cornerstone of Renaissance architecture in the Veneto. And Sansovino's Palazzo Corner della Ca' Grande of 1545–66 in Venice evidently owes something of its facade organization to the Grimani/Canossa design, whose square court with flanking triple loggia

inside the rear entrance appears in the later Venetian palace (though this element may derive more directly from Sansovino's early Palazzo Gaddi begun in 1518 in Rome).

Palladio's first determined orientation toward developed 16th-century classical architecture is exemplified by his particular affinity for the work of Sanmicheli, whom he certainly had come to know well by the winter of 1541–42, when Michele resided in the Pedemuro shop during his extended consultations on the Vicentine Basilica. Even before Sanmicheli's documented visits to Vicenza, however, Palladio would have had numerous opportunities for contact with him in 1539–40 in Padua, where both were associated with closely interrelated circles of the architectural avant-garde (Lewis, 1972 II, pp. 387–388; Lewis 1976, pp. 30–32).

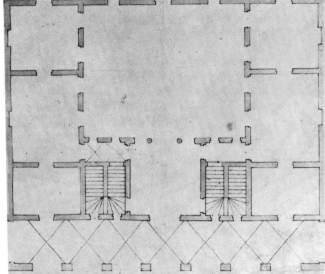

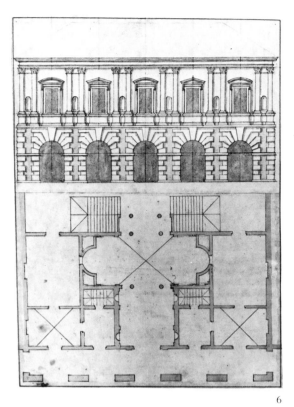

6

Figure 6 above
Figure 7 below

6. FACADE AND PLAN PROJECTS FOR PALAZZO CIVENA, VICENZA

1539–40

RIBA: Palladio XVII/14.

Top sheet 15.3 × 23.2 cm., Talman 257 mark on *verso;* bottom sheet 17.4 × 23.0 cm., Talman 150 mark on *verso;* total size of joined sheets (pasted with 0.4 cm. overlap), 32.3 × 23.2 cm.; no watermarks.

Top, light red siena ink, blond sepia and light brown washes, over umber chalk and very heavy incised lines; bottom, dark siena ink with yellow-gold wash.

Zorzi, 1949, pp. 101–102, fig. 105; Pane 1961, p. 101, fig. 120: 8; Zorzi 1965, p. 185, fig. 148; Forssman 1965, pp. 31–32, fig. 15; Forssman 1972, p. 91, fig. 48; Cevese 1973, p. 245, fig. 156; Puppi 1973, pp. 244–45; Mostra 1973, pp. 94–95 (Cevese), p. 149 (Burns), fig. 103; Arts Council 1975, p. 35, no. 46 (Burns); Berger 1978, pp. 43–56, 199–203, fig. 2; Verona 1980, p. 112, fig. (facade only) p. 117 (Burns).

Royal Institute of British Architects, London.

This handsome small palace is Palladio's first entirely independent work with a firm date (foundation medal 1540, "now constructed" by 7 April 1542), and no less than five plans and two elevations record its careful planning. Since no document or contemporary source names Palladio as the architect, once again, as in the case of cat. no. 4, it is the providential survival of autograph drawings such as these that guarantees Palladio's authorship.

When the Civena family acquired this property from Aurelio dall'Acqua in 1539, it stood beside the west bank of the River Retrone near the city walls, in a district of spacious gardens and arcaded porticoes along infrequent streets. Palladio particularly approved of porticoed side-walks, which he associated with his native Padua (*Quattro Libri* III:ii:8), and their combination with a deep garden on the Civena property in Vicenza seems to have reminded him of the Paduan residence of Alvise Cornaro, where Palladio was first exposed to modern architectural theory and practice during the Paduan sojourns he is assumed to have shared with Trissino between late 1538 and 1540. For this reason it may be appropriate to associate with his Palazzo Civena projects RIBA XVI/6, a very early and heavy-handed design (possibly an exercise preserved from his "student" days in Padua) of a simple "functionalist" house whose sidewalk portico, narrow central hall, and back garden with an ornamental five-bay loggia all closely reflect those of the Cornaro residence.

However, Palladio's first plan that can definitely be associated with the Civena project is RIBA XVI/17 (fig. 7), set between a vaulted portico and a deep garden. The house assumes from the beginning its consistent (and eventually executed) open U-shape of a narrow range behind the entrance portico—with wider rooms extending to the facade above it—and short rear wings embracing a small interior court. This first proposal is larger than its successors, with a portico of seven narrow bays in front, and lateral ranges of three rooms running back along the court: these are reduced to five portico bays and two lateral rooms in the succeeding projects, which omit the garden. It is interesting, however, that the entrance hall (or "atrium") appears here exactly as it was eventually built, with a square plan, four side doors, and one (surviving, though relocated) *serliana* at the end.

The next two plan projects are presented on a single sheet (RIBA XVI/11 top), the alternative being in the form of a flap pasted over the atrium; both propose a wide transverse entrance hall, with a double *serliana* giving access to twin staircases at the back. Palladio's fourth suggestion is the plan component of the present composite sheet, which returns to a square atrium (with the elaboration of lateral pilasters and niches) but follows it with a wide, pilastered transverse hall, into whose ends two apses are inserted as an afterthought—the main stairs thus being forced out onto the garden facade. The patrons must have requested greater economy, for what seems to be Palladio's final plan (RIBA XVI/11 bottom) shows him erasing a similar double-apsed transverse atrium, and reducing this element to the small square hall eventually built, with the further simplifications of lateral doors instead of niches, and a single *serliana* as the garden portal. (Its twin, and the major stair they were intended to introduce, had to wait for their realization until Domenico Cerato remodeled and extended the center of the building, around 1750.)

The present facade design, attached in England in the 18th century to Palladio's fourth plan, could probably equally well have been associated with his second, third, or fifth: the wider first project requires expanded terminal piers (see cat. no. 7). Apart from removing a slightly differentiated bay at each end, this elevation almost exactly reproduces a facade (fig. 6) published in 1575 in Serlio's *Seventh Book* (ch. xxv:63—*cf.* Rosci 1967, p. 16), to whose preliminary drawing Palladio could have had access during Serlio's visits to Cricoli in 1537–38, to Vicenza in January/February 1539, or through Paduan or Venetian intermediaries during the latter or following year.

7. FACADE PROJECT FOR PALAZZO CIVENA, VICENZA

1539

RIBA: Palladio XIII/10.

34.3 × 28.9 cm. (single sheet); watermark, crossed arrows with star (variant of Briquet 6292/6293), "Palladio's standard paper" of c. 1540; Talman 54 mark on *verso*.

Umber ink, thinning to dark auburn/siena.

Zorzi 1949, p. 101, fig. 103; Zorzi 1954, p. 111, fig. 6; Pane 1961, pp. 100–101, fig. 120: 6; Cevese 1964, p. 344, and 1965, p. 344; Forssman 1965, pp. 30–31, fig. 14; Zorzi 1965, p. 184, fig. 146; Puppi 1973, pp. 244–245; Mostra 1973, p. 146 (Burns—as c. 1550); Arts Council 1975, p. 231, no. 408 (Burns—as "XVII/10"); Berger 1978, pp. 43–56, 199–203, fig. 1; Verona 1980, p. 118, no. and fig. V, 2 (Burns).

Royal Institute of British Architects, London.

This magnificent and highly important early drawing—which, with the comparable and contemporary elevation for Palazzo Da Monte (cat. no. 4), marks Palladio's achievement of masterly status as a draftsman and designer—has been unfairly doubted as pertaining to the planning of Palazzo Civena (Cevese, Burns). It is possible, however, to date it confidently to an early phase of the plans drawn for that project between 1539 and 1540, since its wide terminal support and narrow intermediate piers, though here reduced to five bays, relate it uniquely to Palladio's first plan proposal (on RIBA XVI/17—fig. 7). The executed facade (fig. 10) as well as the intermediate elevation at the top of RIBA XVII/14 (cat. no. 6) preserve both the proportions and several of the details of this initial project, particularly the delicate window tabernacles borrowed directly from Falconetto's Loggia Cornaro (fig. 2). In the present design these are set between the boldly projecting shafts of engaged Tuscan columns—doubled at the end, and supporting a richly sculptured entablature—above a basement of heavily rusticated round-headed arches. These individual elements and their strong three-dimensional plasticity derive very directly from Bramante's Palazzo Caprini of c. 1501–10 in Rome (cat. no. 24), which this drawing suggests Palladio must have known through the intervention of Sanmicheli. Wherever Palladio's elevation differs substantially from Bramante's, it comes much closer to Sanmicheli's great Palazzo Pompei in Verona (fig. 8)—so close, indeed (and representing so radical a development for the almost untrained Palladio), as to suggest his intimate knowledge of the Sanmichelian design.

But Palazzo Pompei is undated, and most recent commentators have placed it around or shortly after 1550; while Palladio's related project can be rather precisely assigned, as we have seen, to 1539. Berger and I have independently concluded that this drawing by Palladio provides clear evidence for the traditional dating of Sanmicheli's palace to c. 1530; two supporting arguments which have not yet been mentioned are the numerous prototypes among Serlio's drawings—which left the Veneto in 1541—for Palazzo Pompei's notoriously off-center courtyard (Rosci 1967/Rosenfeld 1978), and a prefiguration of the court's

Figure 8

7

Figure 9

Figure 10

unusual use of columns rather than piers in Sanmicheli's newly discovered palace project of 1528 (cat. no. 5). We do know that during his 1539–40 stay in Padua Palladio would have been associated both with circles that included patrons of Sanmicheli's and, presumably, with the artist himself. And it is also clear that Palladio was looking very specifically at Sanmichelian models as he developed his subsequent facade project for Palazzo Civena (cat. no. 6), in whose rustication Burns has astutely noticed a reflection of Sanmicheli's 1535–40 city front for the Porta Nuova in Verona—a pattern that is also repeated on the executed portal of the Palazzo Da Monte (cat. no. 4), as another proof of that building's Palladian authorship and coeval date. Palladio continued to follow Sanmicheli in basing the closely paired flat pilasters of the executed Palazzo Civena, as well as its smooth and polished rustication, on the elder master's Palazzo Canossa of the same decade (fig. 4). The recessed compartments of Palladio's executed piers form the most self-consciously "modern" element in his final design, with their up-to-the-minute stylishness in quoting a motif from the title page of Serlio's *Third Book*, published in March of 1540 (fig. 9).

---

8. REMNANTS OF A ROMAN TOMB (THE "TORRE SACELLO"), SPOLETO

1540/41

RIBA: Palladio IX/18 *recto*.

44.1 × 29.1 cm. (single sheet); no watermark.

Light umber ink, over brown crayon. *Recto* inscribed in composite handwriting with epsilon and later scripts. At top, rotated detail of entablature of Temple of Antoninus and Faustina, Rome (in isometric projection; compare orthographic rendering in *Quattro Libri*, IV:ix:35). *Verso:* left, corner detail (in isometric perspective) of ENTABLATURE OF "TEMPLE OF SERAPIS" ON THE QUIRINAL, copied from a similar source (reversed with respect to the previous image) as the superb rendition in Codex Coner fol. 81 (Ashby 1902, p. 43), or Serlio's woodcut of 1540 (III:81); inscribed in epsilon handwriting with scale of ⅓ *braccia* = 194 mm. (6½ Vicentine inches), and with label in a hand combining epsilon and later scripts. Right, ENTABLATURE AND BASE PROFILES of the same, labeled in composite epsilon and later handwriting. Zorzi 1956, p. 57, fig. 5 (as Falconetto); Zorzi 1959, p. 75, fig. 157 (as Falconetto, with Palladio inscriptions); Spielmann 1966, p. 146, no. 61, fig. 29.

Zorzi 1956, pp. 57–58, fig. 6 (as Falconetto); Zorzi 1959, p. 102, fig. 253 (as Falconetto, with Palladio inscriptions); Spielmann 1966, p. 178, no. 255 (transcribing inscriptions); Burns 1973, pp. 184, 190 note 27, fig. 132 (as c. 1547/51); Arts Council 1975, p. 147, no. 260 (Burns) Paris 1975, p. 38 (note and ill.).

Royal Institute of British Architects, London.

This sheet is unusual for its finished drawings of unrelated subjects on different axes, and is interesting for its testimony about Palladio's accumulation of such concentrated study drawings. Its date is important to establish, since it influences the chronology of other less informative early sheets. Its visual evidence suggests inquiry along three lines: the sources of its images, their graphic handling, and the handwriting of Palladio's inscriptions.

The bold and beautiful entablature fragment on the *verso* does indeed reflect (as a mirror image) a superb drawing in the Codex Coner of c. 1515, as well as a small detail from Serlio's *Third Book* of 1540. Palladio's drawing is more three-dimensional, however, and it also introduces a substantial variation from the prototypes: the curiously beveled underside of the corona in the main cornice block, above the heavily carved modillions. Moreover, its meticulously measured profile carries annotations which are much more detailed than those in Serlio, and which are similar to but slightly different from those in the Codex Coner. These considerations apply as well to the entablature detail squeezed sideways onto the *recto*, and combine to suggest an independent source.

Although it might be thought that the principal tomb depictions could likewise have been copied from an unidentified source, their images offer hints of a personal formulation by Palladio. The central isometric perspective is handled in exactly the same manner as Palladio's first depictions of other ancient monuments: a main "elevation" tricked out with illusionistic shadows in his early cross-hatching technique, and embellished by a lateral perspective receding in depth. Furthermore, Palladio notes that part of this structure is still buried, and gives the name of its owner, who, as a delegate of the Papal court, might have been recommended or even introduced to him by Trissino. These personal touches are reinforced by the fact that no comparable drafted prototype has yet (to my knowledge) been located, which may in fact mean that Spoleto was rather too distant to have formed part of a standard itinerary for the earlier compilers of Roman sketchbooks. The Umbrian town is, however, on one of the main routes from Florence, Arezzo, and Perugia to Rome: if Palladio and Trissino had taken such a path to or from the Eternal City in 1541, we might thus be able to understand this drawing's measurements in Roman *palmi* (and on the *verso* in Florentine *braccia*—of which Palladio copies out a scale, as if practicing his measures).

A piece of evidence in this regard that so far seems not to have been noticed is that the highly distinctive drafting technique on the rusticated basement of this tomb is precisely identical to that on the 1539 elevation for Palazzo Civena (cat. no. 7). Since Palladio's graphic style was rapidly evolving in these early years, such an absolute identity of form argues compellingly for a close congruence of date. There is good reason to conclude, then, that the present sheet may reflect earlier Roman (and/or Florentine) drawings, on a corrected studio copy that incorporates, in its main images, finished versions of sketches that Palladio himself might have made on site in Spoleto in 1541. The

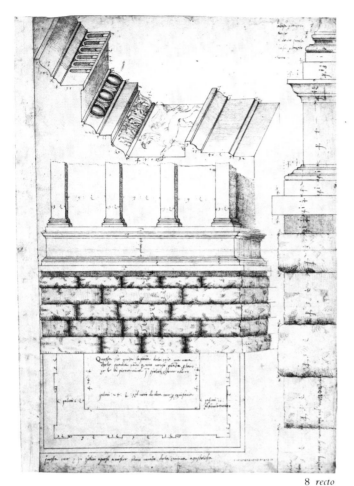

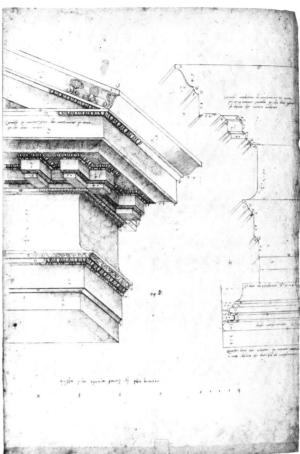

8 *recto*

8 *verso*

closest alternative would be for a similar process to have occurred in 1545 during Palladio's next journey to Rome, when we know that he did pass through Spoleto; but by then his drafting techniques were radically different, and above all he would no longer have needed (or taken the time to produce) such rather ingenuous images of isolated minor antiquities. Their *content* relates these drawings unmistakably to Palladio's eclectic "student" days, and their *style* anchors them securely to the period of his Palazzo

Civena drawings. Since their inscriptions show every sign of being contemporaneous, we are left with the strong probability that already by the time of his first trip to Rome, Palladio's handwriting had begun its evolution away from the arcane neo-Greek mannerism of the "ep-silon" form—a form which was doubtless inspired by Trissino in 1537/38, and of which Palladio would retain at least traces throughout the following first decade of his independence.

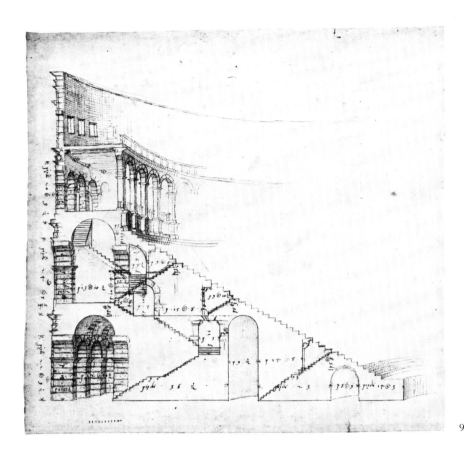

9

9. PERSPECTIVE SECTION OF THE ROMAN AMPHITHEATRE, VERONA

Early 1540s

RIBA: Palladio VIII/19.

27.7 × 28.3 cm. (single sheet); no watermark; laid lines 38.5 mm. apart; Talman 49 mark on *verso*.

Soft umber-brown ink, over pencil or brown crayon; inscribed in epsilon handwriting with measures in feet, with a scale of 10 units = 21.5 mm. (¾ of a Venetian inch).

Zorzi 1956, pp. 58–59, fig. 7 (as Falconetto); Zorzi 1959, p. 97, fig. 234 (as Falconetto, inscribed by Palladio); Spielmann 1966, p. 157, no. 127 (as autograph, before 1550); Arts Council 1975, p. 44, no. 66; Verona 1980, pp. 66–67, no. and fig. III, 41 (Franzoni).

Royal Institute of British Architects, London.

This delicate and appealing little drawing is a working architect's "dissection" of an ancient monument, made in an effort to understand its complex three-dimensional structure; yet in its softly sketched perspectives it catches something of the freshness and enthusiasm of Palladio's first encounters with Roman architecture.

It is hard to judge from this sheet alone whether Palladio's awareness of the Verona amphitheatre at the moment that he made this sketch was firsthand or borrowed. Such oddly composed half-sections of monuments, with the orthographic drawing of the "cut" combined with isometric renditions of the curving elements behind it, were a standard feature of early Renaissance architectural sketchbooks. Images closely analogous to this one occur not only in the

Mellon sketchbook of 1513 at the Pierpont Morgan Library in New York, but also in the Codex Coner at the Sir John Soane Museum in London (Ashby 1902, p. 30, fig. 39). Palladio's "anatomical" drawing follows the established conventions of this type, but demonstrates an unusually particularized detail in its elaborate series of measurements, which seem very likely to record his work in a field survey on the site. He might, of course, simply have entered his measures on a pre-existing drawing that he copied earlier from a sketchbook; but the extensive use of pencil preparations suggests some likelihood of independent composition, and the ink color of the measurements seems very close to that of the sketch.

Zorzi has pointed out (1956 p. 59) that the better-preserved upper levels, which appear in a print of the amphitheatre from Giovanni Caroto's *Antichità di Verona* of 1560, suggest that even though the outer portions survive only fragmentarily today, they may well have been complete enough in the mid-16th century for us to consider Palladio's rendering more in the light of an accurate survey than a hypothetical reconstruction. When Goethe described the structure (as the first great monument of the ancient world that he had seen, on 16 September 1786) only the present isolated "wing" of the outer wall remained, with its four-bay section rising barely above the third-story arcade. The *cavea* is wonderfully intact (though considerably restored), and can still seat some 22,000 spectators for outdoor productions of the summer opera season.

10

10. PLAN AND ELEVATION DETAILS OF THE FIRST TERRACE WALL ABOVE THE ROMAN THEATRE, VERONA

Early 1540s

RIBA: Palladio X/13, restored and remounted as *recto.*

29.0 × 43.6 cm (single sheet); watermark, anchor in circle with star (*cf.* Mošin 748); Talman 49 mark on *recto.*

Siena ink; *recto,* labeled and inscribed with Vicentine and antique feet, and a scale of six units = 43.5 mm. (1½ Venetian in.), first in epsilon script and then in later handwriting. *Verso,* GROUND PLAN OF SUBSTRUCTURES AND TERRACES OF THE ROMAN THEATRE, VERONA, labeled and inscribed with antique and Vicentine feet, and columns of figures, first in epsilon script and then in later handwriting; Zorzi 1951, pp. 7–8, fig. 7; Zorzi 1959, p. 93, fig. 218; Spielmann 1966, p. 154, no. 112, fig. 64 (as *recto*); Zorzi 1969, p. 239, fig. 443; Magagnato 1972, p. 140, fig. 75; Verona 1980, p. 58, no. and fig. III, 34 (Franzoni).

Zorzi 1951, pp. 8–9, fig. 8; Zorzi 1959, p. 94, fig. 222; Spielmann 1966, p. 155, no. 116, fig. 66 (as *verso*); Zorzi 1969, p. 239, fig. 448; Verona 1980, p. 61, no. and fig. III, 37 (Franzoni).

Royal Institute of British Architects, London.

The early first-century Roman theatre of Verona was one of the most impressive of its kind, and remains tolerably well-preserved even today. From a commanding position on the far bank it dominates the great bend of the River Adige surrounding the center of the ancient city, with which it was connected by two symmetrical bridges placed a short distance beyond its outer sides. It backs against a high hill overlooking the city from the northeast, and in this sheet Palladio presents the first of several images which record its most unusual features: a series of superimposed terraces that embellished the upper parts of the slope above

the main architectural fabric (*cf.* cat. nos. 11, 82). Encircling the top of the *cavea* was an outer exterior wall, already exceptional in being raised some twenty feet higher than the customary arcade above the tiers of seats: it evidently functioned as a retaining element for the continuing upward slope behind the theatre, and (with the high stage building opposite) must have given the auditorium an even greater than usual effect of a deep, enveloping space. To counteract this impression, and to gain the greatest sense of architectural and civic drama from the still higher slopes remaining behind, the Augustan architect carved these into a series of shelf-like terraces, cut into the hill's tufa bedrock, and then decorated his superimposed setbacks of vertical cuts with elaborate decorative screens, or "facade" walls. These were executed in the classic *opus reticolatum* of diamond-set pieces of tufa or brick, and Palladio in his sheet shows us the system devised for the first terrace, which defines the back of a broad walkway that extended twenty-five feet back from the apex of the *cavea* (his plan on the *verso* sacrifices this terrace, in compressing all the elements onto a single sheet).

The architectural scheme of a deep semicircular niche, rhythmically flanked by engaged Tuscan columns framing paneled compartments, is both dramatically effective through its patterns of color and light and shade, as well as a subtle recapitulation, on a more human scale, of many solid and spatial shapes prefigured in the ornamental stage backdrop far below. Palladio's sensitive early drawing clearly responds to the "pictorial" and sculptural qualities of this sham facade, and his soft but persuasive chiaroscuro is nowhere more appealingly handled than in the delicately crosshatched shading of this finely detailed elevation.

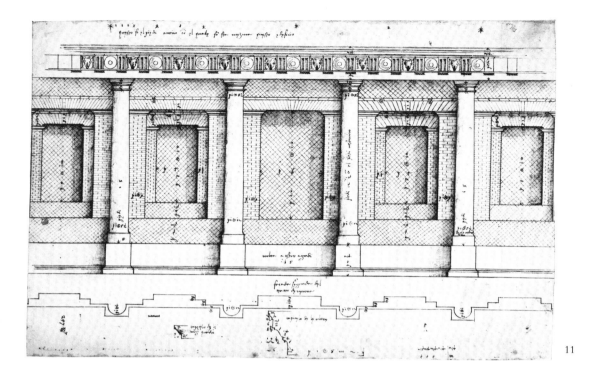

11. PLAN AND ELEVATION DETAILS OF THE SECOND TERRACE WALL ABOVE THE ROMAN THEATRE, VERONA

Early 1540s

RIBA: Palladio XII/22, restored and remounted as *recto.*

28.8 × 43.2 cm. (single sheet); illegible countermark upper left; Talman 257 mark on *recto.*

Recto, dark siena ink, with very pale sepia wash; labeled and inscribed with epsilon handwriting and measures in antique feet (with two in Vicentine feet in later script), and with scale of full antique foot = 29.6 cm. (or 10 Vicentine in.). *Verso,* PARTIAL ELEVATION AND DETAILS OF THE ARCH OF JUPITER AMMON, VERONA (illus. cat. no. 12): dark umber ink, with beige wash; labeled and inscribed in epsilon handwriting with measures in antique feet, and with two scales, of which (lower left) 2 units = 51 mm., and (left center) 4 units = 41.5 mm.; Zorzi 1951, p. 6, fig. 5; Zorzi 1957, p. 68, fig. 2; Zorzi 1959, p. 52, fig. 25; Crema 1966, p. 169, fig. 179; Spielmann 1966, p. 171, no. 219 (transcribing inscription); Brizio 1970, p. 71, fig. 37; Verona 1980, p. x (Magagnato), pp. 52–53, no. and fig. III, 30 (Tosi).

Wittkower 1949/71, p. 85, fig. 30c; Zorzi 1951, pp. 8–9, fig. 9; Zorzi 1959, p. 94, fig. 223; Spielmann 1966, p. 155, no. 117 (transcribing inscriptions); Zorzi 1969, p. 239, fig. 447; Mostra 1973, p. 145 (Burns); Arts Council 1975, p. 111, no. 209 (Burns); Verona 1980, p. x (Magagnato), pp. 61–62, no. and fig. III, 38 (Franzoni).

Royal Institute of British Architects, London.

This drawing depicts the decorated wall at the back of a second intermediate terrace, between the auditorium of the Verona theatre and a final temple platform above it (now covered by the Castel San Pietro). The relationship of the terraces to each other, as well as to the theatre below and the temple above, can be seen in Palladio's ground plan (cat. no. 10, *verso*), in his reconstructed elevation and section of the whole complex (cat. no. 82), and in a section through the front of the hill, whose platform top was thought to have been crowned by a *tempietto* with flanking wings (RIBA IX/4). Although Palladio inserted small access stairs at the outer corners of the successive terraces (not shown in these elevations, but visible in his plan and reconstruction), archaeologically it is not clear whether such connecting flights existed (Marconi 1937, p. 133), and indeed no traces of protective parapets or balustrades seem to have been found on either terrace.

The facade system applied to this second hillside wall is even more fully rendered than the one beneath it (cat. no. 10), which curiously lacks any superstructure. This upper range is shown with a full entablature above its engaged Tuscan columns, and with a still more elaborate layering of thin pilaster-piers, set in receding planes within the compartments between the column shafts. These last (as in the preceding drawing) terminate in vestigial "bases" of a plain vertical profile, which provide a transition to low pedestals. Exactly such simplified and unusual bases were reproduced by Palladio (after he had experimented with other ideas—see cat. nos. 61–63) in his great Basilica at Vicenza, whose invention in the mid-1540s thus provides a probable *terminus* for his notations of an antique prototype on these two sheets. In 1949 Wittkower pointed out that the paneled compartments recorded here could be related to Palladio's similar compositions around the first-floor windows of his later Palazzo Valmarana facade; we might only add that still a third element—the frieze design of alternating *bucrania* and *paterae,* with these two motifs exchanging places at the centers of successive bays—also reappears regularly in Palladio's succeeding work.

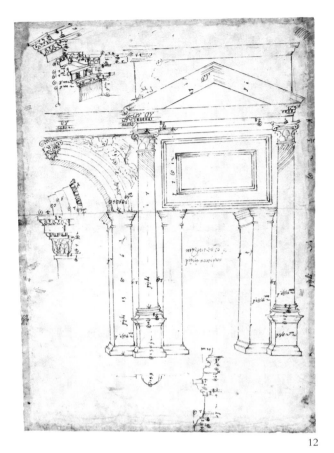

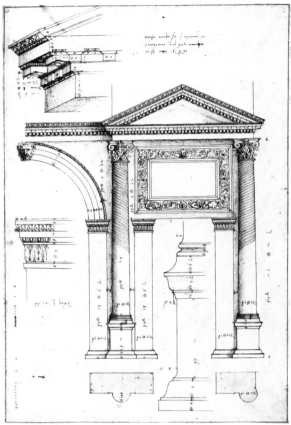

12. PARTIAL ELEVATION AND DETAILS OF THE ARCH OF JUPITER AMMON, VERONA

c. 1540

RIBA: Palladio XII/14.

39.5 × 27.9 cm. (single sheet); watermark, top center, anchor in circle with star, and countermark, lower left, S✝C (much smaller [5.2 × 3.2 cm.] and earlier prototype for Mošin 1114); Talman 49 mark on *verso*.

Very light siena ink; inscribed, in epsilon handwriting, with measures in antique feet.

Zorzi 1951, p. 5, fig. 4; Zorzi 1957, p. 67, fig. 1 (as Falconetto); Zorzi 1959, p. 52, fig. 24 (as Falconetto, inscribed by Palladio); Spielmann 1966, p. 171, no. 218 (as autograph, probably before 1545); Verona 1980, pp. 51–52, no. and fig. III, 29 (Tosi), and pp. 100–101 (Burns).

Royal Institute of British Architects, London.

The *verso* of the preceding sheet presents a finished drawing of this same subject, by which the preliminary image in this much lighter and looser sheet should therefore be identified either as a rough copy from an earlier survey, or as an original annotated field drawing. Points in favor of the latter origin are the slightly skewed horizontals in the panel and attic (Palladio's studio drawings are scrupulously aligned), the painstaking detail in the entablature enlargement (where the surely sketched architectural forms work as an inseparable unity with the hastily inscribed measures), and Palladio's unmistakably autograph notations

of sculpture, most of which are omitted from the clean copy. The three sculptural sketches are in fact diagnostic: none are very good, and they decline sharply in quality from the somewhat caricatured head of Zeus Ammon, on the keystone (much more nobly handled in the finished version, proving that Palladio really could manage quite well with physiognomic detail when he tried), through a stiffly articulated spandrel *Victory,* to the summarily suggested acroterial figure above the pediment—which cogently epitomizes Palladio's very real limitations as a figural draftsman.

This sheet is an early one (as evidenced by its "shading" with close-set parallel strokes), and shows Palladio instinctively still using the old-fashioned three-quarter view to achieve a spatial depth for many details, especially while sketching on site. This habit should probably be tied to his training as a stonemason, and his workmanlike need to visualize clearly the three-dimensional character of each block. He suppresses all these illusionistic devices in his final copy, which is a "pure" elevation (cat. no. 11, *verso*); only the separate entablature detail retains its three-dimensional perspective. It should also be noted that he is in fact using the technique only to emphasize variations from the facade plane: actually this arch (once at the intersection of the Corso Borsari and the Via Quattro Spade, but now destroyed) had a corresponding face set deeply behind this one, with a wide arch in each end (RIBA XII/13); but no such spatial development is visible in this sketch.

13

13. PLAN AND ELEVATION DETAILS OF THE ARCH OF THE SERGII, POLA

c. 1540

RIBA: Palladio XII/9.

50.5 × 38.8 cm. (four pieces of paper joined by Palladio to make enlarged sheet); watermarks, in main piece (upper right center), anchor in circle with star, with countermark (lower left) S‡C (prototype for Mošin 1114); in large left piece, same countermark (lower right), though cut; single Talman 49 mark on *verso*.

Extremely light siena ink; labeled and inscribed in epsilon handwriting, with Veronese measures and scale of 2 feet = 24 mm (2 "antique" inches—*cf.* cat. no. 11).

Zorzi 1955, p. 51, fig. 40 (as Falconetto); Zorzi 1957, p. 69, fig. 3 (as Falconetto); Zorzi 1959, pp. 61–62, fig. 70 (as Falconetto, inscribed by Palladio); Spielmann 1966, p. 175, no. 233, fig. 125 (as autograph, probably between 1541 and 1545); Traversari 1971, pp. 25–26, *disegno* 6 (as RIBA XII/7 [*sic*], as Falconetto); Verona 1980, p. 101 (Burns).

Royal Institute of British Architects, London.

This light and graceful drawing is virtually a twin to the preceding sheet, and is drawn on the same paper; as if to clinch the relationship it is inscribed "*larcha de pola mezurato/ cō el piede veroneze* (the arch at Pola, measured in Veronese feet)." There can be no question of its secure status as a very early survey by Palladio himself (demonstrated by the illusionistic "projection" of relief in depth, the extensive but delicate parallel shading, and the unmistakably characteristic figure sketches and acanthus leaves, as well as by the standard early handwriting). There also can be no doubt that it was drawn on the spot, with its slightly wobbly axes, yet sharply observed small details—as for example in the side elevation shown at the right, with its tilted base but highly detailed frieze.

These considerations should remove any suspicion that geographically incongruous units of measure (*e.g.* antique feet in Verona, Veronese ones at Pola) could alone be taken as evidence of Palladio's copying from borrowed graphic models. This and the preceding sheet are too much alike to support any hypothesis of different draftsmen reaching such results independently; and agreement on a single artist must automatically confirm Palladio's authorship, since so many parallels exist between these early antique sketches and his own documented projects.

The highly decorated little funerary arch dedicated at Pola by the family of the Sergii during the first century A.D. still stands, adjacent to the main *piazza;* Palladio's sketch is extraordinarily accurate, even to the tiny charioteer on the main frieze panel (who drives two horses, however, rather than one). He later produced a finished studio drawing based on this sketch (cat. no. 14).

14

14. PARTIAL MAIN ELEVATION AND SIDE ELEVATION OF THE ARCH OF THE SERGII, POLA

c. 1550

Vicenza: 1950 inv. D-29 *recto*.

41.7 × 28.0 cm. (single sheet with beveled corners); indistinct watermark of curved form in circle, probably anchor or crossbow; no collector's mark.

Siena ink, inscribed in middle-period handwriting with Veronese measures and scale (as in cat. no. 13). *Verso,* PLAN OF THE ARCH, umber ink on pencil underdrawing.

Loukomski 1927, pp. 37–38, fig. V(a); Zorzi 1955, p. 50, fig. 41; Zorzi 1957, p. 70, fig. 6; Zorzi 1959, p. 62, figs. 71 (*verso*), 72 (*recto*); Spielmann 1966, p. 175, no. 234, fig. 124 (as workshop, after 1560); Traversari 1971, pp. 26–27, *disegno* 7; Verona 1980, p. 84 (Burns).

Museo Civico, Vicenza.

The still-open question of whether Palladio made his preliminary sketches for the Pola antiquities—as for example the preparatory study for this drawing of the Arch, in cat. no. 13—as an eyewitness on the spot (as I incline to believe), or from on-site surveys by Falconetto (as Burns proposes) can be put aside when we reach the beautiful finished drawings that were developed from them in the studio. The present sheet is one of the finest of these, and is important in helping to fix a chronology for Palladio's graphic style around mid-century. Spielmann unjustifiably

called it a workshop production from the 1560s, whereas in fact its secure status as a very impressive autograph work from a few years on either side of 1550 can be proven by a series of firm parallels.

The delicately detailed rendering of the Corinthian order, which is subtly reinforced by tiny horizontal shadings in the capitals, is a simplification of the form used on the Minerva temple at Assisi (cat. no. 34), a sheet here dated to 1541—and which in any event cannot be later than 1547. Palladio's soft vertical shadow lines in the attic are exactly comparable to those on his earlier drawing of the Arch of Constantine (cat. no. 37), for which as it happens we do have the useful "control" of another version that is strikingly different, and definitely from the 1560s (cat. no. 38). The exceptional clarity and fineness of line, and the reticent symmetrical inscriptions with measures, are paralleled by similar qualities in the finished Portico of Octavia drawing probably of the middle 1550s (cat. no. 40), but the latter is more boldly rendered and less finicky than the Pola arch. Some of our drawing's closest analogies are to be found in the first Rialto Bridge project of 1552–54 (cat. no. 70), especially in the very rare motif of the beveled "Verona molding" on the top of the attic piers. It is thus possible to suggest that while the shading techniques hold us close to the late 1540s, the other forms of the dawing are closely related to the "Vitruvian" sheets of early in the next decade, and guarantee a date close to 1550.

35

15. EXTERIOR WALLS AND STAIR TOWERS OF THE ROMAN AMPHITHEATRE, POLA

Before 1540

RIBA: Palladio VIII/23 *recto.*

25.5 × 48.6 cm. (two pieces joined by Palladio to make larger sheet, with later hinge on back); watermark, on right piece, ladder in shield below star (Briquet 5933: Verona 1536); Talman 49 mark on *verso.*

Light gray-umber ink; inscribed in epsilon hand with measures in feet. *Verso,* ROUND-HEADED OPENING IN BASEMENT ZONE OF TALL PEDESTALS (left), and ONE BAY OF DECORATED PALACE FACADE (right); pencil sketches; Burns 1979, p. 18.

Zorzi 1959, p. 97, fig. 235; Spielmann 1966, p. 158, no. 130, fig. 78; Paris 1975, p. 38 (note and ill.); Verona 1980, p. 84, with fig. (Burns—as after Falconetto).

Royal Institute of British Architects, London.

This and the following sheet present an interesting reversal of the standard drafting process: in this case the finished drawing of the full monument comes first, and the detailed field sketches made on site represent a later stage in Palladio's study of this still well-preserved and exciting structure. Such an inversion may be explained by the character of the present "view" of the amphitheatre as a studio reconstruction, based on a borrowed graphic prototype, and by the clear evidence that Palladio's later survey (cat. no. 16) was intended to improve details that he had lacked or misunderstood in his earlier source.

The model for this image is not—as might seem logical—the detailed treatment which Serlio gives the Pola amphitheatre in his *Third Book* of 1540 (pp. 77–79), although some of his measures are the same as ones on this sheet; for Serlio's plan includes fifteen lateral bays between the towers, as opposed to Palladio's thirteen, and Palladio's elevations are more particularized than those on the printed plate (though sometimes less true to reality, as a comparison with the monument itself attests). Palladio is therefore working from a still earlier image, produced by a draftsman more interested in dramatic contrasts than in archaeological accuracy: the pilasters that Palladio copies as smooth are actually rusticated throughout, and stand over base pedestals which are also broken forward in a rusticated "pilaster" strip down the center, rather than having uniform blocks from edge to edge. These and several other corrections in the superstructure and the towers are incorporated into Palladio's on-site drawing discussed in the following entry, by which we know that he eventually checked his earlier drawing through a personal field inspection. Palladio's unknown source not only was more complete than Serlio, but may also have introduced the curious ambiguity of a "perspective" view that adopts a three-dimensional illusionism in the towers and more distant terminal bays, but shows a papery flatness in the skin-deep elevation of the nearer flank. Since Serlio provides a good deal of evidence for the development of the piers in depth, it seems probable that Palladio's somewhat credulous drawing—and certainly its retardative prototype—would predate Serlio's publication of the monument in March of 1540. Burns has recently proposed that the sources for Serlio's plates would be on-site drawings by Falconetto, which Palladio could have used as well. The argument independently developed above, and especially the origin and date of the watermark in the paper, support this view.

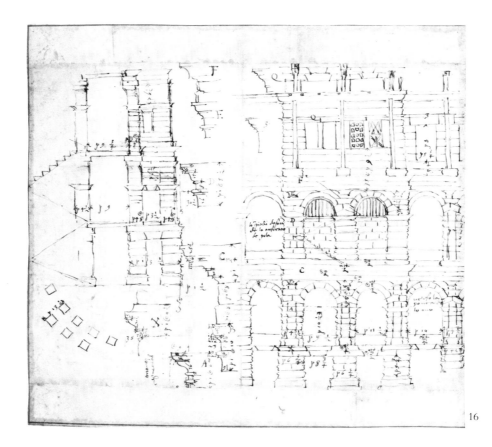

16

16. DETAILS OF PLAN, SECTION, AND ELEVATIONS OF THE ROMAN AMPHITHEATRE, POLA

After 1541

RIBA: Palladio VIII/21 *recto* and *verso*.

28.6 × 37.5 cm. (single sheet, unusually white); watermark (left center), sun with twelve rays, and countermark (lower right), trefoil on staff, with obscure initials (earlier variant of Briquet 13946); Talman 49 mark on *verso*.

Dark umber ink, with later inscriptions in very dark brown ink.

Zorzi 1955, pp. 50–51, fig. 45; Zorzi 1957, p. 70, fig. 7; Zorzi 1959, p. 98, figs. 238 *(recto)* and 239 *(verso)*; Spielmann 1966, p. 158, no. 132 (giving inscriptions, but not distinguishing later labels in heavy dark ink—at center, on *recto*; at lower right, on *verso*—from earlier field notes in lighter ink; and omitting from *recto* "ponta de lo vovo," at lower left, and from *verso* "e dentro," at center); Mostra 1973, p. 142 (Burns); latter two sources give dimensions respectively too small and too large: left margin is actually 28.1 cm. h., right margin 28.6 cm. h.; length is 37.5 as given by Spielmann.

Royal Institute of British Architects, London.

There can be no question at all that this significant early drawing displays a series of field studies made by Palladio on the site of the great Roman circus at Pola. The paper on which it is sketched is a type not normally used by Palladio for finished studio drawings; moreover, the sheet has been folded for easier carrying and use in the field: the *recto* sketches divide at the fold, and all were evidently drawn on a small board. Both vertical and horizontal lines stray significantly from their true axes (a phenomenon so rare as to be almost nonexistent in Palladio's studio productions, but inevitable when drawing on the knee), and there are several instances of blurred or scrubbed lines, where Palladio changed his mind after a closer look. But these carefully interrelated sketches (with such refinements as molding details keyed by letter to their positions on the elevation) are amazingly sure and incisive in their handling, and a comparison with the surviving monument confirms their exceptionally high accuracy as well.

The sheet therefore is important in demonstrating Palladio's increasingly confident command of drawing as an analytic medium for archaeological use in the field. Its early date can be adduced from the "transitional" handwriting of the original field notes (with early *p*'s, but mature *e*'s), and especially by lingering examples of Palladio's early tendency to lapse into the old-fashioned habit of developing "pure" elevation elements in isometric depth. Thus the one full three-story bay on the *verso* has pier capitals and arch soffits drawn (albeit faintly) in perspective—automatic embellishments which Palladio disciplines himself to omit everywhere else. It should be emphasized that although he does show, for example, one pedestal of the main elevation accurately (extreme lower right, on the *recto*), Palladio's principal interest in this sheet is focused on the towers; and the left side of the *verso* is an extremely accurate rendition of the inner wall of one of these four corner pavilions.

17. PLAN AND ELEVATION/SECTION OF THE ROMAN THEATRE, POLA

c. 1540

RIBA: Palladio X/3.

27.0 × 18.7 cm. (single sheet); countermark ИP , lower right; Talman 150 mark on *verso*.

Siena (and some umber) ink, with beige-gray and blue-gray washes; inscribed with measures in *passi* and feet.

Zorzi 1959, p. 93, fig. 216; Spielmann 1966, p. 156, no. 119, fig. 70 (as after 1560); Zorzi 1969, pp. 238–239, fig. 441; Magagnato 1970, p. 140, fig. 73; Arts Council 1975, p. 45, no. 71 (Fairbairn).

Royal Institute of British Architects, London.

This attractive and delicate little drawing has customarily been compared with the plan and elevation details made by Serlio (III:51) to accompany his 1540 account of the ruins at Pola (which were at that time already in a fragmentary state and are now completely lost). But Serlio's plate differs significantly from the images sketched and annotated by Palladio, even beyond the obvious difference that he shows details of the exterior of the *cavea,* while Palladio shows the back of the stage building. How are we to account for the more fundamental differences, when both architects undoubtedly had a firsthand knowledge of the site?

For to judge from the number of enlarged details and the "eyewitness" report in his text, it seems clear that Serlio must have visited Pola personally. And Palladio certainly knew Pola at first hand: located just eighty miles across the Gulf of Venice, at the head of the Dalmatian coast, the Istrian port was important to him and his colleagues not only for its concentration of antiquities, but also for its proximity to quarries that were the primary source of building stone for the metropolitan districts of the Venetian Empire. Indeed, in the last book of his *Quattro Libri* Palladio opens a chapter with a description of the temples, theatre, amphitheatre and arch at Pola which, together with his plates of the temple details, attests to his full familiarity with the site.

The likelihood that Palladio developed this drawing on the basis of a personal visit to Pola (rather than from a drawn or published prototype) is reinforced by the concentration of detailed measurements, which must have been made on the site. Moreover, the reconstruction of the theatre that we see here, with its artificial "cutaway" view and self-conscious impagination, is sufficiently similar to several other of Palladio's small early drawings of ancient monuments to render unlikely any suggestion of his having borrowed the image directly from Serlio or any other source. The unusually clean and careful layout of this and similar early works would in fact suggest that Palladio may have intended to publish a collection of such archaeological images.

In light of these considerations, is it not perhaps possible to detect a particular relevance behind the final comment

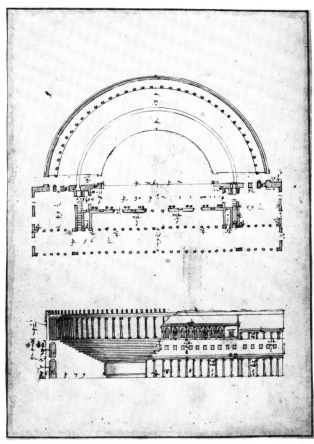

17

in Serlio's description of this theatre in 1540? "You must not be astonished, Reader, if I do not tell you about all the measures minutely and exhaustively, since these things in Pola have been surveyed by a better draftsman, who is an expert in numbers and measures" (III: 72 v). Should we not at least consider the possibility that this report of Serlio's might be the first identifiable reference to a lifelong production of "expertly measured" drawings by Palladio, which he himself felt was one of his major accomplishments? And may we not even wonder, perhaps, whether the young Palladio, carefully preparing his early drawings of antiquity, and the older Serlio, about to publish his own versions of these same subjects, might—just conceivably— have made one of their Istrian trips together? Burns, on the other hand, has recently noticed the same comment of Serlio's, and connected it with a report of Vasari's that drawings of Pola antiquities by Falconetto were published "by others" after his death (Verona 1980, p. 84): and indeed the possibility of such Falconetto sheets having been a common source to both Serlio and Palladio is perhaps even more plausible (see cat. no. 15).

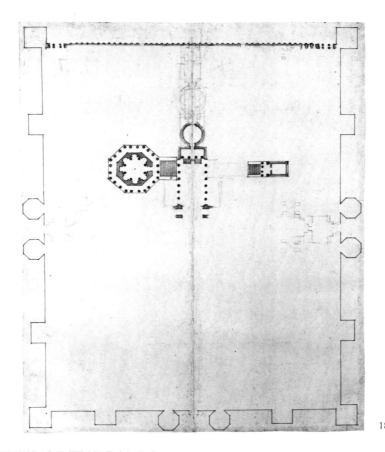

18

18. PLAN ELEMENTS OF THE PALACE OF DIOCLETIAN, SPALATO

1540s

Devonshire Collections, Chatsworth: "Heathen Temples/Plans and Drawings" XXXVI/21.

36.0 × 29.3 cm. (single sheet); watermark, anchor in circle with star, and B beneath (*cf.* Mošin 899); Talman 49 mark on *verso.*

Dark umber ink, with heavy brown wash, over pencil and umber crayon; inscribed upper right, in pencil, □ 17/ρ7/δ9

Magrini 1845, p. 312; Arts Council 1975, p. 105, no. 197 (Burns— "unpublished and unnoticed" [*sic*]).

The Trustees of the Chatsworth Settlement.

The awesome bulk of Diocletian's fortress-villa of A.D. 300–306, built for his retirement on the Dalmatian coast near his native town of Salona, became the nucleus of ancient and medieval Spalato, and still dominates the modern Yugoslav city and harbor of Split. Palladio's crisp measured drawing outlines its main surviving features: the Emperor's octagonal mausoleum, a colonnaded forecourt and entrance rotunda to the palace, and a small classical temple, centered near the south end of a stupendous enclosure of seven-foot-thick and sixty-foot-high walls. These, with their elaborate system of towers and gates, are slightly less regular than Palladio's ideal rectangular plan suggests (the east wall is really skewed outward toward the south by some twenty feet), but his drawing of the surviving central structures is gratifyingly close to a modern archaeological survey (e.g. Boëthius/Ward-Perkins 1970,

p. 525, fig. 200). The three pairs of octagonal gate towers were formerly connected by colonnaded streets, of which Palladio shows part of the crossing, in its relation to the well-preserved palace forecourt; alongside the east and west gates he has made quick pencil sketches of the fortified entrances opening onto these thoroughfares, as well as the first bays of the cross-vaulted arcades encircling the perimeter.

Palladio's tentative pencil development of the main southerly axis through the center of the palace is less successful: he has mistakenly duplicated the rotunda, and subdivided the huge rectangular hall which followed it. This opened onto an immense upper gallery overlooking the sea, whose repetitive piers and terminal pavilions Palladio accurately shows. Between this still-visible element and the entrance rotunda almost nothing of the palace proper has been preserved on the main upper level since medieval times, when its great rooms were first filled with small houses; but its vast basements are being laboriously excavated in our own day, and may now be visited in part.

This carefully detailed but unfinished plan, concentrating on the main elements that were most prominently visible in the 16th century (and for which I believe no prototypes appear in the standard sketchbooks), seems to me to suggest that Palladio may well have carried out an on-site survey within the turn-around time of a vessel calling at Spalato from Venice (or from Pola), and worked up this measured fragment on his return.

39

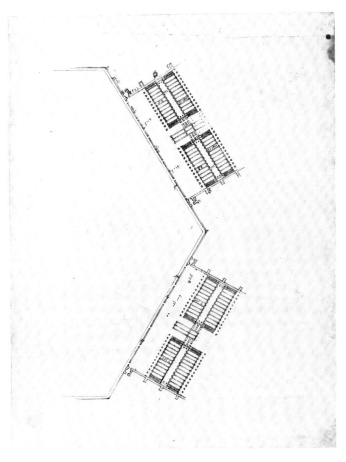

19

19. PLAN OF TWO SIDES OF THE PORT OF TRAJAN, NEAR OSTIA

Early 1540s

RIBA: Palladio XV/4.

39.0 × 28.6 cm. (single sheet); watermark, crossed arrows with star, laid lines 34 mm. apart (variant of Briquet 6292/6293), "Palladio's standard paper" of c. 1540; no collection's mark.

Siena ink, with pencil underdrawing and additions, and extremely pale beige wash; inscribed in epsilon handwriting with measures in feet.

Zorzi 1959, p. 102, fig. 255; Spielmann 1966, p. 178, no. 253, fig. 132.

Royal Institute of British Architects, London.

An ancient coastal monument even greater in size and comparable in architectural drama to Diocletian's Palace—though deriving in this case from the High Empire, rather than from Late Antiquity—is the huge hexagonal harbor a half-mile in diameter that was built in the years around A.D. 103 by the Emperor Trajan, just north of Isola Sacra at the Tiber mouth near Ostia, to be the new port of Rome. The vast basin was accessible to both ocean and river shipping through connection with Trajan's canal, and provided berthing for a hundred ships; adjoining its thousand-foot sides were huge warehouse structures over six hundred feet long, fronted and backed by porticoes, with buttressed ends and ramps as well as stairs for access to upper galleries. The complex is still partially preserved today, on a portion of the Torlonia estates immediately to the south of the Aeroporto Leonardo da Vinci at Fiumicino.

Palladio's meticulous drawing, although highly accomplished technically, is nonetheless a distinctly early work, as witnessed by its tight, painstaking style, and the early form of the epsilon handwriting. For this reason it is particularly revealing to see Palladio's instinctive clarity of design enabling him to make such a brilliant improvement, in his representation of this image, over a parallel such as Serlio's plate of 1540 (III:83). Palladio's bold, spare composition omits two-thirds of the complex, to focus closely on its constituent parts; Serlio crowds the whole plan onto half a page, with major inaccuracies and loss of detail.

Once more with this sheet Palladio achieves a "creative copy," evidently based on some other unusually good graphic prototype—in this case, perhaps that of Pirro Ligorio, one of the mid-16th-century architects who in fact measured the monument at first hand. Palladio's drawing might thus have been drafted quite some time before he actually visited the site: indeed it carries pencil revisions probably of a later date, and Palladio is documented during his last long sojourn in Rome to have visited Porto in May of 1547 (Zorzi 1959, p. 102). Notwithstanding its manifestly early date and quite probable external derivation, though, this drawing's crystalline handling and confident layout show Palladio already mastering an aesthetic mode of real subtlety and sophistication.

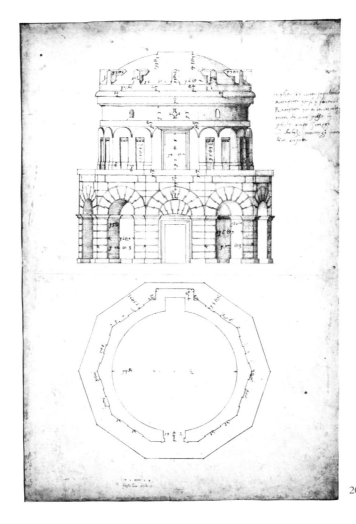

20

20. ELEVATION AND PLAN OF THE MAUSOLEUM OF THEODORIC, RAVENNA

c. 1541

RIBA: Palladio X/19.

43.5 × 28.1 cm. (single sheet of stained and mottled beige paper, no watermark); no collector's mark.

Umber ink, with early brown-ink borders; labeled and inscribed in epsilon handwriting, with labeled scale of 5 feet = 21.5 mm. (¾ of a Venetian inch).

Zorzi 1959, pp. 27 and 102, fig. 254; Spielmann 1966, pp. 176–177, no. 246 (giving inscriptions, but with "sepulcra" for *sepultura*, "pezo" for *peczo*, and "questo" for *questi*; and mistakenly citing a collector's mark).

Royal Institute of British Architects, London

Supposedly erected by the great King of the Ostrogoths in the Western Imperial capital of Ravenna just before his death (in A.D. 526), Theodoric's mausoleum has always excited admiration and wonder: its large structure of closely-fitted ashlar blocks is crowned by a monolithic 300-ton slab of Istrian stone, thirty-five feet across. Palladio notes this singular fact in his caption, along with the tomb's location outside the northeast gates of the city, and gives a correct count of the twelve curious bosses around the edge of the monolith (even Krautheimer [1965, p. 192] gives these as eight). His plan shows the circular burial chamber (but without its porphyry sarcophagus) within the ten-sided upper story, which stands above a vaulted cruciform chamber on the lower level.

Palladio's neatly regular arched panels on the upper zone are actually the ruined imposts of arcuated canopies, which once ran out to a ring of colonettes above the great polyhedral basement, with its massive arches and piers. Apart from this one cosmeticized "improvement," the drawing shows every sign of a sympathetic personal study of the monument. The fact that Ravenna is the first large mainland town on the western shore of the Adriatic below Venice, and that Palladio's drawing displays his early handwriting and drafting techniques (such as illusionistic linear shading and tight cross-hatching), makes it virtually certain that he drew the mausoleum *in situ*, either on his first Roman sojourn of 1541, or conceivably even while calling at Ravenna on a coasting vessel possibly bound to or from other "architectural" ports, such as Pola across the gulf.

Figure 11

21. PLANS, SECTIONS, AND AN ELEVATION, OF THREE ROMAN MAUSOLEA (AFTER SERLIO)

Shortly after March, 1540

RIBA: Palladio VIII/7.

41.9 × 27.4 cm. (single sheet); no watermark; Talman 54 mark on *verso*.

Umber ink and beige-gray wash, over incised lines (one more complete image in such lines, uninked, was left blank in upper center of sheet); inscribed in epsilon handwriting, on curvilinear plan, "finestre" (twice) and "isperoni" (twice).

Dalla Pozza 1943, pp. 68–69, fig. 8, as autograph (cropped to exclude lower two images); Zorzi 1956, pp. 64–65, fig. 24 (as anonymous "Hand 5"); Zorzi 1959, pp. 106–107, fig. 272 (as anonymous); Spielmann 1966, p. 137, no. 7, fig. 4 (as autograph, of [?] 1541); Zorzi 1969, p. 44, fig. 51 (as anonymous); Olivato 1978, p. 159, n. 32.

Royal Institute of British Architects, London.

The four upper drawings on this sheet reproduce—in the same order and relationship—four identical images found in Serlio's *Book Three*, pp. 33–34 (fig. 11), with inscribed measures that are translated from Serlio's text; these last are certainly in Palladio's hand. Such direct copies from published sources are rare among Palladian drawings, but (despite Zorzi's staunch defense of Palladio's greater originality) there can be no question but that these studies are by his hand. They are, however, demonstrably early

works, whose simplifications (as in the silhouettes of the sections) and imperfectly mastered techniques (as in the alternate and sometimes overlapping use of both linear shading and wash) agree with the publication date of their prototypes.

Palladio's unabashedly derivative sketches were doubtless made primarily as memoranda of the buildings (when he later visited the Romulus mausoleum, he carefully improved the rudimentary plan and elevation that appear on the bottom of this sheet), as well as secondarily for practice in draftsmanship. He deftly regularizes Serlio's old-fashioned "perspectival" sections, especially through the orthographic base and bounding lines of that on the left; but he abandons this exercise of graphic updating, as it were in mid-evolution, to render the right-hand section even more "pictorially" than Serlio does.

Dalla Pozza, first publishing this sheet in the context of a claim for Palladio's crucial reliance on Serlio (which, even in these beginning stages, is hardly a general case), followed Rivoira in labeling the upper images as the "sepolcri dei Calventii e dei Cercenii" (1943, p. 68, n. 2). Zorzi suggested an influence of the Romulus elevation on Palladio's "temple-villas" (1969, pp. 44–45), but a considerably more direct influence may be assigned to Serlio's cruciform plan with free-standing corner columns, in inspiring Palladio's elaborate late project for a centralized church of the same basic design (cat. no. 117).

42

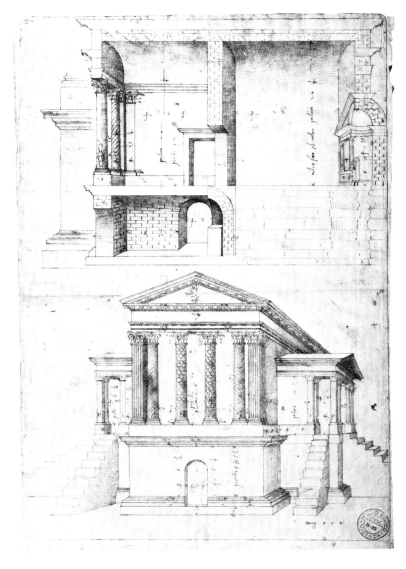

22. PODIUM DETAIL, SECTION, AND PERSPECTIVE VIEW OF THE TEMPIETTO AT THE SPRINGS OF THE CLITUMNUS, NEAR TREVI

1541

Vicenza: 1950 inv. D-22.

42.6 × 28.3 cm. (single sheet with beveled corners); no watermark visible; no collector's mark.

Siena ink (verging toward umber on section); inscribed in epsilon handwriting with note of a measure in *palmi,* and also in mature handwriting with measures in feet; scale of 4 ft. = 25.5 mm. (1 Roman inch).

Zorzi 1956, p. 63, fig. 19 (as ''Author 3''); Zorzi 1959, p. 81, fig. 184 (as unknown draftsman); Pane 1948, pl. IV, fig. 7 (as Palladio); Spielmann 1966, p. 150, no. 82, fig. 41 (as Marc'Antonio Palladio, c. 1550); Gioseffi 1972, p. 57, fig. 20; Mostra 1973, p. 21, no. IIIA, fig. 3 (Forssman—as unknown architect), p. 153 (Burns—as Palladio, after Ligorio).

Museo Civico, Vicenza.

Above the ancient road from Assisi to Spoleto, in central Umbria, the town of Trevi dominates the wide valley of the Clitumnus, a small tributary of the Tiber. The river is attractively augmented by springs a short distance to the south, and some two miles below the town, beside the nascent watercourse and the road, stands the curious little ''tempietto'' which Palladio shows in this drawing. Forssman reminds us that it is probably an Early Christian funerary monument, or even a Carolingian one—which would to some extent account for its unusual shape, with a high chambered podium carrying a portico reached only through lateral porches with tall stairs.

Burns has shown that this perspective rendering exactly parallels a drawing by Pirro Ligorio, and he has demonstrated how that antiquarian architect could have met Palladio through contact with the Trissino circle, during the Vicentines' visits to Rome in 1545 or 1547. It is even possible, according to this view, to see the Central Italian measures on Palladio's drawing of another tomb nearby in

Spoleto (cat. no. 8) as evidence that it too was copied at Rome from a previous drawing made on the site by Ligorio.

But we have repeatedly seen that Palladio's use of non-Venetian measures cannot in itself be taken as an index of copying, any more than Zorzi's old idea that the appearance of perspective renderings (such as this one) would automatically remove a sheet from Palladio's authorship. Nothing would have prevented Palladio from using local measures throughout his travels, and indeed we find him using a scale of Roman inches, for example, consistently through the 1540s. Both the Spoleto sheet and this Clitumnus drawing have precise parallels with Palladio's securely datable domestic projects of c. 1541, but not with his works of the mid-forties. This encourages the conclusion that he either obtained prototype drawings of these Umbrian antiquities from a common source, or met Ligorio during his Roman sojourn of 1541 (see also cat. no. 19).

That Palladio was by 1541 familiar with the Clitumnus temple's design can be demonstrated most obviously through an unpublished component on the *verso* of one of his most celebrated early drawings, RIBA XVII/15 (cat. no. 41). That project's abandoned commencement of a portico motif exactly based on the Clitumnus temple, with a column and a square pier rhythmically paired at the corners, is shown on the *recto* as approached by lateral twin stairs, giving access to entrance chambers on either side of the portico. These elements, together with the strongly accentuated central podium (and perhaps even the number of three pediments in the roof design) can all be said to represent Palladian adaptations of specific motifs from the tempietto on the Clitumnus.

---

23. PLAN AND ELEVATION STUDIES OF THE MAUSOLEUM OF THE DEIFIED ROMULUS, ON THE VIA APPIA

Late 1560s

RIBA: Palladio VIII/1-Left.

28.8 × 20.5 cm. (Single sheet, now detached from the unrelated VIII/1-Right); watermark, cardinal's hat (*cf.* Briquet 3485); Talman 150 mark on *verso,* together with draft apparently dictated by Palladio to his son Silla, for *Quattro Libri* text on Bramante's "Tempietto" (IV:xvii:64, heavily revised): *cf.* Spielmann 1966, p. 148, no. 70 for transcription, omitting however the adjective "Bramante *architetto,*" and other details; see Zorzi 1959, fig. 316 for illustration.

Very light siena ink, with gray-brown wash; later inscriptions in darker ink.

Zorzi 1956, p. 65, fig. 25 (as autograph); Zorzi 1959, p. 80, fig. 181; Spielmann 1966, p. 149, no. 79 (mistaking Zorzi's 1956 attribution), giving inscriptions (of which however "*et e tuto di/ pietra cota*" is also in later ink); Mostra 1973, p. 142 (Burns), fig. 145 (with VIII/1-Right); Arts Council 1975, p. 104, no. 194 (Burns, shortened translation of preceeding), fig. on p. 103; Olivato, 1978, p. 154.

Royal Institute of British Architects, London.

The impressive Late Antique complex which is the subject of this sheet was erected a mile and a half outside the walls of Rome in A.D. 309–312, as a memorial to the youthful son of Maxentius, the last pagan Emperor of the West. Its marble components having long since disappeared, Serlio first reported in 1540 (III:45) that its only visible remains, all in brick, were a vast arcaded court a hundred yards on a side, enclosing at the center the vaulted lower story of a Pantheon-like structure. This structure is creditably reconstructed in his plate, despite the fact that its use for farm animals had almost filled up its interior and rendered it virtually impossible to measure (its portico is still obscured by a farmhouse). As was noted in a preceding entry, Palladio earlier had had access to a substantially less convincing plan, which, with an altogether fanciful elevation, he had copied (cat. no. 21). A more enterprising contemporary—perhaps Ammannati—had, however, produced the better plan preserved in a manuscript codex (Venice, Marciana 5105, fol. 2 *recto*) that was soon copied in the Veneto (Padua, University, Ms. 764) and was quite possibly known also to Palladio (Olivato 1978; 1980, pp. 177–178).

This latter plan may have been one of the sources for the quite beautiful reconstruction in the present drawing, with its "truly happy" reconstitution of a sober yet splendid superstructure, which Zorzi especially praised (1956, p. 65). Burns has suggested its "obvious" relationship in plan with Sanmicheli's Cappella Pellegrini of 1527–29 ff. in Verona (1973, p. 142; 1975, p. 104); but in fact that arrangement of widely spaced engaged *columns,* connected by pediments over the *axial* niches, is a much less precise prototype than the scheme—identical with that of the Romulus rotunda—of paired *pilasters* bracketing the *non-axial* niches, in Bramante's Tempietto (compare the exact graphic analogy in cat. no. 27). Palladio's final version of the Romulus shrine as published in the *Quattro Libri* (IV:xxii:89) retains this ordonnance but introduces a modification, to bring the larger niches into consonance with those in the story below. This he frames at the center of the completed court, in whose plan (as well as in his caption) he very closely follows Serlio's publication of thirty years before.

Burns has also suggested a clear affinity between the hypothetical images on this sheet (those not filled in by wash) and Palladio's design, of over a decade later, for the villa chapel at Maser. And in fact a close iconographical function unites both of them to the present as well, although we cannot say whether Palladio might even have imagined it: the Late Antique tempietto was actually a princely mausoleum, and—through a Papal Bull of Sixtus V on 7 November 1585—Marc'Antonio Barbaro obtained a perpetual right of *giuspatronato* for the owners of the villa at Maser (Basso 1976, pp. 30–34), in whose Palladian chapel the members of the resident family are still being buried even today (visit to the tomb of Marina Luling Buschetti Volpi, 7 September 1980).

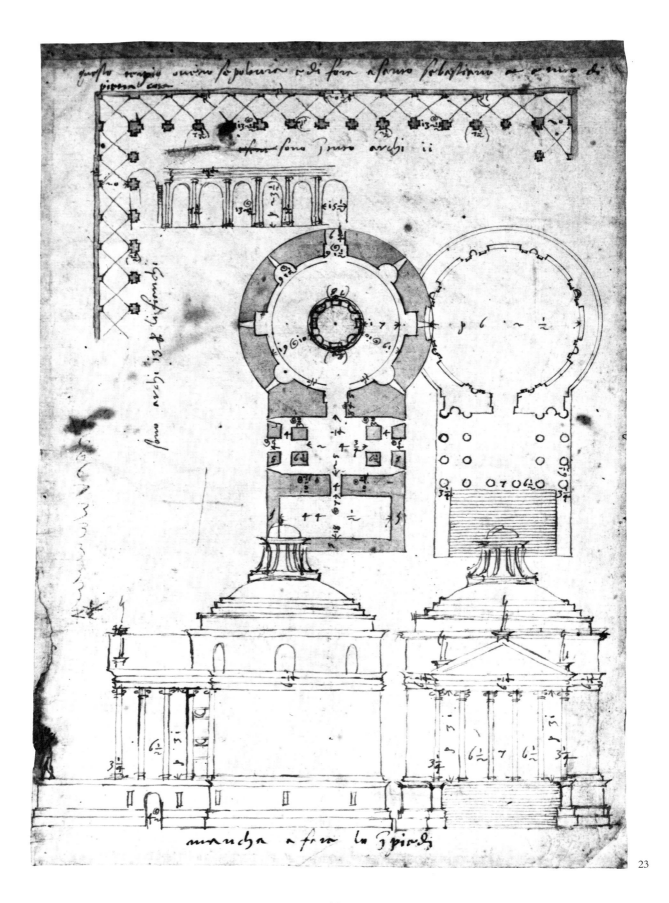

23

24. PLAN, ELEVATION/SECTION, AND DETAILS OF THE "TEMPLE OF VESTA" BY THE TIBER, ROME

Early 1540s

Olin Library, Cornell University, Ithaca: Department of Rare Books, Alphabetical map case.

43.5 × 29.2 cm. (single sheet); no watermark visible; collector's stamp on *verso,* lion within circular inscription, "·ARS ET LABOR· SAMMLUNG L. ZATZKA" (Lugt 2672).

Umber ink, with measures, labels and inscriptions in epsilon handwriting: within plan on *recto,* below scale, "questi sono piedi ·6·/con li quali e mesurato/questo tenpio"; at top of *verso,* "modeno de le finestre"; upper right, "questo sie el sofita/ de dito tenpio coe/soto el portico"; lower right, "modeno dila porta de/dito tenpio".

Phelps 1934, pp. 21–22, figs. 1–2 (as A. da Sangallo the Younger, giving upper inscription on *recto*); Mostra 1973, pp. 141 and 142 (Burns—as Palladio, early autograph); Burns 1973, p. 183.

Department of Rare Books, Cornell University Library.

This sheet—the only known drawing by Palladio in the United States*—was, after a forty-year misattribution to Sangallo, brilliantly restored to the master's *corpus* by Burns' recognition of it (through Phelps' illustration) as an early prototype for Palladio's beautiful drawing on RIBA VIII/1-Right (formerly attached to cat. no. 23), which in turn was the model for the temple's publication in the *Quattro Libri* (IV:xiiii:52–54). The Cornell drawing is twice the size of the later preparatory sketch for the publication, and is an exceptionally handsome and important early sheet. Its crisp and painstaking detail presents a rigorously "archaeological" interpretation: the still-surviving temple was somewhat damaged in transition between an unknown antique dedication and a Christian consecration to St. Stephen (it lost one column, as well as its whole entablature and dome), but Palladio—distinguishing himself from a quattrocento tradition of more descriptive renderings—with this sheet inaugurates its careful reconstruction.

The building's plan and molding profiles were not in question (note Palladio's very early graphic techniques of illusionistic perspectives and shadings on the latter details), but the missing superstructure posed a problem of judicious reinvention. Palladio begins his three-stage restoration of the elevation/section (already in strict orthographic projection) with a very heavy dome that simply continues the full thickness of the wall, and a severely simple entablature with a flat vertical frieze. In his drawing of a quarter-century later, for the *Quattro Libri,* he modifies the former element into a tapering shell whose internal hemisphere is gracefully masked by a low podium and a stepped saucer dome, and actually changes his mind about the frieze (still

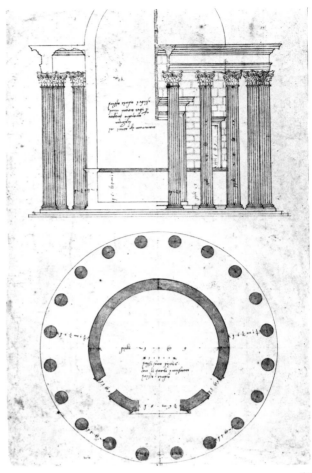

24

flat in an enlarged detail) as he is sketching the elevation/section. The final published version continues this tendency toward decorative gracefulness (even though the block-cutter introduces a stilted, taller podium and a non-tapering dome) by settling on a pulvinated frieze, elaborately sculptured with *bucrania* and garlands.

*The country's unique Palladio drawing is brought closer to home, in its relation to this catalogue, by its most recent ownership: it was purchased in the 1920s in Vienna by my own late friend Dr. Raymond Stites, who presented it to Cornell's College of Architecture some considerable time before taking up his own long-term appointment at the National Gallery of Art. I like to think that he would have taken particular pleasure in seeing it, under its new and more accurate attribution, in his last professional home.

47

25

25. DOMENICO DA VARIGNANA (?): ELEVATION/SECTION OF BRAMANTE'S TEMPIETTO AT S. PIETRO IN MONTORIO, ROME

1513–c. 1520

Morgan Library: 1978.44, fol. 61 *verso*.

20.8 × 14.5 cm. (one half of sheet bound into sketchbook of 83 leaves, including covers); various watermarks; gold-embossed leather collector's stamp on inside front cover (fol. 1 *verso*), sheaf of grain in circle surrounded by inscription separated by oak leaves, PAUL MELLON/OAK SPRING; former owner's name (?) inscribed on last leaf (fol. 82 *verso*), *Dom.co Poltroni*.

Umber ink and gray wash.

For the sketchbook, see Nachod 1955, p. 1ff; Förster 1956, p. 281; most importantly Frommel 1973, II:6 n. 41; for this leaf, Wittkower 1978, p. 95, fig. 107.

The Pierpont Morgan Library, New York.

The Mellon Codex, since its rediscovery in 1955, has become known as one of the earliest and most informative of the architectural sketchbooks of Renaissance Rome. Its title page (fol. 1 *verso*) bears a reworked inscription which now reads ANIBALE FONTANA BONIEN:si / CIVIS · BON: FACIEBAT · /M.D.XIII. When Konrad Oberhuber and I examined this under ultraviolet light at the request of Christoph Frommel in 1972, we felt it was possible to make out, beneath the evidently 17th-century erasure and reinscription, the version reported in Frommel's note attributing the book to Domenico da Varignana: DOMENICUS · HA...(?) S · B(?)...NONIEN · CIVIS · RO · FACIEBAT · M · D · XIII. Frommel's attribution, together with the rich testimony of the codex as an unusually complete compendium of ancient and modern architecture, will be carefully reviewed in a forthcoming facsimile edition, with full commentary, to be published by Wolfgang Lotz of the Bibliotheca Hertziana of Rome.

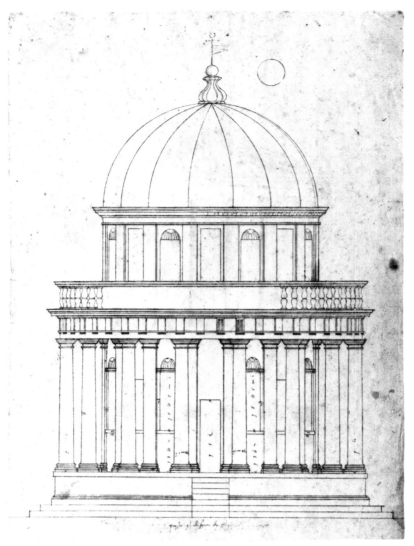

26

Such sketchbooks circulated widely among Renaissance architects. Among the most important for the Veneto are the three famous Destailleur albums at the State Hermitage Museum in Leningrad, of which volume B is labeled on the flyleaf as having belonged to Andrea Palladio. Loredana Olivato has recently discussed these in relation to a well-known sketchbook at the Marciana Library in Venice, and another closely connected example which she found in the library of the University of Padua (1978; Venice 1980, pp. 167–178, nos. 175–176). Others important for the antiquities Palladio studied are the celebrated Codex Coner in the Sir John Soane Museum, London (Ashby 1902), the large folio album with designs after Verona antiquities by Giovanni Caroto (*cf.* Schweikhart 1977), and—for a particularly close parallel of size and character with the Mellon Codex—a small sketchbook in the Biblioteca Comunale at Siena (Verona 1980, p. 39, no. III, 6).

We have already noted that Palladio's curious "cutaway" drawing of an ancient amphitheatre (cat. no. 9) derives from a standard sketchbook type (e.g. Mellon Codex fol. 41 *recto,* Codex Coner fol. 39 *recto*); and the present compendium exhibits several other direct analogies with his graphic work. Fols. 7 *verso* and 8 *recto* show Bramante's corner solution from Palazzo Caprini (or the St. Peter's tribune) of three clustered Tuscan columns, which Palladio used on the corners of his Basilica (*cf.* cat. no. 28, and also fig. 39); fols. 43, 44 depict two antique sarcophagi that Palladio later drew from a similar source (cat. no. 36); and several pages show versions of his elaborate bath plans (*cf.* cat. no. 80, fig. 52). The Mellon sketchbook's rendition of the Bramante Tempietto is highly important for its orthogonal elevation (though its section reverts to perspective), and for the illusionistic "realism" of its literal cut through the facade. Palladio closely followed both the type of projection and the technique of the cut in his Cornell drawing of the round temple by the Tiber (cat. no. 24), and he perfects the orthogonal elevation in his own fine drawing of the Tempietto (cat. no. 26), closely based on images such as that shown on the present sheet.

26. ELEVATION OF THE TEMPIETTO OF S. PIETRO IN MONTORIO, ROME

Early 1540s

Vicenza: 1950 inv. D-26 *verso*.

44.2 × 29.6 cm. (single sheet with beveled corners); indistinct watermark (?); no collector's mark.

Light umber ink, inscribed in epsilon handwriting with measures in feet. *Recto*, ENTABLATURE DETAILS, PERSPECTIVE VIEW AND PLAN OF PORTICO OF OCTAVIA, ROME; umber ink with very dark wash; inscribed in epsilon handwriting with measures and scale in feet: Zorzi 1956, pp. 61–62, fig. 14 (as "Author I"); Zorzi 1959, p. 59, fig. 61 (as anonymous); Spielmann 1966, p. 176, no. 241 (as workshop, before 1550); Mostra 1976, pp. 24–25, fig. 14 (Forssman—as Palladio [?]); p. 154 (Burns); see cat. nos. 39, 40.

Zorzi 1956, p. 62, fig. 15 (as "Author I"); Spielmann 1966, p. 148, no. 71, fig. 37 (as workshop, before 1550); Mostra 1973, p. 154 (Burns).

Museo Civico, Vicenza.

Palladio published a very similar and only slightly elaborated version of this image in the *Quattro Libri* (IV:xvii:66), with a "cutaway" portion on the left to show the section, whose interior details seem to be modeled very closely on the rendering in the Mellon sketchbook (both strangely omit any articulation between the interior pilasters: compare cat. no. 27). There is also a probable influence from Serlio's extended treatment of the monument in his *Third Book* of 1540, with its courtyard, plan, elevation, and section recorded respectively on pp. 41, 42, 43, and 44 (though somewhat more accurately than Palladio's). The shape of the lantern on both the drawing and the print by Palladio differs substantially from that given in the Mellon sketchbook (cat. no. 25), in Serlio, or on the Chatsworth/Cassel drawings (cat. no. 27). There are other elements of fantasy in Palladio's presentation, as for example the figural sculptures with which he fills the external niches. He felt the building to be symptomatic of Bramante's virtual recreation of classical architecture (an opinion which we still follow), and he gave it a place of honor as the sole modern monument among the ancient temples to which his *Fourth Book* was dedicated.

27. FOLLOWER OF BRAMANTE: PLAN, ELEVATION, SECTION, AND DETAILS OF THE TEMPIETTO AT SAN PIETRO IN MONTORIO, ROME

c. 1510–40

Devonshire Collections, Chatsworth: "Drawings/Public Monuments/Arches and Bridges" XXXV/23.

45.2 × 31.2 cm. (two sheets of dark buff-brown paper, pasted with paper backing by original draftsman: top, 22.1 × 25.6 cm.; bottom, 23.2 × 31.2 cm.; the whole laid down on heavy card with gilt border, probably by John Talman (Colvin 1978, p. 801); no watermark visible; collector's mark, lower right, *R* (Lugt 2184), labeled on mount as "J. Richardson Sen./1668–1745."

Light umber ink, used also for original measures, with later inscriptions in much darker ink: at lower center, in a 17th-century Italian hand, "la Capella di S? Pietro / di Bramante nel / cortile del Claustro / di R:R:P:P: Frances = /cani di S? Pietro / Montorio, Roma. / le colonne del Portico son / di granito / bianco. / questo / disegno / è di / Bra = /mante." At top left, 18th-century English inscription, labeled on mount as "Talman's hand": "The original Drawing / for yᵉ little but beautifull / Temple of S! Petro / Montorio in Rome."

Loukomski 1940, p. 73, fig. 10 (as mid-16th century follower of Bramante).

The Trustees of the Chatsworth Settlement.

This highly significant and very beautiful drawing is almost unknown, having been cited only once (in one sentence, in a predominately archaeological journal, during World War II); it is probably exhibited here publicly for the first time. It has an exceptional importance, however, to Palladian studies for the decisive evidence it bears on one of the thorniest problems concerning Palladio's drawings: namely, the authorship of RIBA XIV/11 (cat. no. 28). That equally handsome and much more celebrated drawing of Palazzo Caprini (a building also by Bramante), although preserved within the main collection of Palladian drawings, has been widely doubted as a work from Palladio's own hand. The present drawing of Bramante's Tempietto unexpectedly resolves the question: it may be stated as absolutely certain that both sheets are by the same artist, and (through the incorporation of his non-Palladian handwriting on the Chatsworth drawing) that this artist is not Andrea Palladio.

The demonstration of this useful fact is both interesting and revealing. The London drawing has no inscriptions at all: it shows only parts of a perspective rendering, a linear profile, and an elevation detail. The Chatsworth drawing presents exactly similar techniques and forms in images of the first two of these types, and adds as well an extremely professional plan, together with an illusionistically descriptive section. But while a whole host of identical drafting devices shared by the two perspective renderings make it unquestionably clear that the drawings of both these Bramante buildings derive from a single hand, the identity of their draftsman as Palladio could not be firmly proven or denied without exterior evidence. This is provided by the Chatsworth inscriptions: for although contemporaneous architectural drawings made in the same city will all inevitably share at least strong generic similarities (and most especially so in renderings after coeval buildings of congruent style by a single architect), the individual "personalities" of verbal and numerical handwritings are much more sharply distinctive. In this case not only do the Chatsworth inscriptions describe measures in Roman *palmi* (which Palladio almost never uses), but their calligraphic forms are strikingly different from his, in any period of his life. Once this is seen, the "architectural handwriting" becomes distinguishable as well: this draftsman renders

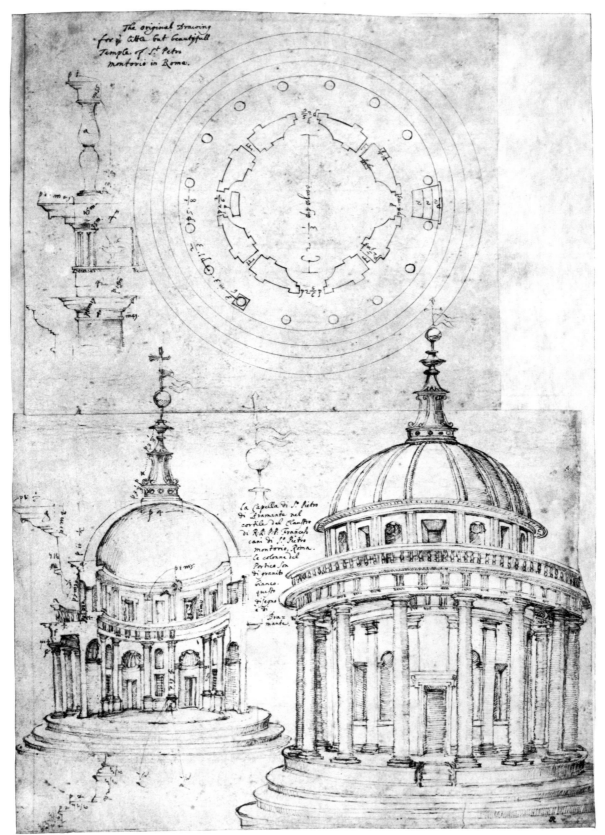

The original drawing
for ye little but beautifull
Temple of St Petro
montorio in Roma.

la Capella di S. Pietro
di Bramante nel
cortile del Claustro
di R.R. P.P. Franceschani di S. Pietro
montorio, Roma.
Le colonne del
Portico Son
di granito
Bianco.
questo
disegno
è di
Bramante.

27

51

shading in very close, mostly curvilinear lines, with a strong preference for the horizontal; whereas Palladio always shades with wider rectilinear grids, including invariably the vertical strokes, and usually (but not always) horizontal hatchings. With surprising consistency Palladio shades the *left* sides of columns, with predominantly vertical hatchings or with wash; this draftsman shades their *right* sides, with tight curvilinear horizontals, and habitually adds a thin line of smaller strokes on their left contour, to sharpen the impression of a left highlight.

The early English sojourn of the Chatsworth sheet in the famous collection of John Richardson—one of the most important early connoisseurs of Old Master drawings—attests to its exceptional distinction, above all for the quality of its graphic technique, but also for its extraordinary architectural accuracy. Its section might be criticized for having stretched the spatial juxtapositions of the interior in an illusionistic distortion that does, however, make the formal structure much more intelligible; and (apart from

its valuable testimony as to the original shape of the lantern) the exterior rendering might be discounted, from a modern perspective, as resembling a bit too uncannily a close wide-angle photograph. But the entablature detail is masterfully deft, and the plan, which deserves to be much more widely known, is one of the handsomest and most accurate that we possess for the monument from the 16th century. (Its forms are closest to the plan on fol. 21 of the Codex Coner at the Soane Museum in London; that image, together with an elevation equally related to Chatworth's, though less convincing [Coner fol. 33], may in fact derive from similar prototypes.) Discounting for a moment the intentional distortion of the stretched-out section (of which a more accurate treatment appears in the Codex Coner, f. 34), all four images on the Chatsworth sheet are immeasurably finer than their corresponding numbers so often reproduced from the treatises of Serlio and Palladio—which in certain respects may well be derivative (and in fact somewhat debased) copies after them.

---

28. FOLLOWER OF BRAMANTE: PARTIAL PERSPECTIVE VIEW, MOLDING PROFILE, AND ELEVATION DETAIL OF PALAZZO CAPRINI, ROME

c. 1510–40

RIBA: Palladio XIV/11.

27.5 × 38.0 cm. (single sheet of pale buff-brown paper); no watermark, laid lines 31 mm. apart; Talman crown mark on *verso*.

Umber ink over pencil; gray washes (used only in elevation detail).

Geymüller 1884, p. 87, fig. 70; Hofmann 1909, col. 118 [and 2nd. ed. 1914, col. 88], fig. 52:dIII; Förster 1956, p. 204, fig. 86, Zorzi 1959, p. 132, fig. 304; Ackerman 1966/1977, p. 30., fig. 3; Smithsonian 1966, no. 3; Barbieri 1968, p. 86, n. 134, fig. xviii; Bruschi 1969, p. 604, fig. 398 (1973/1977 Eng. ed., pp. 173–174, fig. 182); Mostra 1970, fig. 36; Frommel 1973, II:83, no. 4, III: fig. 32b; Arts Council 1975, p. 321, no. 407 (Burns).

Royal Institute of British Architects, London.

One of the best-known of all the drawings attributed to Palladio, this famous sheet with images of Bramante's Palazzo Caprini of c. 1501–10 (usually called "Raphael's House in the Borgo," because of the latter's residence in it from 1517 to 1520) has enjoyed a full century of modern study, as probably the best visual record of the demolished palace. Yet only recently did doubts begin to be published about the drawing's Palladian authorship (Smithsonian 1966, Frommel 1973), and Burns accurately concluded in

1975 that the traditional attribution had no firm basis. In company, perhaps, with other Palladian enthusiasts, I had nonetheless hoped that it might possibly represent a maverick phase of Palladio's earliest graphic style—a view that I continued to hold until accidentally coming across the twin drawing of Bramante's Tempietto at Chatsworth (cat. no. 27), which had apparently escaped the attention of Palladianists by masquerading for some forty years under an improbable title, among "Scamozzi Drawings in London (*sic*)." Now that the two sheets can be put together, however, and the Chatsworth inscriptions compared with Palladio's (see preceding entry), it becomes clear for the first time that the single author of both drawings is definitely not Palladio himself.

Other conclusions, in fact, may well be drawn from the telling juxtaposition of these sheets. Both represent exceedingly famous buildings by Bramante: both structures dated from the first decade of the High Renaissance (and the Tempietto survives as one of its paradigms), both heralded the radically new and gravely monumental "Doric mode," both were small in size but of enormous (and immediate) influence, and both were situated within a short distance of St. Peter's on the Borgo-Gianicolo or west side of the Tiber. There were thus several cogent reasons for which they should both have been drawn by an experienced and talented architectural draftsman, even before we approach the question of his identity.

28

The relationship between the distinguished draftsman-ship of these two sheets and the exalted quality of the buildings themselves provides us with the most likely key to their mutual origins. Precisely such a close congruence of *style,* between the famous forms of the architectural models, and the brilliant mastery of their graphic records, demonstrates at once that their common author was privy to the philosophy and aesthetic of the Bramante circle. Both drawings are dramatically more faithful to the forms of these buildings, as well as more expressive of their spirit, than we could expect of any "outsider": witness, for example, their superiority to images of the Tempietto by Serlio and Palladio. From the fact that the scrupulously executed measured drawing of the Tempietto plan is on a formerly separate fragment, which the draftsman has pasted up in order to add his splendidly controlled freehand

sketches, we might well conclude that this accomplished artist may have had direct access to original drawings of the Bramante shop.

It is of course quite natural that such superlative docu-ments of "the new architecture" should have been imme-diately collected outside of Rome, particularly by the architects of Northern Italy. It is just possible, as Burns remarked about RIBA drawings from the Raphael shop (1975, p. 266), that in this case as well, both Bramantesque drawings in the Devonshire collections may ultimately descend (via Talman and Burlington) from Palladio himself. If we grant the possibility, which is certainly attractive, then all the arguments presented above would make it likely that he would have purchased or even commissioned them—perhaps directly from a survivor of the Bramante shop—upon his arrival in Rome in 1541.

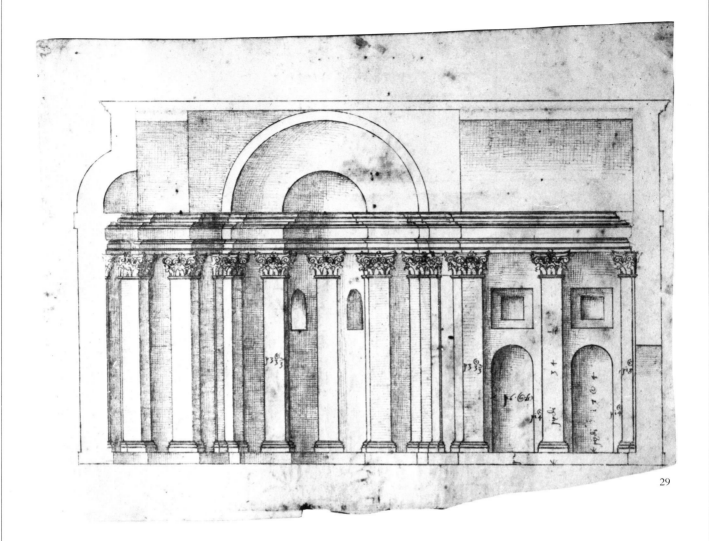

29. LONGITUDINAL SECTION OF BRAMANTE'S PROJECT FOR THE CHURCH OF SAN BIAGIO, ROME

1541

Vicenza: 1950 inv. D-11 *verso.*

20.7 × 26.4 cm. (single sheet with beveled corners); no watermark visible; no collector's mark.

Siena ink with traces of pencil underdrawing; inscribed in epsilon handwriting with measures in feet, and (on *recto*) with scale of 4 units = 46 mm. *Recto,* CORINTHIAN CAPITAL FROM "THE PORTICO OF THE ANTONINES" (i.e. the Baths of Caracalla?); siena ink with traces of pencil underdrawing and very dark sepia wash; Loukomski 1927, pp. 37–38, fig. IVb; Zorzi 1956, pp. 59–60, fig. 9 (as "Author 1"); Zorzi 1959, p. 69, fig. 122 (as unknown); Spielmann 1966, p. 160, no. 144, fig. 81.

Zorzi 1959, p. 70, fig. 125 (as unknown, "Baths of Caracalla"); Spielmann 1966, p. 177, no. 250 (as Palladio before 1550, as "Reconstruction of a Roman Tomb"); Mostra 1973, p. 152, fig. 162 (Burns—establishing correct identification; *cf.* Frommel 1973, II:327–335, III:figs. 145–147); Bruschi 1977, p. 162, fig. 179.

Museo Civico, Vicenza.

This little church of S. Biagio had been intended by Bramante to replace the chapel of S. Biagio degli Armeni, a structure that stands on part of a huge site along the Via Giulia for which Julius II in 1508 commissioned the plans for an imposing new Palace of Justice. Bramante's projected Palazzo dei Tribunale was never completed, though some very powerful blocks of basement rustication can still be seen at its site along the west side of the Via Giulia. The rough brickwork of the new Church of S. Biagio was constructed on the river front—though without its dome— in 1508–13 (Frommel II:333), and it survived into the 19th century, only to be swept away in the regularization of the Tiber banks. Several drawings of its plan and details are known from the early and middle 16th century (Ashby 1902, p. 15, fig. 11, for Codex Coner plan; and Frommel II:330 nos. 3–8), but Palladio's is one of the most coherent, as well as one of the earliest, since its style of cross-hatching, wide capitals, and inscriptions with epsilons tie it securely to his Roman visit of 1541.

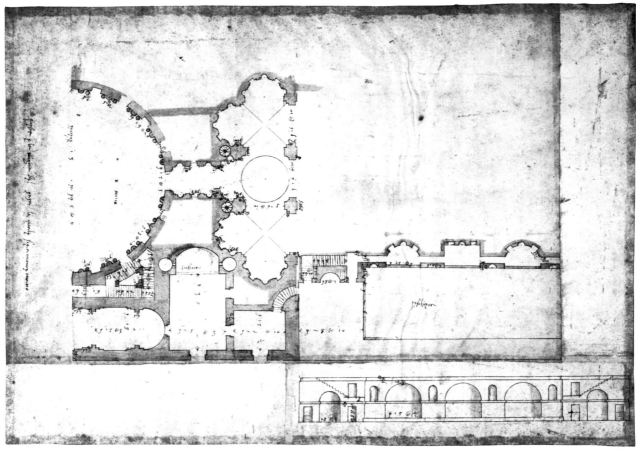

30. PLAN OF EXECUTED PORTION OF THE VILLA MADAMA, ROME (WITH ATTACHED ELEVATION OF TERRACE WALL)

1541

RIBA: Palladio X/18.

33.8 × 46.9 cm. (four sheets joined, probably only in England); no watermark visible; two Talman 54 marks on *versi*.

Very light umber ink, with ochre-beige wash; first inscriptions in epsilon handwriting with same ink ("pertege"/"cusina"/"peschiera"), with scale of which 20 units = 34 mm. (1⅛ Vicentine inches); second inscription in heavy siena ink (but still with epsilons: "questa e la vigna del papa la quale sie a monte mario"); late measures and corrections, evidently on site, in both pencil and pen.

Zorzi 1959, p. 132, fig. 302; Zorzi 1965, pp. 26–27, fig. 4; Zorzi 1969, pp. 88–89, fig. 141; Puppi 1972, p. 44, fig. x; Arts Council 1975, pp. 88–89, no. 163 (Burns), fig. 163

Royal Institute of British Architects, London.

Palladio's familiarity with this great building dates from 1541—perhaps through a Papal introduction via Trissino, when he and Andrea first visited Rome in that year. Palladio's drawing depicts the splendid surviving fabric of what would have been, had it been completed, the grandest Roman High Renaissance villa—a project whose plans involved the collaboration of four great artists.

Around 1516 Raphael had begun work on plans commissioned by Cardinal Giulio de' Medici for a new "vigna" or suburban villa, to be placed high above the Tiber bend on the eastern slopes of Monte Mario, the first great landscape feature on the far side of the broad river plain beyond Castel S. Angelo and the Belvedere, north of the Vatican and the city of Rome. Antonio da Sangallo the Younger superintended the construction (which only proceeded for about five years), and after Raphael's death in 1520 Giulio Romano and Giovanni da Udine completed the stuccoed and painted decoration of the spectacular three-bay vaulted and domed garden loggia (which Palladio draws here—following Serlio, 1540:III:148—with one too many exedrae: it actually has a flat eastern end, where it meets the large living rooms at the northeast corner of the house). All work on the villa stopped in 1523, when the Cardinal was elected Pope as Clement VII; following a sketchy repair after the Sack of Rome, it passed in 1536 to Margaret of Parma, natural daughter of the Emperor Charles V, and from her title of Madama Margherita it takes its name.

The villa still shows the results of this checkered history, with its intended circular central court truncated in both height and extent, and the fragments of its north and east facades patchily composed. The north front, with the garden loggia, shows up in a radically different design in Serlio's treatise (1540:III:148), in a version that Trissino (presumably with Serlio's help) was able to copy almost exactly in his loggia at Cricoli, three years before the design was published. A project drawing for the circular courtyard facade has recently been identified among the RIBA "Palladio" sheets by Burns (1975, pp. 264–266, no. 491), who has demonstrated the probable extent of Palladio's debt to this masterpiece of Raphael's revived antique style.

CHAPTER TWO

Components of a Maturing Technique:

Orders, proportions, and ornaments

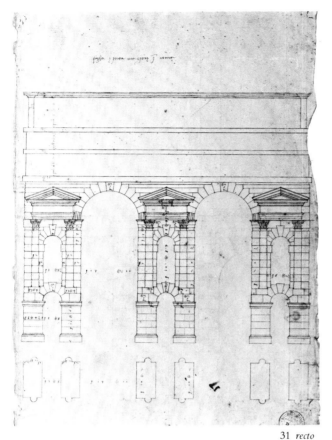

31 recto

31 verso

31. PLAN AND ELEVATION OF THE PORTA MAGGIORE, AND OF A SECTION OF THE CLAUDIANUM, ROME

1541

Vicenza: 1950 inv. D-1 recto and verso.

44.0 × 29.2 cm. (single sheet with beveled corners); unclear watermark, probably crossed arrows with star (variant of Briquet 6292/6293), "Palladio's standard paper" of c. 1540; no collector's mark.

Reddish siena ink, inscribed in epsilon handwriting with measures in feet, and (on verso) with scale of 7 units = 46 mm.

Pane 1948, pl. III, fig. 6; Wittkower 1949/1971, p. 83 no. 3, fig. 29d; Zorzi 1955, p. 48, fig. 32, 36 (as Falconetto); Zorzi 1959, p. 57, fig. 49 (recto), p. 60, fig. 63 (verso); Spielmann 1966, p. 169, no. 204, figs. 110–111 (as workshop, before 1550, and confusing sheet D-1 with Vicenza D-3, representing details from these two monuments); Mostra 1973, p. 25, no. IX.a, fig. 15 (Forssman— as Palladio [?]), p. 150 (Burns).

Museo Civico, Vicenza.

In this sheet Palladio acknowledges that the use of "rustic" orders had dramatic precedent in antiquity. His *recto* shows the great double portals by which the architects of the Emperor Claudius, in A.D. 52, carried two new aqueducts across the junction of a pair of consular highways on the outskirts of Rome; in the 270s the composition was incorporated into the vast circuit of the Aurelian walls, as the easternmost gate of the city. The tall attic which covers the water conduits had been dressed with smooth stone-work, but the whole lower zone, apart from the capitals and pedimented entablature of the columnar tabernacles, had been left in bold, rough-cut blocks of raw stone. Palladio in this early drawing from his first Roman visit subdues and regularizes these antique eccentricities, so that his engaged column shafts, for example, look almost normal; but a later drawing (RIBA XII/14 *recto*) is much more true to the rugged grandeur that caused these Claudian monuments to exert so potent an influence on the more imaginative and expressive architects of the Renaissance.

An even more bizarre and "mannered" conceit distin-guished the upper arcades of the temple terrace of the Claudianum (or Temple of the Deified Claudius) on the crest of the Caelian Hill, which Palladio records—as they are still visible today—on the *verso*. Here a finely detailed order of Tuscan pilasters is conceived as being "imprisoned" within the massive rustication, thus allowing only glimpses of its smoothed shafts to appear between the otherwise uncut blocks. The capitals and entablature are perfectly expressed, but no bases are included; in these details the design is paralleled by Palladio's portal of the Palazzo Civena in Vicenza, completed in 1542, and his drawing of 1542–1546 of a project for the Palazzo Thiene facade (cat. no. 51).

58

32

32. ELEVATION STUDY FOR TWO STORIES OF A THREE-BAY FACADE

c. 1540

Devonshire Collections, RIBA, London: Chiswick 27.

42.6 × 28.5 cm. (single sheet); no watermark visible; Talman 54 mark on *verso*.

Siena ink and umber crayon over heavily incised lines and some pencil underdrawing.

Arts Council 1975, p. 229, no. 403 (as "Vitruvian study").

The Trustees of the Chatsworth Settlement.

This drawing, although much elaborated in its upper portions, may serve to remind us of the highly refined "Doric" (or more properly "Tuscan") order, of which Palladio was such an accomplished master already at this early date. Its severe stereobate is shown with the regulation three steps, the base is simply yet finely detailed, the fluted shaft omits (rather curiously) any trace of entasis, the capital is delicately carved after a model such as Trajan's Column, and (perhaps most interestingly) the frieze eschews any notice of the infamous problem of the corner triglyph by centering that element over the last column (leaving, as

59

Figure 12

Figure 13

Palladio often did in his buildings, a blank strip between the end of the classical order and the actual edge of the structure). This arrangement allowed for the regular spacing of an even number of triglyphs between the columns, with an odd number of metopes, which resulted in the attractively decorative variation of the *bucrania* and *paterae* changing positions at the centers of alternate bays.

The detailed rendering of the order (particularly in such an idiosyncratic detail as the banded *bucrania*) is close enough to RIBA XIII/10 (cat. no. 8) to warrant assignment of this almost unstudied sheet to the same period, that is to around 1539. In that regard the upper zone of the present drawing is especially interesting, since it so clearly recalls the unmolded niches with richly draped figures on the upper story of Trissino's new loggia of 1538 at Cricoli (fig. 1). That design, whose execution Palladio had certainly followed intimately (perhaps even from the stage of Trissino's selection of it in consultation with Serlio, from a drawing by the latter which had been distantly inspired by the garden loggia of the Villa Madama: cat. nos. 1 and 30), also employed the same thinly articulated Ionic pilasters as we find associated with Trissinian niches in the present drawing. Already in comparison with Palladio's first experience of metropolitan "high style" in the loggia at Cricoli, however (which this drawing otherwise so closely resembles), in this sheet—apparently of only a year or two later—he not only shows a much greater mastery than

Trissino and Serlio of correct Ionic proportions, but rather surprisingly presents a Doric order that is almost Bramantesque in its sobriety and power, and strongly reflects Sanmicheli in its sculptural richness.

The question of whether this sheet was intended to have a practical application may be referred by analogy to a parallel design of Tuscan pilasters arranged in three bays, on the Chatsworth drawing XXXVI/33 (fig. 12). This sheet (which does not seem to have been discussed) represents an upper portion of a larger facade, since its supporting moldings continue toward the right. It shows very close analogies with Leonardo Mocenigo's house in Padua (fig. 13), which Palladio remodeled in 1558–1561, according to the testimony of new documents (see cat. nos. 57, 73). The style of the drawing in fig. 12 exactly fits this period, and may in part be based on the prototype of the present sheet.

33. STUDIES OF IONIC CAPITAL AND BASE

Early 1540s

RIBA: Palladio XI/9 *verso*.

43.1 × 26.9 cm. (single sheet, with heavy brown stains); no watermark; Talman 54 mark on *verso*.

Pale, brownish siena ink, directly over incised lines; scale (at bottom) of two starred units = 57 mm. (2 Veronese inches); large module on base *torus* = 51 mm. (2 Roman inches); small module on column shaft = 23.3 mm. *Recto,* LEFT HALF-ELEVATION OF HEXASTYLE SYSTYLE IONIC TEMPLE (AFTER VITRUVIUS), with labeled module of 24 mm.: Zorzi 1959, p. 121, fig. 286; Spielmann 1966, p. 138, no. 15 (but with technical matter applying to XI/10, of which description is given in his cat. no. 16, where technical matter for this sheet occurs; his no. 15 giving inscriptions [in epsilon and transitional handwritings] for XI/9 *recto,* but with substantial inaccuracies); fig. 9.

Zorzi 1959, p. 122, fig. 287; Spielmann 1966, p. 139, no. 18 (as c. 1545–55).

Royal Institute of British Architects, London.

The beautifully severe and simple images on this reverse exercise a striking appeal by their very plainness. They are almost exact illustrations of Vitruvius's instructions to architects (III:v:3, for the Ionic base; and III:v:5–7, for the capital) about how to form the major elements of the Ionic order. No indications of sculptural details have been included, save two minor elements in the curves of the volutes; in particular the main egg-and-dart molding is still missing from the echinus, and the resulting linear simplicity sharply emphasises the underlying structure.

The Ionic temple system on the *recto* again gives visual form to a Vitruvian description (III:iii:1–2), and demonstrates its precocious date not only by a rather stiff graphic style, but by the inclusion of no less than three early handwritings. Very unusually, the first of these in a caption at the bottom is written with Palladio's "mature" form of the *e,* but consecutively followed (i.e. postdated) by an addendum using epsilons. Since all seem to date from the first half of the 1540s, this is one more indication that Palladio's handwriting was beginning to incorporate the "mature" *e* already at an early stage in his development.

Although these images do form the basis for Palladian illustrations in Daniele Barbaro's *Vitruvius* commentary of 1556 (on which Barbaro states in the book that his work began in 1547), they seem likely to have been drawn by Palladio substantially before that period. Trissino too was

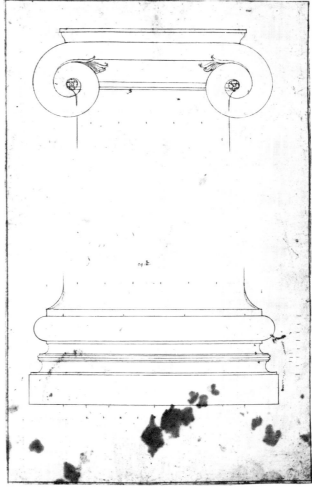

33

a dedicated Vitruvian scholar, and I have already suggested elsewhere (see cat. no. 48) that the circle which he and Palladio are presumed to have frequented in Padua in 1539–40 might easily have brought them into contact with Daniele Barbaro, through several of his relatives, friends, and associates. It is in fact quite possible that such contacts with enthusiasts of the Trissino-Cornaro circle may have helped to develop Daniele's Vitruvian tastes as well as Palladio's.

34 *recto*

34. ELEVATION, PLAN OF COLUMNS AND PEDESTAL DETAIL OF TEMPLE OF MINERVA, ASSISI

1541

RIBA: Palladio XV/9 (now restored and remounted as *recto*).

42.9 × 29.1 cm. (single sheet); watermark, crossed arrows with star (variant of Briquet 6292/6293), "Palladio's standard paper" of c. 1540; laid lines 39 mm. apart; no collector's mark.

Umber ink, with small touches of very light sepia wash; inscribed in epsilon handwriting, and with scale (rt.) of 5 feet = 29.8 mm. (1 Vicentine inch); unlabeled scale (left), of two starred units = 34.5 mm. *Verso,* PLAN AND SECTION OF LATERAN BAPTISTERY, ROME; also inscribed with epsilon handwriting; Zorzi 1959, p. 81, fig. 183; Spielmann 1966, p. 148, no. 68 (giving inscription), fig. 36.

Zorzi 1959, pp. 27, 82, fig. 191; Spielmann 1966, p. 150, no. 84 (giving inscriptions), fig. 44; Mostra 1973, p. 147 (Burns), fig. 155; Arts Council 1975, p. 248, no. 438 (Burns).

Royal Institute of British Architects, London

The splendidly preserved pronaos of the Late Republican temple at Assisi is unusual not in its order—which is represented here by Palladio's version of its strong, simply detailed Corinthian mode—but in its adjustment to its position. Because of the steepness of the site, it was placed at the midpoint of one long side of the city forum, with its internal floor lying substantially higher on the slope. To permit the change of level, the stylobate is cut through at the five intercolumniations, and steps rise ingeniously between the columns (rather than projecting far out into the narrow square) to reach the temple floor, which in fact the level of the column bases represents. When Goethe saw this solution, during his visit to Assisi on 26 October 1786, he was filled with admiration for its "boldness," "logical procedure," and "great loveliness" (Auden ed. 1962, pp. 106–108). But these reactions came at the expense of his severe disillusionment with Palladio, whom Goethe cor-

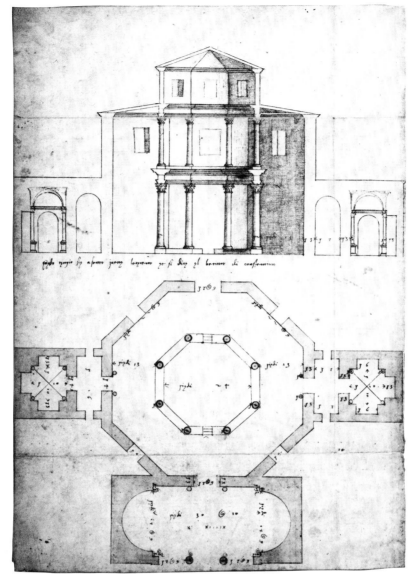

34 *verso*

rectly criticized for having extended the sundered stylobate fragments much higher upward in the form of real pedestals, in his *Quattro Libri* plate (IV:xxvi:105). These upper components of the "pedestals" have no counterparts in reality (Spielmann fig. 43), for the column bases actually stand directly on the lowest molded elements in the drawing, immediately above the accurately depicted steps. (Three or four more continuous steps do descend below the stylobate chunks into the Piazza, as Palladio shows in a slight revision of the drawing in his *Quattro Libri* plate.) Palladio had observed, in the lower caption on this sheet, that the whole substructure in his day was still buried, so that he could only guess at the height of its components. The resulting anomalies of his design, even though distinctly non-archaeological, encouraged him to regard tall pedestals as elements sanctioned by this usage in antiquity; and (as

Burns has shown, 1975) they soon became one of the standard motifs of his own architectural designs.

The two drawings on the sheet seem to have been made during or just after Palladio's trip to Rome with Trissino in 1541; for (despite Goethe's assumption of his ignorance) Palladio does seem to have studied the Assisi temple, as well as the Lateran Baptistery, at first hand. The latter gets a very dull and wooden reproduction in the *Quattro Libri* (IV:xvi:54), which does no justice at all to the delicate subtlety of Palladio's fine early drawing on the reverse of this sheet.

63

35. STUDIES OF COLUMN BASES AT THE LATERAN BAPTISTERY, ROME

1541

RIBA: Palladio XIV/2 *recto*.

40.9 × 26.8/23.1 cm. (single sheet, right corners cut); no water-mark; no collector's mark.

Rich umber ink, used also for touches of wash; labels and inscriptions in epsilon handwriting; scale of 2 starred units = 47 mm. *Verso,* PERSPECTIVAL RENDERINGS OF PANTHEON CORNICE DETAILS: pale umber ink, inscribed in epsilon handwriting, and with scale of 2 starred units = 34.5 mm.; Zorzi 1959, p. 105, fig. 263 (as autograph); Spielmann 1966, p. 148, no. 74.

Zorzi 1959, p. 104, fig. 262 (as Falconetto); Spielmann 1966, p. 148, no. 69 (as autograph, before 1550; giving inscriptions); Arts Council 1975, pp. 258–259 (Burns).

Royal Institute of British Architects, London.

This wonderful sheet is as beautiful for the subtlety of its drafting techniques as for the handsomeness of its subjects. Palladio draws the unusually complex types of bases found in the Lateran Baptistery (cat. no. 34 *verso*), at this very early stage of his graphic career, with a delicacy and elaboration of hatchings and shadings that are extremely rare in his later work. In the upper image, for example, the crisp, sharp profile on the right is touched with very light shading on the shadowed parts. This deepens gradually toward the left, culminating in an opposing profile elab-orated as a contour by a repertory of strokes, barrings, and hatchings that provide exact graphic analogues for its variety of sculptural shapes.

The lower base is depicted with still greater graphic inventiveness, for in addition to the techniques described above, delicate touches of wash are incorporated, together with heavy outlining around the contours of projecting elements. Many of these effects are reproduced with sur-prising fidelity by the block-maker for the illustration of this base in the *Quattro Libri* (IV:xvi:63, and [text] IV:xvi:61). Here Palladio describes having used the curious tall ring of acanthus leaves, between the base and the shaft, on the columns framing the interior facade door of S. Giorgio Maggiore in Venice (Zorzi 1967, fig. 66), where—as he comments about the antique prototype—the purpose similarly had been to raise the bases enough to accommodate some short but spectacular marble shafts, which otherwise would not have fit proportionally.

A beautiful fragment of the Pantheon entablature, on the *verso,* is drawn with equal success and with many of the same devices of three-dimensional illusionism; the label to another sketch of the piece, on a sheet in Vicenza (D-16 *recto*) informs us that the stonemason's shop in which the fragment was copied had been located near S. Marcello al Corso in Rome.

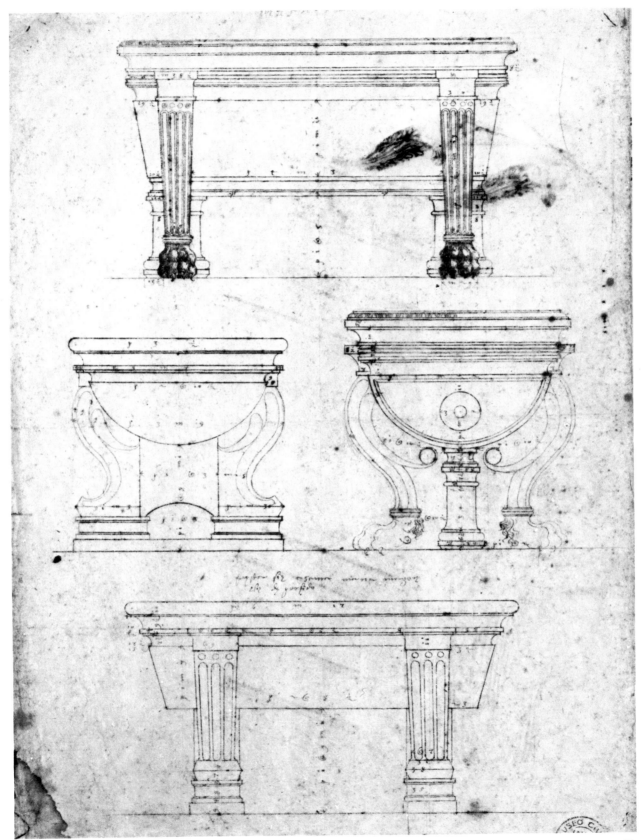

36

36. FRONT AND SIDE ELEVATIONS OF TWO ROMAN SARCOPHAGI

c. 1537(?)–1541

Vicenza: 1950 inv. D-8 *recto*.

43.9 × 29.6 cm. (single sheet with beveled corners); no watermark visible; no collector's mark.

Umber ink, inscribed in epsilon handwriting with descriptions and measures in feet. *Verso,* DETAILS OF CAPITAL AND ENTABLATURE ON THE INTERIOR OF THE PANTHEON, ROME; siena ink with pencil underdrawing, and sepia wash; inscribed in epsilon handwriting with label and measures in feet; Zorzi 1955, p. 43, fig. 11 (as Falconetto); Zorzi 1959, p. 77, fig. 166 (same); Spielmann 1966, p. 149, no. 75 (as Palladio or his shop, before 1550); Mostra 1973, p. 21, no. II.b (Forssman).

Pane 1948, pl. X, fig. 19; Zorzi 1955, p. 43, fig. 12 (as Falconetto); Zorzi 1959, pp. 101–102, fig. 252 (same); Spielmann 1966, p. 149, no. 77 (as Palladio or his shop, before 1550); Mostra 1973, p. 21, no. II.c (Forssman), p. 151 (Burns); Puppi 1973, p. 240, fig. 278.

Museo Civico, Vicenza.

This magnificent sheet, one of the most strikingly designed and beautifully drawn in Palladio's oeuvre, was carefully composed in the studio from sketchbook prototypes, whose ornamental appeal had gained them a wide circulation. The left, bottom, and right images, for example, all appear in virtually identical forms (on fols. 43 *verso,* 44 *recto* and 44 *verso* respectively) in the Mellon sketchbook of 1513–c. 1520 attributed to Domenico da Varignana (cat. no. 25). In the same way, the labels inscribed on the latter images may have been prototypes for Palladio's borrowed inscriptions: "cassa di porfido a santa maria maggiore di roma," which appears on fol. 44 *recto,* is here echoed in Palladio's notation (bottom image): "this is at santa maria maggiore and is of porphyry."

The relative accessibility of these compelling antique designs, the fact that Palladio's colleagues in the Pedemuro shop specialized in exactly the kind of ornamental sculpture that they represent, and Palladio's own sketching of them (with his first handwriting) in a self-consciously pattern-book style, all combine to suggest that this sheet may be an unusually early one, deriving from the days of Andrea's association with his Vicentine masters on programs of decorative sculpture involving just such forms as these. Zorzi in fact proposed, on the basis of this sheet (1966, p. 13, figs. 11–12), that one such collaboration might plausibly have brought the artist into direct partnership with his shop directors Girolamo di Pedemuro and Giovanni da Porlezza, on the tomb they both signed in the Vicenza cathedral for the Bishop Girolamo Schio, whose sarcophagus of 1537 strongly resembles the upper one on Palladio's drawing. Even if this particular sheet is slightly later—though it presumably cannot postdate 1541—the hypothesis may still hold, as Puppi remarked; and these images may simply be improvements or replacements for Palladio's own future use.

37. PLAN AND ELEVATION OF THE ARCH OF CONSTANTINE, ROME

1540s

Vicenza: 1950 inv. D-14.

42.4 × 29.2 cm. (single sheet with beveled corners); unclear watermark, probably crossed arrows with star (variant of Briquet 6296/6293), "Palladio's standard paper" of c. 1540; no collector's mark.

Siena ink, inscribed in epsilon handwriting with label and measures in feet; scale of 10 units = 37 mm.

Zorzi 1955, p. 47, fig. 27 (as Falconetto); Zorzi 1959, p. 55, fig. 34 (same); Spielmann 1966, p. 170, no. 213, fig. 114 (as Palladio or his shop, before 1550); Mostra 1973, p. 26, no. XIIa, fig. 20 (Forssman); p. 152 (Burns).

Museo Civico, Vicenza.

This attractive sheet, which incorporates some of Palladio's most elaborate figure drawings, represents an early phase of his graphic work in which he was still willing to devote painstaking attention to sculptural detail. But while Palladio here includes many decorative elements, he at the same time provides compositional balance by omitting details from the cornice, on the right-hand side where the sculptures are sketched in full. This allows the basic structure of the monument to be immediately perceptible, in keeping with Palladio's lifelong interest in the fundamentals of architectural design.

The sheet was carefully produced in the studio (as one of the items intended to comprise a Book of Roman Arches) in a redrafting of previous studies, either by other architects or Palladio himself. There were quite adequate versions of the monument in various early sketchbooks, as for example in such a possible prototype as fol. 76 *recto* of the Mellon Codex (cat. no. 25). The quality of figural detail indicates that Palladio had studied the arch at least once at first hand, and certain elements of his graphic style (such as the shading techniques) are typical of his drawings from the early 1540s. But the general refinement and delicacy of line, and the measures inserted in such a beautifully symmetrical pattern, anticipate the crystalline precision of Palladio's drawings from the early 1550s, and are characteristic of a transitional period that culminated in his illustrations for Daniel Barbaro's edition of *Vitruvius* (cat. no. 72, figs. 48 and 87). Since the earliest phase of this transition was marked by an emphasis on decorative elements that would not be seen again in Palladio's work until the 1570s, when it re-emerged as one of the principal components of his late style, it is possible that his interest in the most lavish monuments of antiquity—such as those depicted here—came nearer to the end than the beginning of the decade of the 1540s.

37

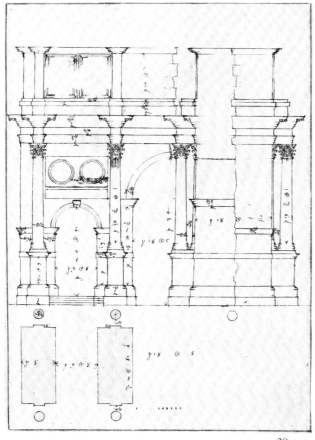

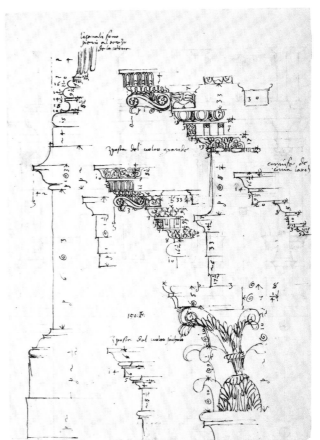

38. GENERAL SURVEY OF THE ARCH OF CONSTANTINE, ROME

Late 1560s

RIBA: Palladio XII/5 *recto* and *verso*.

29.9 × 20.9 cm. (single sheet, unusually clear white paper); countermark Ꞗ E, laid lines 27 mm. apart (Briquet 643: Vicenza 1567); Talman 150 mark on *verso*.

Russet-red siena ink, with light gold-beige wash, on pencil underdrawing (of which a sculptural figure, *recto* upper right, is left uninked); scale of 10 units = 29.8 mm. (1 Vicentine inch) (on *recto*); on *verso*, inscriptions in mature handwriting.

Zorzi 1955, pp. 47–48, figs. 30–31; Zorzi 1959, p. 55, figs. 35, 38; Spielmann 1966, p. 170, no. 214 (giving *verso* inscriptions), fig. 115 (*recto*).

Royal Institute of British Architects, London.

This fine sheet may serve as an exemplar of the graphic canon that Palladio, by now arrived at complete mastery of his medium, had carefully developed for the accurate depiction of ancient monuments (most typically for the purpose of publishing them). The main image on the *recto* is artfully composed of three parts: a half elevation of one of the principal sides, another of a flank, and, between them, a half transverse section; aligned below the main elevation is a half plan, and a corresponding space is even more artfully left blank, for visual relief.

On the *verso* a series of beautifully executed details elucidates every part of the structure: a full pedestal and base profile on the left, and a highly particularized capital and entablature study on the right, thoroughly describe the main order; they are interspersed with four more cornice and impost details of the secondary elements supporting the arches themselves. Not only are the sculptural details sketched with consummate force and beauty, but the rapidly-noted profiles manifest an extraordinary incisiveness.

39. PLAN AND ELEVATION, WITH SKETCHES OF DETAILS, OF THE PORTICO OF OCTAVIA, ROME

Early 1560s?

RIBA: Palladio XI/17 *recto* and *verso*

29.6 × 21.7 cm. (single sheet); watermark, rudimentary angel in oval with star, laid lines 27 mm. apart (probably Briquet 649: Vicenza 1562); Talman 150 mark on *verso*.

Dark-red siena ink, with (later?) flat gray wash; on the *verso*, extensive umber crayon underdrawing, and inscription in mature handwriting.

Zorzi 1959, p. 59, figs. 57–58; Spielmann 1966, p. 176, no. 242 (as after 1562; giving inscription); Gioseffi 1972, pp. 56–57, fig. 14.

Royal Institute of British Architects, London.

The dramatic composition of this image relates it to many similar projects prepared for publication, and we are fortunate in having a series of drawings to record its evolution. Two early sketches with epsilon inscriptions (RIBA VII/5 *verso*, Vicenza D-26 *recto* [cat. no. 26]) are much more tentatively conceived, but the firmly drafted structure and freehand details of this version present the monument in Palladio's standard orthographic elevation, aligned with a restoration of the plan (only a little less than the right half of the portico actually survives). The rather blurred profiles on the reverse, though executed essentially in the same technique as the details in the *verso* of the preceding sheet (cat. no. 38 *verso*), are much less confident and clear: the odd treatment of the secondary frieze (including its strange stripes of gray wash) suggests an auxiliary hand.

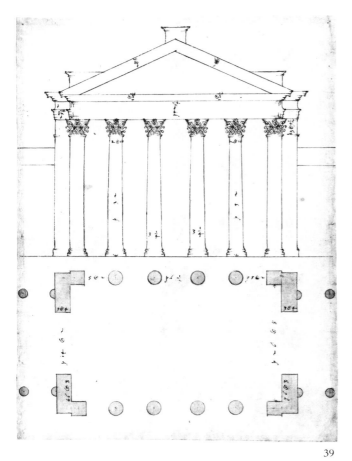

39

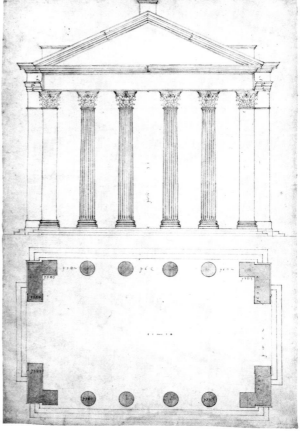

40

69

40. PLAN AND ELEVATION, WITH FLANK AND ENTABLATURE DETAIL, OF THE PORTICO OF OCTAVIA, ROME

Early to middle 1550s

RIBA: Palladio XI/18 recto and verso.

42.7 × 28.9 cm. (single sheet of beige-ivory paper, stained at bottom); watermark, anchor in oval with star (cf. Mošin 788: Fabriano 1552), laid lines 40 mm. apart; Talman 54 mark on verso.

Pale umber ink in very thin lines, with umber-beige wash; starred scale of 5 units = 22.3 mm. (¾ of a Vicentine inch); verso has same drafting ink on umber crayon underdrawing, with measures in siena ink.

Zorzi 1959, p. 59, figs. 59–60; Forssman 1965, p. 125, fig. 59; Spielmann 1966, p. 176, no. 243 (as workshop, c. 1565–1570).

Royal Institute of British Architects, London.

This larger finished drawing is directly related to the preceding model (cat. no. 39), with all the lines mechanically drawn except for the smallest curvilinear details of the capitals; thus the entablature and base moldings, sketched on the companion sheet in Palladio's typical "shorthand" at the edges only, are here carefully ruled all the way across. This change of technique, however, does not necessarily imply a change of hand or a later date, nor even that the two sheets should be read in this order. On the contrary—and in distinction to Spielmann's reliance on "later" versions of standard watermarks, which are generally more flexible in date—I would regard these two sheets, with their brilliant sense of design, but their rather early handwriting, and their inclusion of an isometric "perspective" rendering on the verso of this sheet, as being intimately related, and mutually diagnostic of the first truly mature phase of Palladio's graphic style. We might thus postulate a close stylistic parallel between their clear, crisp renderings and uncomplicated open forms with the similar, highly characteristic handling of Palladio's illustrations for the 1556 Vitruvius edition of Daniele Barbaro. Such an hypothesis might be reinforced by recalling how often Palladio uses such porticoes with arched openings on the sides in his own buildings of the 1550s.

The partially surviving monument which these sheets record stands immediately behind the northwest corner of the Theatre of Marcellus near the eastern shore of the Tiber, in a picturesque and well-preserved corner of medieval and Renaissance Rome. The portico is an entrance added by Septimius Severus around A.D. 205 to a large rectilinear double colonnade, over 150 yards on a side, adjoining the theatre; the whole square had been dedicated, in a rebuilding by Augustus in 23 B.C., to his sister Octavia. Palladio restores the portico as a freestanding structure in this more detailed drawing (which incorporates the old-fashioned perspective element, and distinctly early inscriptions), whereas he correctly includes the lateral colonnades in the quicker and more loosely drawn version of cat. no. 39 (whose inscriptions could well be construed as the later ones). This possible reversal of chronology might suggest (on analogies also between the style of cat. no. 39 and preparatory sheets for the Quattro Libri) that the latter drawing could represent an "improved" version, more rapidly blocked out as a guide to a plate maker for publication. The characteristically more developed details on its verso would support this view as well.

CHAPTER THREE

Domestic Project Drawings of the Early 1540s

41. FACADE AND PLAN PROJECTS FOR VILLA GAZOTO AT BERTESINA, OR FOR VILLA VALMARANA AT VIGARDOLO (?)

1539–41

RIBA: Palladio XVII/15 *recto.*

31.6 × 28.1 cm. (two sheets, pasted with 6 mm. overlap, evidently in England; top, 13.7 × 28.1 cm., watermark, cardinal's hat with B between tassles (Briquet 3437: Vicenza 1539); bottom, 18.5 × 28.1 cm., no watermark; Talman 150 marks on *verso* of both sheets).

Dark siena ink in thin lines, on some pencil underdrawing; pale yellow-gold wash on plan, deeper gold-beige wash on elevation; plan inscribed in epsilon handwriting with measures in Vicentine feet, and wall thicknesses in quarters of feet. *Verso,* siena ink over inscribed lines.

Dalla Pozza 1943, p. 73, fig. 12 (facade only); Wittkower 1945/1974, pp. 166–167, fig. 192 (but describing RIBA XVII/1; which, however—together with the present drawing—is guaranteed to Palladio by extensive autograph inscriptions); Zorzi 1954, pp. 66–67, project no. 9, fig. 9; Pane 1961, p. 109, fig. 132:32; Harris 1966, no. and fig. 7 (as Scamozzi); Ackerman 1967, pp. 3–4, fig. 7; Zorzi 1969, pp. 14, 46–47, project no. 10, figs. 14, 55; Mostra 1973, p. 149 (Burns); Puppi 1973, p. 247, fig. 295; Arts Council 1975, p. 185, no. 326 (Fairbairn); Berger 1978, pp. 64–73ff., fig. 6.

Royal Institute of British Architects, London.

In the year 1541 Palladio seems to have received a pair of almost exactly parallel commissions, which by 1543 resulted in the construction of two small surviving villas, located quite close to each other near what are today the eastern suburbs of Vicenza. Since both projects seem likely to have "started big," but were then more or less sharply reduced in parallel planning stages, it has proved difficult to assign specific drawings, among some ten or a dozen related designs, categorically to the one or the other commission. Indeed until the 1950s and 1960s not only were the two buildings themselves still doubted as works by Palladio, but the undisputedly autograph drawings which in both cases confirm his authorship were rather perversely held to represent "abstract" or "theoretical" studies, from an "early" period (very hazily defined) in which he was assumed to have had so much leisure as to be able to produce a whole host of projects merely for practice (or, as has more recently been proposed, for publication). Since almost all these drawings are of presentation quality, however, and since most of the earliest sheets can be associated in various ways with Palladio's projects of 1537–1543 for actual buildings at Lonedo, Bagnolo, Vigardolo, or Bertesina, we should doubtless accept these interrelationships with the understanding that Palladio would natually have devoted to each of his new villa projects something of the same enthusiasm, inventiveness, and energy that he had expended in these same years, in preparing a comparable number of closely related drawings for his first city palace projects (cat. nos. 2–4 and 6–7).

These celebrated drawings on RIBA XVII/15 are therefore proposed as relating very probably either to the villa for Tadeo Gazoto at Bertesina, or (in my opinion somewhat more plausibly) to that of the cousins Giuseppe and Antonio Valmarana at Vigardolo. The highly idiosyncratic facade, especially in its insistent motif of a *serliana* centered under an interrupted cornice and pediment, exactly parallels Palladio's final design for Vigardolo (cat. no. 36). The direct antique-inspired source for the arrangement of the flanking *serliana,* as well as for the three sequential pediments, may be a hitherto unpublished sketch design on the *verso* of RIBA IX/12 (fig. 14), quite possibly jotted down by Palladio in Tivoli or Rome during the summer of 1541. If the villa design dates from 1539 to 1540, as seems possible from its style and watermark, then the antique sketch may be a slightly later variant of an idea developed in the studio.

The plan presented on XVII/15 was apparently begun on the *verso,* with the initial fragment of an entrance colonnade identical to that of the Tempietto on the Clitumnus (cat. no. 22), but abandoned in favor of the scheme shown. Several commentators have pointed out the relationship of the double-apsed room to the Lateran Baptistery loggia (cat. no. 34 *verso*), although—as Burns implies—the space functions here not as an access loggia (two separate entrances flank it), but rather as the central hall in a divided plan, whose twin halves suggest two patrons (thus possibly the Valmarana cousins, again, at Vigardolo). The exceedingly narrow central staircase, however, recurs almost identically in the following design (cat. no. 42—certainly a specific project for Bertesina), as do also the vaulting patterns (as Fairbairn observed), the character of the inscriptions, and the whole tenor of the drafting style. This plan is part of a very small group of coeval early projects (cat. nos. 41, 42, 44, 45) that show at several points the thickness of the walls, expressed in quarters of feet: in this design Palladio recommends 9-quarter (2′3″) exterior walls, 7-quarter (1′9″) interior ones, and 5-quarter (1′3″) partitions.

Figure 14

41

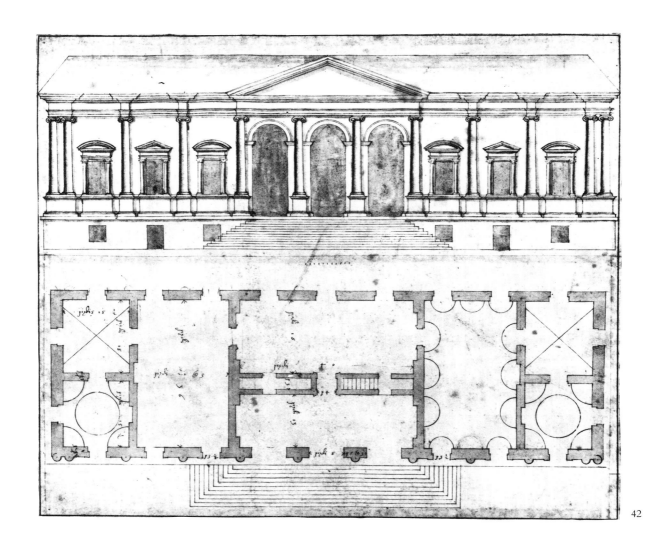

42

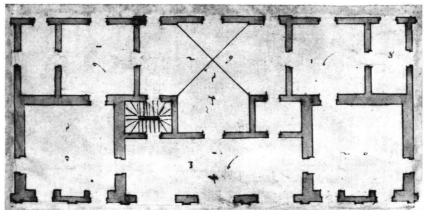

Figure 15

74

Figure 16

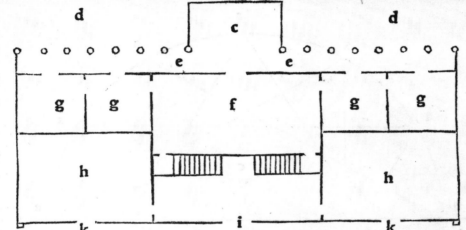

Figure 17

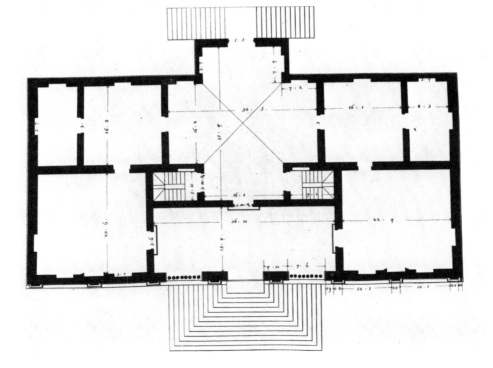

Figure 18

75

42. FACADE AND PLAN PROJECTS FOR VILLA GAZOTO, BERTESINA

1541/42

RIBA: Palladio XVII/27.

32.6 × 37.5 cm. total (two main sheets, pasted with c. 5 mm. overlap, evidently in England: top, 15.2 × 37.5 cm.; watermark, crossbow in circle with fleur-de-lis [variant of Briquet 761/762]; bottom, main sheet 17.9 × 36.5 cm., pieced by adding 1.1 cm. strips left and right with 6 mm. overlaps, making these three 17.9 × 37.5 cm.; no watermarks); Talman 54 marks on *verso* of both main sheets.

Umber ink on facade, siena ink on plan, with pencil or umber crayon underdrawing; pale yellow-beige wash on plan, roof, and illusionistic shadows, darker gold-brown wash in apertures; plan inscribed in epsilon handwriting with measures in Vicentine feet, and wall thicknesses in quarters of feet.

Dalla Pozza 1949, Exhibition; Fiocco 1949, p. 187, fig. 187; Dalla Pozza 1952, Lecture 22 March; Zorzi 1952, pp. 135–138, fig. 143; Zorzi 1954, pp. 68–69, project no. 11, fig. 11; Pane 1961, pp. 101–102, fig. 122:12; Dalla Pozza 1943–1963, pp. 106–118, fig. 8; Zorzi 1969, p. 47, project no. 11, fig. 56, and pp. 67–68 n. 3; Barbieri 1970, p. 68, fig. 88; Mostra 1973, pp. 53–54 (Cevese), p. 149 (Burns), fig. 48; Puppi 1973, pp. 250–251, fig. 298; Arts Council 1975, pp. 183–184, no. 324 (Fairbairn), fig. 324; Berger 1978, pp. 66–68ff., fig. 5.

Royal Institute of British Architects, London.

As Dalla Pozza first demonstrated in the Vicenza exhibition of 1949, by juxtaposing this sheet and Bertotti-Scamozzi's engraved elevation of the Villa Gazoto at Bertesina, there can be no doubt that the upper image on RIBA XVII/27 represents the next-to-last design before Palladio's construction of that facade. His execution is almost identical (fig. 16), the only changes being the omission of one bay at each end (the plan was similarly compressed), his substitution of the drawing's engaged columns with pilasters, and of its alternating-pedimented tabernacles with simpler window frames carrying uniform triangular pediments. Curiously enough, these changes all replace the very elements which had brought the drawing project close to the forms of Raphael's courtyard facade of the Villa Madama (an original affinity that had been pointed out by Fairbairn).

The plan has a more complex relationship to the executed building, for it represents a similarly late phase in a several-stage development, of which—as Barbieri has suggested—at least three previous drawings survive (a more tentative possible fourth is mentioned above, cat. no. 41). These are all very large "double-pile" plans, evidently deriving from Palladio's prolonged revisions (which continued even after completion of the project) to the design for his first large building, the Villa Godi at Lonedo, which was being constructed (presumably with the help of his associates in the Pedemuro shop) in these same years of 1537–42. Palladio's developed "double-pile" projects all show matching domestic suites not only on either side of a central axis containing the loggia and stairs, but also with this entire plan replicated again on the other side of a transverse wall, so as to place identical third and fourth apartments in the rear corners, flanking a large center-axis hall. The most imaginative of these is RIBA XVI/16-C (fig. 51), with three apsidal or segmental-ended rooms, and internal *serliane*; it was apparently too idiosyncratic to be further pursued (though its stairs are the closest to those on the present sheet, and we shall see other echoes of it in the projects for Bagnolo: cat. no. 46). RIBA XVI/16-B, on the other hand (drawn, as is its companion, on "Palladio's standard paper" of c. 1540), presents a "double-pile" plan whose front half forms a close precedent to the full plan on XVII/27, here exhibited; and a larger, slightly simpler plan on RIBA XVI/18 (still on the same paper as the other "double-pile" plans) has a front half not only even closer in general form to our exhibited XVII/27, but also staircases identical to the eventual execution, and the first appearance of pilasters on the facade. Hence, on each of these immensely ambitious plans (but especially on the latter two, XVI/16-B and XVI/18) a blocking-off of the rear halves produces a series of plans directly antecedent to the long, thin shape on the present sheet; and since the last of these (XVI/18) prefigures the stair systems and facade pilasters of the executed house, while its immediately derivative present sheet exactly anticipates the final facade ordonnance, we can thus confidently link all three to the villa at Bertesina, as prototypes for the present image.

Its successor, and immediate model for the construction of the Villa Gazoto, is the strange little plan on RIBA XVI/16-A (Fig. 15). Although actually quite an ingenious compacting of the previous schemes, it is hastily and roughly drawn, on unusual paper, with startling solecisms such as the very odd wall-endings which protrude beyond the flanks. It was quite clearly inspired by the plan of the stage building on fol. 50 *verso* of Fra' Giocondo's *Vitruvius* edition of 1511 (fig. 17), which it more or less exactly repeats. This same source suggested the one embellishment that Palladio seems to have persuaded the patron to add during execution, that is, a large bay projecting from the rear facade to give the hall a cruciform shape; but even so, the villa as constructed (fig. 18) offers hardly any reminiscence of the initial grandeur of Palladio's preceding planimetric schemes.

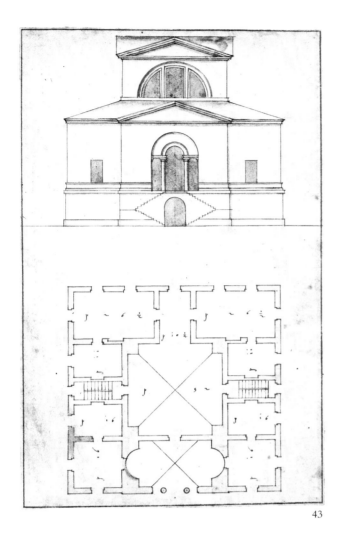

43

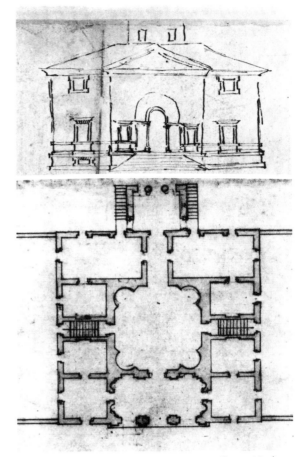

43. FACADE AND PLAN PROJECT FOR VILLA VALMARANA, VIGARDOLO (?)

c. 1540–41

RIBA: Palladio XVII/1 *recto*.

38.2 × 23.5 cm. (single sheet); no watermark, laid lines 33 mm. apart; Talman 54 mark on *verso*.

Umber ink, with pale sepia-beige wash on plan, denser beige-brown wash on elevation apertures, cornices, and roofs; plan inscribed in the same ink with measures in Vicentine feet. *Verso,* umber ink over inscribed lines.

Burger 1909, p. 57, fig. 19:2 (plan), fig. 20:2 (elevation); Loukomski 1938, p. 24; Zorzi 1954, pp. 61–62, project no. 2, fig. 2; Pane 1961 pp. 108–109, figs. 109:31, 132:31; Forssman 1965, p. 28, fig. 11; Ackerman 1966/1977, p. 43, fig. 12; Zorzi 1969, pp. 41–42, project no. 2, fig. 41; Mostra 1973, p. 148 (Burns); Puppi 1973, p. 247, fig. 294; Arts Council 1975, p. 182, no. 322 (Fairbairn); Berger 1978, pp. 64, 79–84, fig. 9.

Royal Institute of British Architects, London.

This sheet mediates directly between the plan projects that can be associated with Palladio's proposals for his patron at Bertesina (cat. nos. 41–42), and those which relate to the evolution of his designs for Vigardolo (cat. no. 44). On its *verso* is the abandoned commencement of a "double-pile" plan very similar to the two in that genre whose front halves are direct prototypes for Bertesina (RIBA XVI/16-B and XVI/18); in this fragmentary plan the twin suites at the rear are brought closer together, across a central hall now only as wide as their individual living rooms. The project on the front of this sheet, however, is directly related to Palladio's final solution at Vigardolo. An ingeniously compact, economical plan of much more plausible functionality, it marks a new departure in Palladio's domestic designs. Apart from its small loggia, for example (which is still open to the out-of-doors, through a large portal in the form of a *serliana*), all of its rooms can actually be closed against the weather. On the other hand

77

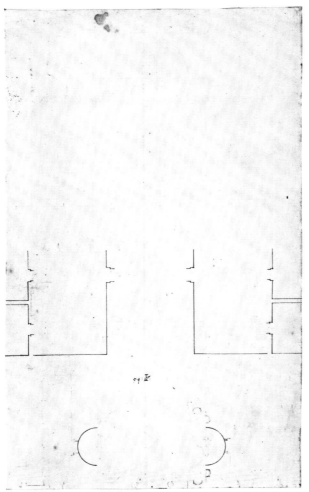

it is a curious fact, characteristic of several of Palladio's plans from this period, that none can be entered from the central hall or from the stairwells that serve it, but only from a little vestibule at the back, and from the entrance loggia, with its attendant risks of draft and damp.

This large presentation plan on XVII/1 is a slightly simplified but otherwise identical replica of one on a smaller sheet, at RIBA XVI/19-B (fig. 20); both have often been related to the plan of the "Odeon" of c. 1530 in Alvise Cornaro's garden at Padua (a genealogy more evident in the smaller, more elaborate version), but all three should be compared with a closely analogous design by Serlio (VII:5), whose drawing was probably brought to the Veneto almost at the same moment as the Odeon was begun. The Serlian scheme, though, is fussy and impractical; in XVI/19-B Palladio's first amalgam of it (?) with Cornaro's Odeon (which he must have studied carefully in 1539–40) recalls Serlio's four square rooms at the corners of a niched octagonal hall, but adds behind these the Odeon's introductory suite (based on Vitruvius: *cf.* Trissino, cat. no. 1-D) of twin rectangular rooms set end-to-end across a narrow vestibule—a pattern that was soon to become a consistent favorite of Palladio's. The present plan retains all these features, save that the domed octagon becomes a corner-buttressed groined hall, and a direct prototype for the Vigardolo drawing in cat. no. 44. It is lighted by a tall cubic attic with four "thermal" windows derived from the Roman baths; this element is paralleled in the beautiful facade sketch on the *verso* of RIBA XIV/4 (fig. 19) which is also closely related by its use of the central *serliana*.

43 *verso*

44. FACADE AND PLAN PROJECT FOR VILLA VALMARANA, VIGARDOLO

1541

RIBA: Palladio XVII/2 *recto*.

40.7 × 26.3 cm. (single sheet of stained and opaque paper); watermark, anchor in circle with star (*cf.* Briquet 480); Talman 54 mark on *verso*.

Siena ink, save for central "30" and vault line adjoining (strengthened in umber); washes varying from light rosy beige (front of plan) and gray-brown (back of plan, where strengthened in umber) to heavy beige-brown (on elevation); plan inscribed in epsilon handwriting with measures in Vicentine feet, and wall thicknesses in quarters of feet. *Verso,* PLAN PROJECT FOR VILLA PISANI, BAGNOLO III; umber ink (no underdrawing); Zorzi 1954, pp. 63–64, project

no. 5, fig. 6; Pane 1961, p. 106, fig. 130:27; Ackerman 1967, pp. 38–39; Zorzi 1969, pp. 43–44, project no. 6, fig. 50; Barbieri 1970; pp. 68, 71, fig. 91; Mostra 1973, p. 148 (Burns); Puppi 1973, p. 255, fig. 311; Arts Council 1975, pp. 187–188, no. 330 (Boucher); Berger 1978, pp. 94–102, fig. 12.

Burger 1909, p. 57, fig. 19:3; Loukomski 1938, p. 24; Fiocco 1949, p. 187, fig. 189; Zorzi 1954, pp. 60–61, project no. 1, fig. 1; Pane 1961, p. 108, fig. 132:30; Dalla Pozza 1964–65, pp. 235–238, fig. 32; Forssman 1965, pp. 28–29, fig. 9; Zorzi 1969, pp. 40–41, project no. 1, fig. 40 (with pp. 60–62, detail in fig. 80); Mostra 1973, p. 51 (Cevese), p. 148 (Burns), fig. 44; Puppi 1973, pp. 245–247, fig. 288; Arts Council 1975, p. 182, no. 321; Cevese 1976, p. 35, fig. 38; Berger 1978, pp. 64, 71–86, fig. 7.

Royal Institute of British Architects, London.

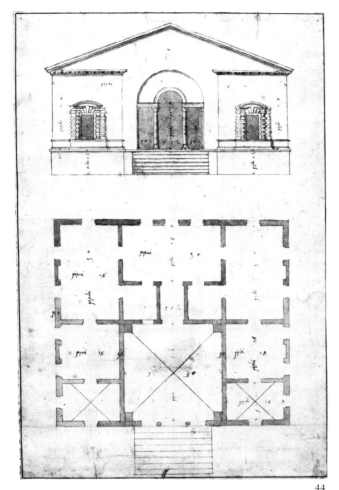

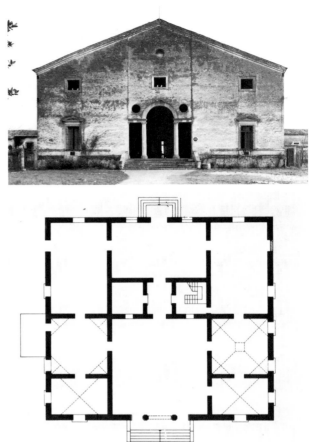

44

Figure 21 above
Figure 22 below

This is one of the key sheets in Palladio's oeuvre, and the interpretation of its role at Vigardolo has involved many of the controversies which have plagued his drawings. A lengthy debate ensued, for example, over the question as to whether it was an autograph *elevation* (cat. no. 42, RIBA XVII/27, championed by Dalla Pozza) or an equally exact drawing of the executed *plan* (fig. 15, RIBA XVI/16-A, advocated by Zorzi) that proved Palladio's authorship of the parallel and coeval villa at Bertesina. In the present case one should note immediately that the plan on RIBA XVII/2 is an almost precise recreation of the one by Trissino—or, just possibly, on the evidence of this and the following sheet (cat. no. 45), by Palladio?—that was executed in 1537–38 at Cricoli. Unfortunately a universal agreement that the plan in this drawing is identical—even to the exact correspondence of its measures, including wall thicknesses—to the executed plan (fig. 22) at Vigardolo (a realization dating from the first connection of the drawing with the building by Loukomski in 1938, though this publication has never been mentioned in the subsequent literature) has not prevented many critics from continuing to doubt the building, because of an allegedly poor resemblance of its simplified facade to the elevation at the top of this sheet—an attitude which ultimately led to the absurdity of disassociating the drawing from Vigardolo altogether.

But the very fact that this project *survives,* with its elaborately decorated facade tricked out with fashionable Roman and Mantuan motifs, proves that it was certainly not a working drawing used in actual construction (such sheets were inevitably destroyed, through daily consultation on the building site). Quite clearly, its complex and expensive window tabernacles were vetoed by the patrons at Vigardolo, who chose the simpler—and in fact more characteristically Palladian—window frames that are among the finest details of the executed fabric. They did intend to follow this project (that is, its more simply decorated successor) in carefully centering the facade windows within "projecting" wall segments, actually to be differentiated by a slight recessing of the wall around and above the portal: for corresponding stone segments of the socle stringcourses are executed only to the appropriate points, equidistant from the window centers with the corners of the facade. But the (unsupervised?) brick masons mistakenly (or too hurriedly?) filled in the intended recesses all the way to the portal, and then carried their lines directly upward, without curving one inset over the *serliana,* and

79

framing that composition with another, bounded by the ends of the stone moldings. Once these changes had been introduced, the execution of the corresponding cornice segments became problematical, and compromise solutions were reached in providing an upper register of fenestration.

The lower stringcourses placed in exact conformity with this penultimate project, however, prove that the Vigardolo facade was certainly *begun* in strict fidelity to Palladio's model; and although it bears witness to a last-minute change of design (possibly *for the purpose* of suppressing the upper paneling and cornices, in order to include the three windows whose positions they would have blocked), still the fenestration of the flanks is beautifully executed, and highly characteristic of Palladio; as are the vaultings of the forward rooms, and the internal molding details (including the notorious off-center doors, characteristically suppressed in this drawing, that were introduced—probably over Palladio's protests—to provide access from the atrium to the lateral apartments). Although the rear facade has much

simpler moldings (and, around the door, much later ones), it seems to me that the evidence of the elaborate Palladian moldings on the flanks, as well as the exact and complete execution of the Palladian plan, argue for a unified construction of the whole fabric; the back door may simply have been embellished with more "elegant" moldings in the following century. (The problematical eight-sided bases in the central *serliana* are in fact normal Palladian bases, whose corners have been roughly chopped off.)

Since the present drawing was thus manifestly used as a presentation proposal to a real client (who, fortunately for us, rejected it), and since Palladio pulled it out of his portfolio—quite possibly in the presence of other contemporaneous clients at Bagnolo (as discussed below, cat. no. 46)—to sketch another plan proposal on its reverse, it thus enables us to see even such formal layouts as a standard part of his normal working method for actual commissions, rather than as "abstract" studies for the embellishment of his repertory, or for publication.

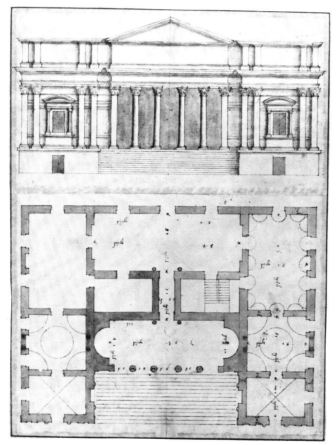

45

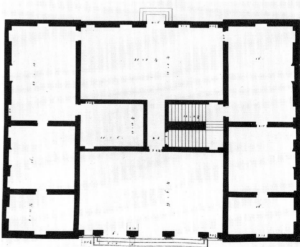

Figure 23

80

45. FACADE AND PLAN PROJECT FOR VILLA PISANI, BAGNOLO (I)

1539–40

RIBA: Palladio XVII/16.

37.0 × 27.3 cm. total (two sheets pasted with 6 mm. overlap, evidently in England: top, 16.0 × 27.3 cm., no watermark; bottom, 21.6 × 27.2 cm., watermark, anchor in irregular circle with star [cf. Briquet 480]; Talman 150 marks on verso of both sheets).

Umber ink, over heavy incised lines (without pencil, save for erased plan of groin vault in back hall), with dark umber-beige wash; plan inscribed in epsilon handwriting with measures in Vicentine feet, and wall thicknesses in quarters of feet.

Zorzi 1954, pp. 67–68, project no. 10, fig. 10; Pane 1961, p. 110, fig. 133:33; Forssman 1965, pp. 29–30, fig. 10; Zorzi 1969, pp. 45–46, project no. 9, fig. 54; Barbieri 1970, pp. 68, 71, n. 81; Arts Council 1975, pp. 236–237, no. 421 (Fairbairn)—for text only: technical information refers to RIBA XVII/17; Berger 1978, pp. 64, 76–79, fig. 8.

Royal Institute of British Architects, London.

This spectacular design represents the culmination of Palladio's "apprenticeship" under the humanist tutelage of Trissino, and can be dated with some certainty to the two years of their joint sojourn in Padua, immediately after the completion of Trissino's manor at Cricoli (cat. no. 1). In both conception and handling it stands midway between Andrea's earliest, most eclectic essays (cat. nos. 2–3, here dated c. 1538/39), and his first achievement of a distinct architectural and graphic style, in such a sheet as the closely related final design for Palazzo Da Monte (cat. no. 4, here dated c. 1540–41). These four elevations, studied in such a sequence, reveal the near identity of many details on this beautiful facade—such as the window bays, with their segmental-pedimented tabernacles, secondary cornice bands, and framing Corinthian pilasters—with the same elements in cat. no. 2; as well as extremely precise analogies with the drafting techniques of cat. no. 3, which together with the present elevation immediately precedes the somewhat more resolved idiom of cat. no. 4. The plan offers further illuminating parallels with these designs, as for example in the same elaborate central doors that we have encountered on cat. nos. 2 and 3.

As the unique villa plan to survive from this earliest period, alongside the very rudimentary city palace plan already mentioned on RIBA XVI/6 (cf. cat. no. 6), it is particularly appropriate that this scheme should be based so precisely on that of Trissino's villa at Cricoli (fig. 23), while in turn the urban design in XVI/6 should recall so specifically the arrangement of Alvise Cornaro's house and garden in Padua, interpreted in a graphic style strongly reminiscent of Serlio's. With growing imagination Palladio does add to the present plan (in the place of Cricoli's deep and rather empty entrance loggia) a dramatically recessed access stair, as well as a loggia more interestingly composed of sketchbook quotations from the Portico of Octavia (for the colonnade: cf. cat. nos. 39–40), and the Lateran Baptistery (for the apses and the door: cf. cat. no. 34 verso). But the plan reflects in every other detail a diagnostic borrowing from Palladio's experiences of the two preceding years at Cricoli, as a kind of homage to the primacy of that work as an inspiration to his early career.

46. PLAN PROJECT FOR VILLA PISANI, BAGNOLO (II)

1541

RIBA: Palladio XVII/18 verso [misidentified as recto in previous literature].

41.9 × 27.3 cm. (single sheet); watermark, crossed arrows with star (cf. Briquet 6292/6293), "Palladio's standard paper" of c. 1540; Talman 54 mark on verso, i.e. this face.

Umber ink, with some underdrawing or corrections in umber crayon; dark umber-beige wash; partially inscribed in early handwriting with measures in Vicentine feet. Recto (of cat. no. 46), PLAN AND ELEVATION STUDIES OF A TEMPIETTO-TABERNACLE (illus. at cat. no. 71). Very dark siena ink, over incised lines; Zorzi 1966, p. 26, fig. 25; Puppi 1973, p. 266; Arts Council 1975, p. 204, no. 366 (Burns); Berger 1978, p. 260 n. 279, and p. 288 n. 679.

Burger 1909, p. 47, fig. 10:1; Zorzi 1954, p. 63, project no. 4, fig. 5; Pane 1961, p. 106, fig. 130:26; Dalla Pozza 1964–65, p. 213, fig. 10; Zorzi 1969, p. 43, project no. 5, fig. 49; Barbieri 1970, pp. 68, 71, fig. 92; Mostra 1973, p. 149 (Burns); Puppi 1973, p. 255, fig. 312; Arts Council 1975, p. 188, no. 331 (Boucher)—but with measures not matching p. 204, no. 366 (see recto above); Berger 1978, pp. 98–101.

Royal Institute of British Architects, London.

The surprising observation that the three-room suites along the flanks of this project for Bagnolo exactly match those of the preceding design—in mutual derivations from the Cricoli plan, in vaulting patterns, in scale and dimensions (hence in actual size on the sheet), and even in colors of ink—has prompted the assimilation of that earlier drawing on RIBA XVII/16 into the graphic corpus for the Villa Pisani, now increased to five sheets, of which it is here proposed (cat. no. 45) as the first of the series. (Franco Barbieri intuitively proposed a similar relationship and destination for it and the present sheet [1970, pp. 68, 71], in his brilliant elucidation of a suggestion by Dalla Pozza [1964–65, p. 213] that there in fact existed a "fifth" Bagnolo project, "one of two to be drawn with an elevation.") Exactly as in the case of the Vigardolo plan (RIBA XVII/2 recto, cat. no. 44), Palladio's development from a direct recall of the spread-out Cricoli scheme in Bagnolo I (RIBA XVII/16, cat. no. 45) to the much more imaginative arrangement here expressed in Bagnolo II, involves him in an exercise of lateral compression. Cricoli's sequential three-room suites are kept intact in all three designs, but their diffuse and unexciting central connections in the first

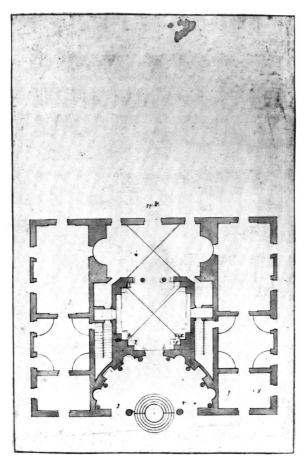

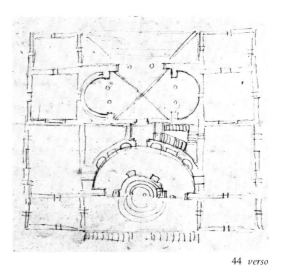

44 *verso*

46 *verso*

Bagnolo project are tightened into a much more compact relationship in the second, and finally in the Vigardolo plan compressed still further, until the unified atrium between their smaller rooms has become a perfect square, a shape also harmoniously reflected in the plan of the whole.

As proof of these interconnections of the Villa Valmarana and Villa Pisani projects, the *verso* of the Vigardolo sheet XVII/2 bears a hastily sketched plan which can now be identified as Bagnolo III (cat. no. 44, *verso*). It carries the tendency to lateral compression so far as to become deeper than it is wide, in a rather clumsy "double-pile" arrangement of two distinct planimetric units, separated by a continuous transverse wall. Through the evidence of this latter characteristic it may well be contemporaneous with the prototypes for the Bertesina project (*cf.* cat. no. 42), with the exhibited version of which it shares an exceedingly narrow central vestibule, and (on its rear facade) a grand pyramidal stair. Its intervening element of a groin-vaulted double-apsed loggia entered through a *serliana* reappears in one of those Bertesina-related designs (RIBA XVI/16-B), while another of them (RIBA XVI/16-C [fig. 51]) has groin-vaulted halls—alternatively with heavy corner buttresses and apses—associated with the *serliana* as an internal feature, as well as stairs placed behind a curved and niched atrium wall, in ways closely parallel to similar components not only in Bagnolo II but also in Bagnolo III.

It has long been customary to see the bold entrance hemicycles of the successive Bagnolo designs as evidence of a strong enthusiasm that Palladio acquired in 1541 for Bramante's culminating exedra in the Belvedere court—or, as has been more recently suggested, for Raphael's unfinished semicircular "entrance" court at the Villa Madama. Both sources are probably reflected in these drawings, but another important line of influence comes through Serlio. Two of the projects eventually published in the latter's *Seventh Book* (fols. 13, 39) show similar hemicycles with concave-convex stairs, as entrance loggie *incorporated within the block* of comparable villa plans. Both indeed frame this element between projecting wings, exactly as Palladio does at the front of his third sketch for Bagnolo—thus retaining a device that he had pioneered (with straight stairs) on Bagnolo I, and in fact repeats at the rear of his sketch for Bagnolo III. The crucial difference is that Bramante's, Raphael's, and Serlio's hemicycles are all open-air, while those that Palladio suggests for Bagnolo are all roofed. The suggestion for the change may have come to him through a third design in the same collection of Serlio's (VII:5), which we already have seen as a potent influence on two contemporary Palladian projects (cat. no. 43): it provides not only a roofed loggia recessed behind a *serliana* over a concave-convex stair, but also the curious angled passageways at the corners of the main hall, as in Bagnolo II.

47. SITE AND PLAN PROJECT FOR VILLA PISANI, BAGNOLO (IV)

1541

RIBA: Palladio XVI/7.

38.3 × 25.3 cm. (single sheet of buff-beige paper, with remains of serious water stain lower left); watermark, crossed arrows with star (*cf.* Briquet 6292/6293, "Palladio's standard paper" of c. 1540); Talman 54 mark on *verso*.

Umber ink, with umber crayon underdrawing, and very pale sepia wash; labeled and inscribed in epsilon handwriting with measures in multiples of Vicentine feet.

Burger 1909, p. 45, fig. 11:1 (detail of house and kitchen only); Zorzi 1954, p. 64, project no. 6, fig. 7: Pane 1961, pp. 106–107, fig. 130:28; Dalla Pozza 1964–65, pp. 212–213, fig. 9 (detail of house only); Zorzi 1969, p. 42, project no. 3, fig. 47; Forssman 1969, pp. 149–151, fig. 84; Barbieri 1970, pp. 70–72, fig. 93; Mostra 1973, p. 147 (Burns); Puppi 1973, p. 255, fig. 313; Arts Council 1975, p. 187, no. 329 (Boucher), fig. 329; Berger 1978, pp. 99–100.

Royal Intitute of British Architects, London.

This extraordinarily fine drawing is as important as it is beautiful, for it represents the key piece in Palladio's series of proposals for the Villa Pisani. Together with the immediately successive plan on RIBA XVII/17 (cat. no. 48)—on whose model the surviving construction was begun—this expansive design ties the whole series to the site at Bagnolo, a tiny village on the river Guà in the extreme southwest corner of the Vicentino. At the bottom of the drawing (the eastern side of the site) Palladio's delicate graphic symbol for the stream is labeled "river," as is the separate "kitchen" alongside the house to the north; while the large ceremonial court on the landward or western side is given the measures it closely retains (36 by 34½ "*pertiche*" or—these being units of six feet—216 by 207 feet). Its long lateral colonnades with simple shed roofs would have looked rather like ancient stoas: indeed, the left-hand one is designed as a purely ornamental feature, being backed only by a bounding wall. It is shown as giving access through a small gate into a plantation lane, beyond which lay a great walled park (fig. 24); perhaps for the reason of its functional superfluity this southern portico seems never to have been built, although the wall, the gate, and the lane all survive. On the other hand Palladio draws its northern counterpart as backed by a solid building, whose undifferentiated (and thus pre-existing?) interior is broken only by a symmetrical vehicular access to the colonnade and the court. It thus assumes the form of a standard *barchessa*—the dialect name in the Veneto for a long barn, fronted by a roofed shed that stands open (preferably, as here, toward the south) through a series of piers or columns, and whose enclosed rear portions might contain storage lofts above, and stables, storerooms, or even residential quarters below.

All these functions are still served by the fabric surviving (or more probably rebuilt) in this position at Bagnolo; though it should be understood that whenever the main house was actually occupied by the owners, such a building as this would never have functioned in a utilitarian way for "the uses of the farm," notwithstanding all of Palladio's theoretical argumentation to that effect. It would have been used instead—sparingly, and discreetly, because of the potential distractions to the relaxing patrons of the inevitable noises, smells, and invasions of the privacy of the outdoor living space that both they and Palladio wished to control—only for their own saddle stock, their carriages and coaches (as these came to be used, after mid-century), their staff accommodations, and the bulkier storage of their prime agricultural products, especially wine and grain. Such exclusively owner-oriented rather than farm-oriented use of the *barchesse* adjacent to large houses is abundantly demonstrated by documents: we know definitely that the near-contemporaneous *barchessa* adjoining Palladio's Villa Cornaro at Piombino, for example, was used restrictively as a service support for the main house, from the 16th century continuously to the mid-20th. Indeed we see exactly such restricted use by the proprietors surviving today in all of Palladio's still-inhabited buildings that were actually executed with such structures (even though he propagandistically claimed "agricultural" functions for them), namely at Angarano, Fanzolo, and Maser. Just as in all these estates four hundred years after his death, so here at Bagnolo at the beginning of his career we can find Palladio's frank acknowledgement of the fact that in practice these closely adjoining structures would be reserved for residential support functions. The demonstration of that circumstance at Bagnolo is strikingly proven by the continuing existence there, exactly as at all the other estates just named, of a large and distinct agricultural complex sharply separated from the residential center, though absolutely essential to successful functioning of a large farm.

Palladio very rarely drew these crucial elements (cat. no. 69-B is the exception, though cat. no. 54 should also be mentioned as a kind of compromise), and even more rarely let their images creep into the *Quattro Libri* (Angarano is the unique example with an actual working courtyard, at II:xv:63; though the plate for Lonedo might also be claimed, as showing a pre-existing barn that may really have functioned as such: II:xv:65). They have consequently been neglected almost utterly since his time; although the functions of neither Fanzolo nor Maser, for example, can be even minimally understood without reference to the "plantation centers" that stand separated by short but decisive distances from the residential blocks with their ornamental wings. In fact only the great fabric for agricultural functions here at Bagnolo, built on the other side of the lane in an angle of the park, and well beyond the upper left-hand corner of this drawing (but visible in a survey map of 1569, fig. 24), is so large, so strikingly handsome, and so well connected with plausible documents, that it has indeed been published—uniquely, among such fully detached structures—as a work by Palladio (bibliography in Arts Council 1975, p. 189, no. 334, Burns; see also the drawing at cat. no. 69-B, where, however, Palladio was probably only sketching an existing farmyard).

Whether or not Palladio himself actually designed these distinct but essential farming complexes—and only at Angarano (1548), Piombino (1553), and here at Bagnolo (1562) do we have any evidence that he did—they can

83

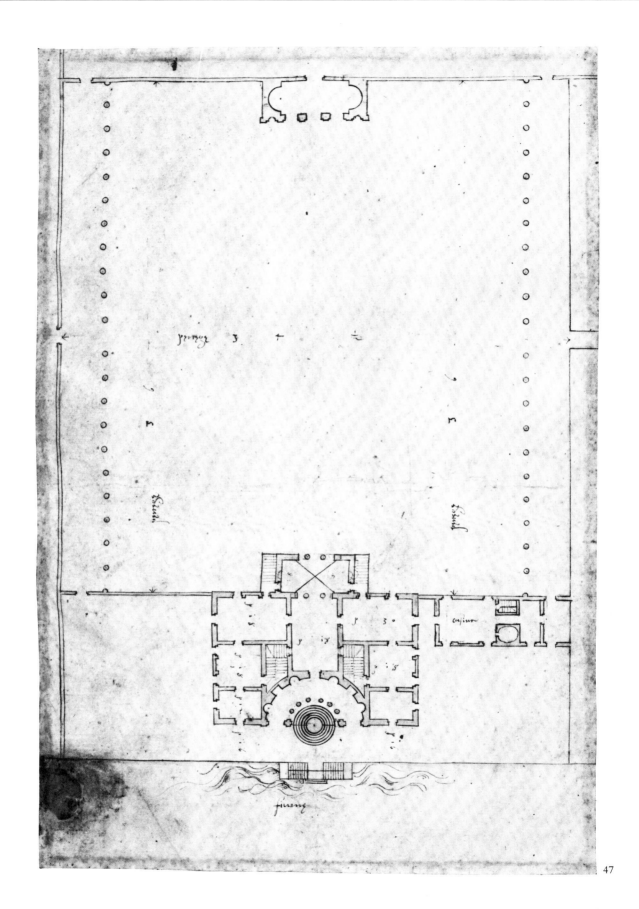

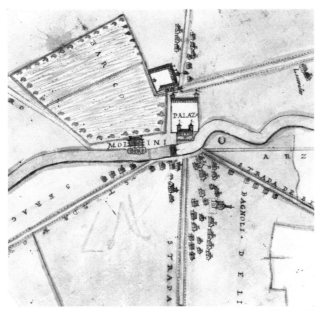

Figure 24

always be presupposed. They usually pre-existed, since their farms had almost all been functioning for generations, if not centuries, before Palladio's patrons (as here) decided to renew a manor house within its immediate setting. These considerations explain why Palladio's clients were able to request such comprehensive formal designs for the ceremonial centers of their estates, that is, the areas over which they, rather than their overseers, had direct control. They were free *within these limits*—which explains the omission of real farming complexes from Palladio's designs—to make correspondingly aesthetic rather than practical decisions about his proposals, to an extent that would never have been possible had truly functional farm requirements been involved. The result was that Palladio's ideas, even for the basic arrangements of these large courts, could change considerably (as is apparent whenever we have a chance to see them in sequence, as for example in cat. no. 58, for Poiana). In just such a way, the lateral porticoes and terminal loggia proposed here for Bagnolo seem to have been replaced in execution by a terminal *barchessa*—which, however, does not survive—in addition to the one probably pre-existing on the north, and the great farm court to the southwest (as can be seen in maps of 1562, 1569 [fig. 24], and 1572).

The distilled and perfected plan of the manor house, on this sheet, is one of the most masterly achievements of Palladio's whole career. Studied, equilibrated, and supremely concise, it represents a quintescence of his early planning, and closely recalls RIBA XVI/19-B (fig. 20), whose porch and garden loggia it shares. The L-shaped arrangements of its three-room suites form a paradigm for Palladio's maturity, and indeed the entire plan (though shorn of its porch and with a rectangular loggia) reappears in the later 1540s as the Villa Zen (fig. 25). With all this evidence of Palladio's originality and satisfaction in the design, it is interesting to note its almost exact derivation from a drawing reproduced in Serlio's *Seventh Book* (fol. 13).

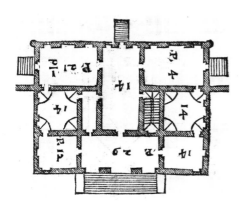

Figure 25

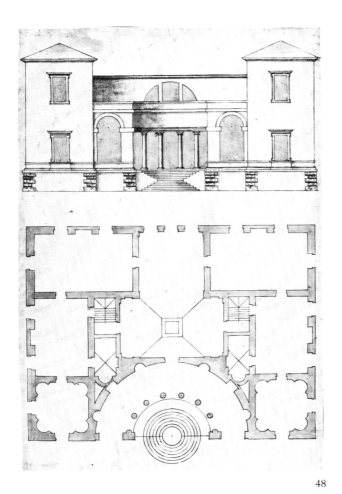

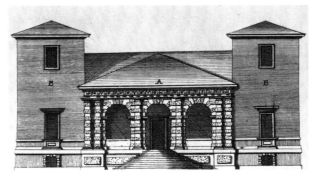

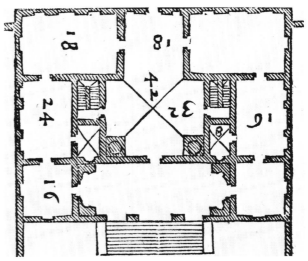

48

Figure 26 above
Figure 27 below

48. FACADE AND PLAN PROJECT FOR VILLA PISANI, BAGNOLO (V)

1542

RIBA: Palladio XVII/17.

41.5 × 27.8 (single sheet of beige paper, stained at top); no watermark visible; Talman 54 mark on *verso*.

Very dark umber ink, on pencil underdrawing, with light sepia-gold wash (on elevation) and blue-gray wash (on plan, and in light touches on elevation).

Burger 1909, p. 46, fig. 11:3; Zorzi 1954, pp. 62–63, project no. 3, fig. 4; Pane 1961, pp. 106–108, fig. 107:29, fig. 131:29; Dalla Pozza 1964–65, pp. 213–214, fig. 12; Ackerman 1967, pp. 38–39, fig. 39; Zorzi 1969, pp. 42–43, 53–58, project no. 4, fig. 48; Forssman 1969, pp. 149–151, fig. 85; Barbieri 1970, pp. 68, 72, fig. 94; Mostra 1973, p. 149 (Burns); Puppi 1973, p. 255, fig. 314; Arts Council 1975, p. 188, no. 322 (Boucher); Berger 1978, pp. 100–102, fig. 14.

Royal Institute of British Architects, London.

The testimony of unpublished documents from the Pisani archive clarifies the chronology of Palladio's successive projects for Bagnolo, including this fifth and final design. Through this evidence, summarized below, we may conclude that construction of the Villa Pisani was apparently begun in 1542 according to the project shown on this sheet,

but executed with the changes of design in the loggia and hall that we find expressed in the surviving fabric (as dramatically restored by the Pisani descendents in 1977–78), and already recorded (for the elevation [fig. 26]) on a map of 1562, and (for the plan) on Palladio's *Quattro Libri* plate of 1570 (fig. 27).

The identity of the villa's Palladian patron can now be reestablished in conformity with the published 16th-century sources and documents, beginning with a tax declaration of 1545, continuing to Vasari's description in 1568, and including Palladio's text of 1570—which all name Vettor Pisani uniquely, or list him first among three brothers. His primary role in the villa commission was thrown into doubt as early as 1909 by Burger's publication of a date for his birth that was eight years too late—a date which unfortunately has been followed ever since; even though Zorzi (who in 1969 published Vettor's correct date of marriage, from the same standard Venetian genealogies) noted how curious it would be if that event had occurred in Vettor's fourteenth year. But Vettor Pisani was actually born on 17 September 1520 (ASV, Avog. di Comun, *Nascite,* b. 68; private archive, Venice, *Libro d'Oro,* II:1133), married Paola Foscari on 27 September 1542 at the age of twenty-two, and died—outside of Venice, presumably

86

from the plague—in July of 1576 (*ibid.*). He had been the presumptive head of his family since his father Giovanni had died in the Pisani palace at S. Paternian in Venice on 12 May 1528 (ASV, Avog. di Comun, *Necrologio* I), and—because of that long gap in succession—had in fact been promoted to full nobility by enrollment in the Maggior Consiglio immediately after his eighteenth birthday, on 3 October 1538 (ASV, *Secr. alle Voci*). We can thus understand the importance of his lengthy residences in Padua (when he was not at Bagnolo itself, which was of course much easier to reach from the university city than from Venice) during the period beginning on 18 April 1537 that is covered by a personal account book, preserved in a private archive of Pisani materials ("*D̲ de Mobelj di Casa/N̲o 19,*" with following citations to dates and pages; preliminary notice about this archive having recently been found, in Lewis 1973, p. 378 n. 18).

Vettor was busy throughout the spring and summer of 1537—presumably having just moved to the mainland to take up his studies—in acquiring at Padua (e.g. 23 August, f.19) various provisional furnishings *p portar a bag̲lo,* "to take to Bagnolo" (18 April, 16 June) where he evidently began personally to supervise the family's vast agricultural properties, and to realize the urgent need for a new residential and administrative center on his neglected estates. A fortunate entry (f. 19 *verso*) in fact records his dutiful purchase of a new income ledger on 17 March 1539, and another on 15 August of the same year notes his shipment to Bagnolo of a special wine cask. These notices are providential, for they record Vettor's presence in Padua—with Bagnolo strongly on his mind—during the very season of Trissino's coming into residence there (late 1538/early 1539), with Palladio in accompaniment. I have already outlined elsewhere (1972-I, pp. 5–13; 1972-II, pp. 387–393) several of the ways in which this very young but very rich and well-connected Venetian nobleman could be expected to have been brought into their circle: through the agency of his princely relation, the Cardinal-Bishop of Padua, Francesco Pisani (presumably a friend of Trissino); through that prelate's architectural and artistic advisor, Alvise Cornaro (certainly a friend of Trissino, and the joint patron of Falconetto); through their mutual relation (and Sanmicheli's illustrious patron of the same moment, for

the Paduan city walls) the Venetian governor Girolamo Cornaro—whose accompanying son Zorzi, almost the same age as Vettor Pisani, was similarly to profit from these Paduan connections in commissioning his own villa from Palladio, at Piombino; or finally, and most importantly and directly of all, through Vettor's own very close cousin Daniele Barbaro, the brilliant associate of all these luminaries and architectural enthusiasts, whose oration for his doctoral examination galvanized the city on 19 September 1540. Daniele's mother was Elena Pisani, of the same immediate family as Vettor's late father: I believe the conclusion is inescapable that Palladio would certainly have been introduced through Trissino and Alvise Cornaro to both Vettor and Daniele in Padua (as well as to his third future patron, Zorzi Cornaro, and above all to Sanmicheli) during the residences of all of them there in 1539–40.

Thus the chronology here proposed of Palladio's projects for the Bagnolo commission would begin already in the immediate context of his earliest training at Cricoli and Padua (for the Cricoli plan with Paduan details, cat. no. 45, drawn up as a result of his first contacts with Vettor Pisani in Padua in 1539), and proceed through evident analogies (in cat. nos. 46 and 47) with his successive designs for Palazzi Civena and Da Monte (1540), as well as for villas Gazoto and Valmarana (1541), to the catalyzing moment, for the present design, of Vettor's marriage (1542), and Bagnolo's certain period of construction (1543), to reach the inscribed date of completion that Magrini (1845:79) found in a lost fresco (1544), and that we have seen confirmed in Vettor's first tax declaration (1545), announcing his possession of "a palace in Bagnolo, newly built."

Any possible foundations for a hemicycle lie buried within the solid core (as at Piombino, no basement was excavated beneath the loggia and hall), so the date of its biapsidal replacement is unclear. The cruciform hall, thus extended, has a closed groin vault rather than the open *impluvium* suggested here (following the correct interpretations of Zorzi, 1954 and 1969, rather than the "closed compartment" interpretations of Pane, Barbieri, Boucher and Berger: the downward-sloping roof, not visible in elevation, makes the feature quite clear).

Figure 28

49. HALF ELEVATION PROJECT FOR FACADE OF PALAZZO THIENE, VICENZA (I)

1542–46

RIBA: Palladio XVII/6 *recto*.

39.3 × 26.2 cm. (single sheet of unusually thick, heavy paper); no watermark visible; Talman 54 mark on *verso*.

Umber ink over heavily incised lines with pencil and umber crayon underdrawing; deep beige-gold wash. *Verso*, SKETCHES OF DORIC ENTABLATURES, WITH PARTIAL ELEVATION OF AN ALTAR OR CHIMNEYPIECE(?): extremely light pencil, in very pale lines; Burns 1979, pp. 17–18 (but *cf.* Puppi 1973, pp. 237–238, fig. 273).

Zorzi 1954-II, pp. 111–112, fig. 7; Pane 1961, p. 165, fig. 179:23; Zorzi 1965, p. 205, fig. 203; Mostra 1973, p. 148 (Burns); Puppi 1973, pp. 253–254, fig. 306; (?) Arts Council 1975, p. 232, no. 412 (Burns)—neither measures nor inventory number coincide with the present sheet, though description implies it is being discussed; Berger 1978, pp. 167–170; Verona 1980, pp. 117, 119, no. and fig. V:4 (Burns).

Royal Institute of British Architects, London.

49

On 10 October 1542 Palladio was witness to a contract between Marc'Antonio Thiene and three stonemasons "for the building and making of a residence" evidently on the site of the present-day Palazzo Thiene: Palladio's title is also given simply as "stonemason." Through letters written by Alessandro Vittoria on 16 April 1552 and 7 January 1553 we know that at least between these dates he was decorating rooms in the portion of the building that was executed; its facade and courtyard stringcourses carry inscribed dates of 1556 (east range) and 1558 (north range). Palladio published the palace in the *Quattro Libri* of 1570 as his own work (II:iii:12–15, mentioning Vittoria and the other decorators); but during a visit to Vicenza in 1613–14 the great English architect Inigo Jones was told by Vincenzo Scamozzi—and also by other, perhaps less prejudiced informants—that for this palace Palladio had only executed "designs of Giulio Romano" (see cat. no. 50).

Giulio in fact is documented to have been present in Vicenza for consultations on the restoration of the Basilica for a period of fifteen days during December of 1542 (Zorzi 1937, pp. 52–55), two months after the building contract for Palazzo Thiene had been signed in the presence of Palladio. The present drawing (though certainly drafted by Palladio) is indeed a kind of Giulian pastiche, in that the ground-floor relationships of larger and smaller rectangular

88

windows on a rusticated wall with a large central portal do strongly recall the west facade of Giulio's Palazzo del Te in Mantua, while the drawing's upper stories almost exactly reproduce the fenestration systems of his north and south courtyard facades in the same building.

But this very piling up of two Giulian facades on top of each other demonstrates an eclectic approach, involving Palladio's assimilation of Giulian motifs into a personal idiom that incorporates other influences as well. As Burns has suggested (1975), the most obvious of these come from Sanmicheli. The lower floor of Palladio's drawing, for example, is directly based on the reinterpretation of Giulian ideas that Sanmicheli presents in the facade of Palazzo Canossa, completed in 1537 (*cf.* cat. no. 5, fig. 4). Probably the most important prototype for this design, however, is Sanmicheli's lost Villa Soranzo of c. 1539 near Castelfranco, whose tall facade pioneered the use of rustication through three stories, including even a heavy attic. The reconstruction of its elevation presented here (fig. 28) is redrawn to newly discovered measurements, and emphasizes Palladio's debt in this drawing to its proportions as well as its general forms.

Figure 29

50

50. ANONYMOUS: ENTRANCE TO THE HOUSE OF GIULIO ROMANO, ROME

c. 1530?

Devonshire Collections, Chatsworth: "Drawings / Public Monuments / Arches and Bridges" XXXV/53.

28.1 × 20.4 cm. (single sheet); no watermark visible; no collector's mark.

Brownish siena ink on pencil underdrawing, with several tones of umber wash; *verso* carries labels in Italian for PLAN OF PART OF THE VILLA MADAMA, and in German for ANTIQUE BASE AT SAN MARCO, ROME.

Loukomski 1940, p. 73, fig. 11 (as traditionally attributed to Vignola, but 'probably by Giovanni Antonio Dosio'); Arts Council 1975, p. 37, no. 49 (Burns—as German?).

The Trustees of the Chatsworth Settlement.

This is apparently the earliest of five related drawings that afford us our only images of Giulio's small house, built for himself around 1523/24 on a corner of the Macello de Corbi opposite S. Maria di Loreto, near Trajan's Forum. Frommel (1973, II:218, III, figs. 86a, b, c) dates a more spontaneous partial sketch by Aristotele da Sangallo (Uffizi 2692) also to the period before 1550, and to c. 1570 a tight orthographic elevation in the Biblioteca Nazionale in Florence (Cod. Magliab. II:i:429). The fourth and latest version, drawn shortly before 1600 by Giovan Antonio Dosio (original at Uffizi 2691, copy at Albertina 1228) is most similar to the Chatsworth drawing, and may be based on it; this is the only version to articulate the attic window, and to add a roof. The Chatsworth sheet appears by far the most accurate, particularly in the handling of the architectural details (although it raises the sarcophagus-shaped bench beside the portal, and omits the aperture cut into it that Burns has interpreted as a basement window).

Gombrich (1935, p. 138) first connected Giulio's extraordinary main window frame, on this facade, to the almost identical ones (taller by one projecting block) that Palladio executed on the upper story of the Palazzo Thiene in Vicenza (cat. nos. 49, 51–52, fig. 29). The connection is indeed so close as to give a considerable degree of likelihood to a comment about the Thiene facade recorded in his copy of the *Quattro Libri* by Inigo Jones in 1613–14: "Scamozo and Palmo saith that thes designs wear of Julio Romano and executid by Palladio & so yt seemes" (Allsopp 1970, but corrected from the original; most published versions give 'adjusted' instead of 'executed': *cf.* Forster and Tuttle 1973, p. 118, n. 2). Another of Jones's comments on the same point strikingly recalls the two documents of 1542, mentioned in cat. no. 49, that record a visit by Giulio to Vicenza within two months of Palladio's witnessing the palace contract as a "stonecutter"; "this capitell was carved by Palladio his owne hands as y^e masons at Vicensa tould mee:" (Allsopp 1970, II:iii:14).

51. HALF ELEVATION PROJECT FOR ONE STORY OF PALAZZO THIENE, VICENZA (II)

1542–46

RIBA: Palladio XVII/7.

21.5 × 34.6 cm. (single sheet of very thin paper): watermark, large cardinal's hat flanked by initials A P, laid lines 33.5 mm. apart (variant of Briquet 3465); Talman 54 mark on *verso*.

Umber ink, in various strengths and techniques (with some touches of siena, lower left) and pencil (as subsequent amplifications, rather than underdrawing).

Zorzi 1954-II, pp. 111–112, fig. 8; Pane 1961, p. 165, fig. 179:21; Zorzi 1965, pp. 205–206, fig. 204; Mostra 1973, p. 148 (Burns); Puppi 1973, pp. 253–254, fig. 307; Arts Council 1975, pp. 37–38, no. 50 (Burns); Berger 1978, pp. 167–170, fig. 24.

Royal Institute of British Architects, London.

This very beautiful and interesting drawing shows on the left and right Palladio's first "quotations" of the Giulian window from Rome (cat. no. 50), set on either side of a variant with a segmental pediment. All are interpreted with the projecting, uncut blocks of the engaged column shafts set very tightly together in alternate widths, as every other block is diminished just enough to show a trace of smooth shaft above and below (*cf.* cat. no. 31 *verso*, the Claudianum, on which this order is based). The tabernacles are set into a rhythmic pattern between single pilasters marking the bays: but the pilaster strip to the right of the segmental-headed window is articulated also as the outer edge of a whole projecting wall plane, elaborated with a triumphal arch motif of further-projecting paired pilasters enclosing small windows, on either side of a standard tabernacle framing a central aperture. It is unlikely that this latter element is an upstairs window rather than a downstairs door (per Burns 1975), since such configurations represent one of Palladio's normal types of ground-floor entrances (*cf.* cat. no. 65), since the whole design is borrowed very directly from Giulio's west facade portal of the Palazzo del Te, and since the considerable height of the story drawn on this sheet exactly equals that of the tall ground floor (to the main window-sills) on RIBA XVII/6, in cat. no. 49—thus making the design a spread-out version of a similar project, to a similar scale.

The Giulian prototypes for this design again give a striking point to the remarks about the executed portal made by Inigo Jones in 1613–14: "this Enterance is to be Imitated and is of Julio Romano [and the manner of all y^c Pallas] yt Palladio sets yt downe as his owne!" (rather than "yet Palladio has made it his own," as misquoted in Forster and Tuttle 1973, p. 111). These early drawings, however, contradict Jones's (and some modern scholars') too credulous acceptance of the Scamozzian denigrations: they show Palladio imaginatively combining and recombining many Giulian and Sanmichelian motifs, in thoroughly characteristic and personal ways that go far beyond any mere reproduction of Giulio's designs.

---

52. CORNER AND ADJOINING BAY OF FINAL FACADE ELEVATION FOR PALAZZO THIENE, VICENZA (III)

Late 1560s

RIBA: Palladio XVII/10-Right.

27.7 × 19.3 cm. (single sheet, formerly attached—but only in England—to XVII/10-Left, although with different page layout in *Quattro Libri*); watermark, small anchor in circle with star, laid lines 31 mm. apart (*cf.* Briquet 520); Talman 150 mark on *verso*.

Warm siena ink, with very pale yellow-gold wash, strengthened to beige in upper left and lower right windows; reddish umber inscription (in the hand of Palladio's son Orazio) "faccia della casa del c. ottavio," and scale of 10 units = 41.5 mm. (1$^5/_{12}$ Venetian inches).

Pane 1961, pp. 165–166, fig. 179:22; Zorzi 1965, p. 208, fig. 213; Bassi 1971, p. 54, fig. xxvi (detail); Mostra 1973, p. 148 (Burns); Puppi 1973, p. 254, fig. 305; Arts Council 1975, p. 38, no. 52 (Burns).

Royal Institute of British Architects, London.

With certain changes, the elements of facade organization in RIBA XVII/7 (cat. no. 51) are reused for the upper story of the Palazzo Thiene as executed (fig. 30), and as shown on this sheet. These changes are all diagnostic of their origins: the heavily rusticated short pilasters become tall smooth ones, as in this same pattern on the west facade of the Palazzo del Te (though with Corinthian rather than Doric capitals, as befitting an upper rather than a lower story); the window tabernacles now precisely reproduce the prototype on Giulio's house in Rome (cat. no. 50), with equal alternating courses of cut and uncut blocks; and the tall, rusticated wall surfaces above them seem to have been intended quite possibly for the inclusion of just such small "attic" windows as in fact appear on both north and west facades of the Palazzo del Te.

These simplified and derivative relationships introduce a new aspect, in comparison with cat. nos. 49 and 51: namely, that of direct copying. In the ground floor another "quotation" occurs: the recessed panels over the windows, with a set of strongly projecting keystones, both within and without, are borrowed via Giulio's own house in Mantua (which is also the source of the superimposition in the stories of smooth over rough rustication) from the model of "Raphael's House" by Bramante in Rome (cat. no. 28).

All these Giulian borrowings in the final facades of the Palazzo Thiene may indicate directions that Palladio was obliged to follow after 1546, when Marc'Antonio Thiene's knighthood was confirmed, and when the project—perhaps delayed because of the patrons' possible dissatisfaction with Palladio's early and more inventive designs—may have taken on a more intentionally Giulian

Figure 30

52

cast; such wishes of the patrons', of course, might quite naturally have engendered comments such as Jones heard from Scamozzi in 1613–14. This drawing was made a full ten years after the completion of the palace, as a prepa-

ratory design for the woodcut in the *Quattro Libri* (II:iii:14). It thus represents a somewhat revised rendering of the finished building, rather than a stage in its development.

---

53. COMPANION SKETCH PLANS FOR THE FULL BLOCK OF PALAZZO THIENE IN VICENZA, AND FOR VILLA THIENE AT QUINTO, ON A SHEET OF ROMAN FIELD NOTES

1545/46

RIBA: Palladio XIV/4 *recto.*

42.5 × 29.5 cm. (single sheet, folded in quarters and eighths for sketching in the field); no watermark visible; no collector's mark.

Umber ink, with subsequent lighter ink and pencil notations, in mature handwriting; as also in the comparable SKETCHES OF BATH AND FORUM PLANS, on the *verso* (Zorzi 1959, p. 66, fig. 97; Spielmann 1966, p. 165, no. 177).

Zorzi 1959, p. 74, fig. 146; Spielmann 1966, p. 145, no. 51 (as after 1560, and giving inscriptions); Burns 1973, pp. 181–182, 189–190 n. 25, fig. 136; Arts Council 1975, p. 38, no. and fig. 51 (Burns); Berger 1978, pp. 223–224, fig. 19 (detail of palace plan only); Burns 1979, p. 13, insert.

Royal Institute of British Architects, London.

Two recent students of Palladio's drawings (Burns 1973, Berger 1978) have published their independent identifications of the larger sketch plan (of 5.5 × 11 cm.) near the bottom of this sheet as a study for Palazzo Thiene in Vicenza, but neither apparently noticed (until Burns's lecture of 1979) that just three inches above it, and tucked into the cornice details of an antique entablature, Palladio also drew a tiny sketch (3.7 × 1.5 cm.) of his first idea for the plan of the Villa Thiene at Quinto. The rapidly sketched plan of the villa assumes an importance far beyond the single square inch of its form, since its juxtaposition on this sheet with a simultaneous sketch for the full block of the Palazzo Thiene solves several outstanding problems about these city and country projects for the same patrons.

First, we are enabled to clarify their dates. As we have seen (cat. no. 49), there are no clear dates for the Palazzo Thiene, between its mysterious initial contract of 1542 and Vittoria's stucco decoration of its partially executed fragment ten years later. But the villa at Quinto was a joint

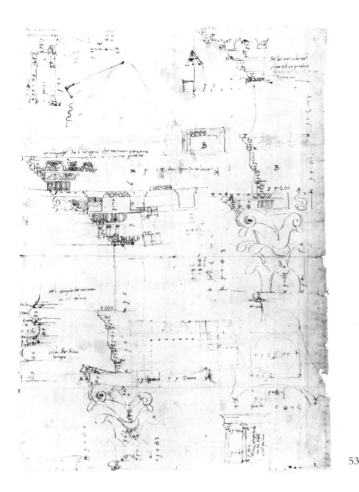

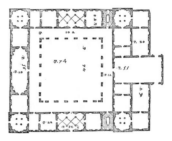

53

Figure 31

commission of Marc'Antonio Thiene's in association with his brother Adriano (Palladio, *Quattro Libri* II:xv:64); and the latter fled from Vicenza under a suspicion of heresy in 1547 to the court of Henri II of France, where as a celebrated expatriate he wrote his will on 29 January 1550 and died shortly afterward (Marzari 1591, II:196; Stella 1967, p. 56; Zorzi 1969, p. 109; Mantese 1969–70, p. 90 n. 32). Since Palladio's first ideas for the house that was actually built at Quinto are sketched on a sheet of antique studies, made during a Central Italian sojourn when we know him to have been traveling in fact with members of the Thiene family around Rome and the Campagna (Puppi 1973, p. 312), we can thus confidently assign the impulse for these twin designs to conversations with Marc'Antonio and Adriano in 1545 or at the latest in the spring of 1546, when Palladio was briefly back in Vicenza to present his model for the reconstruction of the Basilica (among whose Deputies was another relative of the Thiene brothers). This dating also exactly fits the best interpretation of stylistic evidence for the Vitruvian plan projected in the villa at Quinto (Puppi 1973, p. 262, deciding on 1546), and furthermore represents the moment of Marc'Antonio Thiene's confirmation to the honor of a knighthood (Zorzi 1965, p. 206). The latter development may well have been the essential catalyst in encouraging the new and much grander project for the city palace that we see Palladio

addressing for the first time on this sheet, in conjunction with his twin commission for the recreation of an antique *villa rustica* in the country manor at Quinto (cat. no. 54).

There has already emerged a consensus (Puppi 1973, Burns 1975) that Palladio's second and determining stage of the work on the Palazzo Thiene—in which he would have revised his earlier designs (cat. nos. 49, 51), and have had perhaps some opportunity to redirect any construction that might have been begun under the 1542 contract—is a phase in the building's history which can be dated to this crucial moment of 1546. It was almost certainly from this point (the date also of Giulio Romano's death) that the existing upper floor began to receive its more personalized Palladian details, and both patrons and architect, perhaps under the necessity of making new decisions in the wake of Giulio's demise, began to think of the possibility of extending the project to a monumental facade on the Corso, whose angled sidewalk is drawn in this sketch. Berger has suggested that Palladio's development of this southern range occupied him through a period embracing the later 1540s, but the sketch which she has proposed as intermediate between this image and the *Quattro Libri* plate (fig. 31) may not in my view be any later than c. 1546/47 (see cat. no. 65 *verso*), and thus a more or less immediate development from the present sketch upon Palladio's return from Rome to Vicenza in July of 1547.

93

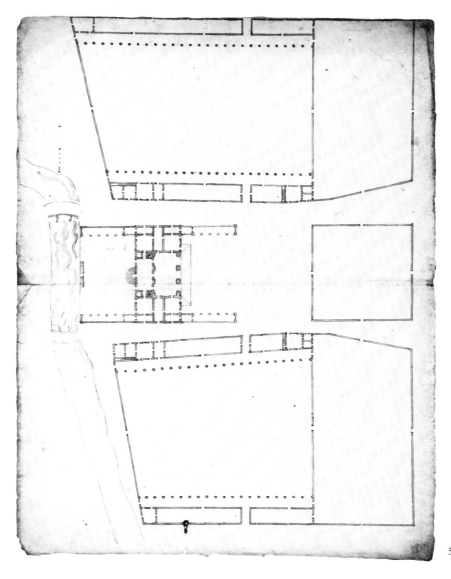

54

54. SITE AND PLAN PROJECT FOR VILLA THIENE, QUINTO

1546

Worcester College Library, from Inigo Jones album no. I/90, now designated H.T. 89 (supplementary series).

58.7 × 44.4 cm. (single sheet); watermark, small anchor in circle with star, and countermark CA (variant of Briquet 507); circled identification number 58A in pencil on *recto* (Gotch no. I/58A).

Siena ink over strongly incised lines, with sepia wash; inscribed with transitional handwriting in river courtyard "p. 70," and with scale of 50 Vicentine feet = 49 mm. (1⅔ Vicentine inches); different (and slightly later?) ink in hatching inserted to shade arms of landward entrance court.

Harris 1971, p. 34, fig. 38; Barbieri 1971, pp. 43–52, fig. 14; Mostra 1973, pp. 56–57 (Cevese), 149–150 (Burns), fig. 56; Puppi 1973, p. 261, fig. 322; Arts Council 1975, p. 191, no. 339 (Fairbairn); Berger 1977, p. 85–88, fig. 2; Berger 1978, pp. 126–129; Harris and Tait 1979, p. 54, no. 128.

The Provost and Fellows of Worcester College, Oxford.

Since John Harris first published this splendid drawing exactly ten years ago, it has become a touchstone of controversy in Palladian studies. The preliminary sketch plan which is its immediate prototype (cat. no. 53) has until now been lacking from the debate; for although the sheet of Roman studies on which it appears had frequently been reproduced, the sketch for Quinto had not been publicly discussed until Burns mentioned it in a lecture at Vicenza in 1979. For comparison with the Worcester sheet the only elements available—in addition to the heavily changed building itself (fig. 32)—were thus the very different image prepared by Palladio more than twenty years later, for publication in the *Quattro Libri* in 1570 (fig. 33); a sketch of the executed fabric made in his copy of that book by Inigo Jones during a visit to Quinto on 13 August 1614 (preserved as well in Worcester College Library); and the sections of his great *Architettura di Andrea Palladio* (cat. nos. 128–130), in which Francesco Muttoni published the results of a campaign of restoration that contemporary

Figure 32

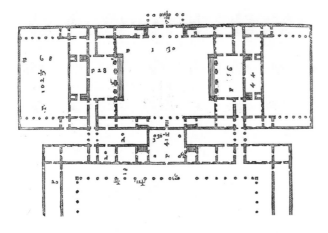

Figure 33

Quinto, having been acquired intact around 1724 by the donor who gave it to Worcester in 1736; (b) the Worcester sheet is in perfect condition; and (c) Muttoni refers to Palladio's autograph working drawing at Quinto as a sheet that showed the correct design of the attic, whereby we know that it was certainly a facade elevation.

The Worcester drawing of the site thus stands on its own as Palladio's unique surviving image of the actual planimetric details at Quinto, but its accurate depiction of these is strikingly reinforced by the juxtaposition that can now be presented with its sketchy yet informative prototype in cat. no. 53. The RIBA sketch plan shows two light curving lines extending north and south from short distances beyond the western corners of the fabric (both sheets are here oriented with north at the top, as is Palladio's *Quattro Libri* plate). These are the Thiene farmyard walls bordering the north-south road and embankment alongside the river Tèsina, while the spaces left beside the house are the east-west roads intersecting it: all are precisely rendered with topographic accuracy on the Worcester sheet, together with their symmetrical bridges over the Tèsina itself, by which Palladio frames the approaches to the manor house. The architect was particularly proud of his own work in regularizing and beautifying these roads at Quinto (*Quattro Libri,* III:i:7). We may more readily appreciate both his enthusiasm and his siting when we remember (as has not yet been noted in Palladian literature) that the still-functioning main road along the northern side of the villa Thiene is the ancient *Via Decumana* of the "Agro Patavino" established by Augustus, the main "cross street" to the Via Aurelia, by which one would have passed "Quinto"—the "fifth" milepost—on the direct route from Vicenza to the sea; as the principal east-west road of the province it was

members of the Thiene family had commissioned him to accomplish at Quinto shortly before (1740, I:39–40, figs. XL–XLII). In his work of completing the exterior decoration of the attic, which Muttoni had found inadequately rendered by the original builders, he commented that his 18th-century patrons had enabled him to base his restoration "on the actual autograph drawing by Palladio, in large part torn and frayed." Barbieri correctly followed Magrini (1845, p. 302) in recognizing that precious but completely deteriorated working drawing to have been lost: Puppi is certainly wrong to have identified it with the present sheet "that has been found among the graphic collections of Inigo Jones," since (a) the Oxford portion of that collection had been complete since before Muttoni even went to a monumental thoroughfare sixty-five feet wide, and survived virtually intact even until the present century (Benetti 1974, pp. 44–45, fig. IV). Palladio borders it with courtyard walls framing not only the Thiene's private river garden, but also the landward-facing main entrance: the presence of these walls in the RIBA sketch happily cancels all suspicions (Burns 1973, Fairbairn 1975) that they might have been later additions to the Worcester plan. In the same sense the latter's assymmetrically adjusted farmyard courts instantly distinguish themselves as functional solutions to specifically considered agricultural needs, and as such are rare to the point of uniqueness in Palladio's work (*cf.* cat. nos. 47 and 69). They thus offer a precious testimony of actual working usage, to set against the ideally perfected schemes (intended to be generally applicable) in Palladio's much later treatise. The Worcester drawing, in sum, is one of our sole images to offer any evidence for Palladio as a working architect (in his role as a designer of villa complexes) rather than as a propagandizing theorist.

In a magisterial analysis written during the year in which this sheet was discovered, Barbieri demonstrated its vital importance in documenting Palladio's detailed responses to the practical requirements as well as the topographic exigencies of such elaborate commissions. John Harris had already pointed out the crucial significance of its "coming to more realistic terms with a situation and site" than we are ever able to see "embodied in the ideal project[s] for the *Quattro Libri*," and indeed these achievements of the Worcester sheet are impossible to overstress. But its boldly pragmatic forms are inevitably corrosive to preconceptions in favor of a graphic "purity" such as that which the elderly Palladio so rigorously imposed on the publication of his own works; and since 1971 its commentators (apart from Puppi) have regarded it with distrust, if not outright disapprobation. The tenth anniversary of its discovery may thus be an appropriate moment in which to reaffirm its transcendent importance to this question, as well as its great intrinsic beauty.

55. ANONYMOUS: CASTLE COMPOUND, GARDENS, ORCHARDS, PARK, FARMYARDS, AND MILLS OF THE VILLA GIUSTINIAN, RONCADE

1536

Biblioteca Comunale di Treviso, Pergamene Giustinian, no. 4.

81.3 × 58.4 cm. (highly irregular single parchment); identification stamp on *recto,* shield of Treviso in circle, inscribed BIBL. TARV.

Umber ink, with brown, red, pink, green, yellow-green, and blue washes; labeled with sheet number and date ("Charte 4"—later replaced as "·CAR··IIII·"—and "Anno dñi 1536"), cardinal directions, and scale of 110 Trevisan *pertiche* = 12 Trevisan inches; extensively inscribed with topographic measures and descriptions. *Verso* dated, and inscribed "Il castello da Roncade, con li Molini, e casete (The Castle at Roncade, with its Mills and [farm]houses)."

Botter 1955, pp. 14–15, with detail as frontispiece; Puppi 1972-II, p. 93, fig. 4; C. K. Lewis 1977, pp. 19–27, p. 173 n. 39, and Appendix I, pp. 222–224 (giving transcription and translation of inscriptions), figs. 74–76, 81.

Biblioteca Comunale, Treviso.

The Villa Giustinian at Roncade, near Treviso, can be securely attributed to the Venetian architect-sculptor Tullio Lombardo, as a work of c. 1511–13 (fig. 34). Its importance, as witnessed by the present drawing, is manifold: it is the earliest surviving 16th-century villa in the Veneto (as this drawing is also the earliest accurate representation of one); its manor house has a universal significance—crucial to Palladio—as apparently the first secular building of the Renaissance with a fully expressed classical pediment; and the design as a whole forms a vital link in the history of villa types, by presenting the earliest and finest replica of a lost building complex which pioneered its proto-Palladian

scheme, with a country palace set inside a symmetrically walled enclosure, whose forecourt is bordered by twin *barchesse* (*cf.* cat. no. 47).

That prototypical masterwork was the "Barco" or royal country residence of Caterina Cornaro, former Queen of Cyprus and "Lady of Asolo," who ordered it built in 1491 outside the village of Altivole, near Castelfranco (C. K. Lewis, pp. 157–166 and 270–287, figs. 97–134; Kubelik 1977, pp. 73–75, no. 22, figs. 2–3, 174–186). Queen Catherine was a lady of the highest Imperial connection: her grandmother, Valenza Commenus Paleologus, had been a Princess of Byzantium, the daughter of the Emperor of Trebizond; and Caterina herself, before she had abdicated in the forced "donation of Cyprus," had been the sole reigning monarch in the whole history of the Venetian state. It is thus thoroughly comprehensible that when she was obliged to retire to the Veneto she should have chosen as an architectural frame for her court a walled palace compound reminiscent of that which the Emperor Diocletian had created twelve hundred years before, when he retired to his comparable palace complex on the Dalmatian coast (cat. no. 18). Spalato, then, was not only an eminently acceptable paradigm for the courtly residence of a retired monarch of Imperial rank or pretention; it was also a prominent port within Venetian dominions, which Queen Catherine would have passed at least twice, and which her courtiers and architects would also have known. In the circumstances its reproduction at Barco (like the Carolingian revivals of its contemporary monuments) was more faithful to its iconographic shapes and arrangements than to specific forms: Barco accurately reproduced the planimetric and hieratic *idea* of Spalato, but was substantially smaller, and—appropriately to its patron—much more

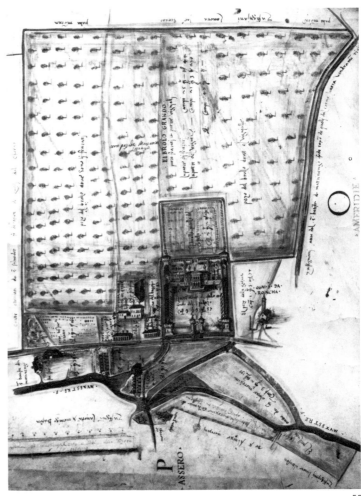

Figure 34

55

delicately articulated, as we know from a surviving fragment of its purely residential and ornamental eastern *barchessa*.

A drastically inadequate knowledge of Barco (and even of Roncade) has enabled a rather lopsided debate to go on for far too long about the supposedly mysterious origins of such formal, *barchessa*-flanked entrance courts in Venetian architecture of the 16th century, above all in the early works of Palladio. A currently fashionable idea—predictably persuasive to our populist age—is that indigenous rural building types must have played a strong part in their development, whereby certain particularly impressive local tendencies would have become isolated and perfected in Palladio's inventions. It would be wrong to exclude the

likelihood of a contribution from this tradition; but it would probably be still more unwise to deny that Caterina Cornaro's first truly monumental achievement of such a form, in the whole perspective of the Italian Renaissance, was probably based for iconographic reasons on specific palatine prototypes; and that, in the year that she died, the nearby Villa Giustinian was designed for a competitively ancient and prominent Venetian family—whose members claimed descent from the Emperor Justinian—with equally ornamental ranges of *barchesse* to frame its emulation of her palace. The Queen, after all, never farmed at Barco: and Roncade reminds us, with its decisively separated farmyard (to the left of the castle compound), that neither were such functions anticipated here.

56. SITE AND PLAN PROJECT FOR VILLA MOCENIGO, DOLO (I)

1544/45

RIBA: Palladio XVI/2.

40.3 × 25.8 cm. (single sheet); watermark, anchor in circle with star, laid lines 34.5 mm. apart (variant of Briquet 502); Talman 54 mark on *verso*.

Pale, grayish siena ink, with some pencil underdrawing, and light beige-tan wash; later pencil or umber crayon suggestion for double apses and groin vault in hall; inscribed with measures in Vicentine *pertiche* and feet, and with scale of 30 feet = 28.9 mm. (one Venetian inch).

Burger 1909, pp. 119–120, fig. 47:1; Zorzi 1969, pp. 90–91, fig. 145; Lewis 1972, pp. 12–14; Puppi 1972, p. 43, fig. vii; Mostra 1973, p. 147 (Burns); Puppi 1973, p. 360, fig. 493.

Royal Institute of British Architects, London.

This carefully executed sheet and its companion (cat. no. 57), both finished presentation drawings, as well as two sketchier but comparable designs subsequently developed from them (cat. nos. 72 *verso* and 73), are all tied to "a commission from the distinguished Knight Sir Leonardo Mocenigo, for a site that he owns on the Brenta," by Palladio's caption to a fifth such project, published in the *Quattro Libri* (II:xvii:78, fig. 50). Ever since Bertotti-Scamozzi in 1778 called the latter an "imagined and unexecuted invention," Palladian commentators have almost unanimously assumed that no version of the project was ever constructed. When in the 20th century the associated drawings were published (in full and in correct sequence only by Zorzi, figs. 145–149), these were assumed to represent other unrealized projects, only problematically associated with the Mocenigo commission. This lack of credence even extended so far that it became a commonplace of Palladian criticism to doubt whether the architect or his patron had even had a specific site in mind: the alleged vagueness of a collocation "sopra la Brenta" was considered as evidence that all these plans "for Leonardo Mocenigo" were essentially only abstract exercises.

Yet a quarter of a century ago Rodolfo Gallo, in an article all too prophetically devoted to "Some poorly known buildings by Palladio," published two undated documents recording Palladio's contracts with stonemasons "for the building at Dolo," on the Brenta, of "that distinguished Knight" (1955:29–30). Gallo did not specifically mention that the contractual reference to "4 bases for columns that will be 4 feet in diameter" exactly fitted the size and number of columns on at least two of the porches in each of the Mocenigo designs except the third, but that fact clinches the connection of all the projects sharing this constant characteristic to "la fabricha del Dolo." Gallo also tried to dispense once and for all with the topographic ambiguities, by quoting through a 19th-century scholar a ruling of 3 April 1551 from the Venetian board of water control, which thoroughly described the older "casa da Cha' Mocenigo," on the left or north bank of the Brenta just above Dolo, as having to its west a watercourse whose

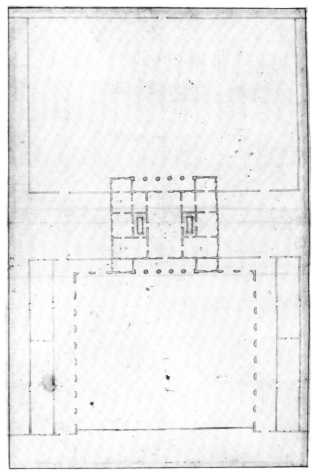

56

channel was to be extended eastward "behind the Mocenigo park" to a boundary between convent and monastery lands, marked by a road leading north toward Arino (original document now cited in Tiepolo 1980, p. 42, no. 83). And precisely such a configuration, identical in every detail, was depicted in 1754 on a fine survey map of the property, published by Gallo and here reproduced (fig. 49).

But the 1754 map, as well as a slightly earlier view of the villa from the river by Gian Francesco Costa, both labeled the property as belonging to the Tiepolo family; and neither shows a main building that could be considered to resemble very clearly any of the Mocenigo projects sketched or published by Palladio. Gallo did show that the Mocenigo estates had indeed been inherited toward the turn of the 18th century by the descendants of Lucretia Mocenigo and Alvise Tiepolo; but the architectural impasse remained, and with it any specific knowledge of Palladio's commission for Dolo was suspended, until the presentation of further historical, contextual, and documentary information, as summarized in association with the related designs (cat. nos. 57, 72 *verso* and 73).

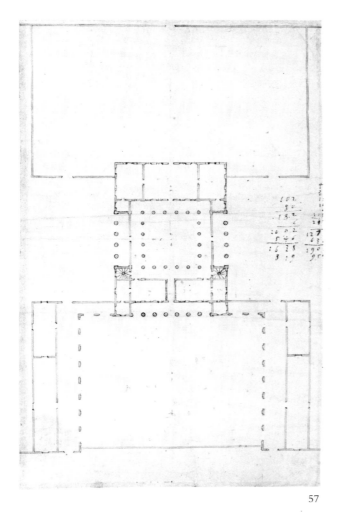

57

57. SITE AND PLAN PROJECT FOR VILLA MOCENIGO, DOLO (II)

1544/45

RIBA Palladio XVI/1.

40.1 x 25.1 cm. (single sheet); countermark in lower right corner, BC (variant of Briquet 502), laid lines 34.5 mm. apart: same paper as XVI/2 (cat. no. 56), possibly same sheet; Talman 54 mark on *verso*.

Pale, grayish siena ink, with pencil underdrawing, and light beigetan wash; later figure calculations, right center, in deep umber ink; inscribed with measures in Vicentine *pertiche* and feet, and with scale of 30 feet = 28.9 mm. (one Venetian inch).

Burger 1909, p. 120, fig. 47:3; Zorzi 1969, p. 91, fig. 146; Lewis 1972, pp. 12–14; Puppi 1972, p. 44; Mostra 1973, p. 147 (Burns); Puppi 1973, p. 360, fig. 494.

Royal Institute of British Architects, London.

Leonardo Mocenigo was probably Palladio's most faithful and consistent patron. He employed the architect on his palace in Padua (*cf.* cat. no. 32, figs. 12, 13), on two large country villas at Dolo and Marocco, at the church of Santa Lucia in Venice, and even to create for his collection of medals an ebony cabinet "resembling the Arch of Constantine," which after his death in 1575 his son offered to the Grand Duke of Tuscany (Zorzi 1965, p. 135). Leonardo was born—not registered at his majority, per Zorzi: his parents were only married in March of 1522—on 23 January 1523 (1522 *m.v.*); his younger brother Tomà was drowned at eighteen in a shipping disaster on 7 April 1544, and seven months later Leonardo married Marina Capello, on 26 November 1544. His bride was a niece of the Cardinal-Bishop of Padua, Francesco Pisani, whose relative Vettor had commissioned the villa that Palladio was completing at Bagnolo in this same year (cat. no. 48). A natural circle of friends and relations would thus have encouraged the bridal pair to request a design from Palladio for the riverfront property between Venice and Padua that Leonardo was already using—probably for its convenience to the latter as the university town.

The first of the sheets here proposed as results of such a commission, in fact, presents a Palladian design (cat. no. 56) based very precisely on Falconetto's Villa Vescovile for the princely uncle of the bride, a building to an almost exactly similar plan that was being decorated at this same moment, under the supervision of Palladio's Paduan acquaintance Alvise Cornaro. The alternate proposal on the present sheet is similarly retrospective, with its strong reminiscences of Giuliano da Maiano's villa of Poggio Reale near Naples of 1487–88. Palladio's early projects for Dolo display progressively shallower U-shaped courts on the side toward the river; but the fact that both are walled against the entrance of vehicular traffic emphasizes once more their formal, ornamental, and private nature, a use made particularly clear here by the fact that farm functions were essentially nonexistent in this well-appointed extra-urban pleasure palace (*cf.* cat. nos. 47, 55). Both courts are bounded by flanking *barchesse* with arches between pilasters, the latter doubled at the ends; Palladio executed a closely similar but still shorter example at Cicogna, whose full plan also contains many further reflections of the Dolo projects (*Quatro Libri*, II:xv:62; Puppi 1973, pp. 310–313). These earliest Mocenigo drawings are tentative or even banal in their room arrangements (except for the grand and precocious stair systems of the first), and finicky in their draftsmanship. They closely precede the comparable center portion of the site and plan project for Quinto (cat. no. 54), whose loggia-to-wings relationship of pilasters-to-columns they exactly reverse. Their plan systems of four free-standing columns between corner piers, flanked by tiny rooms enframing the entrances, are identical (as are other details) among all three of these near-contemporaneous, and increasingly "Vitruvian," schemes.

Although Palladio and his subcontractors began assembling materials for the Villa Mocenigo at Dolo early in 1554 (the newly discovered documents are summarized at cat. no. 73), actual construction at the site did not begin until after 17 April 1561, apparently on 15 September; the same documentation dates Palladio's completion of Leonardo Mocenigo's house in Padua (*cf.* cat. no. 32) from 19 January 1560 to 4 January 1561. As an explanation of this chronology we should note that Leonardo and Marina Mocenigo received three almost simultaneous legacies from Leonardo's father, Procurator Antonio Mocenigo, who had died on 13 March 1557; from Marina's father, Cavalier Zuanne Capello, who died on 20 September 1559; and from Leonardo's grandmother Pellegrina Foscari, whose estate was divided between him and his uncle Francesco Mocenigo, on 30 January 1560. Thus for the first time we can assign understandable dates to the rapid sequence of Palladio's three domestic commissions for Leonardo Mocenigo. The final campaign on his palace in Padua dates from the same month as the last of these inheritances, and was completed early the next year. The immediately subsequent construction of Villa Mocenigo at Dolo was quickly executed in 1561–62. Finally, in the latter year Palladio built at least a substantial portion of another Villa Mocenigo at Marocco north of Mestre, on land that Leonardo had just obtained in the division of his grandmother's property. Burns has recently found Palladio's autograph sketch for the villa at Marocco (Archivio di Stato, Venice, *Confini, busta* 262: Arts Council 1975, p. 223, no. and fig. 392); and I can confirm Magrini's date for the construction, of 1562 (1845, *Annotazioni*, p. xxiv, n. 47), by my own rediscovery on the site by the River Dese of the inscribed stone tablet that he quotes, which for over a century and a quarter has been assumed to have been lost.

CHAPTER FOUR

Private Commissions and Public Projects
in Vicenza and Venice, 1544-1554

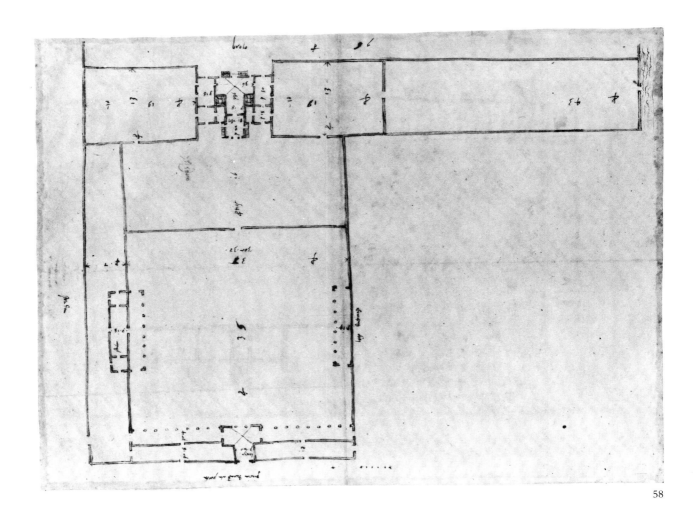

58. SITE AND PLAN PROJECT FOR VILLA PAGLIARINO, LANZÈ(?), AND FOR VILLA POIANA, POIANA MAGGIORE

1544

RIBA: Palladio XVI/3.

30.4 x 40.1 cm. (single sheet); watermark, angel in oval with star, and B beneath (Briquet 670 *bis*: Vicenza 1544, original sheet size 33 × 43 cm.); Talman 54 mark on *verso*.

Siena ink, roughly applied with imperfect pen, and yellow ochre wash, also hastily applied; *recto* roughly inscribed with measures in Vicentine *pertiche* and feet, scale of 10 *pertiche* (60 feet) = 37 mm. (1¼ Vicentine inches), and the words "brolo / loza 18 / strada / piacia davanti ala porta / larga: p. 20 / stala / logo da tinazi"; *verso* inscribed (in same ink) "al cavalier / paiarino / i⁻ vinetia" and (in later, umber ink) "deseḡno."

Burger 1909, p. 98–102, fig. 38:1; Ackerman 1967, p. 63, fig. 9; Zorzi 1969, pp. 62–63, fig. 86 (as for Villa Contarini, Piazzola); Lewis 1973, pp. 370, 377 n. 8 (publishing *verso* inscription, watermark, and date); Mostra 1973, pp. 64–65, p. 123 n. 34 (Cevese), p. 147 (Burns—as workshop); Puppi 1973, pp. 274–275, fig. 343; Arts Council 1975, pp. 192–193, no. 342 (Fairbairn—as workshop); Berger 1978, pp. 183–185; Burns 1979, p. 16.

Royal Institute of British Architects, London.

This rather rough, quickly sketched project is evidently similar to Palladio's site plan for Bagnolo (cat. no. 47), with its long rectangular court entered through a loggia opposite the house. It is even closer to Tullio Lombardo's "castello" at Roncade (cat. no. 55) in that the flanking *barchesse* do not run whole length of the forecourt, but stop short of a transverse wall defining a second courtyard. This space, in conjunction with a "brolo" or park behind, and two walled gardens at the sides (one of which is here extended via a walled access to a neighboring stream) is all reserved as the private domain of the manor house, which is thus successively sheltered from the "road" and "piazza" of the village outside.

The project on this sheet has consistently been associated with Palladio's spectacularly handsome and original manorial complex at Poiana Maggiore, an ancient fiefdom in the southernmost Vicentino, opposite Montagnana. But there were some subtle difficulties with the association. On the other hand, the successive walled courts of Palladio's curiously old-fashioned "castellated" plan might be seen as a response (either directly or indirectly—*cf.* Canova and Mantese 1979, pp. 168–171) to the impressive bulk of a still-surviving medieval castle with a high tower, directly across the road: Guglielmo da Poiana had encircled it with

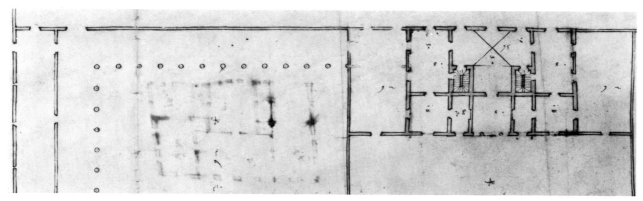

Figure 35

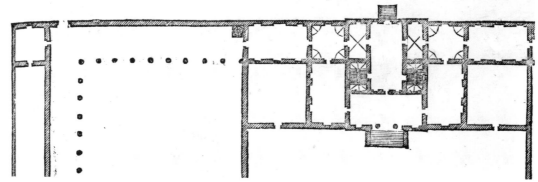

Figure 36

crenelated walls in the early 15th century. But the space between that dominant relic and Palladio's new site was not so much a "piazza," as a narrow medieval highroad; the "strada" alongside his new court was only a farm lane, apparently shown open in a map of Poiana of 1629, but walled off very shortly afterward; and a small tributary of the Ronego did flow past on the opposite side, though perhaps not quite so close as the stream shown in this drawing. Most curiously of all, the eventual building at Poiana is manifestly a work of Palladio's emerging maturity and was still being finished in 1554: whereas this much earlier drawing is executed on paper that is a full ten years older (Lewis 1973), and shows a plan whose suites of rooms are exactly reversed with regard to the executed fabric.

When I suggested eight years ago that the watermark in this paper might encourage a substantially earlier dating for Palladio's Villa Poiana, I had been assuming that the address he had inscribed on the *verso*, and that I had rendered "to the Cavalier Poiarino [*sic*] in Venice," could be interpreted as rather whimsical evidence that Palladio might have had an even more informal approach to spelling than certain youth of today. But the ancient family of the Counts Poiana bore as their heraldic device—and their name—an absolutely household word; for a "poiana" is none other than a common buzzard (*Buteo buteo*), and is not likely to change its orthography as easily as its feathers. Further inspections also convinced me that what Palladio had actually written was "*paiarino*"; and now Howard

Burns has brilliantly resolved this part of the difficulty (1979, p. 16) by connecting the drafted site with an exactly analogous property in the village of Lanzè, just east of Quinto, that was owned in 1544 by Cav. Bartolomeo *Pagliarino* (of whose name, in rapid speech, the *gl* is quite appropriately silent). This rich Vicentine nobleman was married to a cousin of Palladio's patron for Palazzo Porto (cat. nos. 64–67), and is known to have spent substantial time "*in vinetia*"; his death in c. 1545 explains the uniqueness of this "castellated" project, which was neither developed nor executed for the site at Lanzè.

But Palladio, astutely salvaging a good idea, got the sheet back (as its survival in the main Palladian collection attests), and—perhaps even on the stimulus of the similarity of name?—resubmitted it, apparently at once and with complete success, at least for the design of the manor house, to Cav. Bonifacio *Poiana*. Its plan was subjected to various modifications to adapt it to the new site (figs. 35–36), including its reversal of orientation through 180°, with the park facade's transverse groin-vaulted room now serving as an entrance loggia. A confirming fact which has never been pointed out is that Poiana's foundations and full basement story were built precisely to the plan in *this* drawing (which is unique in the four-part sequence for its design), with a heavy transverse wall beneath the *salone*, now supporting nothing, but intended as a substructure for the entrance to the loggia—that is the "*loza*" of this drawing, now turned toward the park.

59. PROTOTYPE FOR THE PORTICOES OF VILLA POIANA AND VILLA FORNI, DRAWN AS AN ENTRANCE TO THE THEATRE OF MARCELLUS, ROME

1545–47 or 1554

RIBA: Palladio XIV/3 *verso*.

41.7 × 28.9 (single sheet of stained and dirty paper, folded in quarters for sketching in the field); watermark, five crescents with Greek cross in circle (Heawood 882; *cf.* Briquet 5376–5380: Rome, 1540–1565); no collector's mark.

Warm reddish siena ink, interspersed with details in umber; mature handwriting. *Recto*, PLAN SKETCHES OF BUILDINGS AT BAIA AND POZZUOLI; Zorzi 1959, p. 98, fig. 240; Spielmann 1966, no. 128.

Zorzi 1959, p. 68, fig. 114; Spielmann 1966, p. 167, no. 191 (as after 1560); Burns 1973, p. 171, fig. 125 (detail of another image on the sheet); Arts Council 1975, p. 248, no. 437 (Burns).

Royal Institute of British Architects, London.

Figure 37

This attractive sheet of quick sketches after the antique records Palladio's study of several monuments: at the top right is part of a temple plan, below it a courtyard elevation and a porphyry urn from the Baths of Caracalla, and at the bottom a sketch plan of the Baths of Agrippa. Most interesting as prototypes for Palladio's own designs are the plan at top left, and the partial section at top center, of one of the two groin-vaulted entrance halls that flanked the stage building at the Theatre of Marcellus: Palladio frequently used the scheme in his own projects (in RIBA XVI/12 precisely, even to the apse), and he executed a beautiful example at the Palazzo Barbaran (cat. no. 99). Even more cogently the entrance portico, of which he sketches the facade superstructure with an entablature detail alongside, is a direct source for several of his domestic designs. The most immediate of these are the porticoes of the Villa Poiana (cat. no. 58, fig. 37) and the Villa Forni (cat. no. 60, fig. 38), whch both use its motif of a *serliana* with square piers, centered under a pediment, as a dominant entrance feature. In the Villa Forni the proportions of the whole pavilion are similar, and the apertures (as in the drawing) are unmolded. At Poiana the frontispiece is broadened to include lateral windows with eccentric flat frames, and an open pediment; but the bold Bramantesque shapes above the portal only emphasize once more the crystalline sharpness of its unmolded piers.

Palladio's "stripped style" as exemplified in these buildings is so idiosyncratic as to be unique to him, and to this phase of his work: it was recognized by Ackerman (1966/1977, pp. 22–24; 1967, pp. 3–4, 59–64), indeed, as being the touchstone by which both the Villa Forni and the Villa Poiana could be assigned to Palladio's activity in the 1540s. It would thus be interesting to know to which of Palladio's Roman journeys we should date the present sheet. Its drafting style on the whole seems early (especially in the hatchings for three-dimensional effect), but the annotations are late. This may, of course, be only one that has survived among several studies that Palladio might have devoted to the Marcellus theatre at different times, during his principal Roman sojourns of 1541, 1545–47, or 1554. We are not even clear as to whether he was depicting an element no

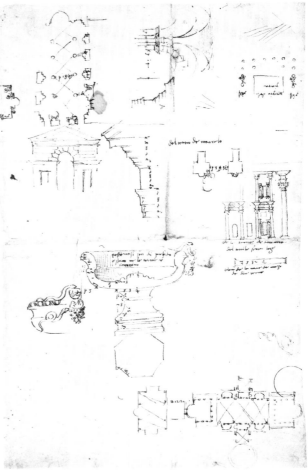

59

longer extant, or developing a plausible reconstruction from its remains. One clue to his precocious interest in the building is provided by the exact reproduction of its vaulted hall in RIBA XVI/12, cited above: the sheet can certainly be assigned to the early 1540s, as one of Palladio's first plans to be based specifically on his experience of Roman prototypes.

104

Figure 38

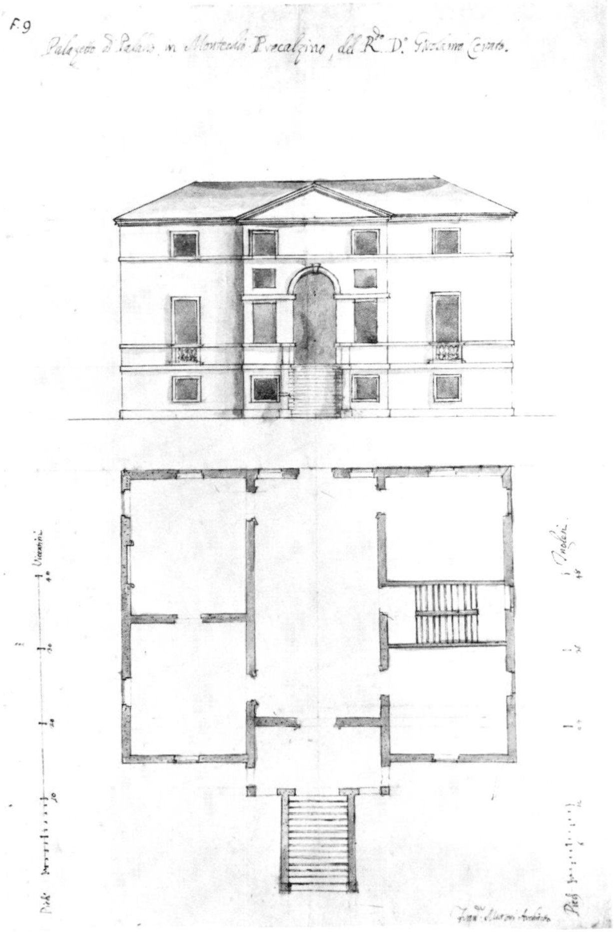

60

60. FRANCESCO MUTTONI: ELEVATION AND PLAN OF VILLA FORNI-CERATO, MONTECCHIO PRECALCINO

Shortly before 1740

Devonshire Collections, Chatsworth: Muttoni F.9.

45.6 × 29.2 cm. (single sheet); watermark, three diminishing crescents in line (Heawood 871: Venice 1740); no collector's mark; inventory number F.9, top left. .

Brownish black ink, with some siena ink, and gray wash, on pencil underdrawing; inscribed at top, "Palazetto di Paladio, in Montechio · Precalzino, del R.ᵈᵒ D.° Girolamo Cerato."; signed bottom right "Fran:ᶜᵒ Mutoni Architetto," and inscribed with scales in Vicentine feet (40 ft. = 14.7 cm.) and English feet (48 ft. = 14.9 cm.).

Arts Council 1975, p. 203, no. 362 (Burns); Barbieri 1980, p. 230, fig. 11.

The Trustees of the Chatsworth Settlement.

This is one of some dozen drawings by Muttoni at Chatsworth, which are discussed below as a group, in cat. nos. 128–130. A particular importance attaches to this sheet, for its caption constitutes the first known ascription to Palladio of the fascinating but undocumented Villa Forni (fig. 38). Muttoni published the attribution in the letterpress accompanying a Veneto map that he issued in 1739 as a prospectus for his great *Architettura di Andrea Palladio*, and since then the building has been widely acclaimed as a particularly handsome early work by the master. Its startingly plain "stripped style" portico refers exactly to Palladio's Theatre of Marcellus facade sketch and to Poiana (cat. nos. 58, 59), while the moldings of its lateral windows, balustrades and cornice closely reflect other Palladian structures of the 1540s. The simple, clear room sizes also demonstrate Palladian patterns: the 8-by-16-foot loggia is symmetrically followed by a 16-by-32-foot *salone*, and the four smaller rooms, all 15 feet wide, are 13½, 14, 17½, and 18 feet deep; only one is drawn with a fireplace.

No record of the building or the property has yet been found that predates the drafting of a will in 1610 by its owner Girolamo Forni, who had probably housed his friend Alessandro Vittoria in the villa during the plague years of 1575–1576; the originals of the modern facade sculptures are thus customarily attributed to him. Notwithstanding the mysterious silence of the documents, Ackerman has demonstrated convincingly (1967, pp. 59–60) that the genesis of the design—to a commission as yet unknown—must refer to the clearly circumscribed period of the 1540s that culminated in the building of Villa Poiana.

105

61. PARTIAL ELEVATION OF PROJECT I FOR THE BASILICA, VICENZA

1540/41

RIBA: Palladio XVII/22.

15.8 × 28.6 cm. (single sheet of extremely clear white paper, cut along left margin); no watermark visible; Talman 150 mark on *verso*.

Light gray-umber ink, strengthened by heavy dark siena, with faint pencil underdrawing or revision, and gold-brown wash; inscribed in epsilon handwriting with measures in Vicentine feet, of which a scale of 9 feet (interrupted by cut at left edge) = 25 mm.

Pée 1939/1941, pp. 21–22, fig. 5; Dalla Pozza 1942, pp. 126–128, fig. 3 (cropped at 3rd bay); Dalla Pozza 1943, pp. 102–103, fig. 25; Pane 1961, p. 145, fig. 152:7; Dalla Pozza 1964–1965, pp. 215–216, fig. 16; Zorzi 1965, p. 45, fig. 36; Lotz 1967, pp. 14–15 and 17, fig. 4; Barbieri 1968, pp. 67–68, fig. xv; Zorzi 1969, p. 61, fig. 73; Mostra 1973, p. 113 (Cevese), p. 149 (Burns); Forster and Tuttle 1973, fig. 72; Puppi 1973, p. 269, fig. 328; Arts Council 1975, p. 31, no. and fig. 36 (Burns); Berger 1978, pp. 162–167, fig. 22; Verona 1980, p. 118, no. and fig. V, 1-a (Burns).

Royal Institute of British Architects, London.

This extremely beautiful and impressive design marks the culmination of Palladio's early eclectic style. Its delicate draftsmanship makes it a small masterpiece of refined technique—as for example in its wonderfully regular shaded areas of "dry-brush" freehand hatching, where the pen is used almost pictorially.

The drawing documents not only Palladio's artistic development, but also the history of the reconstruction of the great Palazzo della Ragione or city hall of Vicenza, known since Palladio's time as the "Basilica." The site had been occupied by a communal council building for perhaps half a century before an associated Palazzo del Comune was built alongside it in 1222; both these buildings were badly damaged in fires of 1290 and 1378, and were on the point of collapse when the Venetian Senate in 1444 voted a large subsidy for their renewal. Domenico da Venezia provided the design for the resulting structure of 1449–60 that still survives, incorporating a huge 52-by-21-meter upper hall with a great curving timber roof, erected over a ground-floor complex of shops set in double rows between open passageways. From 1481 to 1494 Tommaso Formenton surrounded this core with his two-story loggias of broad arches on slender columns, but the whole west tract of these galleries collapsed, almost as soon as they were finished, on 20 April 1496. There then followed a frustrating fifty years of indecision, prolonged by the wars of the League of Cambrai, during which no less than eight of the greatest architects in Northern Italy were consulted for their views on stabilizing and completing the fragmentary structure. Their roster reads like a roll-call of the generation of transition from the "Early" to the "High" Renaissance in the Veneto. They begin with Pietro Lombardo, who came to advise Formenton in 1495/1496; Antonio Rizzo, called immediately after the collapse, in May and July of the latter year; and Giorgio Spavento, as the last of the "pre-war" consultants, whose recommendations were considered on 22 March 1498. With the return of peace, more up-to-date stylistic currents were represented by visits of Antonio Scarpagnino in May 1525 and May 1532; Jacopo Sansovino in January and April of 1538; Sebastiano Serlio, paid on 15 February 1539; Michele Sanmicheli, who stayed in the shop of Palladio's associated stonemasons during his visits of November 1541 and

Figure 39

January 1542; and finally the great Giulio Romano, who was brought from Mantua with great fanfare in December of 1542.

Palladio was born in the year that marked the beginning of the wartime hiatus (1508), and had enrolled in the guild of Vicenza stonemasons by the spring of 1524. He would thus have been working as a younger fellow professional during the visits for consultation on the Basilica by Scarpignino, Sansovino, and Serlio. He would also have encountered Sanmicheli personally, through the latter's residence in the Pedemuro shop—although in this case Andrea would almost certainly have known the senior architect already for some three years, since their presumed association in Padua in 1539 (cat. no. 48). Palladio in fact is now usually assigned responsibility for a fine portal of 1536, between the Basilica and the adjoining palace of the Venetian governor, so that he may already have been emerging as the local architect of greatest authority (and with the greatest interest in the Basilica) by the time of Sansovino's and Serlio's visits in 1538 and 1539. The dates of these latter consultations by "outside experts" of course also exactly correspond with the period of Palladio's emerging friendship with Trissino, in many ways Vicenza's "elder statesman" and senior arbiter of taste. We have seen (cat. no. 1) how strongly the evidence of Trissino's loggia at Cricoli suggests that Serlio himself had actually been a collaborator on its design by 1537; and thus he too, through Trissino as well as through Alvise Cornaro in Padua, would have been well acquainted with Palladio by the time of his return visit to Vicenza. Jacopo Sansovino, finally, had just begun his great Library of St. Mark at the moment of his Vicentine consultations, and as state architect of Venice may have seemed somewhat more officially remote to the twenty-nine-year-old Andrea: but through Vasari's description we know Jacopo to have had an essentially modest and affable manner, and he was closely associated with Serlio.

It is therefore not at all surprising that this sheet with Palladio's earliest independent ideas about the Vicentine Basilica should show a Sanmichelian vocabulary of heavily rusticated arches and piers, together with superimposed Serlian motifs that are paralled by coeval villa projects (cat. nos. 41, 43–44), being assimilated into a low horizontal design—whose subsequent development, especially in its corner bays (cat. nos. 62–63), brings it consistently closer to Sansovino's Library. This drawing's clear association with the period just before Palladio's first trip to Rome, and its one Sansovinesque detail, even help to confirm a date of c. 1540 for an undocumented design by the older master. The lightly penciled small arches above the side apertures of Palladio's *serliane* exactly reflect Sansovino's central window for the church of San Martino in Venice; the motif ultimately derives from Bramante (choirs of S. Maria delle Grazie and St. Peter's), though a more direct inspiration for these revivals may be the treatment of the end walls on Giulio Romano's garden loggia at the Palazzo del Te in Mantua.

62. PARTIAL ELEVATION OF PROJECT II FOR THE BASILICA, VICENZA

1545/46

RIBA: Palladio XIII/9.

35.8 × 28.3 cm. (single sheet); no watermark; Talman 54 mark on *verso*.

Umber ink over heavily incised lines, with gray-umber wash.

Pée 1939/1941, pp. 15–16, fig. 3; Dalla Pozza 1942, pp. 125–126, fig. 2; Dalla Pozza 1943, p. 102, fig. 24; Pane 1961, p. 145, fig. 152:6; Zorzi 1965, p. 46, fig. 37; Lotz 1967, pp. 14–15 and 17, fig. 6; Barbieri 1968, pp. 61–62, fig. xiv; Mostra 1973, p. 113 (Cevese—as workshop), p. 146 (Burns—as Palladio or workshop), fig. 135; Forster and Tuttle 1973, p. 116, fig. 74; Puppi 1973, pp. 269–270; Arts Council 1975, p. 31, no. 35 (Burns); Berger 1978, pp. 162–167; Verona 1980, p. 118, no. and fig. V, 1-b (Burns).

Royal Institute of British Architects, London.

Following the intense activity of the Vicenza council in requesting expert recommendations about the completion of the Basilica in 1538, 1539, 1541, and 1542 (cat. no. 61), a further delay of more than three years occurred, which we must imagine to have been occupied with considerable behind-the-scenes maneuvering, since the prevailing mood was clearly one of dissatisfaction with the professional advice. Finally on 5 March 1546 the Council voted 84 to 19 to authorize the construction of a trial bay in wood, according to a new design which had just been submitted by Giovanni da Pedemuro and Andrea Palladio. Successive payments of 30 *scudi,* 12 *ducati,* and 13 *troni* were appropriated for this large structure on March 6th, on May 24th, and on January 31st, 1547; these were followed by a silence of more than a year and a half, until on 6 September 1548 three civic commissioners were selected for the building project. One of their first acts was to pay Palladio 50 *lire* for the production of further drawings; these were then pondered for another six months, while more wooden models were made.

Palladio's appointment as architect of the Basilica was thus by no means easy (he was even obliged to present his first proposal in association with his former master), and in view of the august consultants called earlier by the city council, we can understand in what a broad and competitive context he was being judged. It has consistently been assumed that the present drawing represents a stage close to his official presentation project of 5 March 1546, and indeed the conclusion seems plausible. Puppi has even suggested (1973, p. 269) that Trissino might well have arranged their second sojourn to Rome, from September 1545 to February 1546(?), precisely in order to give Palladio the more developed firsthand knowledge of antique classicism which this drawing seems to reflect. It is perhaps less likely that Palladio could have passed from the stage represented here to his final design in just one more step (represented by his "four drawings" of October 1548), and

62

Figure 40

108

this sheet's still very strong reminiscences of RIBA XVII/22 (cat. no. 61) probably serve to anchor it to a preliminary phase of Palladio's "Romanizing" of that earlier design. There are still strong Venetian reflections as well: the addition of the Doric frieze makes the lower level even more Sanmichelian, while the upper Ionic pilasters and wide arches recall Falconetto's Odeon Cornaro and Villa Vescovile, which Palladio had recently experienced in Padua. The advantage of making the superimposed openings a uniform large size was both a functional and an aesthetic gain; but the very broad piers would still have obscured light from the interior, and they offered no real means of expanding or contracting the arches (whose heights had to be uniform, to meet the pre-existing loggia vaults), whenever the transverse passageways or surrounding loggias changed widths.

Palladio's 1548 drawings and wooden model presumably proposed the much improved scheme which we see now in marble (fig. 39). His model was debated in a final Council session on 11 April 1549, where it was eloquently supported by the two commissioners Gian Alvise Valmarana and Girolamo Chiericati, both already committed partisans of the architect (*cf.* cat. no. 88). Even though competitive models had been prepared to show Antonio Rizzo's and Giulio Romano's earlier projects, Palladio's

carried the majority by a vote of 99 to 17. He was at once appointed superintendent of the huge undertaking, and work began in May, with his visits to the quarries at Piovene and his trips to Venice and Padua to enlist stonemasons.

I am not sure that the exceptionally close parallel of this drawing to the Venetian "Loggia Nuova" at Candia in Crete has ever been noticed (see Gazzola 1960, pp. 183–185, fig. 205). Sanmicheli had spent several years in the late 1530s working on the fortifications at Candia, and in 1541 he is named in a document referring to the desirability of the loggia (which was built and functioning by 1576). The usual argument that its strong Sanmichelian character must be fortuitous, since it is known to have been completely rebuilt in the 1620s, loses force when we find it again being successfully reassembled—as I did in 1975—after yet another rebuilding, with the same stones (a process which in this seismic area seems inevitable and continuous). It thus seems to me to be very highly probable that Michele would have brought back to the Veneto a drawing of the proposed Cretan loggia—indeed the document states that information about the project could be had from him—and that Palladio's design on this sheet may therefore be likely to refer to a specific rather than a generic Sanmichelian prototype.

63

Figure 41

63. ELEVATION AND CORNER BAY OF THE UPPER ORDER OF THE BASILICA, VICENZA (PROJECT DRAWING III)

1564/65

RIBA: Palladio XIII/8.

45.9 × 37.1 cm. (single sheet of heavy paper); no watermark; Talman 49 mark on *verso*.

Umber ink on pencil underdrawing, with scale of 2 Vicentine feet = 29.8 mm. (1 Vicentine inch).

Dalla Pozza 1943–I, pp. 242–243, fig. 7; Zorzi 1965, p. 47, fig. 39; Barbieri 1968, p. 80, fig. xvi; Mostra 1973, p. 113 (Cevese—as workshop, after 1549), p. 146 (Burns—as Palladio or workshop); Puppi 1973, pp. 270–271, fig. 329; Arts Council 1975, p. 31, no. 37 (Burns).

Royal Institute of British Architects, London.

Palladio's "Basilica" is not really an independent building, but a double screen of superimposed vaulted galleries, surrounding and buttressing a Gothic core: even so, the execution of such an immense structure, entirely in marble, took a very substantial time. By 23 July 1561 the lower range toward the main piazza had been finished, but it was only on 6 March 1564 that a vote was taken to proceed with construction of the upper level, of which Palladio had just prepared a detailed model. This was slightly modified before 18 April 1566, by the insertion of a base molding beneath the pedestals. The present drawing (for the northwest corner of the upper level, where the new construction was to begin) lacks that element, as well as the pulvinated frieze common to cat. no. 62 and to the executed fabric; and also, most importantly, the decorative moldings at the level of the capitals, on the small piers immediately flanking the columns and apertures (which have yet to be expanded slightly) of the secondary order. It must therefore record an intermediate phase associated with the working out of the detailed design of the upper loggia, to be assigned in all probability to the period of contract negotiation in 1564/65.

Cevese's and Burns's doubts expressed in 1973 about the autograph status of this drawing and cat. no. 62 are borne out by the rough, heavy-handed, and irregular drafting of both sheets. Their technique is virtually identical with the Chatsworth drawing of Sanmicheli's Porta Nuova in Verona, attributed to Marc'Antonio Palladio, nephew of the architect, who is documented to have assisted his uncle on the Basilica (Verona 1980, pp. 119–120, no. and fig. V,5, Burns). We should therefore consider it an open possibility that these two sheets may have been partially drawn or redrawn by him, perhaps as records of stages in the presentation projects, which Palladio may have wished to keep by him in his studio.

The architect was immensely proud of his great achievement in the Basilica, which takes such prototypes as Sansovino's Library of 1537, or perhaps even more closely one of Serlio's plates from the *Fourth Book* of the same year (fol. 32 *recto*), possibly reflecting one of his ideas for the Basilica (fig. 40), and makes of these heterogeneous sources a compelling new invention. "I do not doubt," wrote Palladio in 1570, just as the upper level of the west range was being finished, "that this structure could well be compared with ancient buildings, and enumerated among the greatest and most beautiful fabrics that have been made from the time of the ancients to the present day; both for its size and its decorative ornaments, as well as for its material, which is all extremely fine cut stone, whose blocks have all been ordered and assembled with the highest degree of diligence."

The Basilica is indeed one of those rare masterworks whose perfected solution sums up an age. The graceful, expansive rhythms of its *serliane,* spatially broadened and structurally refined to afford maximum light to the galleries, have inevitably been baptized "Palladian motifs" (figs. 39, 41). No matter that their dramatically punched roundels reaffirm the Bramantesque origins of much earlier examples that Palladio had seen in Rome and translated only tentatively into his own designs for Vigardolo (cat. no. 44) and Poiana (cat. no. 58), largely on the example of popularizations by Serlio (fig. 40). Ever since the eventual completion of the Basilica in the second decade of the 17th century, at the moment that is of the fateful visits of Inigo Jones, the splendor of its forms have perfectly epitomized Palladio's genius, and have become, along with the *Quattro Libri,* the principal source of his reputation to the world.

---

64. PLAN PROJECT FOR PALAZZO PORTO, VICENZA (I)

c.1549

RIBA: Palladio XVI/10.

28.5 × 26.8 cm. (single sheet, with repair strip pasted over fold on *verso*); watermark, cardinal's hat with A alongside (part or variant of Briquet 3465); Talman 54 mark on *verso*.

Umber ink on (earliest?) lines of property divisions; siena ink on plan; some few pencil or umber crayon additions; very pale light beige wash with rose tints.

Zorzi 1954, p. 116, fig. 18; Zorzi 1965, pp. 32–33, fig. 21; Mostra 1973, p. 147 (Burns).

Royal Institute of British Architects, London.

This splendid and impressive plan for an urban site in Vicenza was the subject of a memorable analysis by Zorzi (1954/1965), who was unable to connect it with any known commission; Burns in 1973 tentatively proposed that it might represent an ambitious and optimistic proposal for the site owned by Montano Barbaran (*cf.* cat. no. 99), but this is contradicted by our certain knowledge that his property occupied a long narrow corner site, until it was expanded slightly (along quite different lines) by acquisitions made only in 1569/70.

It is in fact possible to establish through two independent lines of evidence that this design securely refers to Palladio's planning of Palazzo Porto. A closely related sheet (RIBA

XV/1, fig. 42), apparently unpublished and undiscussed, can be unequivocally identified as a large site plan encompassing almost the whole area between Contrà Porti (on the right, or east), Contrà Pedemuro S. Biagio (north, at top), and the Strada dei Stalli (west, left). It embraces virtually the whole north end of the "Porto block," which below this site of Iseppo da Porto's, to the south, was almost filled with the large palaces of his relations. The proof that Palladio's sheet XV/1 refers definitely to this area is provided by its triangular sidewalk on the lower

64

right margin, occupying the set-back between Iseppo's future facade and that of the existing Casa Muzan-Poloni to the north. All these elements are still in place (cf. fig. 45 for the sidewalk), and the large modern site plan in the *Corpus Palladianum* monograph on Palazzo Porto (Forssman 1973, fig. I) exactly reproduces the major dimensions, proportions, and relationships of Palladio's plan. Its sheet is further embellished with a spectacular miniature sketch for the facade of the new palace, a quickly rendered prototype for several subsequent designs (cat. nos. 65, 66, 101).

With the large plan on RIBA XV/1 should clearly be associated a smaller one, on XVI/8-D (fig. 43): in this case Burns did note in 1973 (p. 147) that the relationship of the two facade walls is indeed "paralleled by that of Palazzo Porto and the building to its right." In this cleaner and more finished drawing we can thus see a design immediately subsequent to the roughly blocked-out plan on the site survey: both are unquestionably studies for Palazzo Porto, and both offer independent evidence to connect our exhibited sheet to the same commission.

The large site plan (fig. 42) shares with modern measured drawings a successively angled line at the top left, where Contrà Pedemuro S. Biagio curves southwest toward the corner of the Strada dei Stalli. Palladio renders two segments of this line, on either side of a small service alley giving access to the inner courtyard, with angles respectively of 11° and 21° to the main east-west walls. Our large finished drawing here exhibited shows an exactly intermediate 16° on the beveled line of this same corner, as Palladio strove to regularize the curve with one median angle (the modern

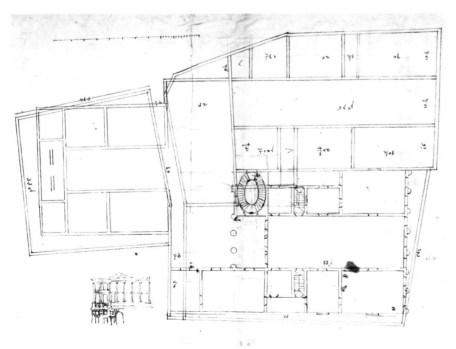

Figure 42

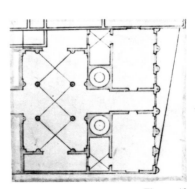

Figure 43

111

survey gives the basic 21°). All three images show the path of the service alley intersecting the north-south walls at a uniform 79°. The exhibited plan thus differs from Palladio's survey of 1549, and CISA's of 1972, only by setting the block of its projected palace well back from the street line on Contrà Porti, to a point exactly athwart the service alley—a solution the neighbors would presumably have discouraged. It also shows their older houses continuing beyond the sheet at the top right, where indeed several older houses still exist to the northeast of Palazzi Porto and Muzani. Palladio in both these larger plans is assuming that the latter house could be incorporated in his designs: but Iseppo da Porto evidently could not acquire it, thus enabling us to appreciate its fine Gothic facade even today.

The smaller plan illustrated here (fig. 43) thus restricts itself—as do all subsequent proposals for Palazzo Porto—to the narrower site that was actually used. It provides an independent demonstration that our exhibited plan was intended for the same commission, by exactly replicating its extremely idiosyncratic transverse hall, with a triple groin vault set within perimeter walls of recessed panels framed by engaged columns. The identical designs of this feature in the two drawings, and even more strikingly that of the vast central atrium in the exhibited plan, exactly recreate the long groin-vaulted entrances of the Theatre of Marcellus, as elements of classical planning that were particular favorites of Palladio's during the decade of the

1540s. At the far end of the longer atrium a pair of magnificent oval stair systems mark the first appearance of this motif in all of Palladio's work. (A single stair on a truly elliptical plan had been included on the associated sheet in fig. 42, and several more were sketched at exactly this moment on cat. no. 102 *verso*.) These beautiful double stairwells with deep niches in the walls of their apsidal landings are one of the architect's most splendid inventions. They were first executed in 1551–52 at the Villa Cornaro in Piombino, where they are also the unique survivals in their original form; a twin pair (now unfortunately re-modeled) were built immediately afterward in 1553 at the Villa Pisani in Montagnana (cat. no. 98).

The facade projected on this exhibited plan for Palazzo Porto is a direct parallel, with flat pilasters, for the more muscular version using engaged columns on the villa facade in cat. no. 68. Both are very closely related to the coeval projects of 1548/1549 for Palazzo Chiericati (cat. nos. 91–93), with their pedimented centers and coupled shafts at the sides of the projecting frontispiece. This doubling of the supports also occurs in a rhythmic repetition at the outer corners of the facade; when read with the innermost of the single pilasters set between the intermediate bays, it causes an apparent trebling of the order as a frame to the central pavilion, again as on the associated villa facade and Palazzo Chiericati.

---

65. FACADE PROJECTS FOR PALAZZO PORTO (II)

1542/46

RIBA: Palladio XVII/12 *recto* and *verso*.

28.4 × 41.8 cm. (single sheet of heavy paper); countermark, upper left corner, B; Talman 54 mark on *verso*.

Siena ink, darker in ruled lines, on pencil underdrawing; extremely pale biege wash on upper walls, heavier beige-tan wash to shade cornice and upper windows, and dark siena to umber brown wash on lower apertures. *Verso*, PROPOSALS FOR GROUND FLOOR OF PALAZZO PORTO FACADE, INK SKETCHES OF DOMESTIC PLANS, AND PENCIL SKETCHES OF VILLA PORTICOES: very dark siena ink on facades, umber ink on sketches; extensive pencil. Zorzi 1954, p. 113, fig. 10; Forssman 1965, p. 86, fig. 41; Zorzi 1965, pp. 187–188, fig. 157; Forssman 1973, p. 25, fig. vii; Lewis 1973, pp. 370–376, fig. 198; Mostra 1973, p. 149 (Burns); Puppi 1973, p. 280, fig. 353 (facades only).

Dalla Pozza 1943-I, p. 240, fig. 4, and 1943-II, pp. 73–74, fig. 13; Zorzi 1954, p. 113, fig. 11; Forssman 1965, p. 86, fig. 39; Zorzi 1965, p. 188, fig. 158; Forssman 1973, p. 23, fig. v; Mostra 1973, p. 149 (Burns); Puppi 1973, p. 280, fig. 351; Arts Council 1975, p. 234, no. 416 (Fairbairn); Berger 1978, 170–171.

Royal Institute of British Architects, London.

Iseppo da Porto would certainly have met Palladio through his betrothal in 1542 to Livia Thiene, whose brothers Marc'Antonio and Adriano were at that moment negotiating construction of the nearby Palazzo Thiene (cat.

nos. 49–53), and by 1545/46 were to commission the villa at Quinto (cat. no. 54). A document of 28 February 1542 set Livia's dowry at 4000 ducats (Forssman 1973, p. 20 n.5), but we are not certain of the actual moment at which her marriage to Iseppo may have occurred. It seems most likely to have been the catalyst for the construction of their palace, on whose facade Temanza read the now-cancelled inscription *JOSEPH. PORTO. MDLII.* (1778, p. 295), and on one of whose chimneypieces, now also lost, Da Schio in the early 19th century recorded a similar inscription with the same date of 1552 (Ms. quoted in Zorzi 1965, p. 194 n. 27). The testimony of Palladio's drawings themselves is therefore our best guide to the dating of his successive projects for Palazzo Porto, during this decade of silence in the documents.

The present sheet offers two early proposals for the facade, with some associated variations. The full elevation on the *recto* has always been compared to Palladio's similar design with tall Corinthian pilasters at Palazzo Civena, of 1540–42 (*cf.* cat. no. 6, fig. 7). The relationship of the order to the large wall area above the windows also recalls Palazzo Da Monte of the same years (cat. no. 4, fig. 3), the coeval facade design for Bertesina (cat. no. 34), with the engaged Ionic columns that soon became standard on the Porto projects, and especially the nearby and closely related Palazzo Thiene (fig. 30, cat. no. 52), whose similar high

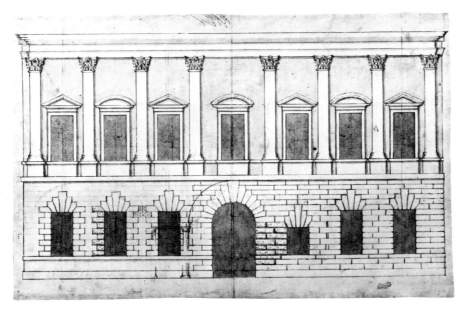

65 recto

65 verso

basement, tall pilasters and large wall planes were being gradually selected between 1542 and 1546. The treatment here of heavy rustication with infilling brick around the basement windows, on the left, is exactly paralleled in the second of the Thiene facade drawings from this period of transition (cat. no. 51). The unmolded pedestals of these upper windows and pilasters are duplicated at Vigardolo (c. 1541–43; fig. 21), and in both Basilica designs (cat. nos. 61–62) of the period from c. 1541 to 1546.

Palladio's alternative proposal on the *verso* of this sheet shows the rusticated keystones of the lower windows set within semicircular panels that are smoothed-out versions of those used in the final design for Palazzo Thiene (*cf.* figs. 30 and 45). Most curiously of all, he experiments on this sheet with proposals for an entrance atrium of four free-

standing Tuscan columns with a groin vault (as eventually executed, again on the pattern of a simultaneous design for Palazzo Thiene—*cf.* fig. 31 and cat. no. 53); but he shows their forms strangely projected onto the facade plane, as if this were in part transparent. [Only the "projection" on the *verso* is to be considered autograph: that on the *recto* is an interpolation that does not align with the necessary window, has much cruder moldings, and shows a column shaded on the opposite side and a different technique from Palladio's.]

The close connections that are manifested throughout this drawing with Palladio's final revisions of c. 1546 for Palazzo Thiene encourage the conclusion that Ursel Berger is probably right (1978, pp. 223–225, esp. n. 621 and figs. 19–20) to associate the largest of the plans sketched on the

113

upper half of this *verso* with the ideal extension of the Thiene block to a facade on the Corso. The idea of a great southern range of reception rooms that would allow Palazzo Thiene to culminate in a projecting frontispiece on Vicenza's central thoroughfare, is prefigured in 1545/46 on the site sketch in cat. no. 53, and published in 1570 in the *Quattro Libri* (fig. 31); Berger has suggested that the present *verso* study would immediately follow the general sketch, as a detailed working out of the room arrangement. Although I had suggested in 1973 (p. 372, following Puppi) that this plan study seemed possibly to be a first idea for Palladio's 1548–49 "remodeling" of the Villa Godi at Lonedo (a campaign we can now demonstrate to have been fictitious— see cat. no. 89), I recognize that Dr. Berger is persuasive in associating it instead with the revision of Palazzo Thiene, which is reliably dated to the middle 1540s. This revision has the advantage of also fixing an earlier date of c. 1546 for the design of Villa Zen at Cessalto (whose plan prototype here overlaps that of the south range for Palazzo Thiene): we have already seen evidence that this sketch, and its executed *Quattro Libri* plan (fig. 25), in fact constitute close reworkings of Palladio's superb plan proposal of 1541 for Bagnolo IV (cat. no. 47). The third ink sketch on this *verso,* and its associated pencil designs for porticoes, offer related evidence for the chronology of Palladio's common plan for Villa Chiericati at Vancimuglio, and Villa Foscari at Malcontenta (cat. no. 88).

66. FACADE PROJECTS AND PLAN PROPOSAL FOR PALAZZO PORTO, VICENZA (III)

c. 1546/47

RIBA: Palladio XVII/9 *recto* and *verso*.

28.2 × 40.6 cm. (single sheet); watermark, large anchor in circle with star (no identifying marks visible); Talman 54 mark on *verso*.

Siena ink on pencil underdrawing, with beige wash; inscribed with measures in Vicentine feet, and scale of 10 feet = 51 mm. (2 Roman inches); *verso* includes castle-villa plan entirely in pencil (see Burns 1975 below), and (unrelated?) scale of 10 units = 17.5 mm.

Dalla Pozza 1942, pp. 189–190, fig. 17, and 1943, pp. 168–169, fig. 37; Wittkower 1949/1971, pp. 75–76, fig. 25 b; Zorzi 1954, pp. 113–114, figs. 12, 13; Pane 1961, p. 226, fig. 242:12; Forssman 1965, pp. 86, 90, figs. 40, 43; Zorzi 1965, pp. 188–189, figs. 160, 161; Forssman 1973, pp. 23–24, 26–27, figs. vi, ix; Mostra 1973, p. 148 (Burns); Burns 1973, p. 180; Puppi 1973, pp. 280–281, figs. 346, 352; Arts Council 1975, p. 200, no. and fig. 357 (*verso*— Burns), p. 233, no. and fig. 415 (*recto*—Fairbairn); Berger 1978, pp. 171–176, fig. 25; Verona 1980, p. 116 with fig. (Burns).

Royal Institute of British Architects, London.

This is one of the most refined and elegant of all Palladio's facade designs, and offers the patron a choice of two quite different solutions. That on the right is superficially similar to the early proposal on RIBA XVII/12 (cat. no. 65 *recto,* left), but much more carefully developed and tightly organized. The completely rusticated basement is taller, with narrower wall segments and wider windows, whose delicate frames would have contrasted intriguingly with the heavy surrounding blocks. Palladio even considered pushing this contrast further, by adding decorative lintels on pendant brackets at the tops of the frames: since these components were executed at Poiana (fig. 37), but are otherwise unique, the Porto drawing provides one more testimony for Villa Poiana's final design being settled in the mid-1540s. The drawing's handsome attic windows with their double projections top and bottom recall Vigardolo and Bagnolo as well as Poiana, while the uneasy relationships of framing strips and base-molded pedestals, around the main windows, repeat the missed vertical alignments of these elements at Bertesina.

The very elaborate left-hand proposal with Ionic half-columns is essentially the one that was selected, although it was executed without the bothersome window-framing strips, with a plain flat frieze instead of a rounded one of wreathed garlands, and with basement window lintels simplified from Palazzo Thiene, on the model of a previous design (cat. no. 65 *verso*). This project's decorative ground-floor roundels may reflect the same motif at Palazzo Civena (fig. 10), where parallel *tondi* were executed on an identical field of smooth-surfaced ashlar rustication. Bertotti-Scamozzi engraves the Civena facade with sculptured busts in these apertures, as we see also sketched on the Porto design; in its execution (fig. 45) these became lavishly carved keystone heads with bizarre physiognomies. Their startling differences from the hard-edged blocks around them form one reminder of the sharp contrasts of medium and form that Palladio had contemplated in these designs.

The splendidly resolved plan on the *verso* of this sheet represents a magisterial solution to the problems of the site (cat. no. 64); its immediate prototype has long been recognized to be the small sheet at RIBA XVI/8-C (fig. 44). These drawings had previously been connected with the property mainly through the presence of one of them on a sheet with Porto facade proposals, and through the close approximation on that *verso* plan of the executed room arrangement; but we are now able to recognize also our familiar northwest corner angle in their dotted extensions at the rear. Both are among the most extraordinary plans in Palladio's oeuvre (and indeed in the whole Italian Renaissance) by virtue of their vast, "baroque" stair systems. These exceedingly precocious schemes show parallel twin flights rising along the sides of huge halls (which are open across their whole width on the upper levels), and turning through 90° to mount pyramidally toward central landings. In the prototype plan this stair structure extends beyond a "Marcellus theatre" groin-vaulted atrium to project boldly into an elaborate court, at whose far end appears a spectacular guest house, amalgamating elements

66 *recto*

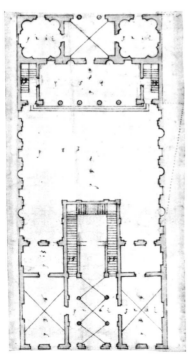

Figure 44

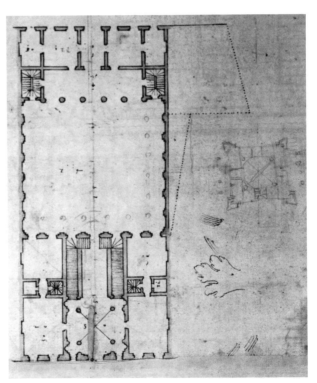

66 *verso*

115

from both the Loggia and Odeon of Alvise Cornaro. These reminiscences are interpreted through the intermediary of what may well be Palladio's earliest surviving drawing, RIBA XVI/6, which we have already encountered at cat. nos. 6 and 45; a somewhat parallel design (XVI/19-A), in this case intermediate between the Civena and Porto palaces, strongly simplifies the guest pavilion, and offers it covered access to the main block by means of arcades along the sides of the court—both ideas being reflected in our *verso*

design. Other projects played a part in this planimetric development, notably RIBA XVI/19-C (fig. 68—for the twin light wells and twin stair systems of the project in cat. no. 64), and XVI/8-B, with its apsidal hall recalling the Marcellan prototype (*cf.* XVI/12 and cat. no. 59). I am not sure whether the latter's striking descendant lightly sketched on this *verso* plan has ever been noticed: a great apsidal projection with a full "ambulatory," which Palladio places on the facade toward the garden.

---

67. HALF ELEVATION OF FACADE AND HALF SECTION THROUGH PROJECTED COURTYARD OF PALAZZO PORTO, VICENZA (IV)

Late 1560s

RIBA: Palladio XVII/3.

28.8 × 37.3 cm. total (two sheets, abutting but not overlapping, joined in England with connecting strip: left sheet, 28.7 × 18.9 cm., watermark a bull's head with cross [*cf.* Briquet 14526]; right sheet, 28.8 × 18.4 cm., no watermark; laid lines on both sheets 29 mm. apart); Talman 150 mark on *verso* of both sheets.

Dark siena ink for ruled lines, bright reddish siena ink for freehand details; pale cool blue-gray wash; scale of 5 Vicentine feet = 23 mm.

Wittkower 1949/1971, pp. 77–78, fig. 25a; Pane 1961, p. 160, fig. 172:7; Zorzi 1965, p. 192, fig. 168; Gioseffi 1972, p. 61, figs. 32, 33; Forssman 1973, p. 32, fig. x; Mostra 1973, p. 107, figs. 119 (Cevese), p. 148, fig. 157 (Burns); Puppi 1973, p. 281, fig. 349.

Royal Institute of British Architects, London.

This stunningly beautiful sheet is actually a composite made by John Talman, who had marked each piece individually before he later joined them: the two Palladian drawings refer to two separate pages in the *Quattro Libri* (II:iii:9 as a rendering of the executed facade of Palazzo Porto, and II:iii:10 for the section through a newly-designed courtyard, supposedly to be associated with it); they are in fact printed overleaf from each other, and not even as a spread. Talman's montage has the effect of representing the lateral extent of the palace as a whole, but with the right half "transparent" (or the left half "opaque," depending on one's reading). It is undeniably useful in affording a visualization of the ostensible rapport between the facade of 1547–52, and the imaginary courtyard published in 1570; but since the latter element must be construed as more or less visionary, the gain is adventitious. It has lulled unwary critics into thinking that Palladio could have derived from it his "subsequent" facade design for Palazzo Valmarana (which however must predate 14 December 1565, whereas this drawing may be as late as 1569), on the analogy of the "step-down" effect of this courtyard's secondary order closing the edge of the composition, beyond the colossal Corinthian order at the center.

Figure 45

This project for a huge courtyard at Palazzo Porto, densely ringed with colossal column shafts and connecting galleries, is a "Vitruvian" development from the small courts of the preparatory drawings. It was to have been followed (again theoretically, as an essentially abstract idea) by an exact duplication of the main palace block (!), to form an equally magnificent guest house; the concept derives ultimately from Vitruvius's description of "the private house of the Greeks" (VI:vii:1–7), and is much more practically developed in cat. no. 95 below.

It has usually been said (at least since the relatively recent consensus that such images refer to later *Quattro Libri* plates, rather than to preparatory studies from the phase of execution—*cf.* cat. no. 52) that these sheets are in fact the direct prototypes for the published woodcuts. But they are not: a substantial number of variants—above all in the mezzanine windows on the courtyard side of the main block (*cf.* Forssman 1973, fig. 39), and in the facade frieze and sculptures—attest to their status as intermediate stages in the process of arriving at images for the treatise that would be at once accurate and persuasive. The final drawings handed to the block cutter would have been consumed during his work of transferring them, and none indeed are known to survive. The present conjoined sheets are therefore precious testimonies to Palladio's painstaking effort to make his published images as attractive and informative as he could. Although he had much studio assistance at this stage in his career, these images seem to be completely his own, and show the feathery grace and incisiveness of his late style.

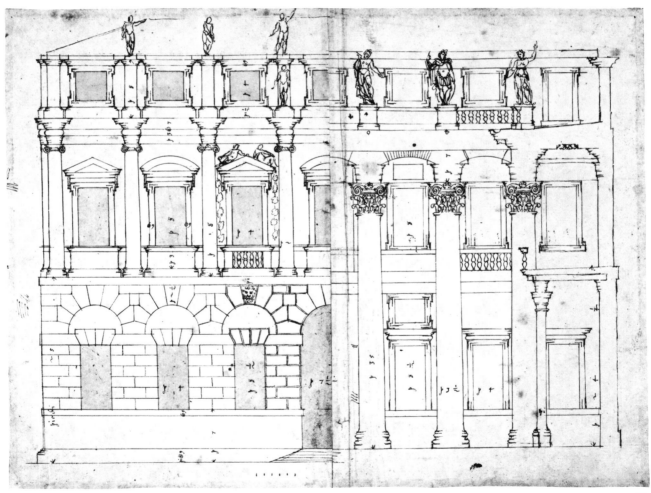

67

117

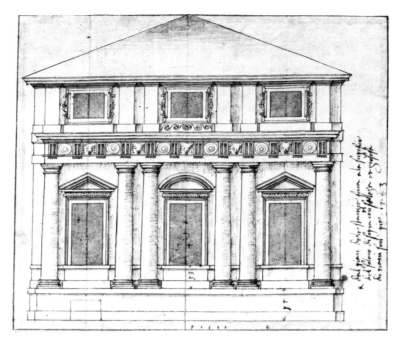

Figure 46

68. FACADE PROJECT FOR A SMALL VILLA (PERHAPS FOR VILLA ARNALDI, MELEDO ALTO?), POSSIBLY LATER ADAPTED FOR VILLA MUZANI, RETTORGOLE

1547/48

RIBA: Palladio XVII/21.

20.7 × 31.2 cm. (single sheet); countermark, upper right, AP (part of Mošin 879 [?], by extension with anchor watermark on companion sheet, XVII/24); Talman 150 mark on *verso*.

Sepia ink over heavily incised lines (somewhat lighter ink on freehand details); rich gold-tan wash, applied illusionistically in stripes (on roof), and together with linear shadings throughout; inscribed with measures in Vicentine feet, and with scale of 10 ft. = 51 mm. (2 Roman inches).

Zorzi 1954, pp. 70–71, figs. 15, 17; Pane 1961, p. 110, fig. 134:35; Zorzi 1969, p. 49, fig. 60; Arts Council 1975, p. 237, no. 422 (Fairbairn—as "clearly not earlier than about 1549"); Berger 1978, pp. 136, 181–182, fig. 26.

Royal Institute of British Architects, London.

This drawing has an exact pendant in RIBA XVII/24, an elevation to the same scale of the three bays forming the left side of the same villa, with identical forms and technique (fig. 46): it bears Palladio's note that "from the level of the main floor rooms to the surface of the floors in the attic, including the thickness of the beams and the terrazzo paving, is 17 ft. 3 in." (Palladio's word *salezà*—misinterpreted by Zorzi—is the Venetian dialect term for paving, *salizà* [Boerio 1856/1971, p. 594]; Fairbairn was incorrect to read the dimension as "the height of the rooms *to* the beamed ceiling," which would have been a standard 16 feet; the "17 ft. 3 in." falls within the Doric frieze, and leaves barely 9 vertical feet for the attic wall, thus explaining Palladio's concern about its height.)

This project is a maverick in Palladio's production. Villas small enough to have only three windows on their flanks are rare in his work: related arrangements occur only at Finale, Poiana, and Fratta, and no executed design aligns them, as here, in three regular bays. Indeed Palladio's note about the limited height strikingly emphasizes the project's miniature scale. Its plan measures only 59½ by 37 feet (Fairbairn's comparable measurements suffer misprints on both their initial digits), and even the tiny Villa Saraceno at Finale—Palladio's smallest country house—at 65 by 43 feet is almost 28 percent larger.

For a design so small as to be virtually a "toy" villa, it is all the more surprising that Palladio's elevations for this project are more sculpturally plastic, and more lavishly detailed, than any other of his works. The projecting pedimented portico, with a weighty Tuscan order rhythmically gathered into dense columnar triads at the corners, is very similar to the project for Palazzo Chiericati, whose design was evidently undertaken in 1548. Elements of a similarly rich decorative vocabulary occur in Palladio's drawings for that facade (*cf.* esp. cat. no. 92), as well as for Palazzo Porto's (esp. cat. no. 66, of c. 1547), in both of which the same tightly banded garlands bulge outward in the friezes, or hang loosely between the Doric capitals. Another design very closely related—for these elements, for the same intercolumnar relief panels, and for an identical graphic technique—is the beautiful tempietto-tabernacle of RIBA XVII/18 *recto* (illus. at cat. no. 71); and Palladio's associate Zamberlan does show small windows with these same elaborate strapwork frames on one other Palladian drawing, a later design for the interior of the palazzo municipale at Brescia (Zorzi 1965, fig. 78).

Since at least one if not two of these latter parallels treats an interior design, the comparable elaboration and tiny scale of this villa-pavilion might suggest its appropriateness as one of the small ornamental buildings, with a few

68

rooms, that Palladio sometimes shows (often approached by such lateral stair systems) inside the courts or gardens of his city palace plans, at exactly this period (*cf.* cat. no. 66 *verso* and fig. 44). But the special attention to its richly decorated side facades seems to contradict this potential destination for the project, since Palladio always shows his city garden pavilions as contained between solid walls, offering them no apertures and no visibility on their flanks.

A more standard attempt to relate the project to a known villa commission is rendered difficult not only by its miniature scale, but also by the uniqueness of its design. The band of horizontal attic windows between short piers is paralleled only—and in a quite different context—by the final project for Palazzo Porto (cat. no. 66). Its comparable use in a single-story frontispiece over a loggia occurs on no other Palladian building (if we discount Inigo Jones's indistinct sketch of the attic at Quinto, and its questionable recreation by Muttoni), unless we consider its somewhat grander reappearance in the Villa Muzani at Rettorgole as an autograph work. In fact, that lost but evidently handsome building, brought close to the Palladian canon by the near-identity of the present design, seems to me to have been unfairly doubted: its plan, too, has a precise Palladian model in RIBA XVI/16-A (fig. 15), once we remove two distracting partitions, and slightly increase some of the dimensions. Exactly such a situation is reported in the one document for Rettorgole (Dalla Pozza 1943, pp. 213–215), where Pietro da Nanto has made (i.e. redrawn?) and annotated with measures a plan and an elevation, for whose walls Palladio is authorized to set a cost per linear foot. And we might remember that Casa Muzani in Vicenza was apparently being considered, during the very period of our "problem" project, for potential Palladian amalgamation with the next-door palace of Iseppo da Porto (cat. no. 64).

If we acknowledge, however, that the present designs would indeed have needed significant redrafting in order to expand them to the size of Rettorgole (a building executed in 1559 at some 85 by 46 feet), then the commission which is by far the closest to them in both size and date is represented by Vincenzo Arnaldi's remodeling of his *villino* at Meledo Alto in 1548–49. Palladio was certainly involved in consultations on it at this point (which thus corresponds exactly with the clearest stylistic date for these drawings), although in this case as well a document from as late as 1565 reminds us how long many of these projects continued to occupy both patron and architect. But the autograph Palladian sketches of 1547/48 for the Villa Arnaldi here exhibited (cat. no. 69) show a left flank with three windows, and a facade portico of three wide and two narrower apertures between six supports, flanked by single windows lighting stairs—thus elegantly accounting for the off-center placement of the windows on our elaborate facade, whose hitherto most puzzling feature had been their exact alignment on precisely *half* their available space; this is now clearly to be understood in terms of their being positioned to provide axial illumination to one of two contiguous flights. The dimensions seem to correspond almost exactly: on a measured drawing in the Arnaldi portfolio (cat. no. 69-D) Palladio shows the two large rooms behind the loggia as 18 feet deep, and the portico with its bounding walls as 33⅓ feet wide (the comparable measurement on our elaborate elevation being 32 feet), while from the sketches and from Palladian practice we can estimate its depth as 14 feet. When the 2-foot columns and standard 1½-foot walls are added, these measurements produce an overall dimension for the depth of Villa Arnaldi—at least as Palladio was considering it in these drawings—of exactly 37 feet, or (perhaps uniquely among Palladian buildings) the exact breadth of the lateral facade associated with the present project.

119

69. TWO SKETCH PLANS FOR VILLA ARNALDI, MELEDO ALTO, AND ONE FOR A SERVICE COURT IN MELEDO BASSO

1547/48

Biblioteca Bertoliana: Gonzati 28.1.4 [= 471].

42.4 × 32.2 cm. (single sheet of rough gray paper with water stains at bottom, folded to make two leaves of 21.2 × 32.2 cm.); watermark, small anchor in circle with star; Gonzati (?) album nos. in top right corners of the two leaves, *11/12*. Associated with a bound booklet of three other such sheets with a different loose sheet (here designated Drawing D) of VAULTING PLANS FOR TWO ROOMS BEHIND A LOGGIA, of 23 February 1565; 21.4 × 31.2 cm., foxed paper, watermark an orb with cross.

Drawing A, fol. 11 *recto,* umber ink, inscribed in Vincenzo Arnaldi's hand (as are all following inscriptions) *Meledo alto* (illustr. as cat. no. 69-A); Drawing B, fol. 11 *verso,* umber ink, inscribed in spine *Meledo basso;* Drawing C, fol. 12 *verso,* umber ink, no inscription; Drawing D, siena ink, inscribed *Loza* and *Strada* (illustr. as cat. no. 69-D).

Temanza 1778, pp. 312–313 (for full text of letter associated with Drawing D, "with Counts Fabio Arnaldi and his brothers in Vicenza"); Magrini 1845, pp. 74–75 (for Drawing D as autograph, but A through C as by Arnaldi); Zorzi 1969, pp. 17, 227–228, figs. 22–23 (for letter and Drawing D, agreeing with Magrini's attributions); Puppi 1973, pp. 371–372, figs. 517–518 (same conclusions as preceding); Puppi 1974, pp. 96–97, figs. 124 (Drawing C—as by Arnaldi) and 125 (Drawing D—as by Palladio); Arts Council 1975, pp. 221–222, no. 390 (Burns—all four drawings as Palladio), fig. 390 (detail of Drawing C, as "the only surviving drawing of a chimney pot by Palladio"); Venice 1980, pp. 274–275, no. 447 (Bassi—for letter of 23 February 1565, and Drawing D); Burns 1980, Lecture of 31 August (with reconstructions of Palladio's project).

Biblioteca Civica Bertoliana, Vicenza.

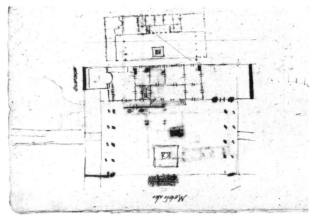

69 A

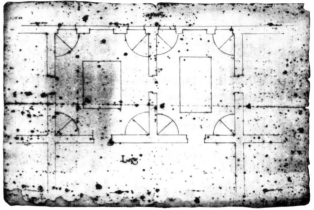

69 D

Vincenzo Arnaldi assembled this booklet of memoranda to record the reconstruction of his small country house in the hamlet of Upper Meledo, in the hills south of Vicenza. He possessed considerable agricultural property in the lower village of the same name, and one of the drawings on this sheet by Palladio that Arnaldi bound into his dossier (B, fol. 11 *verso*) shows a sketch of the lower walled court with its service buildings. As we have seen (cat. no. 47), drawings of actual farmyards are extremely rare in Palladio's work. Indeed, this is the only known "working drawing" of such a complex; the equivalent service courtyards on the presentation site plan for Quinto (cat. no. 54) have been regularized and formalized by comparison, as—to an even greater extent—have the only published examples, at Angarano and Lonedo (*Quattro Libri* II:xv:63, 65). Here on Arnaldi's smaller estate Palladio may only be sketching a pre-existing farmyard: this he apparently did in order to offer a suggestion for the overseer's house, which is shown in a partial cancelled sketch, as well as a larger plan with a separate inner court, an access to the highroad, and a kitchen garden. We have no evidence, however, that anything was done at Meledo Basso as a result of his visit.

But for Arnaldi's own house at Meledo Alto (which survives, though somewhat modified), we can trace successive stages in Palladio's involvement with actual construction. The patron's dossier begins in 1547 (fol. 6) with a very long list of questions about remodeling the existing house; with these he presumably interrogated Andrea, most likely on the occasion of the visit recorded by our drawings. Palladio's sketches are on the folded inner (farmyard) and outer (upper villa) faces of a sheet matching the client's other papers—we can thus imagine him being handed a pen on the spot and being asked to start drawing! Arnaldi's leaves 10, 13, 14, and 15 are all records of construction activity in 1548, by which time at least a good deal of Palladio's recommended facade was built; fols. 17 and 20 bring us into 1549, the last with a letter of May 2nd about the construction, and fol. 21 carries a final entry for the project, on 8 April 1550. Palladio wrote from Venice on 23 February 1565 to send a further drawing (here illustrated as cat. no. 69-D) with which he proposed vaulted ceilings for the two rooms behind the loggia; but no further work seems to have been undertaken after the brief campaign of 1548–49. It is suggested above (cat. no. 68) that an otherwise highly idiosyncratic and enigmatic Palladian project could perhaps be interpreted as a full-scale effort to persuade Arnaldi to embark on a major remodeling of the villa's facades. This seems quite likely, from a comparison of the drawings; but nothing surviving at Meledo or in the documents reflects that larger intention.

70. ENTRANCE FACADE OF AN EARLY PROJECT FOR THE RIALTO BRIDGE, VENICE

1554

Vicenza: 1950 inv. D-19.

38.1 × 56.9 cm. (single sheet); no watermark visible; no collector's mark.

Siena ink and sepia washes; scale line of 5 (presumably Venetian) feet = 25.5 mm. (1 Roman inch).

Magrini 1845, pp. 301–302; Pée 1939/1941, p. 145–147, fig. 38; Pane 1961, p. 357; Zorzi 1965, p. 174, fig. 142; Venditti 1969, pp. 31–33, fig. iii; Mostra 1973, p. 153; Puppi 1973, p. 378, fig. 528.

Museo Civico, Vicenza.

This interesting project has unfortunately been much misunderstood, since the existing interpretations of it as a variant for the Loggia del Capitaniato (Pée, Pane), or for the ceremonial arch to welcome Henri III into Venice (Zorzi), only made it appear as an unusually thin and tentative interloper among those robust representatives of Palladio's later style. Recent commentators have either downplayed it because of perplexity over the ambiguities resulting from such a dating (Puppi), or simply referred to its destination as unknown (Burns). But in fact it represents a portico very nearly identical to those shown dominating the pedestrian approaches to the Rialto Bridge project, published in the *Third Book* of Palladio's treatise (see cat. no. 123, fig. 86). The *Quattro Libri* design has long been

recognized as the architect's second major proposal for a great stone bridge over the Grand Canal in Venice, and Puppi has tentatively dated it to 1565 (1973, p. 302, followed by Burns, Arts Council 1975, p. 126). An earlier project was known to have been prepared by Palladio and presented in 1554 (*ibid.*, pp. 124–125), through the evidence of an imposing plan and river elevation preserved on a large drawing in Vicenza (1950 inv. D-25). Burns recently recognized another Vicenza drawing as being a variant facade for one of the ends of the bridge as projected in the 1565 design (cat. no. 109), but a corresponding entrance facade has not until now been identified from the first stage of Palladio's work on the project in the early 1550s.

The present design clearly dates from that period, yet it is closer to the *Quattro Libri* plan assigned to 1565 than to the Vicenza plan assigned to 1554; this may mean that the treatise plan will have to be given an earlier date, or that at least its entrance pavilions can be recognized as closely reflecting an alternate plan from the early fifties, of which the present sheet is a surviving elevation. Our facade drawing depicts a monumental entrance pavilion on a high podium, approached by axial and lateral stairs exactly as in the *Quattro Libri* plan. It shows a five-bay screen of arches between square piers faced by larger engaged columns, supporting a tall attic crowned by sculptural allegories and decorated with heraldic heads of the Lion of St. Mark. It thus precisely parallels the five apertures between six columnar supports, with interwoven major and secondary orders, as shown in its revised version on the

Quattro Libri plates. Here again the outer elements take the form of piers faced with applied columns (this time on the sides toward the river, and with the relative size of the orders reversed): the four central supports, in the publication of 1570, have become tightly spaced free-standing columns.

Indeed Burns has shown this latter development to have constituted the fatal flaw in the treatise plan (*op. cit.*, p. 126); for even though Palladio suppressed all its measurements, these can be calculated as providing a clear space of only some three feet between the bases of the column screens. The entrance pavilions of the published plan fell into this difficulty by the fact that they presented lateral facades only as wide as the main roadway over the bridge. But the entrance courts of the 1554 plan (on Vicenza drawing D-25) frame bridge facades that are 75 feet wide, according to the inscribed scale. Burns had already calculated, in the different context of an "unknown destination" (1973, p. 153), that our present facade has a total width of 80 feet; and indeed the decorative part—such as would have been visible between the colonnades of a forecourt as projected on the contemporaneous Vicenza plan—has an exactly corresponding width of 75 feet. The present project is thus precisely related in size to the bridge facades on the 1554 Vicenza drawing, but also intimately related in plan to those on the subsequent proposal in the *Quattro Libri*.

It may safely be construed to stand between them, and to represent a lost plan reusing the measures of the Vicenza project, but prefiguring (probably in a close chronological relationship) the raised, five-bay design of the treatise project, with the variation of offering apertures wide enough for an easy flow of traffic.

The reidentified Rialto facade of 1554 is guaranteed a firm dating within the preceding one or two years by its very close relationships of motif and drafting style with the last facade project for Palazzo Porto (completed 1552—cat. no. 66), with the facade for a small villa of the years just before mid-century (cat. no. 68), and especially with the identical draftsmanship of the Halicarnassus facade, evidently commissioned but not used for Barbaro's *Vitruvius*, of the years immediately after (cat. no. 71). Burns has already shown (Arts Council 1975, pp. 124 and 126) that Bernardino India is the likely author of the figures along the skylines of both the 1554 river elevation (Vicenza D-25) and the c. 1565 entrance elevation (Vicenza D-20, cat. no. 109) of Palladio's two previously identified Rialto projects. Since India worked directly with Palladio on the decoration of Palazzo Thiene in Vicenza in 1552, the attribution to him of the closely corresponding figures here provides one more clear indication of the date of this sheet in the year or two preceding the known submission of Rialto bridge projects in 1554.

---

71. RECONSTRUCTION OF THE MAUSOLEUM OF HALICARNASSUS, FOR BARBARO'S *VITRUVIUS*

1554

Devonshire Collections, RIBA: Chiswick 26.

37.6 × 49.6 cm. (single sheet); watermark, very heavy crossed arrows: *cf.* cat. no. 91 (different and evidently later variant of Briquet 6292/6293 than "Palladio's standard paper" of c. 1540); no collector's mark, save for small *70* in gray ink on *verso*.

Light siena ink, over heavy incising and some pencil underdrawing; rough pencil lines on right margin; inscribed with measures in feet.

Image unpublished: *cf.* Arts Council 1975, p. 252, no. 456 (Burns).

The Trustees of the Chatsworth Settlement.

This spendid drawing was restored to Palladio's corpus by a notice in Burns's Arts Council catalogue of 1975, although the omission of an upper pyramid caused Burns to question whether the sheet did in fact pertain to the Mausoleum. However, the description of the Mausoleum's pyramidal steps in the account of Pliny the Elder (*Natural History* xxxvi:30–31) is the most ambiguous part of a confused account; and Vitruvius, the other principal antique source for the structure (fragments of which were not excavated until 1857), omits altogether any reference to such a feature. Thus Palladio, working to the commission of an illustration for the text of *Vitruvius*, may have felt that the five diminishing steps between his magnificent

main facade and the supporting tall podium constituted an adequate homage to Pliny.

But in fact there also survives a preliminary drawing for the upper zone (mentioned but unidentified by Burns; inventoried in the Devonshire Collections, RIBA, as Chiswick sheet 28; 24.6 × 37.3 cm., with design of identical dimensions and form save for unfluted column shafts), above which Palladio has lightly penciled the alternatives of three small sequential pediments, a square central attic, or an embracing pedimental "pyramid." In our more finished drawing on Chiswick 26 exhibited here, he may have deferred making a decision in favor of one or the other of these choices simply because of the reduced space at the top of the sheet. He presumably would have resolved this issue one way or another had the design been selected by Barbaro for publication.

A curious series of clues confirms the identification of our main sheet, and at the same time links it to another heretofore enigmatic Palladian drawing. This latter is the very beautiful "tempietto-tabernacle" (cat. no 46 *recto*) shown here, whose secure dating to this period is assured by the identity of all its architectural motifs and drafting techniques to those on the small villa facade of 1547/48 (cat. no. 68), and of its mask-supported garland festoons to those on the Rialto bridge project of 1554 (cat. no. 70). These dates fall precisely within the period of Daniele Barbaro's "nine years' work" on his Vitruvian edition of 1556, which thus began (presumably with Palladio's col-

71

46 *recto*

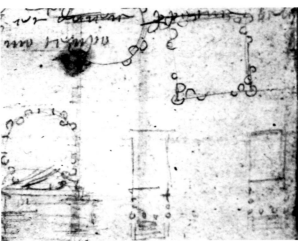

Figure 47

laboration) in 1547. We are therefore justified in assuming a potential Vitruvian context for the "tempietto."

And in fact the tempietto drawing and our main Mausoleum sheet are both given exactly such a Vitruvian destination by a series of tiny plan sketches that Palladio jotted on the edges of a draft letter (RIBA XVI/9-B *verso*) to Gian Giacomo Leonardi, Venetian ambassador of the Duke of Urbino, and an expert on military architecture. Palladio's letter concerns a model for the port of Pesaro, and either the subject matter or Leonardi's architectural expertise evidently called to mind Vitruvius's enthusiastic report of the port and fortifications at Halicarnassus (II:viii:11), for Andrea has annotated the draft with sketches of the theatre, shrine of Venus and forum which Vitruvius described. The draft letter also contains sketches of a large square structure whose sides are symmetrically decorated with niches between engaged columns: the concept appears nowhere else in Palladio's work save on the corresponding podium of our Mausoleum reconstruction (fig. 47).

On the left, immediately adjacent to the most fully developed of these "Mausoleum" plans, Palladio twice sketches the plan of a small circular structure with eight engaged columns, flanking portals or pedestals: the parallel with our "tempietto" elevation is as exact as it is unique, and justifies that drawing's tentative identification as a possible reconstruction (on the analogy of the round "temple of Vesta" in cat. no. 24?) of a temple to the feminine deity of King Mausolus's "shrine of Venus."

The fact that these "Halicarnassian" drawings are somewhat more fanciful than Daniele Barbaro's Aristotelian practicality might have countenanced could well explain why they remained unpublished.

---

72. PLAN OF THE ROMAN THEATRE AT VICENZA, SUBSEQUENTLY ADAPTED FOR BARBARO'S *VITRUVIUS*; AND SKETCH OF PLAN PROJECT FOR VILLA MOCENIGO, DOLO (III)

Early 1540s (*recto*), and 1554 (*verso*)

RIBA: Palladio X/1 *recto* and *verso*.

28.7 × 41.1 cm. (single sheet); watermark, crossed arrows with star (variant of Briquet 6292/6293), "Palladio's standard paper" of c. 1540; Talman 49 mark on *verso*.

Reddish siena ink, warm beige wash; *recto* inscribed in epsilon handwriting (at two periods) with measures in feet; *verso* inscribed in later hand "*Brolo,*" "[*C*]*ortile da* [?] *Batere* [?]*,*" and with measures in *pertiche* and feet.

Zorzi 1959, p. 95, fig. 224 (*recto*); Forssman 1965, pp. 58–59, fig. 26 (*verso*); Spielmann 1966, p. 140, no. 22, fig. 13 (*recto*); Zorzi 1969, pp. 91–92, fig. 147 (*verso*), p. 240, fig. 450 (*recto*); Magagnato 1972, p. 140, fig. 74 (*recto*); Puppi 1972, p. 44, fig. ix; Mostra 1973, p. 144 (*recto* and *verso*—Burns); Puppi 1973, p. 343, fig. 466 (*recto*), p. 360 (*verso*); Puppi 1974, p. 292, fig. 157 (*recto*); Arts Council 1975, p. 45, no. 69 (*recto*), and p. 223, no. 393 (*verso*—both Burns).

Royal Institute of British Architects, London.

The striking and celebrated drawings on this sheet at first glance might seem to date from Palladio's maturity, since both refer to the Vitruvian interests that culminated in his illustrations to Barbaro's translation and commentary of 1556. But the paper on which they are drawn is one that Palladio used most frequently in the early 1540s, and his handwriting on the theatre plan still uses epsilons. The latter drawing may indeed be one of the last to retain this feature: its clear, delicate lines and symmetrically centered inscriptions do make it transitional to the Vitruvian drawings of the years around 1550, and in fact Palladio reused it almost unchanged for the Barbaro edition (fig. 48), adding only another file of rooms and a rear colonnade to the stage building, very much on the model of Serlio's 1540 publication of the theatre at Pola (*cf.* cat. no. 17). There was so little left of the great Teatro Berga of Vicenza, even in Palladio's day, that the addition can hardly be condemned for changing the archaeological "accuracy" of his rendition. The small details of its sections (one extended in perspective) are standard derivations from early sketchbooks, and reinforce the rather abstract character of Palladio's reconstructed plan. We have seen him returning to it in sketching a theatre for the ideal re-creation of Halicarnassus (cat. no. 71), and his inclusion of it on that sheet of 1554, with the triangular scenery panels that appear in its 1556 publication but are missing from the 1540s plan, is one of the clearest indications of its return to a prominent place in his portfolio during the period of preparation of Barbaro's *Vitruvius*.

As we have seen (cat. nos. 56, 57), the first projects for a great riverside villa of Leonardo and Marina Mocenigo at Dolo on the Brenta can be dated to a relatively short period following their marriage of 26 November 1544. The present sketch represents a renewed campaign of a decade later, and of Palladio's five projects it shows the most fidelity to the site when compared with an actual land survey (fig. 49; *cf.* cat. no. 56). The sketch reveals a degree of detail that suggests a personal visit by Palladio during his travels to and from Venice along the Brenta. Since we can now document construction at Dolo to have begun in August of 1554 (cat. no. 73), and since we know Palladio spent a large part of that year in the company of Daniele Barbaro, we can thus consider his villa sketch on the *verso* of this Vitruvian theatre drawing to be a "side effect" of one of the trips he made to Venice for consultations with Daniele in that same year.

The drawing has a distinguished place in the history of architecture because of its introduction of a motif which not only was to become characteristic of Palladio but was destined to revolutionize Late Renaissance, Baroque, and Neoclassical planning. This is the large curving colonnade which Palladio here for the first time sketches over his cancelled rectilinear service building, as a frame to the entrance court. He quickly became entranced by it: the sketch project of Dolo IV (cat. no. 73) shows the motif as a wide pair of welcoming arms, and the *Quattro Libri* project of Dolo V (fig. 50) presents it as a symmetrical scheme, front and back. "Thes circular logges" fascinated Inigo Jones (Allsopp 1970, p. 33), and Tait has provocatively suggested (1970, p. 235) that through his enthusiastic adoption of the form, "this villa was indeed the root of the English Palladian movement."

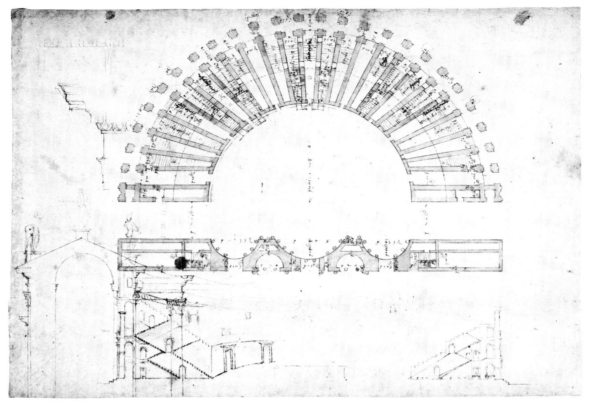

72 verso

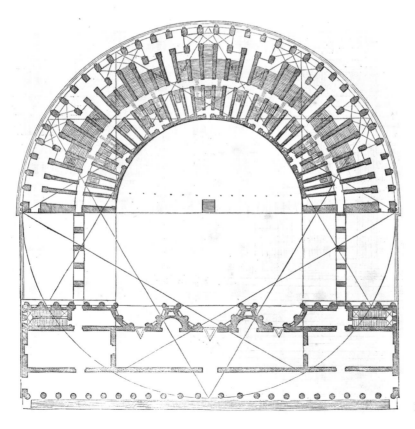

Figure 48

125

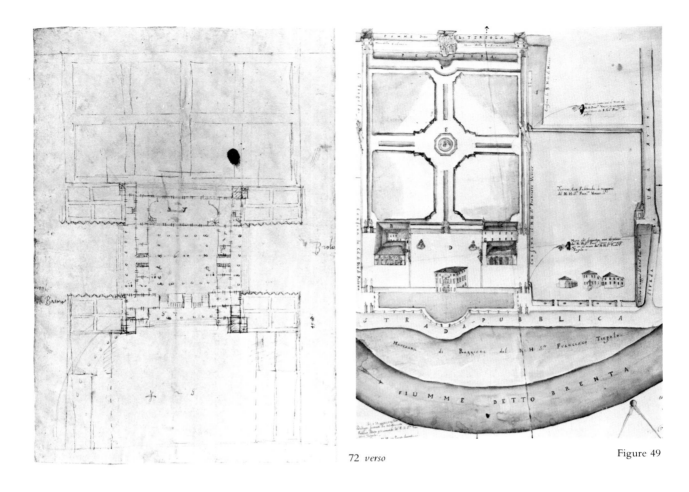

72 *verso*

Figure 49

73. SKETCH OF PLAN PROJECT FOR VILLA MOCENIGO, DOLO (IV)

1554

RIBA: Palladio X/2 *recto*.

43.5 × 28.5 cm. (single sheet); no watermark visible; Talman 49 mark on *recto*.

Gray-brown umber ink, inscribed with measures in feet (erasures of earlier inscriptions in epsilon handwriting, beside steps). *Verso*, SECTION OF ROMAN THEATRE, VICENZA; umber ink; Zorzi 1959, p. 95, fig. 225; Spielmann 1966, p. 158, no. 133; Zorzi 1969, p. 92, fig. 453; Puppi 1974, p. 292, fig. 138.

Burger 1909, p. 120, fig. 47:2; Zorzi 1959, p. 103, fig. 258; Spielmann 1966, p. 177, no. 249; Zorzi 1969, p. 92, fig. 148; Puppi 1972, p. 44, fig. xi; Mostra 1973, p. 144, fig. 150 (Burns); Puppi 1973, pp. 360–361, fig. 495; Arts Council 1975, p. 223, no. 393 (Burns).

Royal Institute of British Architects, London.

The history of this sheet is intimately associated with the preceding (cat. no 72), since two of its images (a pair of tombs on the lower part of the *recto,* here masked), drawn in the early 1540s, were plan reconstructions of Roman antiquites for which Palladio has provided labels in his earliest handwriting; the *verso* had subsequently been used to sketch a section through the *cavea* of the Teatro Berga of Vicenza, and is annotated in mature handwriting. In the course of consultations with Daniele Barbaro concerning the adaptation of the theatre drawings as illustrations for their joint edition of *Vitruvius,* Palladio would have been carrying the still partially blank sheet with him as he passed the site of the Mocenigo villa at Dolo on the Brenta, standing as it does alongside both the land and water routes to Venice. We can now document the moment of this passing consultation at Dolo with precision: for in addition to the near certainty of Barbaro's accompanying the architect to Rome for extended discussions of antiquities in 1554, we also know specifically that Palladio was in Venice on 26 July of that year, undoubtedly to confer with Daniele about the rapidly approaching publication of the *Vitruvius* (*cf.* Lewis 1972, p. 385, for the document).

A newly discovered portfolio of "Drawings and Receipts for the Building of the Palace at Dolo, that is near Fiesso" deriving from a private archive of the Mocenigo family allows us to date the commencement of Leonardo Mocenigo's villa on the Brenta, so long considered a mere fantasy from the *Quattro Libri* (*cf.* cat. no. 56), to the very month

126

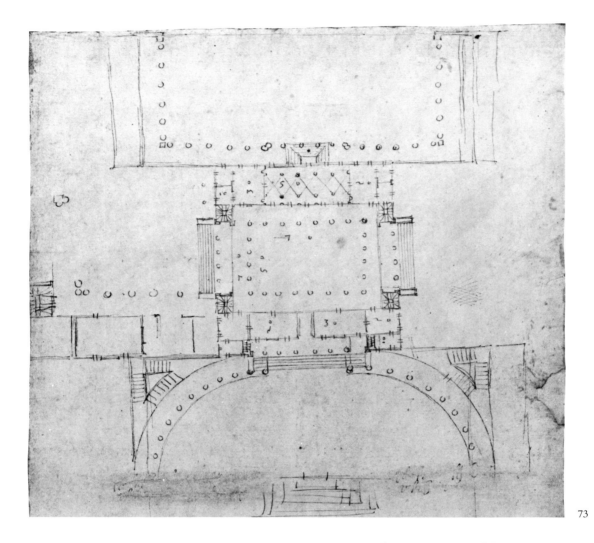

73

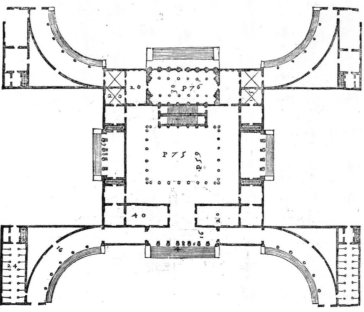

Figure 50

of Palladio's midsummer visit to Venice in 1554. In February of that year Palladio had arranged for a Venetian stonemason, a Master Antonio, to begin work on the large number of carved stones that were to be used in the grandiose project; from the attached drawings we learn that the villa plan was very close to that of Palladio's earliest proposal, on cat. no. 56. Antonio was paid periodically from 14 August through 6 October 1554. We can thus understand one of the necessities for Palladio's presence in the city during the last week of July, and can postulate that he would have been occupied also at least through the first fortnight of August in completing for Master Antonio the working drawings of profiles and sections that are mentioned by the documents. It would therefore evidently have been during one of Palladio's trips into Venice for this purpose, during the summer of 1554, that he would have produced the two beautiful quick sketches—on sheets previously used for the Vitruvian theatre, and present for that reason in his traveling portfolio—in a last attempt to obtain Leonardo Mocenigo's approval of a still grander scheme for the villa about to rise on the banks of the Brenta.

Palladio, presumably through the exhibition of his new sketches, seems to have been persuasive enough to occasion a substantial delay in the execution of the earlier plan, for when we next hear about the works for Dolo (in September of 1561), Master Antonio has died and his stonework for the villa is being sold by his son Silvestro to a Master Pasqualin. Pasqualin executed the building speedily, under Palladio's supervision: by 1563 painting was in progress and the gardens were being carefully laid out, and in 1564 the garden gates were ordered and the last glazing was installed in the main house. The Palladian palace at Dolo stood for barely twenty years, however, for Leonardo Mocenigo died in the plague months of December 1575–January 1576, and his son Alvise commissioned a drastic remodeling of the whole house. It was rebuilt in 1581–82, and its facades so thoroughly reworked that Inigo Jones was unable to recognize any trace of a Palladian design when he visited Dolo in 1613–14. The house stood in the form we see in Costa's print and Brandolese's map (fig. 49) until it was demolished in 1835. Palladio, in the meantime, published a final fifth version of his grandiose project in the *Quattro Libri* of 1570 (II:xvii: 78—fig. 50) as a memorial to his own Vitruvian visions.

CHAPTER FIVE

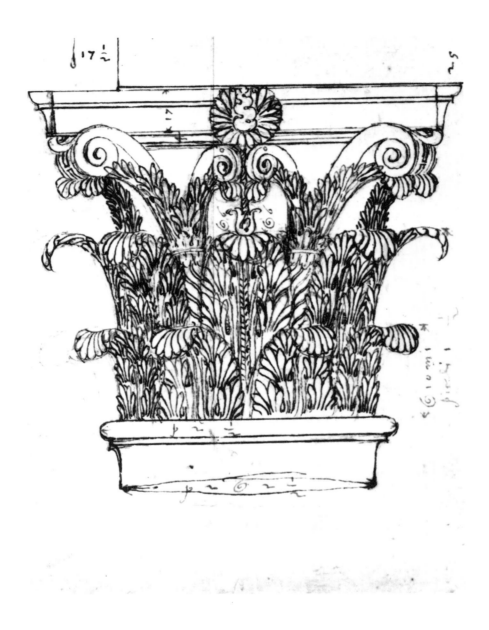

The Experience of Rome (I):

Reconstructions of the Imperial Baths

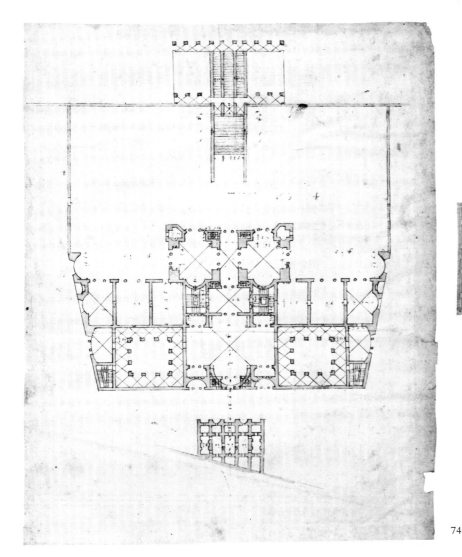

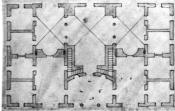

Figure 51

74

74. RECONSTRUCTED PLAN OF THE BATHS OF TITUS, ROME

c. 1541 RIBA: Palladio II/1.

36.3 × 28.1 cm. (single sheet); no watermark; no collector's mark (Burlington purchase, 1719).

Reddish-brown siena ink with sepia-rose wash; inscribed with measures in feet and *pertiche,* of which a scale of 5 = 18 mm.

Burlington 1730, p. 31, pl. 5; Bertotti-Scamozzi 1785/1797, p. 21, pl. 5; Krencker 1929, p. 265, fig. 396; Zorzi 1959, p. 65, fig. 90; Spielmann 1966, p. 163, no. 166, fig. 92; Boëthius/Ward-Perkins 1970, p. 226, fig. 94.

Royal Institute of British Architects, London.

Palladio devoted much of his working life to a continuing study of the great Roman Imperial bath complexes. He was drawn to the baths by previous architects' renderings which he could have seen through sketchbooks (*e.g.* fig. 52), or through such images as Serlio had published in 1540 of the Baths of Caracalla, Diocletian and Constantine (*e.g.* fig. 53); but he was also attracted to these spectacular monuments by the imposing remains of the structures themselves, with which he became familiar during his own visits to Rome between 1541 and 1554.

These ruins were generally much better preserved in the 16th century than they are today, and this impressively complete drawing of the great forerunner of the whole type, the public bathing establishment which the Emperor Titus built in A.D. 79–80 to celebrate the opening of the Colosseum, is a perfect illustration of the point. The only remnants that survive today are fragments of one of the porticoes, so that our entire knowledge of it as a monumental whole depends exclusively on Palladio. Yet it is by no means clear on what authority Palladio's image was composed. There are no obvious sketchbook prototypes that are equally detailed, yet he was in Rome so briefly in the fall of 1541 that it seems dangerous to assume that he could have made the necessary archaeological test pits and on-site measurements himself. He even tells us, on captions to other drawings, that "these baths, opposite the center of the Colosseum at the foot of the Esquiline Hill, are very badly ruined."

This important drawing is definitely not a late work, in

130

which Palladio could have availed himself of years of familiarity with the surviving remains. On the contrary, its drafting style clearly ties it to the early 1540s (though its inscriptions may have been added a bit later, as was often the case). Indeed, a firm piece of evidence for such a date, which seems not yet to have been discussed, is a plan for a bath-like project for the Villa Gazoto at Bertesina (RIBA XVI/16-C, fig. 51), whose hall is unquestionably derived from the triple-vaulted double-apsed hall at the upper center of this plan. Since the Bertesina sheet cannot date later than c. 1542, the plan of Titus's baths must certainly have entered Palladio's consciousness through his Roman sojourn of 1541, either through borrowed images or personal experience. The present sheet is thus most plausibly identified as a studio piece based on prior studies by Palladio or a near contemporary.

75. RECONSTRUCTION SKETCH PLANS OF THE BATHS OF AGRIPPA, ROME

c. 1554

RIBA: Palladio VII/6 verso.

31.2 × 21.7 (original drafted sheet; has been pieced by two blank additions, at bottom and right); watermark, an orb with star; laid lines 30 mm. apart (cf. Briquet 3077); no collector's mark (Burlington purchase, 1719).

Reddish siena ink. Recto. SKETCHES OF BATHS OF AGRIPPA AND SKETCH PLAN OF THE "TEATRO MARITTIMO" OF HADRIAN'S VILLA, TIVOLI; reddish siena ink, with sums in umber-brown ink; Zorzi 1959, p. 72, fig. 141; Spielmann 1966, p. 167, no. 190, fig. 104; D'Ossat 1973, p. 35, fig. 17; Arts Council 1975, p. 249, no. 445 (Burns—as verso).

Zorzi 1959, p. 72, fig. 142; Ackerman 1966/1977, pp. 171–174, fig. 93; Spielmann 1966, pp. 166–167, no. 189, fig. 103; Zorzi 1967, pp. 33–34, fig. 40; Puppi 1973, pp. 273–274, fig. 339 (detail of tombs).

Royal Institute of British Architects, London.

These superbly free and inventive sketches show Palladio experimenting with a series of ideal reconstructions of the Baths of Agrippa. They had been constructed in c. 25-12 B.C., to the south of the original Agrippan Pantheon and Basilica of Neptune, and apparently had exercised a formative influence on the development of the classical Imperial bath that appeared in the succeeding century (cf. cat. no. 74). But a disastrous fire in A.D. 80 destroyed most of Agrippa's monumental buildings in the Campus Martius, and a convincing restoration of his bath complex has been notoriously difficult.

While Palladio's sketches on this sheet are mostly fanciful and inventive, they are nonetheless based on reliable precedent. On one of his earliest visits he had made a large survey plan (RIBA IX/14 verso) which, although fragmentary, is a marvel of archaeological accuracy: surviving walls are indicated by shading, while the hypothetical ones are left in outline; and its rendition of the partly assymmetrical south halls appears as an almost miraculous replica of the ancient drawing on the Severan marble plan of Rome (Boëthius and Ward-Perkins 1970, p. 207, fig. 87). Unfortunately the whole of the axis that would have extended the bath complex toward the back of Hadrian's reconstructed Pantheon had vanished even before the 16th century, leaving only two great apses that could be construed as framing a vast central hall. It is on the plausible development of the space between these elements that Palladio lavishes his attention in this sheet, with the addition

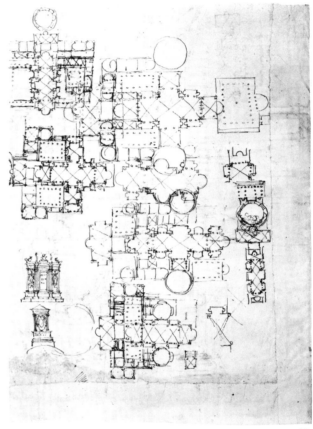

75

of flanking halls and colonnaded courts that are wholly imaginary. (These configurations formed the basis for his final plan on the Vicenza drawing D-33, which was to achieve unwarranted but extensive publication through Lord Burlington's and Bertotti-Scamozzi's editions of the 18th century.)

Zorzi proposed that the tomb monuments sketched at the lower left probably document Palladio's design of the Gritti tombs in the chancel of San Francesco della Vigna in Venice, and the connection is convincing. As Puppi has cautioned, however, Zorzi's date of 1548 is unsupported; actually, the style of draftsmanship on the sheet as a whole links it most clearly to the sketches on RIBA XVI/9-B verso (cat. no. 71, fig. 47), and establishes a persuasive date of c. 1554.

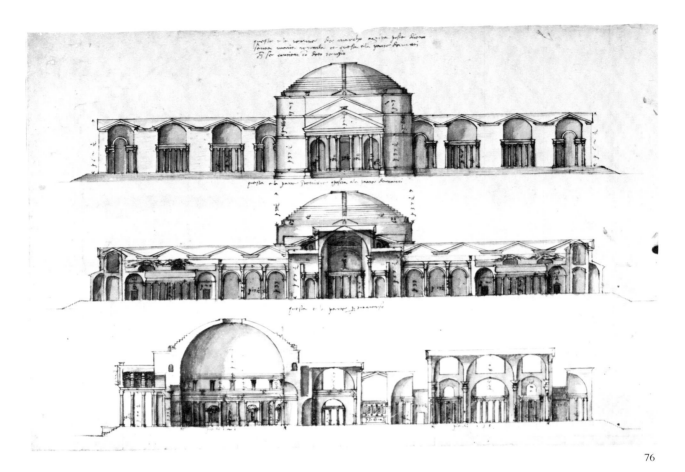

76. RECONSTRUCTED FACADE AND SECTIONS OF THE BATHS OF AGRIPPA (INCORPORATING THE PANTHEON OF HADRIAN), ROME

1550s?

RIBA: Palladio VII/3.

28.7 × 42.0 cm. (single sheet); countermark AP in upper left corner; laid lines 29 mm. apart; no collector's mark (Burlington purchase, 1719).

Reddish siena ink with warm siena wash; inscribed in mature handwriting with labels, and measures in feet.

Burlington 1730, pp. 23–26, pl. 2; Bertotti-Scamozzi 1785/1797, p. 16, pl. 2; Zorzi 1959, p. 72, fig. 143; Spielmann 1966, p. 167, no. 196; Arts Council 1975, p. 249, fig. 446 (Burns).

Royal Institute of British Architects, London.

These powerful, impressive images incorporate the results of Palladio's ideal re-creation of the Agrippan baths (cat. no. 75), and translate his reconstruction dramatically into view by means of the vertical development of orthogonal projections, with three-dimensional illusion accomplished through bold contrasts of color and light and shade.

Of the north facade elevation at the top Palladio writes, "these are the Baths of Marcus Agrippa behind S. Maria Rotonda [the Pantheon, consecrated as Saint Mary of Ancient Martyrs], and this is the part at the front, which adjoins the church." He gives a simplified but clear view of the existing Pantheon, flanked by wide lateral wings with suites of changing rooms, which he had imaginatively developed as framing elements in his ideal plan. These are further revealed in a complicated but clearly legible central section from the south ("this is the interior part, seen from the other side"), in which we glimpse some of the smaller heated rooms at the extremities, with views onto two sets of courtyards: an outer pair with colonnades ringed by barrel vaults, then large interior ones to accommodate the open pools, whose access corridors open through large triple arcades.

At the center of the whole complex Palladio shows a high, groin-vaulted hall, seen through its short axis in the middle image, and through its long axis in the transverse section at the bottom ("this is the part across the center"). There we find it as the most important element of the bath building proper, detached from a lesser duplicate of itself (alongside the Hadrianic rotunda) by means of a small open court with screens of columned niches. It represents Palladio's reconstitution of the lost structure that would have stood between the surviving but distant double apses (cat. no. 75), here seen as tall, half-domed hemicycles establishing great volumetric containers of space, in a hierarchy of progressively loftier and larger bays culminating in the vast central hall.

77. UNFINISHED LONGITUDINAL SECTION OF THE GREAT HALL OF AN IMPERIAL BATH BUILDING

Early 1570s?

RIBA: Palladio V/8.

21.7 × 28.3 cm. (single sheet); watermark, anchor in circle with star; laid lines 32 mm. apart (*cf.* Mošin 1461: Venice 1573 *ff.*); Talman 49 mark on *verso*.

Umber-brown ink on left half, with black-brown on right; light blue-green wash for middle distance, and deep green-gray wash for space behind; elaborate system of incised lines.

Zorzi 1959, p. 71, fig. 133; Spielmann 1966, p. 162, no. 158 (as Burlington purchase [*sic*], and as workshop (?), after 1570); Paris 1975, p. 36 (note and illustration).

Royal Institute of British Architects, London.

This spectacular drawing is unusual to the point of uniqueness in Palladio's work, both for the scale of its images from antiquity, and especially for its color. It has usually been identified as showing the *frigidarium* of the Baths of Diocletian (which space was converted by Michelangelo in 1561 into the nave of a new church for Saint Mary of the Angels), but both the existing structure and Palladio's known rendition of it (on RIBA V/2) suggest otherwise. The present section in fact bears less resemblance to the Diocletian section (RIBA V/2) than to the great thermal hall of the Baths of Agrippa shown in the preceding entry (cat. no. 76).

Most importantly for this identification, the cornice of the colossal order (whose columns are suggested here by incised lines) is shown near the level of the crown of the most distant central arch, rather than near its base as in the Diocletian hall. The use of dark wash to indicate interior spaces beyond the hall is no more relevant to the Diocletian baths than to Palladio's reconstruction of the Agrippan, and thus may be a later addition. Both monuments (in Palladio's reconstruction) had column screens giving directly or through windows onto open spaces, with cold plunges behind the screens in the lateral bays, and open pools in the courts beyond. It is thus relevant to note that this drawing (uniquely among Palladio's baths, save for the Agrippan plan preserved in Vicenza) did not remain at Maser and Venice to be bought by Lord Burlington from the Barbaro-Trevisan descendants in 1719, but came through Jones and Webb, and was bought by Burlington in 1721 from John Talman.

78

78. COLUMN BASES AND CAPITALS, WITH ENTABLATURES, OF THE TEMPLE OF HADRIAN (RIGHT), AND THE BATHS OF CARACALLA (LEFT)

Early 1550s

RIBA: Palladio VI/9.

30.9 × 41.1 cm. (single sheet, with considerable staining and wear at left and top; left corners lost); watermark, angel in oval with star; laid lines 28 mm. apart (*cf.* Briquet 647); no collector's mark (Burlington purchase, 1719).

Dark umber-brown siena ink, on pencil underdrawing; inscribed in mature handwriting (in at least two campaigns) with later labels and descriptions, and with (mostly much earlier) measures in feet, with various scales (4 units = 20 mm., left, and 4 units = 32 mm., right) and modules.

Burlington 1730, pp. 55–57, pl. 24 (Hadrianeum), pl. 22 (Caracalla); Bertotti-Scamozzi 1785/1797, p. 34, pl. 24 (Hadrianeum), pl. 22 (Caracalla); Zorzi 1959, p. 69, fig. 120; Zorzi 1965, p. 158, figs. 75/79; Spielmann 1966, p. 160, no. 149, fig. 82; Paris 1975, p. 36 (note and ill.).

Royal Institute of British Architects, London.

This spectacular sheet presents two of the most splendidly decorated orders of Roman Imperial architecture, and in their juxtaposition Palladio anticipates the stylistic comparisons of modern art-historical analysis. The substantially surviving Temple of the Deified Hadrian, of A.D. 138–145, reflects in its ornament one of the revolutions which that most architecturally minded of all emperors achieved, in this case by his importation of models and even workmen from Greece and Asia Minor: namely, an almost austere clarity of design, overlaid with elaborate surface ornament as well as larger decorative elements such as the convex or "pulvinated" frieze. Palladio brilliantly achieves these same effects with his strong, clear profiles and delicately embroidered ornamentation.

The colossal composite order on the left side of the page comes from the great open pool on the north side of Caracalla's baths: as Palladio comments in the caption, he has marked with the letter G the column screens in which it appears on the bottom section in cat. no. 79, and on the plan in cat. no. 80. Although the baths were finished a full two generations after the Hadrianeum (being built between A.D. 206 and 216), their ornamental details revert to models created under the Flavian emperors of the first century—as for example in the decorative bands below and above the freize, the "arrow-heads" in the egg-and-dart molding just above the intermediate dentils, and a general tendency toward exuberant richness of detail, together with strong effects of light and shade (Robertson 1929/1959, pp. 215–217, 261). Since the Baths of Caracalla may well have been executed by workmen trained on the restoration of the Flavian Palace (von Blanckenhagen 1940, pp. 90–99), this reversion may easily be explained; it is equally indicative that Caracalla's Temple of Serapis (cat. no. 105) consciously revived the "eastern" ornament of the Hadrianeum (Boëthius/Ward-Perkins 1970, pp. 274–275). As the most unusual types in the repertory of Roman ornament, Palladio devoted to these last an especial attention and sympathy; they form a major ingredient, and their drafted images are perfect exemplars of what we have here identified as his "first decorated style," of c. 1548–c. 1554 (see esp. cat. no. 70).

134

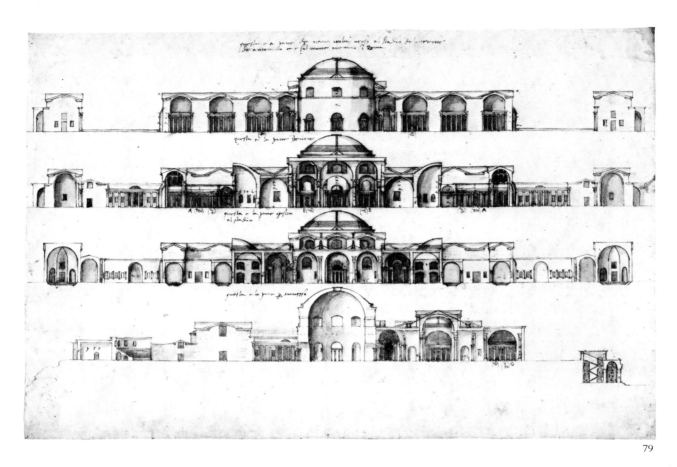

79. RECONSTRUCTED FACADES AND SECTIONS OF THE BATHS OF CARACALLA, ROME

1540s

RIBA: Palladio VI/4.

28.8 × 43.2 cm. (single sheet); watermark, probably anchor in oval with star (?); laid lines 37 mm. apart; no collector's mark (Burlington purchase, 1719).

Dark brown siena ink, with unusually dense siena wash; inscribed in mature handwriting (in two campaigns) with later labels and with earlier measures in feet.

Burlington 1730, pp. 40–41, pl. 10; Bertotti-Scamozzi 1785/1797, p. 25, pl. 10; Loukomski 1938, fig. on p. 26; Zorzi 1959, p. 68, fig. 115; Pane 1961, p. 76, fig. 89:1; Ackerman 1966/1977, p. 172, fig. 92; Spielmann 1966, p. 159, no. 143, fig. 83; Ackerman, 1967, p. 12, fig. 22; Bieganski 1968, p. 20, fig. 6; Mostra 1973, p. 142 (Burns); Paris 1975, p. 36 (note and ill.).

Royal Institute of British Architects, London.

Palladio's celebrated reconstruction drawings of the Baths of Caracalla do full justice to one of the most impressive monuments in the whole history of architecture. As the third-century culmination of the fully developed Imperial bathing establishment, whose type had been successively refined since the mid-first century baths of Nero and Titus (cat. no. 75), the Baths as here reconstructed present in perfected form the spectacular achievements of High Imperial concrete vaulting—which Palladio evidently understood, but could not adequately study in the damaged superstructure—and an equally extraordinary planimetric sophistication; on these well-preserved remains Palladio in fact based many of his essential architectural principles of bilateral symmetry, interlocking vistas and hierarchy of parts (Ackerman 1966/1977, pp. 171–174).

He begins his beautiful four-part plate with what Ward-Perkins has characterized (1970, p. 272) as the most interesting and expressive facade of an Imperial bath, the great southwest elevation, and the parallel with his restored north facade of the *Thermae Agrippae* (cat. no. 76) reveals the cogency of that reconstruction. This time it is the great Pantheon-like *caldarium,* boldly projecting by more than half its circumference from the line of the facade, that Palladio emphasizes as the dominant feature of the whole. With an interior span of 115 feet this vast rotunda was more than four-fifths the diameter of the Pantheon itself, and much taller; although in relation to it the huge hall of the *frigidarium* would have loomed higher, in a more balanced spatial equipoise (it stands in front of the rotunda in Palladio's second and third views—respectively a longitudinal section and a partially cut-away north elevation—and at right center in his transverse section, at the bottom). Palladio shows both these colossal spaces, perhaps correctly, as united formally and luminously through their great rings and rows of clerestory windows at identical heights. He suggests the perceptual excitement and exhilaration that would be engendered by coming upon their crescendo of dramatic shapes, as culminating experiences in the symmetrical twin circuits that were followed around the outer sequence of bathing rooms. At the climax of the architectural composition, marking the intersection of the longitudinal axis and the heart of the central core (the main transverse axis of *caldarium-tepidarium-frigidarium* and open pool), the gigantic hall of the *frigidarium* was punctuated as Palladio shows it in his sections by the vast monothic shafts of colossal columns, above which its soaring groin vaults would have appeared more to be restrained in the manner of insubstantial, billowing colored canopies than actually supported as titanic shells of concrete masonry. At 170 feet long by 82 wide by more than 100 feet high, this perhaps most sublime of all antique secular spaces richly

deserved the careful attention Palladio devoted to its reconstructions, as well as those of its predecessors (*cf.* cat. no. 77). He achieved one comparable though more human-scale reminiscence of it, with his "thermal hall" as the groin-vaulted cruciform *salone* of the Villa Foscari at Malcontenta (fig. 56). In that plan the prototypical lessons of the Roman baths—bilateral symmetry, interlocking vistas, and hieratic spatial sequences—culminate in an interior whose austere grandeur is brilliantly accentuated by Palladio's, Franco's, and Zelotti's lavish fresco decorations (*cf.* cat. no. 87), in a striking demonstration of the degree to which Palladio understood and espoused the principles of High Imperial classic architecture.

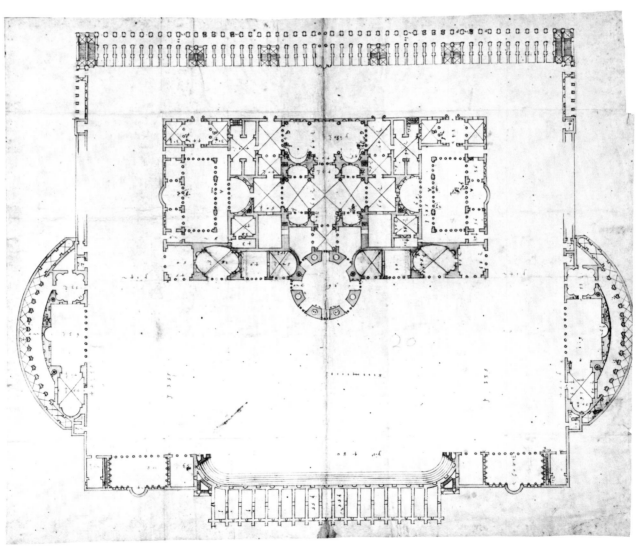

80

80. RECONSTRUCTED PLAN OF THE BATHS OF CARACALLA, ROME

1540s

RIBA: Palladio VI/1.

39.5 × 46.5 cm. (single sheet; left edge trimmed at the corners); watermark, anchor in circle with star; countermark in upper left corner is cut, but apparently shows part of *B*; laid lines 34 mm. apart; (*cf.* Mošin 895/862); no collector's mark (Burlington purchase, 1719).

Original dark umber ink, with later light reddish siena ink and pencil for added details and measures; inscribed (in at least two campaigns) with measures in feet, and scale of 10 units = 40 mm.

Burlington 1730, pp. 39–40, pl. 9; Bertotti-Scamozzi 1785/1797, p. 25, pl. 9; Zorzi 1959, p. 68, fig. 110; Spielmann 1966, p. 159, no. 142, fig. 84; Mostra 1973, p. 141 (Burns).

Royal Institute of British Architects, London.

The cyclopean complex of the largest and finest Imperial Roman bath is organized around the sides and at the center of an enormous quadrangular platform, 1100 feet on a side, enclosing a vast terrace some 20 feet high, and almost 50 acres in extent. On a map of Rome it looms larger than virtually any other structure; the main bath building alone, which is set in the northern half so as to leave the south terrace open for gardens, at 700 by 360 feet is equally as wide and somewhat longer than St. Peter's. This stupendous scale has combined with a most unusually complete preservation (of the substructures and walls—except the rotunda's—though not of the vaults), to make the monument consistently popular among students of antiquity: indeed, we have at least three earlier drafted reconstructions against which to judge the achievement of Palladio's version on this sheet.

By far the best of these is the "extremely fine plan" published by Ashby (1902, p. 21) from fol. 22 in the Codex Coner of c. 1515, which is an extraordinary early achievement of accurate archaeological investigation. We have already commented on its pioneering use of shaded double lines for standing walls, with open or omitted lines for

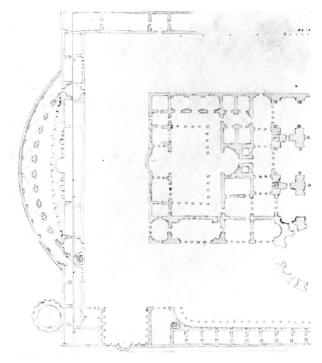

Figure 52

hypothetical ones (cat. no. 75); in all its details it constitutes one of the earliest masterpieces of the modern approach to archaeological precision, and it underlies many of Palladio's best interpretations of obscure points.

A nearly contemporary version (1513–c. 1520) is that on fols. 48 *verso* and 49 *recto* of the Mellon Codex in the Morgan Library (fig. 52—*cf.* cat. no. 25), which is more fully though less reliably reconstructed. It seems to depend from a late 15th-century prototype, rather than a "modern" archaeological investigation from the moment and the circle of Raphael's appointment as Superintendent of Antiquities at the papal court. It does give several interesting

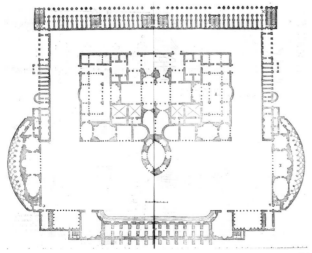

Figure 53

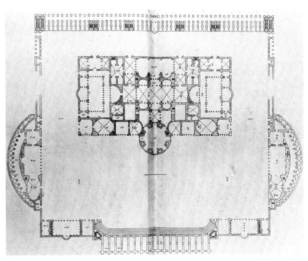

Figure 54

new details for the main block, but it shifts the great segmental-curved exedrae (which contained libraries and other cultural offerings) into axial alignment with the bath building, and thus adversely affects the proportions as well as the design of the whole.

Sebastiano Serlio's large plan issued in 1540 is the first well-known published example (III:88–89—fig. 53), and it too is astonishingly accurate in detail—some of which seems based on the "Coner" prototype—in addition to being fully persuasive as a total restoration (per the "Mellon" type). Palladio's plan in most major respects is an improved copy of the Serlio version, and it is interesting that many of his improvements to Serlio's plates seem to come from a "Coner" prototype. Others may well derive

from on-site corrections (the plan includes some erasures and alternate notations), but in general Palladio's version must be said to sum up a development which was coherent and complete by 1540, rather than representing any major new departure. An element of youthful naïveté that demonstrates the early date of Palladio's rendition is provided by the "anecdotal" double-arched supports at the ends of the stadium seats: these are illusionistic carryovers from his earliest tendencies toward "perspectival" draftsmanship and are of course completely inappropriate on a vertically projected plan. Nevertheless, even Lord Burlington's engravers take over this motif exactly (fig. 54), injecting an artisan's convention into the rarified world of Neoclassicism.

---

81. RECONSTRUCTED PLAN OF THE BATHS OF CONSTANTINE, ROME

Middle or late 1540s

RIBA: Palladio I/1.

51.9 × 31.6 cm. (single sheet); watermark, angel in oval; laid lines approximately 33 mm. apart; (cf. Briquet 644); no collector's mark (Burlington purchase, 1719).

Reddish-brown siena ink, with light beige-brown wash; inscribed in mature handwriting with measures in feet, of which scale of 36 = 23 mm.

Burlington 1730, pp. 50–51, pl. 14; Bertotti-Scamozzi 1785/1797, p. 31, pl. 14; Krencker 1929, p. 282, fig. 422a; Zorzi 1959, p. 65, fig. 84; Speilmann 1966, p. 164, no. 175, fig. 97; Boëthius/Ward-Perkins 1970, pp. 507–508, fig. 193; Puppi 1973, fig. 334.

Royal Institute of British Architects, London.

More than a century after Rome's great sequence of Imperial bath buildings had culminated in the masterpiece of the Baths of Caracalla (cat. no. 78–80), the Emperor Constantine ordered the creation of a final, much smaller, retrospective example; it appeared in the ancient capital at the moment of the pagan Empire's metamorphosis into the Early Christian world of a new state religion, in A.D. 320—just ten years before the Imperial government was shifted to Constantinople. In such a context Palladio's fine plan (which here again is our standard for the perished structure) shows its forms as being fewer and more simply composed, though individually much elaborated. The suites of large south rooms display a striking virtuosity in their varied shapes; the great hall of the *frigidarium* is strongly emphasized in its cruciform character, as the central crossing-point of two great axial sequences; it is formally isolated by a big square space for the open pool to the north, and a large, clearly defined service court on the south, shaped exactly like a Constantinian transept in one of the Emperor's new foundations of the basilican churches. Standing apart at the center of this T-shaped space is an elegantly centralized *tepidarium*, that Palladio shows with four outward-swelling walls of expansive, curvilinear shape. At quite modest scale it is the fitting prelude to one last soaring, domical *caldarium*,

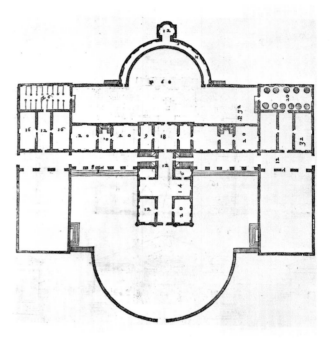

Figure 55

the final triumph of the Imperial bath buildings in Rome. Its representation is also a small masterpiece of clarity and beauty in Palladio's graphic oeuvre: he carefully shades its immense supporting drum, so that the four vast piers that he fills with wash stand out as the basic cylindrical skeleton. This, however, he shows dramatically broken open by three boldly projecting apses, to contain the hot pools around the *caldarium*. Palladio brilliantly differentiates a narrower superstructure with four great double-curving arches above the apses and the *tepidarium*, and further depicts this upper drum as scalloped by very broad, segmentally curved exterior niches—which open, above tiny spiral stair systems, in four great clerestory windows

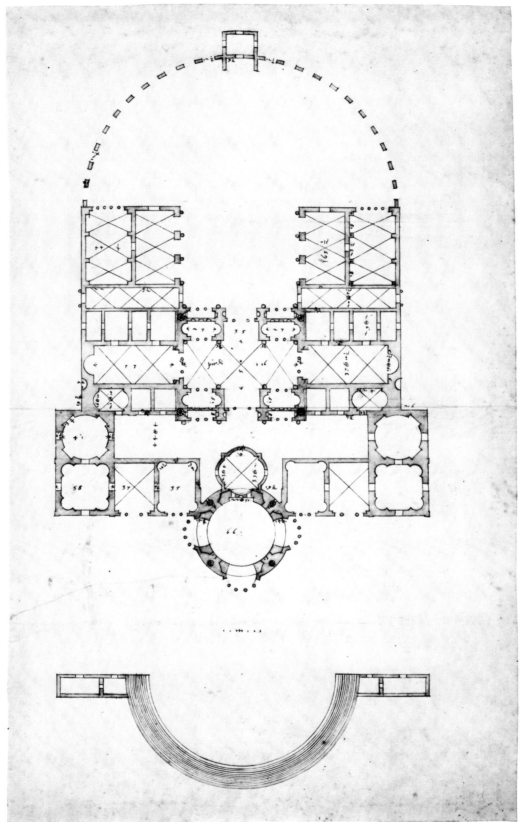

that are rhythmically offset (in an alternating X-axis) to the cardinally aligned cross-axis of the projecting pools below.

The clarity and elegance of Palladio's highly sensitive rendition of this compact and even intimate Late Imperial bath clearly justify our investigation of its resonances in his own work. And immediately, in his 1551–58 design of the Villa Barbaro at Maser (especially as we see it in the *Quattro Libri* plate of 1570, fig. 55) the parallels are striking indeed. The whole general shape of the plan is congruent, with the big southern hemicycles of garden walls (lined by stadium seats on the Quirinal, and driveways at Maser) answered by similar exedrae at the north (an open arcade at the bath, a niched nymphaeum wall at the villa), the latter directly associated in both cases with pairs of service wings extending northward to frame open pools and enclosed gardens, with a small square chamber/grotto at the end of the axes.

The central structures are closely analogous as well, with the powerful projections of the *caldarium* and the main palace block providing boldly three-dimensional frontispieces, to be followed by three major cross-axes (one open-air, between two closed) as their transverse spines are integrated into the longitudinal extensions of the wings. The projecting blocks both have strong internal cross-axes; as we move northward in both complexes, through narrow spaces providing access from the service areas, we emerge into a centralized hall with the longest lateral vistas into the wings (whose alternations of wide and narrow room shapes are identical in the northernmost tiers of both designs), and these halls look directly out into the northern pools, gardens, and exedras, of both configurations. In considering the many similarities in overall conception, general shape, and specific detail, we should note that Palladio devoted a full five lines out of twelve, in his own description of the layout at Maser, to a discussion of its water engineering (1570: II:xiiii:51). On this basis it seems plausible to recognize an evident inspiration of the Maser design (cat. no. 90) in this beautifully coherent plan of the last and most adaptable of the Imperial baths.

CHAPTER SIX

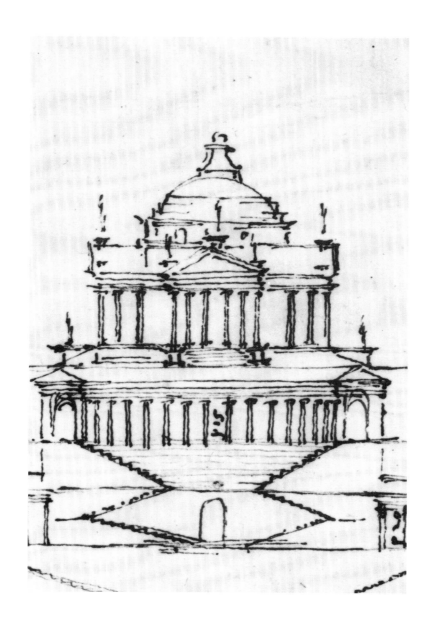

The Experience of Rome (II):
Imperial multi-level monuments restored

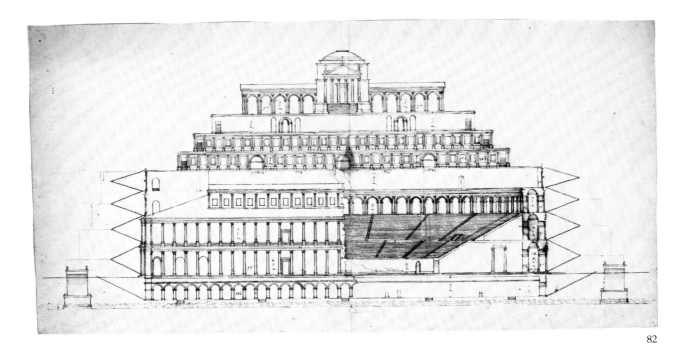

82. RECONSTRUCTED ELEVATION AND PARTIAL SECTION OF THE ROMAN THEATRE, VERONA

Probably early to middle 1550s

RIBA: Palladio IX/10.

27.8 × 54.9 cm. (single sheet); watermark, coronet with star; laid lines 35 mm. apart (*cf.* Briquet 4834); no collector's mark (Burlington purchase, 1719).

Dark siena ink; inscribed in mature handwriting with measurements in feet.

Loukomski 1938, fig. on p. 17; Zorzi 1951, pp. 9–11, fig. 12; Zorzi 1959, p. 94, fig. 219; Forssman 1965, p. 111; Crema 1966, p. 171, fig. 171; Spielmann 1966, p. 155, no. 113, fig. 63; Zorzi 1967, p. 170, fig. 116; Tafuri 1968, p. 68, fig. 41; Zorzi 1969, p. 239, fig. 445; Mostra 1973, p. 143, fig. 147 (Burns); Arts Council 1975, p. 110, fig. 208 (Burns); Verona 1980, p. 60, no. and fig. III, 35 (Franzoni).

Royal Institute of British Architects, London.

This carefully composed masterwork beautifully represents Palladio's most sensitive, but most responsible restoration of ancient monuments. As we have seen (cat. nos. 10–11), the important Roman theatre at Verona stands on the left or east bank of the Adige, at the apex of a sweeping curve made by the river around the promontory of the town, onto the center of which the theatre looks from across the stream. Behind it rises the hill of San Pietro (partly cut by the river into a naturally amphitheatrical shape), whose successive antique, medieval, and Napoleonic fortresses now cover the two uppermost levels shown in Palladio's reconstruction. We have already looked in some detail at the first (cat. no. 10) and second (cat. no. 11) richly articulated terrace walls that are set into the slope of the hill between its crest and the top of the *cavea*, perhaps to provide access from the latter to a monumental complex

such as Palladio restores at the top of the composition here (his connecting stairs at the ends of the terraces, however, are conjectural). Below the niched walls of these terraced walkways Palladio cautiously shows only a plain retaining wall at the top of the *cavea*, though older 16th-century commentators suggested a second superimposed loggia, on the analogy of the two lower ones supporting the sides of the *cavea* (visible in Palladio's cutaway view on the right), whose existence is well attested. Archaeological work of the last two decades suggests that there were in fact two upper loggias (Verona 1980, pp. 55–56 [Franzoni], with figs.); but in defense of our conscientious architect we can note that this result would probably have astonished Vitruvius just as much as it evidently did Andrea.

Recent archaeological findings have proved Palladio's elaborate stage building to be exactly the correct length (*ibid.*, p. 55); he shows its bluntly arcaded basement as washed by the Adige, whose symmetrical bridges frame the whole complex (the Ponte Pietra survives, reconstructed, on the left). The superstructure of the stage building, its towered flanks (left) and the stair systems against the hill, on the other hand, are as conjectural as are the crowning terraces, with their tempietto and flanking arcades.

For all these latter elements, it has usually been suggested that Palladio's reconstruction refers to the impressive plate in Giovanni Caroto's printed compendium *Dele antiqità di Verona* (1560: XIV), which is based in turn on an immense drawing in Caroto's sketchbook (Biblioteca Civica, Verona, Ms. 978, fol. 36 *verso*). But it is worth noting that Palladio's own drawing may predate 1560 as well. The only stylistic indicator through which I can suggest a specific date is provided by the motif of doubled pilasters at the ends of the top-most loggias: these are distinctly rare, but are found in the (shop?) drawing on RIBA XVII/

20, which was executed as a *barchessa* of the Villa Thiene at Cigogna, a work Palladio states in the *Quattro Libri* to have been built by a patron who died in 1556 (Puppi 1973, p. 311). In fact, both the style and content of the present sheet encourage its assignment to these very years of Palladio's work on Roman antiquities for the *Vitruvius* edition, in which of course a theatre was involved (cat. nos. 71–73). When we notice, as a corollary to this suggestion, that Caroto's crowning tempietto is only lightly sketched as a subsequent addition on his sketchbook drawing, and then heavily reworked before the printing of its published plate (Verona 1980, pp. 58/60, figs. III, 33a/III, 33b), we can argue with considerable conviction that the direction of borrowing may well have been reversed. Palladio's superbly coherent image might evidently have proved irresistable to Caroto, who may first have sketched a reminiscence of it in his album, and then added a finished version of it to his plate.

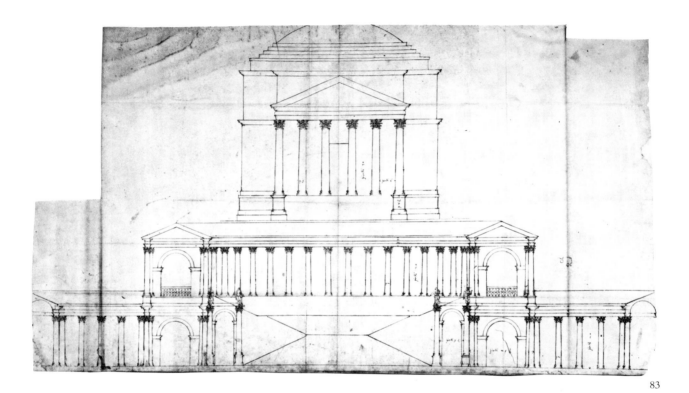

83

83. IDEALIZED RECONSTRUCTION OF THE UPPER TERRACES AND TEMPLE OF FORTUNA PRIMIGENIA, PALESTRINA

Late 1560s

RIBA: Palladio IX/9 *recto.*

45.2 × 76.4 cm. (single sheet); watermark, coronet with star (*cf.* Briquet 4834); no collector's mark (Burlington purchase, 1719).

Umber-brown ink; inscribed in mature handwriting with measures in feet.

Zorzi 1951, p. 151, fig. 5 (cropped to fold on left); Zorzi 1959, p. 85, fig. 204; Spielmann 1966, p. 153, no. 102; Puppi 1973, p. 388, fig. 538; Fancelli 1974, pp. 58–60, 83, 125, fig. 27; Arts Council 1975, p. 250, fig. 449 (Burns).

Royal Institute of British Architects, London.

This grand and imposing drawing is a conceptual hybrid, since it combines the pedimented, Pantheonic rotunda from the top of Palladio's Verona theatre reconstruction (cat. no. 82) with the rather similar terraces of another, earlier site. This was the great Hellenistic sanctuary of Fortuna Primigenia at Praeneste, or Palestrina, at the southern end of the Sabine Hills above the Roman Campagna. Several spots on a steep hillside above the forum of that town had become celebrated in association with an oracle of Fortune that was told by the casting of lots; in a rebuilding under the Roman conqueror Sulla around 80 B.C., these sites were connected through seven superimposed terraces, culminating in a small round temple above a final theatrelike area at the summit. The latter element is represented by the beautiful curving Corinthian hemicycle at the center of Palladio's drawing, with its schematic indications of steps beneath (Palladio's sketch plan of a slightly modified variant

143

is shown on cat. no. 84; modern archaeologists prefer a single axial stair, and a *"cavea"* coming only as far down as Palladio's first zone beneath the hemicycle—that is, roughly to the top of the arcade, which was probably continuous across the center). The hemicycle colonnade, its two-story terminal pavilions, and the rectangular court of the sixth terrace beneath, are all remarkably close to current archaeological restorations (*cf.* Boëthius/Ward Perkins 1970, pp. 140–146, fig. 78–79). But Palladio's massive rotunda dwarfs its substructures in a way he knew to be unfaithful to the remains: he had often drawn a correctly

delicate little tempietto (in plan, on RIBA IX/1; in section, on IX/2, 3, and 5; and in elevation on IX/6), so his choice of a huge Pantheonic hall doubtless reflects his use of such a feature on the Verona theatre reconstruction somewhat earlier. Puppi has plausibly dated the finished Palestrina sheets to Palladio's campaign of the late 1560s of designs for the Villa Trissino at Meledo, which would have the further advantage of bringing this "Pantheon" elevation into a range closely synchronous with his similar drawing of the Romulus tomb (cat. no. 23).

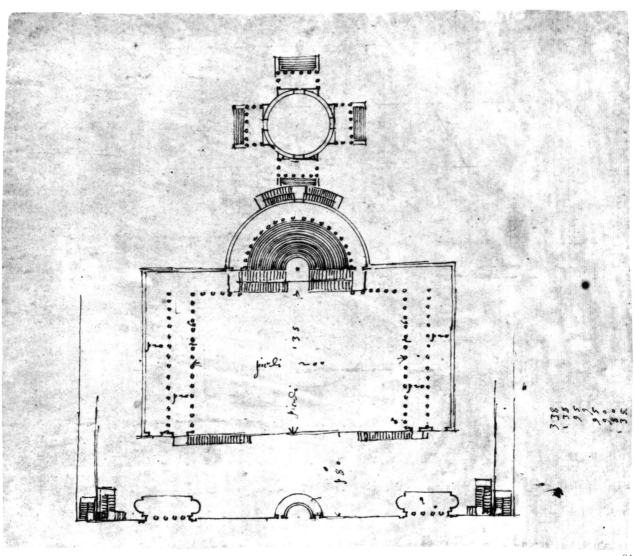

84

84. FANCIFUL SKETCH PLAN OF THE UPPER TERRACES AND TEMPLE OF FORTUNA PRIMIGENIA, PALESTRINA

Late 1560s

RIBA: Palladio IX/8.

24.0 × 27.5 cm. (single sheet); watermark, angel in circle with star; countermark, S C in shield surmounted by trefoil; laid lines 27 mm apart (Briquet 649); no collector's mark (Burlington purchase, 1719).

Dark reddish-brown siena ink; inscribed in mature handwriting with measures in feet.

Burger 1909, p. 113, fig. 44:2; Zorzi 1957, pp. 158–159, fig. 15; Zorzi 1959, p. 89, fig. 210; Spielmann 1966, p. 154, no. 107; Ackerman 1967, p. 18, fig. 36; Semenzato 1968, p. 16, fig. vii; Zorzi 1969, p. 125, fig. 214; Puppi 1972, p. 42, fig. vi; Mostra 1973, p. 143 (Burns); Puppi 1973, pp. 310, 388, fig. 539; Fancelli 1974, pp. 71–83, 125, fig. 31; Arts Council 1975, p. 251, fig. 452 (Burns—as IX/18).

Royal Institute of British Architects, London.

This tiny little jewel is, in its way, one of the most enchanting of Palladian drawings. It forms a continuation of the plan on RIBA IX/7 (cat. no. 85), extending the image of that largely imaginary sanctuary through three more superimposed terraces to a charmingly nonfunctional pinnacle, in a tempietto consisting entirely of four "false fronts," with nothing inside. The two-sheet scheme is ostensibly meant to refer to Palestrina, as is clear from a similar but unified image on RIBA IX/1: in that plan the forum and all seven terraces above it are shown as tightly concentric rectangles, like a child's nested puzzle, with the tempietto as a kind of jack-in-the-box at the center. Something of the same effect obtains here, but the terraces are all rearranged and have been given fanciful forms. Once more, the plan of the lower terrace—with its central exedra and stairs ideally concentrated at the corners—strongly recalls Palladio's partly hypothetical reconstructions of the levels above the Roman theatre at Verona—of which cat. no. 82 is certainly one of the sources as well for this splendid but empty tempietto.

As a technical note on Palladio's working procedure, we might observe that he first mechanically drafted his major elements—the drum of the rotunda, the hemicycle wall and steps, and the bottom niche—and then went on to improvise entirely in freehand. The lacy refinement of detail appealingly sets off a clearly expressed confidence in structural massing, and both characteristics emphasize Palladio's quality as one of the most imaginative and inventive of the professional architects of the Renaissance.

---

85. FANCIFUL SKETCH PLAN OF THE FORUM, AND ELEVATION OF THE FORUM AND SANCTUARY OF FORTUNA PRIMIGENIA, PALESTRINA

Late 1560s

RIBA: Palladio IX/7.

39.6 × 29.0 cm. (single sheet); watermark, angel in circle with star; countermark, S C in shield surmounted by trefoil; laid lines 27 mm. apart (Briquet 649); no collector's mark (Burlington purchase, 1719).

Dark reddish siena ink, with some additions in very light siena ink; inscribed in mature handwriting with measures in feet.

Zorzi 1957, pp. 158–159, fig. 14; Zorzi 1959, p. 88f, fig. 209; Forssman 1965, p. 55, fig. 23 (detail); Spielmann 1966, p. 154, no. 106, fig. 59; Ackerman 1966/1967, pp. 174–177, fig. 94; Semenzato 1968, p. 16, fig. viii; Zorzi 1969, p. 125, fig. 215; Puppi 1972, p. 42, fig. viii; D'Ossat 1973, p. 32, fig. 14 (detail); Mostra 1973, p. 143, fig. 146 (Burns); Puppi 1973, p. 388; Fancelli 1974, pp. 71–83, 125, fig. 31; Paris 1975, p. 38 (note and ill.); Arts Council 1975, pp. 250–251, fig. 451 (detail—Burns).

Royal Institute of British Architects, London.

Justly praised by generations of commentators, this pyrotechnic display of dazzling virtuosity represents Palladio's most unfettered exercise of pure invention on a recognizable theme. Fancelli has demonstrated that the direct translation of measurements from Palladio's "archaeological" survey plan of the forum and sanctuary at Palestrina (RIBA IX/1) guarantees a connection of this great project with the site, even if only as an ideal recreation of what might have been. The plan is a model of a clear, coherent description of a complex scheme in simple terms: essentially it takes two decorative hemicycles on the hillside at Palestrina and aligns them with forum colonnades below the sanctuary, to produce the truly breathtaking images at the bottom of this sheet. Similarly the elevation is a marvel of adaptation, whose uppermost levels (for example) repeat the carefully drafted forms of RIBA IX/9 (cat. no. 83), though with a considerably expanded verticality. The design has deservedly been linked with the planning of the Villa Rotonda near Vicenza and the Villa Trissino at Meledo, but it easily surpasses them both. Even more than the *Quattro Libri's* grandiose plans of Meledo or the Dolo villa of Leonardo Mocenigo (fig. 50)—the two images usually taken as paradigms of Palladio's most visionary schemes—the almost hallucinatory elaboration of this megalomaniacal *tour de force* places it at the forefront of an architectural tradition more usually associated with Juvarra, the Bibiena, or Piranesi, and not comparably re-elaborated until the great age of Beaux-Arts fantasies at the turn of our own century.

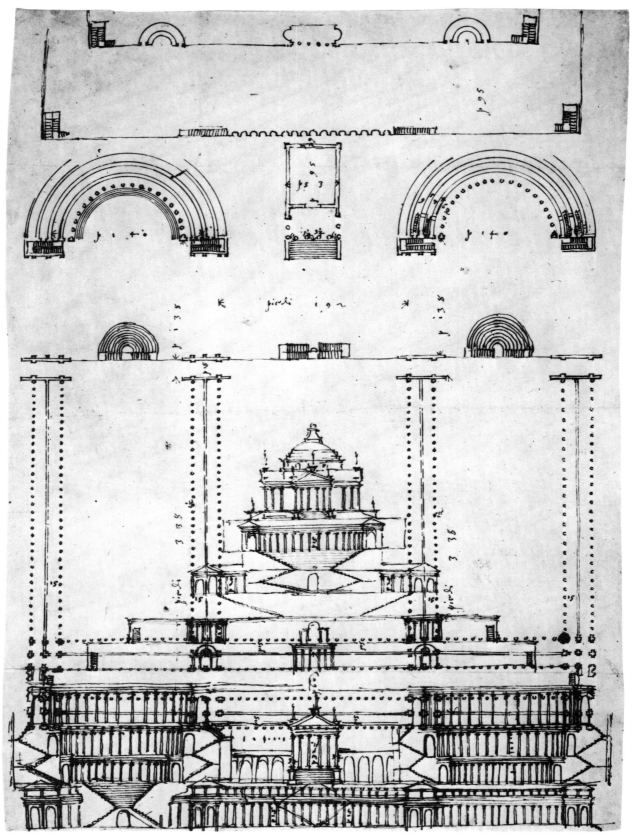

85

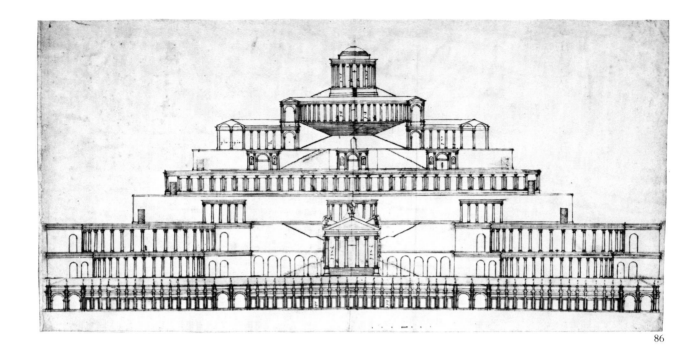

86. IDEALIZED ELEVATION OF THE FORUM AND SANCTUARY OF FORTUNA PRIMIGENIA, PALESTRINA

1560s

RIBA: Palladio IX/6.

28.5 × 56.0 cm. (one main sheet, including strip 4.7 to 5.1 cm. high added along the bottom, and superimposed patch of 6.7 × 5.2 cm. added with temple facade at center); watermark, three mounds with fleur-de-lis in shield (earlier variant of Briquet 11936); no collector's mark (Burlington purchase, 1719).

Dark reddish siena ink, tending toward umber at top; gray-brown umber ink on patch applied at center; inscribed in mature handwriting with measures in feet, of which a scale of 60 = 51 mm. (2 Roman inches).

Burger 1909, p. 113, fig. 45; Loukomski 1938, fig. on p. 17; Zorzi 1957, pp. 159–160, fig. 16; Zorzi 1959, p. 89, fig. 211; Chastel 1965, p. 19, fig. 14; D'Ossat 1966, p. 36, fig. 39; Spielmann 1966, p. 154, no. 109, fig. 61; Zorzi 1967, p. 170, fig. 117; Semenzato 1968, p. 16, fig. vi; Tafuri 1968, p. 68, fig. 42; Mostra 1973, p. 143 (Burns); Fancelli 1974, pp. 49–52, 125, fig. 25.

Royal Institute of British Architects, London.

In its solemn monumentality this large finished drawing is at least as impressive as its quickly sketched predecessor (cat. no. 85). Burns has noted that in this more rationalized form, Palladio's carefully measured elevation of a reconstructed hilltop sanctuary (though still very closely related to the dramatic *bravura* performance on the preceding sheet, in cat. no. 85) has become a kind of ideal compendium of motifs from a whole repertory of such Late Republican and Early Imperial sites. The crowning tempietto and its supporting amphitheatrical hemicycle are highly accurate reflections of Palestrina. But their two successive terraces of long straight wings embracing a rectangular piazza, with triple-arch motifs on the face of its retaining wall, are borrowed from Palladio's reconstruction of the Roman theatre at Verona; and in fact the next facade, with its rectilinear compartments and lateral stairs, is an almost exact rendition of Palladio's second terrace wall above the Verona theatre (cat. nos. 10 and 82). The large temple standing isolated at the center (framed by long colonnaded wings), while suggesting several of the Imperial forums, is probably a direct reference to the sanctuary of the Victorious Hercules at Tivoli. This is a monument which Palladio drew archaeologically several times, and also added as an ingredient to a number of these conflated restorations (it is also included, for example, in the more fanciful sketch on the preceding sheet). The two great columnar exedrae that frame the whole complex are the components for which the sources are the most elusive. Spielmann, followed by Burns, suggested analogies with the lateral apses (toward the slope of the Quirinal) of Trajan's Forum, but they are in fact too close together, have no axial centerpiece, and no symmetrical colonnades—in the case of the one centered on the open Forum—that would have extended outward from the hill. These latter elements however are all present in Pirro Ligorio's as well as Palladio's more strictly archaeological surveys at Palestrina (*cf.* RIBA IX/1, or Ligorio's Turin drawing in Fancelli 1974, fig. 33), and even in certain modern reconstructions of the Temple of Hercules Victor (*e.g.* Canina's of 1848—Zorzi 1957, fig. 2). It thus seems more plausible that Palladio's inspiration for his twin apsidal-ended stoas would have come from one of these sites in the Campagna, of which the precedents at Palestrina are probably the most suggestive (see cat. no. 87).

87. (Recto) PALLADIO: STUDY SKETCHES OF PLAN AND DETAILS OF A FORUM; (Verso) BY OR AFTER BATTISTA FRANCO: SKETCH STUDIES AFTER MICHELANGELO'S *LAST JUDGMENT* AND PARMIGIANINO'S *DIOGENES*

1554

RIBA: Palladio VIII/10 *recto* and *verso*.

43.3 × 28.0 cm. (single sheet); no watermark visible; Talman 49 mark on *verso*.

Gray-brown umber ink, with partial (later?) sepia wash on *verso*; *recto* inscribed in mature handwriting (in two campaigns, the second in light siena ink) with labels, descriptions, and measures in feet.

Zorzi 1957, pp. 157–158, fig. 13 (*recto*, as Temple of Hercules, Tivoli); Zorzi 1959, pp. 87–88, fig. 206 (same); Spielmann 1966, p. 153, no. 104 (*recto*, as Forum of Trajan, Rome); Fancelli 1974, pp. 60–64, 125, fig. 28 (*recto*, as site plan, 2nd version, of Palestrina); Rearick 1980 (*verso*: letter to the author of 10 December 1980).

Royal Institute of British Architects, London.

The unpublished *verso* of this sheet is one of the most important drawings in the Palladian corpus; on the basis of both style and content it can be associated very closely with the Venetian draftsman and painter Battista Franco. It documents an unexpectedly close relationship between Franco and Palladio, for it is evidently a drawing which they used together to design the fresco decoration of the Villa Foscari at Malcontenta (cat. no. 88). It therefore demonstrates another example of Palladio's intimate involvement in the interior decoration of his buildings, a process in which we can now show him (here and in cat. no. 89) to have taken an active and creative part. Because of its evident reference to Palladio's trip to Rome with Daniele Barbaro and other Venetian friends in 1554, the sheet also serves the important function of dating the house at Malcontenta before that year, and the Villa Barbaro nymphaeum at Maser (which Palladio prefigures on its *recto*) to the period immediately after.

The central figure on the *verso* is a highly accurate copy of Caraglio's Roman engraving of *Diogenes* (Bartsch XV:94:61) after Parmigianino. Caraglio was a native of the Veneto, and the young Franco might well have acquired a print of the *Diogenes* in his native Venice before he set off for Rome in the early 1530s (Rearick 1958–1959, pp. 107, 112 and 121). In October 1541 Franco returned to the Papal capital for the unveiling of Michelangelo's Sistine Chapel fresco of the *Last Judgment*, and was so fascinated by the work that he determined to remain in Rome, as Vasari records, to make drawings of it (Milanesi ed. 1881, VI:578). Three of the results are assembled on this sheet, surrounding the *Diogenes*: Franco's upward-gesturing figures are all quoted from a tightly interconnected group on the left middle margin of the Sistine fresco, in the first cloudborne rank of the Elect ascending to Paradise. Franco later moved to Urbino, where he worked with his close friend Bartolomeo Genga at the Ducal court for most of the decade 1544–54. We might remember that Palladio comments on

having visited Urbino in his letter, evidently of the spring of 1554, telling the Duke's ambassador about his recent meeting with Genga in Venice (cat. no. 71). Battista Franco—for whom Palladio came to have an exceptional esteem, calling him "one of the very greatest draftsman of our time" (*Quattro Libri*, II:xiiii:50), had returned to residence in Venice by this time, as we learn from his first payment of rent on 28 November 1554 to his new Venetian landlords.

These were Girolamo and Piero Foscari, who were the patrons of one of Franco's first Venetian commissions. Their patronage provides three highly important links to our present context. First, their sister Paola's marriage in 1542 to Vettor Pisani (cat. no. 48) had precipitated the construction of Bagnolo by Palladio, whom the Foscari brothers can thus be assumed to have known well for some ten or a dozen years. Second, Piero had married Elena, daughter of the Patriarch of Aquileia, Marco Grimani, whose youngest brother (and succeding Patriarch) Giovanni, was to become Franco's greatest Venetian patron with his commission for the decoration of the Grimani Chapel at S. Francesco della Vigna. (However, neither this commission nor Palladio's commission for the facade could be carried out until the death in August 1558 of Giovanni's and Marco's brother, the Procurator Vettor Grimani, who, as the initial Sansovino patron, controlled both the chapel and the facade.) And third, a final recommendation from Franco's prominent Venetian hosts can be added on the direct evidence of our sheet: its left-hand *Saved Soul* and central *Diogenes* appear frescoed together on the south curve of the barrel vault over the eastern arm of the cruciform central *salone* of Palladio's villa at Malcontenta, commissioned and constructed in the 1550s by two cousins and contemporaries of Franco's landlords, the brothers Nicolo and Alvise Foscari.

The notorious problems of assigning exact dates to Palladio's designs as well as to Franco's paintings for this celebrated monument are thus handily solved by the apparition of our jointly invented drawing of 1554. It demonstrates, first, that the Palladian house at Malcontenta by then existed, and was ready for its frescoes. This date accords perfectly with the villa's style (see cat. no. 88), and with an obvious but undiscussed testimony about its patronage. A large facade inscription proclaims the structure as the work of NICOLAVS ET ALOYSIVS FOSCARI FRATRES, that is the collaborative commission of two bachelor brothers: its fully developed bilateral arrangement confirms its planning in two independent units, and—crucially—its frescoes appropriately celebrate the liberal arts, civic virtues, and Bacchanalian subjects, without any hint of the standard themes of conjugal and dynastic virtue, that appear in all of Palladio's villas connected with recent or forthcoming marriages. Yet Nicolo Foscari *was* married during this period, in May of 1555, to Isabella Dolfin Pisani: thus the completion of the house at Malcontenta and at least the commission of its fresco cycle must certainly predate the spring of 1555. Our drawing dates probably from the spring of 1554; it documents Palladio's and Franco's discussions about frescoed elements for the ceiling of the

149

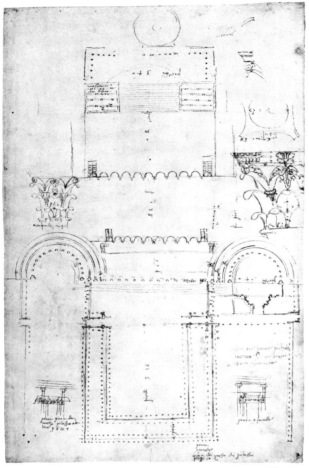

87 *recto*

Malcontenta hall, which survive in Franco's style; and we can now assign the distracting campaigns of both artists at S. Francesco della Vigna, under the patronage of the Patriarch Giovanni Grimani, to a date shortly after 22 August 1558. It therefore seems inescapable that the Malcontenta villa was built in the years between about 1550 and 1553; that—on the evidence of this drawing and the frescoes themselves—its paintings were begun by Franco and carried at least around the frieze of the *salone* and the walls of the eastern square room in 1554–1558; and that it was the imperious demand of the Patriarch of Aquileia, rather than Franco's death, that first suspended the execution of the cycle. Battista died (regretted by Palladio, who eulogizes him in the *Quattro Libri*) in 1561; but Nicolo Foscari had predeceased him on 6 December 1560, and it was evidently the combination of these events that obliged Alvise as the surviving patron, and Palladio as his intermediary (see cat. no. 89) to secure the services of Giambattista Zelotti to complete the fresco decorations of the Villa Foscari.

On the *recto* of this sheet Palladio sketches one of his most imaginative recombinations of plan elements from the hillside monuments of Rome, Tivoli and Palestrina (cat. nos. 83–86). In an intriguing innovation, however, he screens the right-hand large hemicycle with a small but deep apsidal structure placed opposite, rather like the central bay of an antique stage building. The diagnostic draftsmanship of this element offers a firm date of 1554 for the sheet (through its identity with the same and other elements on RIBA XVI/9-B *verso*, fig. 47). More importantly it also gives us the date of inception for the garden nymphaeum of the Villa Barbaro at Maser—of which its deep curve, flanked by single ornamental bays on the front plane, and with round and rectangular niches framing a square chamber at the center, are all direct prototypes.

CHAPTER SEVEN

Professional Maturity:

Built and painted architecture at mid-century

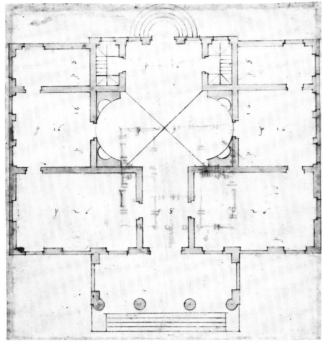

88 *recto*

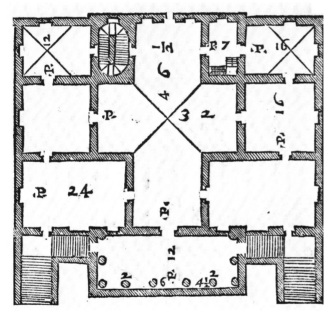

Figure 57

Figure 56

88. PLAN PROJECT FOR VILLA CHIERICATI, VANCIMUGLIO, AND FOR VILLA FOSCARI, MALCONTENTA: SKETCH PLAN FOR VILLA CALDOGNO, CALDOGNO

1547/1548 (*recto*), and 1548/1549 (*verso*).

RIBA: Palladio XVI/20-A *recto* and *verso*.

21.1 × 19.4 cm. (single sheet, now detached from the unrelated XVI/20-B: see cat. no. 97); watermark, cardinal's hat surmounted by Maltese cross with buttons (Briquet 3416/3417: Venzone 1540, Padua 1541, etc.); Talman 150 mark on *verso*.

Orange-red siena ink with beige-pink siena wash, on pencil underdrawing, with pencil sketch of alternate plan lower right; inscribed with measures in feet, at scale of 10 feet = 1 Vicentine inch of 29.8 mm.

Zorzi 1954, p. 65, project no. 7, fig. 8A; Pane 1961, pp. 109–110, fig. 133:34; Zorzi 1961, pp. 179–184; Dalla Pozza 1943–1963, pp. 128–130, fig. 15 (first recognition as Vancimuglio plan, related to Malcontenta); Ackerman 1967, p. 73, fig. 42; Zorzi 1969, pp. 44–45, fig. 53A, pp. 156–160, fig. 277; Lewis 1973, pp. 369–376, fig. 195, and fig. 197 (first publication of *verso*); Mostra 1973, p. 148 (Burns); Puppi 1973, pp. 296–297, fig. 377; Arts Council 1975, p. 195, no. 350 (Fairbairn/Burns), and p. 190, no. 336 (Burns—mentioning Caldogno sketch, but without identification as *verso*).

Royal Institute of British Architects, London.

The three villas whose executed plans derive from this sheet pose no problems in terms of the clear relationships of their forms to Palladio's drafted images. As Dalla Pozza first pointed out, Palladio's plan on the *recto* is identical with the villa of Giovanni Chiericati at Vancimuglio just southeast of Vicenza (fig. 56), save that the double apses in its hall were economically omitted, and its stairs pushed into the adjoining *camerini* to leave the executed *salone* as an unimpeded cubic space. Dalla Pozza also commented on the drawing's virtual reuse as the plan for Malcontenta (fig. 57): this relationship has been minimized in the literature, but in fact it combines with the evidence presented in cat. no. 87 to disprove an alleged late date for the Villa Foscari, repeated by all commentators since Burger (1909, p. 89). In the same way, the identity of the Villa Caldogno plan (fig. 58) to Palladio's sketch on the *verso* of this sheet—a particularly fine autograph study that perhaps (as Burns hints) records a partially pre-existing state—so far affords our only unimpeachable document for the Palladian paternity of this fine house (fig. 59).

Whereas the relationships of these drawings to Vancimuglio, Malcontenta, and Caldogno are unequivocal and assured, no such obvious concurrence is available to confirm the respective chronologies, either of the drafted images or the executed buildings. The latter have proved extraordinarily difficult to date, although Burns (1975, p. 190) has now established a documented period in the 1540s for the "improvements" at Caldogno that are recorded by our *verso* sketch. For an investigation of the finished design

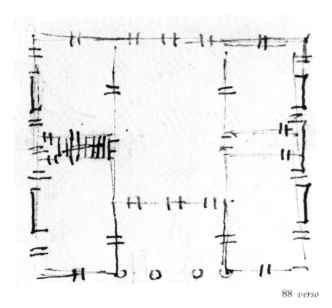

88 *verso*

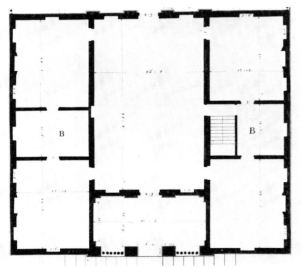

Figure 58

that precedes it on the *recto,* we might note first that their common paper bears a Veneto watermark of the 1540s. Its measured plan is composed from the amalgamation of an ink sketch (for the room arrangement) and a pencil design (for the portico plan) on the *verso* of RIBA XVII/12 (cat. no. 65). Palladio would have laid aside that sheet of Palazzo Porto facade studies shortly following his return from Rome in the autumn of 1547, since by some point soon after that date Palazzo Porto and its facade would certainly have been rising, in time to receive their exterior and interior inscriptions by 1552 (the year also of the decoration of Palazzo Thiene, which in many ways is a prototype for the Porto design). That Palladio would have reached for the partially blank sheet of cat. no. 65 *verso* around 1547 is demonstrated by the sketches he added to it: in addition to one for the proposed extension of Palazzo Thiene (cat. no. 53), and to those for the Vancimuglio plan and portico (which are most plausibly datable by documents to 1547), they include a sketch plan for the villa of Marco Zen at Cessalto. This undated villa's plan and courtyard facade exactly parallel those at Bagnolo, completed in 1544/45 (see cat. no. 47); and the execution of the Villa Zen finds its closest connections with the twin designs of Malcontenta and Piombino, executed in c. 1550/51–53.

If Palladio's rough sketches preparatory to these designs date most probably from 1547, the present finished drawing can be dated to the same moment, through some neglected but definitive evidence of patronage. Early in 1546 Girolamo Chiericati, Giovanni's brother, was knighted as a result of his congratulatory embassy to the newly elected Doge Francesco Donato (Tomasini 1677/1976, p. 69), and the brothers—evidently planning conspicuous improvements—divided their properties on 5 November 1546 (Puppi 1973, p. 296). Meanwhile on 5/6 March 1546 a tightly knit clique of the Vicentine aristocracy had engineered the acceptance of Palladio's first project for the Basilica. This group was headed by Pietro Godi, the patron

Figure 59

of Palladio's first villa, at Lonedo, and Gabriel Capra, who proved lavish in the discharge of his duties as civic supervisor for the production of Palladio's wooden mock-up (cat. no. 62). A noble Caldogno and a Chiericati cousin were also among the deputies making these decisions, but it is even more interesting to find that this early group, so well-disposed toward Palladio, included as well Vincenzo Arnaldi (Zorzi 1965, pp. 54–55). Palladio's sketches for his villa of the same moment of 1547/48 (cat. no. 69), so exactly analogous to the sketch for Villa Caldogno on the *verso* of our present sheet, thus take on a significant import—especially as a parallel to the forthcoming Chiericati projects—in establishing a pattern of domestic works undertaken by Andrea for the committed noble partisans who were lobbying for his greatest civic appointment.

In this reciprocal process of public and private patronage both Chiericati brothers were intimately involved. Giovanni's interest in Palladio may have come first, for his son was married to Gabriel Capra's daughter (Tomasini p. 68), and the present drawing for his splendid house at Vancimuglio is clearly to be dated to a moment shortly following his property division of November 1546. His brother Girolamo was not long delayed in joining and enjoying the perquisites of this Palladian coterie, for he was elected on 6 September 1548 as one of three official commissioners for Palladio's Basilica. It has long been recognized as no coincidence that Girolamo Chiericati should record on 15 November 1550 that he had paid Palladio four golden escudoes "over the course of the last many months, for drafting the plan project and making the facade elevation for the new palace that I have decided to build on the Isola" in Vicenza (Zorzi 1965, p. 203, Doc. 2: see cat. nos. 91–93 for the drawings themselves).

We need only emphasize, finally, the analogous situation with his brother's villa at Vancimuglio. Giovanni Chiericati was just as promiment (his knighthood in fact came from the next Doge, Marc'Antonio Trevisan), and just as committed to Palladio. His will of 1557 exhorts his descendants to complete the house at Vancimuglio which he had begun, to a Palladian plan reflected on this sheet, *before* 1554— rather than after, as has been misconstrued from the one early document. Giovanni's tax declaration of that year lists not only "an old house," but also an as yet "less valuable private residence" (Dalla Pozza, p. 126); this can only be the 1547–54 commencement of the Palladian house, whose fine basement is executed in Palladio's best style of these years. We know that the main floor (save the portico) had been constructed to the level of the windows by the time of Giovanni's death in 1558. Its measures are taken directly from this drawing, and executed with a high degree of accuracy. The idiosyncratic vaults of the square rooms are paralleled in the coeval houses at Montagnana and Malcontenta, and the details, as in the fireplace moldings, are matched in those two houses and in Poiana (which was being completed in May of 1555). The semicircular back stairs projected on this drawing and executed at Poiana belong of course to the earlier stages of design and foundation-building of these two contemporaneous projects, that is, just after Palladio's return from Rome in 1547. Since it is clear that Vancimuglio was certainly in progress by that date or the following year, we can understand the availability of this unneeded sheet to provide space for the sketch of Caldogno during the following few months (in a campaign documented within the 1540s), and for Palladio's reuse of its measured plan at Malcontenta shortly after.

---

89. DESIGN FOR FRESCO DECORATIONS ON THE WEST WALL OF THE *SALONE* OF VILLA GODI, LONEDO

4 July 1550 (Date on which Palladio was paid for the sheet)

Devonshire Collections, RIBA: Chiswick 37.

41.4 × 45.7 cm. (single sheet of beige/ivory paper, foxed and stained; cut on left side, possibly by about 11 cm.); watermark, three indistinct objects in circle with star; no collector's mark (Burlington purchase, 1719).

Reddish siena ink; inscribed, probably in the hand of *"Nad Bav"* (? monogram signature lower right), with scale of 6 Vincentine feet = approx. 3 Vicentine inches (89 mm.), and with labels as follows, from bottom to top: *"testa de la salla de sig^n Godi a lonedo, larga Piedi n° 24—questa faciata è richisima de hornamenti simile à l'altre / Portello Principale che porta D'Logia in salla / cartelon finto D'oro con figure / tutti trofei militari / figure / festoni / cornise con modiglioni simile à l'altre / straforo / figure / trofei / figure / cornise simile à l'altre."*

Unpublished.

The Trustees of the Chatsworth Settlement.

In some respects this is the most important drawing in the present exhibition. Its pre-eminent status accrues not only from its novelty, as one more unnoticed item of Palladiana, nor even from its intrinsic interest as an unusually handsome, well-proportioned and carefully drafted sheet, from a rare period in the architect's oeuvre. Its importance derives rather from its precious character as one of only a half-dozen documented drawings in the Palladian corpus (among which it is the unique early sheet with a fixed date), and above all because its subject represents an aspect of Palladio's artistic creativity that has been unsuspected—but which, through the impeccably documented testimony of this sheet, has the potential of revolutionizing our view of his work. Its rediscovery affords the occasion for an appropriate offering of American scholarship with which to celebrate the artist's four hundredth anniversary year, and provides one of the principal justifications for the retrospective comprehensiveness of this exhibition.

Or rather its second rediscovery: for although the drawing has lain unremarked at Chiswick for more than two

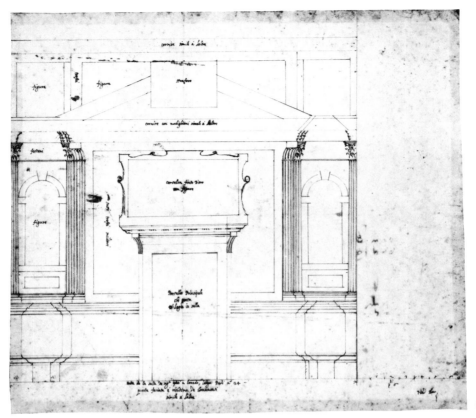

89

and a half centuries, Bertotti-Scamozzi two hundred years ago discovered the documents for it and its fellows, and fully recognized their import, even without the benefit of visual evidence. This signal triumph of historical imagination—which should be useful as well in correcting our view of Bertotti-Scamozzi as a dry and chilly Neoclassicist—was made possible by his hospitable reception during a visit to Lonedo by the then owner of the villa, Contessa Violante Godi-Porto, who made available to him *"two manuscript Books, wherein were listed all the payments . . . made to Palladio for the work he had done; several of which I believed it to be incumbent upon me to transcribe, and they are as follows.* [Eight exactly comparable entries are then quoted from a year earlier and two years after this note by Pietro Godi:] *'Palladio. Gave him today, 4th July [1550] for the drawing of the Hall, one Hungarian crown [worth] 7 lire 14 soldi'."* Bertotti-Scamozzi's nine almost equal entries evidently record Palladio's payments, from 1549 to 1552, for drawings of the nine rooms at the Villa Godi. His two immediately preceding citations described Pietro Godi's paying Palladio "for having made for me the compartmentation of the Room toward the Garden" (5 September 1549), and "for his drawing of the Room beside the loggia" (22 June 1550). Bertotti fully recognized this evidence as decisively documenting that "Palladio himself was the designer" of the Villa Godi's "admirably ingenious framework" of fictive architectural frescoes (1778, II:24–25).

But Bertotti's was a lone voice, and his own publication was partially responsibe for a "puristic" view of Palladio

Figure 60

155

that has clouded the last two centuries of Palladian criticism. This aesthetic viewpoint has insisted (in broad terms) on a Palladian architecture of pure whitewashed spaces, proportionally conceived, and sparingly (if at all) filled with stone moldings of rigorously chaste profile. Stucco and painting were usually regarded as interlopers in this purified world, whose abstraction appealed enormously to late 19th- and early 20th-century functionalists. This became so extreme a view that Palladio was even charged with having *disapproved* of the great fresco cycle at Maser (*cf.* cat. no. 90). Finally, because that house is so perfectly and richly decorated, he was increasingly (and perversely) held to have designed less and less of it (Cevese, in Mostra 1973, pp. 78–81; Huse 1974, pp. 106–122).

The present drawing, and others that may now be recognized through its example, should help to sweep away the remnants of this "reductionist" view of Palladio as a kind of Bauhaus functionalist *avant la lettre*. Its delicately proportioned and executed pilasters, and elaborate dado and attic (elements substantially changed in execution, proving this to be not merely a copy) all fit handsomely within Palladio's purely architectural vocabulary of the years around 1550 (*cf.* cat. nos. 14, 40, 70), while its decorative intention exactly matches the tendency of this same period toward lavish sculptural ornament that we have characterized as Andrea's "first decorated style" (*cf.* esp. cat. nos. 66, 68, 71, 78, 92, 100, 105, etc.), and which reaches its culmination in a whole range of exuberant masterworks from his later period after c. 1565. The drawing was brilliantly translated into a masterpiece of fictive architecture, full of illusionistic marvels, by Zelotti (fig. 60)—who again, as at Malcontenta, was called upon to replace a deceased colleague, the considerably less distinguished Gualtiero Padovano.

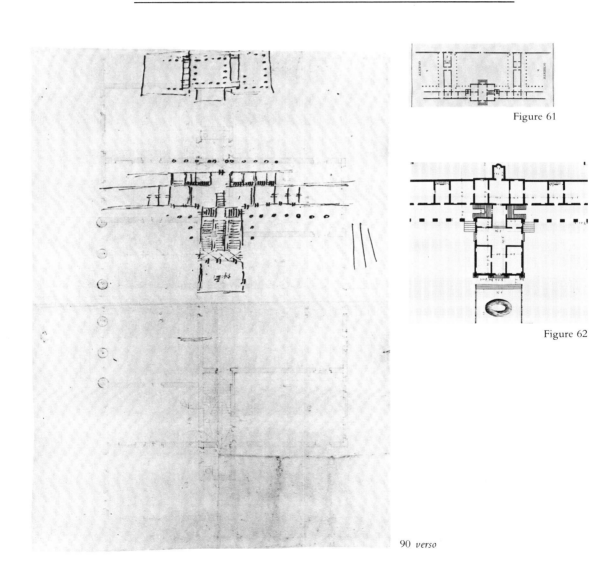

Figure 61

Figure 62

90 *verso*

156

90. PLAN SKETCHES FOR VILLA ANGARANO, ANGARANO AND VILLA BARBARO, MASER

1548/49

RIBA: Palladio XVI/5 *verso*.

37.2 × 26.2 cm. (single sheet); watermark, cardinal's hat surmounted by Maltese cross, with countermark B; laid lines 30 mm. apart (Briquet 3467/3488); Talman 54 mark on *verso*.

Heavy umber ink. *Recto,* SANMICHELIAN VILLA PROJECT, heavy umber ink over extensive umber crayon, with pale yellow to beige-tan wash, heavily inscribed in very early or different hand, with measures in feet.

Burger 1909, p. 95, fig. 36:1 (*recto,* as Piombino); Loukomski 1938, pp. 21, 26 (*recto,* as Montagnana); Zorzi 1969, p. 183, fig. 344 (*recto,* as neither); Lewis 1973, pp. 369–376, fig. 190 (*recto,* as project of c. 1535–40), figs. 191–193 (first publication of *verso*); Puppi 1973, p. 294, fig. 372 (*recto,* as possibly Piombino); Arts Council 1975, p. 194, no. and fig. 347 (Boucher—*recto,* as Piombino).

Royal Institute of British Architects, London.

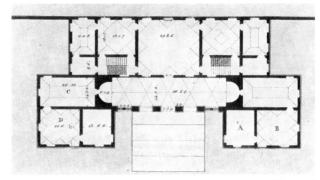

Figure 63

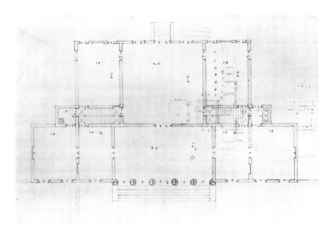

90 *recto*

The very beautiful and spontaneous drawings on this *verso* include what is certainly the finest first sketch of a design idea yet to be discovered in Palladio's oeuvre, the magnificent plan (at the center of the sheet) for the Villa Barbaro at Maser (*cf.* fig. 62). It is quite beyond question (*cf.* Huse 1974, p. 119 n. 6) that this quick graphic record represents Palladio's first proposal for integrating the pre-existing medieval castle (whose walls survive to the height of the projecting block—Basso 1976, pp. 6–29) into a new and much grander scheme, involving a vast cross-axial structure that would extend east and west across the entire space within the former moat, and run parallel to the slope of the hill that rises behind. One of Palladio's most brilliant solutions to the iconographic preservation and "adaptive reuse" of ancient monuments is his decision to retain at Maser the image of a high, imperious castle keep, by placing the main living floor of the new Villa Barbaro a full story above the ground-level entrance to the facade. He thus inserted it, over a tall ground floor, at very nearly the level of the old *soler* (the present attics being nearly at the height of a former third floor in the old castle, as the remains of medieval fireplaces in their walls attest). In one of his finest demonstrations of a mastery of three-dimensional planning he continued this main living level right across the new north range, extending it as a high, enclosed garden through to the flank of the hill, where it terminates in a spectacular sculptural hemicycle with a fountain grotto placed over the source of ancient springs (*cf.* cat. no. 81, fig. 55, and cat. no. 87).

In his first sketch of this idea Palladio's concern is thus concentrated on the considerable problem of the villa's major change in level, which is the most striking and dramatic element in its design. The hidden, quiet garden at the back, cooled by its plashing fountain, is rendered inaccessible from without through the fact that the steep northern slope is met at its sides by the closed tops of the lower service wings (evidently ancient structures along the moats, omitted in Palladio's sketch). The sequential living

suites of Palladio's long transverse wings stand athwart its southern side as a huge retaining wall, thus allowing them to open privately onto the secret garden through doors at their upper floor level, but dropping the whole composition by a full story, toward the plain, by their inspired device of great upper windows looking out onto a very tall two-story arcade with suites of service rooms directly underneath, on the ground or entrance level shared by the old projecting block. On the upper level of this, standing forward of the superimposed intersections with the cross-axial wings, the main reception rooms sweep outward as a high, triumphant image of the patrons' domination over their vast estates, overlooking them from the vantage of three exposures—through tall windows that open into real space the illusionistic vistas of Palladio's and Veronese's sublimely frescoed halls (*cf.* cat. no. 89).

Palladio's sketch for Maser is certainly to be dated not later than the month between the death of the patrons' father Francesco Barbaro in April 1549, and the departure of Daniele as Ambassador to England in early June (Lewis 1973, pp. 373–374). It is interesting that in the ground floor of its projecting medieval tower Palladio should return to the same dreams of vast stair systems that had formed so extraordinary a part of his slightly earlier proposals for Palazzo Porto (cat. no. 66 *verso,* and fig. 44). And indeed, while those had prefigured parallel outer flights joining across a central landing in shorter, opposed ramps on an

157

essentially U-shaped plan, the Maser proposal picks up an idea from Leonardo's sketchbooks, with parallel flights along the outer walls leading across a continuous landing to a reversing third flight, standing free at the center. The first well-known example of this so-called Imperial type to be built was the great Escorial stair, begun in 1563 (Wilkinson 1975); it is thus fascinating to find in Palladio's sketch of 1548 or 1549 for Maser an Italian prototype that might very well have been built—had not what were probably more practical considerations intervened—when the villa was executed in 1551–58.

The small sketch at the top of the sheet is almost certainly a first idea for the villa of Palladio's close friend Giacomo Angarano, which was apparently begun to this plan (cf. fig. 61) on that nobleman's ancient fief near Bassano, during or shortly after Palladio's documented residence at the site in May, June, and July of 1548 (Puppi 1973, p. 273). Since we know Palladio to have traveled together with Angarano to Venice in September of that year (Zorzi 1950, p. 142; 1965, pp. 35–36), where Daniele Barbaro was already hard at work on the *Vitruvius* edition that Palladio

was illustrating for him (cf. cat. no. 71), it may thus be easy to understand why Andrea should have used the same blank page in his traveling portfolio (which seems to have contained his half-used sheets: cf. cat. nos. 72–73) to sketch his first ideas for both sites—particularly since he would probably have stopped off at Maser on his way, in which case our sketch should be dated some eight months earlier.

The awkward, imprecise, and frequently mistaken drawing on the front of this sheet is either Palladio's earliest surviving attempt at draftsmanship or more probably a learning effort by one of his sons (Zorzi has proposed Leonida [1969, p. 183]). It is a weak copy after Sanmicheli's famous plan of "La Soranza" outside Castelfranco (more precisely the Villa Soranzo at Treville), whose date, although undocumented, is probably around 1539 (fig. 63). Since we can assume Palladio to have been in contact with Sanmicheli by that very year (cf. cat. no. 48), the possibility exists that this is a Palladian *incunabulum* based on a drawing for the Villa Soranzo, or reflecting a visit to the site; but I prefer Zorzi's hypothesis of its being a student effort by one of his sons.

---

91. UPPER PART OF ELEVATION PROJECT FOR PALAZZO CHIERICATI, VICENZA (I)

1546–48

Worcester College Library, from Inigo James album no. I/93, now designated H.T. 93 (supplementary series).

44.6 × 59.0 cm. (single sheet); watermark, very heavy crossed arrows (left center) with countermark B (upper right): cf. cat. no. 71 (different and evidently later variant of Briquet 6292/6293 than "Palladio's standard paper" of c. 1540); circled identification number 58E in pencil on *recto* (Gotch no. I/58E).

Umber ink (for order, etc.) and siena ink (for windows) over heavily incised lines.

Harris 1971, pp. 34–37, fig. 40; Mostra 1973, p. 150 (Burns); Puppi 1973, p. 284, fig. 356; Arts Council 1975, p. 40, no. 57 (Burns); Harris and Tait 1979, p. 54, no. 129.

The Provost and Fellows of Worcester College, Oxford.

One of the most wonderful of Palladio's works, the great facade of Palazzo Chiericati dominates a large open space called the Isola, at the east end of the main Corso, and forms one of the first impressions of Vicenza for every visitor arriving by the road from Venice. This public function is one of the most important aspects of the palace, and was clearly foreseen by the architect and patron. Already in the Chiericati brothers' division of their property on 5 November 1546 (cf. cat. no. 88) the building of a new palace on this site was anticipated. It has generally been assumed from the specificity of the document (Magrini 1855, pp. 57–58) that Palladio's plan may have been settled at least in outline by that point, since Girolamo and Giovanni Chiericati were probably by then both involved in helping to arrange Andrea's appointment as architect of the Basilica. The first step toward this goal had been realized eight

months before, by the city council's dramatic vote of 5 March 1546 to consider his first plans—a victory which the Chiericati brothers, together with their kinsman Gabriele Capra, may well have helped to achieve. As we have noticed (cat. no. 88), Girolamo himself became one of Palladio's direct supervisors and protectors in his election of 6 September 1548 as a Basilica commissioner; he gave an oration in praise of the final design on 11 April 1549, as a result of which it was approved; and eighteen months later he opened a new account book to record the construction of his palace by Palladio, whom he first paid for his prior work of "many months" on its drawings.

This and the following sheet must therefore certainly predate 15 November 1550, and by a substantial distance—since from that date the palace accounts record the rapid construction of the portion that was built, to the substantially changed design that we see (in completed form) today. The Worcester drawing is clearly the earliest of Palladio's projects to survive, for it proposes a Composite order for the upper floor, whereas the executed facade uses Ionic. In the more elaborate order, as in its central pediment or pyramidal roof, it probably reflects an impressive invention from Serlio's *Third Book* (1540:153—fig. 64), as Dalla Pozza pointed out in 1943 (I, pp. 247–248, figs. 10–11; II, p. 77, figs. 16–17). The capitals are prototypes for rather than parallels to the ones in cat. nos. 70 and 71, from just after mid-century: in the Worcester versions we might note in particular the still upward-flaring abacus and shaded leaves, elements which disappear from Palladio's graphic canon before 1550. The drawing is thus substantially earlier than has been construed, and in fact its tightly spaced row of pedestals and window aprons is identical to the same zone (as the windows are closely parallel as well) in cat. no. 66, the Palazzo Porto facade drawing of

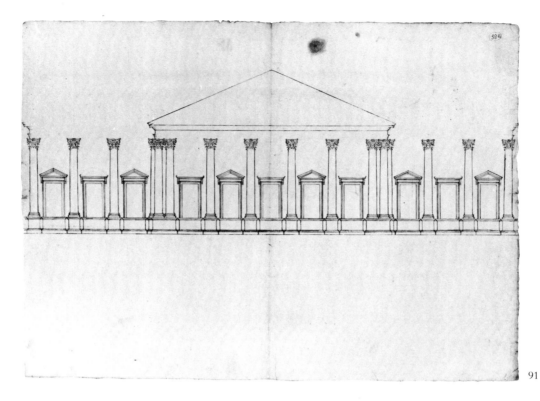

91

c. 1546/47. We have seen above that Palladian drawings for Palazzo Chiericati can credibly be assumed to have been in progress by the autumn of 1546; this beautiful sheet may well be one of them, reflecting a design stage (most likely a flat wall with a slight projection at the center, as shown for example on the plan in cat. no. 64) earlier even than the ones the patron was shown, in the "many months" before the fall of 1550. In this regard it is also extremely interesting to note its striking relationship to Ursel Berger's recon-

structed façade of the Villa Thiene at Quinto (1978, fig. 17, based on Muttoni 1740, pl. 41), also of c. 1546 (*cf.* cat. nos. 53–54). Here again the five bays of a slightly projecting central element end with rhythmically coupled pilasters, beyond which extend three-bay wings. Even the order of the lower floor at Quinto is a heavily detailed Doric, a close prototype for the one eventually executed on the ground floor of Palazzo Chiericati some five years later.

---

92. PARTIAL ELEVATION PROJECT FOR PALAZZO CHIERICATI, VICENZA (II)

1547–48

RIBA: Burlington-Devonshire VIII/11.

40.3 × 56.9 cm. (single sheet); watermark, tree with star-shaped leaves (later variant of Briquet 773, adding superimposed star); collector's numbers (?) *15* on *verso,* and *35* on *recto* (Burlington purchase, 1719?).

Umber ink (roughly applied) and very light wash, over heavily incised lines, and extensive pencil underdrawing.

Forssman 1962, p. 36, fig. 8; Barbieri 1964, pp. 328–329; Forssman 1965, p. 84, fig. 37; Forssman 1972, p. 92, fig. 46; Puppi 1973, p. 284; Arts Council 1975, p. 40, no. 56 (Burns).

Royal Institute of British Architects, London.

This sketchily handled but elaborate design brings us substantially closer to the final form of Palazzo Chiericati, with its richly sculptural Doric order supporting a decorated Ionic. The closest parallels for their graphic treatment are the Ionic façade of the Palazzo Porto (cat. no. 66) and the Doric small villa (cat. no. 68), of 1546–47 and 1547–48 respectively. But the present façade is still more comprehensively ornamented, and handsomely inaugurates the period we have called Palladio's "first decorated style," beginning around 1548 (cat. nos. 70, 78). Its plan also comes closer to the executed form, for its step systems and illusionistic shadow lines show it to have a now strongly projecting central frontispiece, open as a loggia on the ground floor, but walled as the front of the *salone* above; the lateral walls are shown solid, and held to the same rear plane as the back of the loggia. The unusual baseless Doric order appears on a Vitruvian palace façade in cat. no. 94, and in the execution of the Villa Pisani at Montagnana (cat. no. 98).

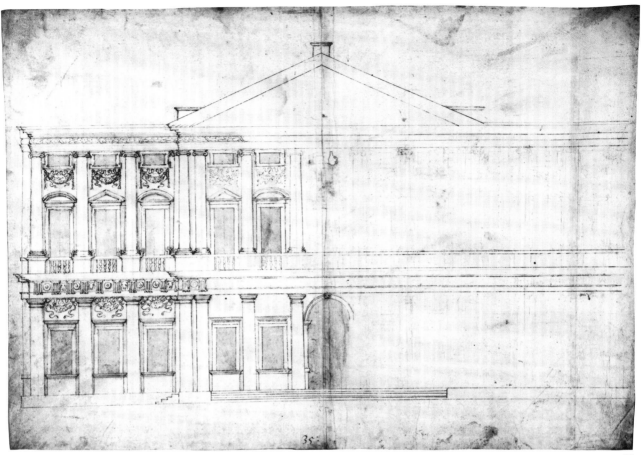

92

Figure 64

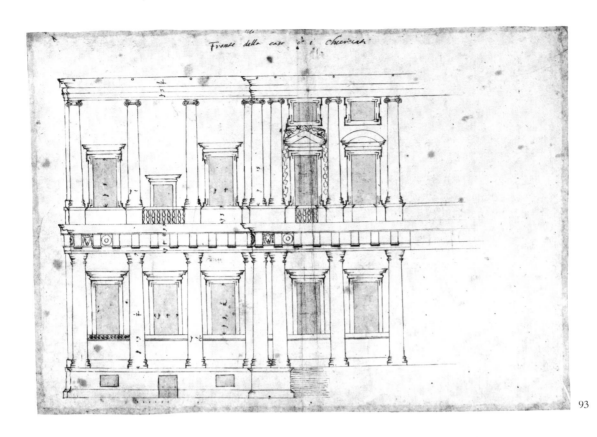

Frante della casa de i Chiericati

93

93. LEFT HALF OF FINAL FACADE ELEVATION FOR PALAZZO CHIERICATI, VICENZA (III)

Late 1560s

RIBA: Palladio XVII/5.

28.7 × 39.5 cm. (single sheet); watermark, anchor in circle with star, countermark AC; laid lines 27 mm. apart (Mošin 1618); Talman 150 mark on *verso*.

Dark siena ink, with lighter reddish ink for details; cool gray-blue wash, tending to beige; inscribed in late handwriting with measures in feet, and scale of 10 feet = 44.5 mm. (1½ Vicentine inches); with a later inscription in the hand of Orazio Palladio, "Fronte della casa de i Chierecati."

Loukomski 1938, fig. on p. 22; Pane 1961, p. 163, fig. 174:13; Zorzi 1965, pp. 197–198, fig. 193; Mostra 1973, pp. 100–101, fig. 113 (Cevese), p. 148 (Burns—correctly identifying Orazio's hand; *cf.* cat. no. 52); Puppi 1973, p. 283, fig. 358; Arts Council 1975, p. 40, no. 58 (Burns).

Royal Institute of British Architects, London.

Figure 65

This drawing is a superb example of Palladio's elegant and economical late graphic style. It was created shortly before 1570, as a stage in the preparation of the *Quattro Libri* plate of Palazzo Chiericati, published that year (II:iii:7), and is thus a record after the fact rather than a preliminary study of the facade. It is entirely autograph, save for the caption added by Palladio's son Orazio (*cf.* Zorzi 1965, fig. 383); the decorative as well as the architectonic details are therefore helpful indicators of Palladio's hand in the less secure drawings of the period. The splendid woodcut

161

illustrating the palace is one of the most beautiful in Palladio's treatise (fig. 65). It eventually concentrated only on the middle section of this drawing, that is, on the three bays flanking the corner of the central projection. The latter—being, as we have seen in cat. nos. 91 and 92, difficult to decipher in its transitions from solid to void—was partly misunderstood by the block cutter, who, as a Venetian, did not have easy access to the palace itself: he shows the corner's upper intercolumniation as open, whereas in fact it is filled by part of the *salone* wall. The peccadillo is certainly minor, and the plate otherwise succeeds supremely well in transmitting a vivid impression of this spectacular design, whose bold architectonic massing is the powerful frame for a rich and festive sculptural embellishment.

Palladio's final recommendation for the facade was put before the city council in Girolamo Chiericati's famous petition of 19 March 1551, in which he asked for permission to extend the front of the palace by 13 feet into the square, so as to provide "greater convenience and greater honor both to myself and to the public, and the ornamentation of the entire city" Zorzi 1965, p. 203, doc. 1; transl. and commentary in Ackerman 1966/1977, pp. 164–167). Thus Palladio's initial flat wall broken slightly forward at the center section (cat. no. 91, analogous plan cat. no. 64), evolving through a fully projecting center section (cat. no. 92, analogous plan fig. 31), culminated—through the Vicenza council's enthusiastic approval—in the complete translation of the whole facade line a full 13 feet to the east. It thereby encloses a magnificent stoa-like loggia on the ground floor, and a much expanded *salone* (behind its only solid wall) on the *piano nobile;* this is flanked by corresponding upper loggias, and creates a novel rhythm of five great open sections enclosing a single solid plane, itself almost dissolved away under a rich sculptural decoration.

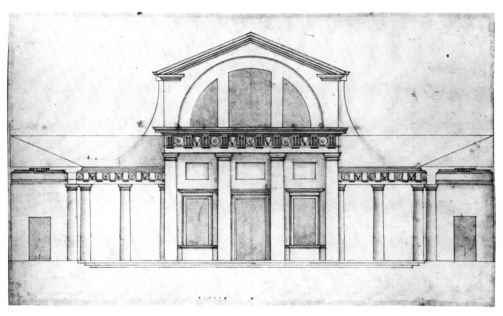

94

94. COURTYARD ELEVATION OF THE "GREEK HOUSE," AFTER VITRUVIUS

c. 1547/48

RIBA: Burlington-Devonshire VIII/16.

26.6 × 43.0 cm. (single sheet); watermark, anchor in circle with star (to associate with cat. no. 95, as variant of Mošin 919?); Talman 54 mark on *verso*.

Very dark siena ink, and light sepia-tan wash, with some pencil underdrawing; inscribed with scale of 10 Vicentine feet = 44.5 mm. (1½ Vicentine inches).

Unpublished (though evidently mentioned, with collocation as B-D VIII/11 [*sic*], by Burns 1979, p. 17).

Royal Institute of British Architects, London.

Lord Burlington acquired this exceptional drawing in his block purchase of 1721 from John Talman, but left it as a loose sheet, deciding not to include it in his bound albums of Palladian materials (perhaps he doubted its attribution to Palladio). Through the fact that almost all scholarly attention to Burlington's Palladian drawings now at the RIBA has been concentrated on those in the albums, this sheet has gone virtually unnoticed until very recently, when Howard Burns and I independently recognized that it represents the courtyard elevation of a well-known Palladian plan (cat. no. 95). Burns arrived at this conclusion from his analysis of the design as a possible working project, on a commission from a real patron "who may not have liked stairs" (1979, p. 17)—although the other side of the house does have staircases that must have led to a full attic, such as the one in cat. no. 68 (a design it very closely resembles). Indeed the design is so idiosyncratic—especially in the interior elevation—that attempts to suggest "requirements of patronage that might have pushed Palladio toward such an unusual invention" (*ibid.*) are probably not feasible.

I was brought instead to a recognition of the elevation as that of an ideal Palladian courtyard by noticing its near-identity in plan to that of "the private house of the Greeks" on page 44 in the *Second Book* of Palladio's treatise; that plan, in turn, has close analogies with the one on RIBA XVI/15 (cat. no. 95), and affords the connection between the two sheets. The intimate parallel with the theoretical reconstruction in the *Quattro Libri*, moreover, provides the key to the drawings' real identity: they, like the woodcut,

are illustrations of Vitruvius's chapter on "the Greek house" (VI:vii:1–3), as Palladio reminds us in his text (1570, II:xi:43). The London drawings may be seen as his effort to "modernize" the type, and in them he produces a much more pragmatic design than the diffuse, "archaeological" reconstruction in the treatise. Whether he can actually have hoped to convince any real Vicentine patron to build a city or suburban "Greek house" according to this more simplified scheme is hard to say. Palladio's most committed supporters were distinguished by great loyalty to his ideas, as he himself acknowledged in a moving passage (*Quattro Libri* II:iii:4). And Francesco Pisani, who was Palladio's contemporary and closest friend among his great Venetian patrons, did build at Montagnana a house on a narrow plot just outside the city walls that has very close analogies with this design (cat. no. 98).

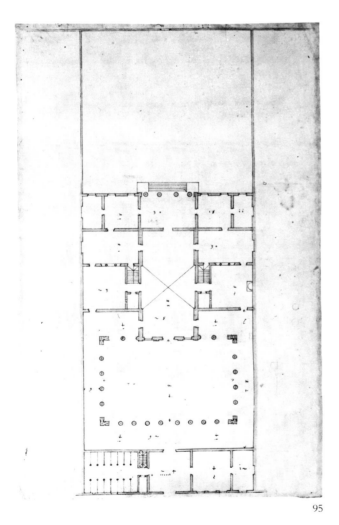

95

95. PLAN OF THE "GREEK HOUSE," AFTER VITRUVIUS

c.1547/48

RIBA: Palladio XVI/15.

43.1 × 27.0 cm (single sheet); countermark B C (to associate with cat. no. 94, as variant of Mošin 919?); Talman 54 mark on *verso*.

Russet umber ink, and gray-umber to light tan washes, with pencil or umber crayon underdrawing, and additions (of columns etc.) in left margin; inscribed with scale of 10 Vicentine feet = 15 mm. (½ Vicentine inch).

Zorzi 1954-II, pp. 116–117, fig. 19; Zorzi 1965, p. 33, fig. 23; Arts Council 1975, pp. 194–195, no. 348 (Burns); Burns 1979, p. 17.

Royal Institute of British Architects, London.

As Palladio quotes Vitruvius in the *Quattro Libri* (II:xi:43), "the Greeks make tight, narrow entrances to their houses, with the stables on one side and servants' rooms on the other. From this first space one enters the courtyard, . . . which has sumptuous porticoes and ampler sets of apartments. It has either four colonnades of equal height, or else the side which faces south is higher than the others and is called a Rhodian peristyle. Such apartments have fine entrance courts with imposing front doors of their own; [the colonnades are decorated with polished stucco in relief, and coffered ceilings of woodwork,] and they were occupied only by the men of the house. Within are various rooms, which we might call antechambers, chambers, and smaller rooms behind, from the fact that they follow in sequence. [These] are the spaces for dining, sleeping, and other such necessary activities of the family" (in part rearranged, and quoted also from Morgan 1914/1960, pp. 185–187; bracketed portion omitted by Palladio).

This passage is so clearly a description of the present plan and its courtyard elevation (cat. no. 94) that it does not require much more extended comment. The style of the two drawings, however, may remind us of some opportune parallels. The garden facade at the top of the plan (which despite the elegance of its portico is the secondary front, as is proven by the insignificance of its associated postern gate) is remarkably close to the "small villa facade" of 1547/48 (cat. no. 68), and has analogies through its podium design and draftsmanship with the Vancimuglio plan of the same years (cat. no. 88). It does present an early appearance of one of Palladio's most significant inventions, on which he specifically comments in the published text: that is the proportionally sequential suites of three rooms of graduated sizes, in all of which one dimension is constant (here 30 by 18 feet, 18 by 18, and 18 by 11). This invention had been tentatively prefigured in his earlier work (cat. no. 41 of 1539–41 is a precocious example with identical measurements), but it makes its principal and definitive entry in this period (cf.

cat. nos. 65 *verso*, 88, 97, 98, 99-B), to become Palladio's most characteristic and most successful technique of organizing domestic interiors.

The triumphant solution of this forward-looking scheme contrasts oddly with the almost archaizing quality of the rest of the project: it returns to the motif of the *serliana* (an early example of which had also used baseless Tuscan columns— cat. no. 43), it shows a projection of the main hall into the courtyard "peristyle" that is not exactly authorized by Vitruvius but is extremely close to the Plazzo Porto projects (cat. no. 66), and the whole flavor of the design is backward looking and "primitive" in a way which the same elements composing the Palazzo Chiericati facade (cat. no. 92) definitely are not.

96

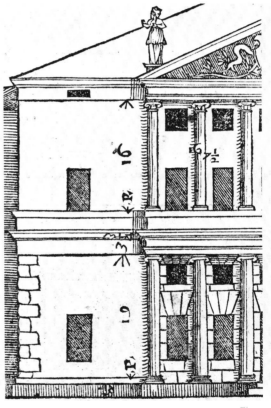

Figure 66

96. PARTIAL FACADE ELEVATION OF PALAZZO ANTONINI, UDINE

c. 1570?

RIBA: Palladio XVII/25.

25.2 × 18.7 cm. (single sheet); countermark, plain five-lobe "flower" lower right (*cf.* Briquet 6464); Talman 150 mark on *verso*.

Dark red siena ink, with flat gray wash.

Loukomski 1938, p. 24 (as XVII/28); Dalla Pozza 1943-I, p. 251, fig. 13; Dalla Pozza 1943-II, p. 80–81, fig. 19; Zorzi 1965, p. 227, fig. 256; Zorzi 1969, p. 183, fig. 343; Puppi 1973, p. 307, fig. 398.

Royal Institute of British Architects, London.

This is a puzzling drawing, for it represents one of Palladio's early mature palace designs, yet its drafting style is either late or at least partially by another hand. Perhaps the wisest course at present is to call it a later studio copy after a project drawing of c. 1550. There is not much possibility of Palladio's collaboration on this version: the capitals are clumsier and more summary than his, as are the hastily sketched molding corners; the use of brushed wash independent of inked lines (as in the entablature) is very rare in Palladio, and the curly scrolls on the bottom of the upper window frame are quite unknown. The dull,

164

heavy gray wash is uncharacteristic of his drawings, though evidently a stock-in-trade of this draftsman, who uses it for several different effects. (A very slight chance that this sheet might be a copy after Palladio by Inigo Jones should perhaps also be mentioned, although I doubt its likelihood.)

The original project was a drawing for the east or garden facade of the palace of Florio Antonini at Udine in the Friuli, by a wide margin Palladio's easternmost work. The facade stands essentially in the same form today (Zorzi 1965, fig 251), but with radical changes in the window frames, upper entablature and roof. For this reason the *Quattro Libri* plate of the west or street side is used as a comparison (II:iii:5, fig. 66), though its windows are missing their frames altogether, and in proportion are less true to reality than those in the drawing. On the street facade the columns are engaged in the walls of the upper and lower halls, rather than free-standing before two-storied open loggias. The design upon which our sheet is based for the first time introduced this motif of superimposed porches, unless the lateral facade loggias of Palazzo Chiericati precede it: they were designed in the late 1540s and executed from the autumn of 1550 (cat. nos. 91–93), whereas Palazzo Antonini and its designs unfortunately have never been dated. It is, however, a close prototype for the Villa Cornaro at Piombino, which was designed in

1551 and completed by 1553; indeed this drawing has sometimes erroneously been connected with that palace, though the Villa Cornaro stands on a very tall podium, has no projecting quoins but rather fully drafted fictive rustication inscribed on its coat of stucco, and (on the garden facade with open loggie) four small windows rather than two big ones on each side.

The drawing project—and the Palazzo Antonini as executed—are both related even more closely to the Villa Pisani at Montagnana, apparently planned a bit earlier, but executed in 1552–53. This relationship has just been dramatically reinforced by Howard Burns, who has shown that a sheet of Webb's sketches at Worcester College, which clearly reproduces the present drawing, also depicts two other project images for Udine that are now lost. These included fully rusticated facades, such as prefigured in cat. no. 49, and barrel- or groin-vaulted halls, exactly as in the contemporary case of Montagnana.

We may thus understand that the corpus of Palladian drawings for Udine was once larger by at least two sheets than it is now; and that, during the period of its planning, Palladio's design for the Villa Pisani was also being worked out. Piombino's perfected derivation puts the date of these experiments to the winter of 1550–51 or earlier: thus our best date for Palazzo Antonini is still c. 1550.

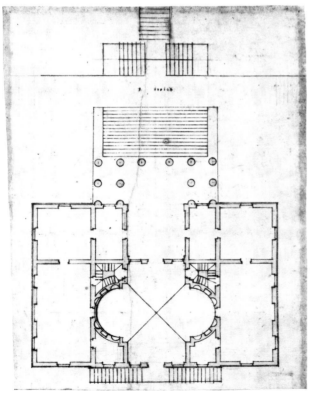

97

97. PLAN PROJECT FOR AN ARCHAEOLOGICAL VILLA

c. 1550

RIBA: Palladio XVI-20-B.

25.7 × 19.5 cm. (single sheet, now detached from the unrelated XVI/20-A); watermark, angel in oval with star and B beneath (Briquet 669: Vicenza 1542); Talman 150 mark on *verso*.

Umber ink and umber-gray wash, with some pencil underdrawing and additions; inscribed with scale of 10 Vicentine feet = 20 mm. (⅔ of a Vicentine inch).

Zorzi 1954, pp. 65–66, no. 8, fig. 8B; Pane 1961, pp. 109–110, fig. 133:34; Zorzi 1969, p. 45, no. 8, fig. 53B; Lewis 1973, p. 369, fig. 195; Mostra 1973, p. 148 (Burns); Puppi 1973, p. 297, fig. 377; Arts Council 1975, p. 195, no. 350 (Fairbairn/Burns).

Royal Institute of British Architects, London.

This beautifully simple, grand, and imposing plan has been variously interpreted, with only modestly convincing results. Long associated with the Vancimuglio/Malcontenta project of c. 1547–48 (cat. no. 88), with which it was fortuitously connected for mounting in the Burlington albums, it actually has almost nothing to do with either of those buildings. It is composed instead from the *alternative* sketches to theirs, on RIBA XVII/12 *verso* (cat. no. 65 *verso*), that is, from those proposing a columnar temple-portico rather than one with lateral screen walls (as drawn on cat. no. 88, and built at Vancimuglio, fig. 57); to this extent alone it does recall Malcontenta, though that plan lacks its pair of interior portico columns.

These near-contemporaneous "square block" plans of the early 1550s can be easily distinguished by the arrangement of their three-room living suites. Independent of Palladio's rapidly changing ideas about the loggias and halls, the twin apartments that enclose and define these elements form true "signature motifs" that are nearly autonomous for each project. The first type, pioneered at Bagnolo (cat. no. 47), Cessalto (fig. 25), and Vancimuglio/Malcontenta (cat. no. 88), reached its perfected form at Piombino: its long rooms parallel the facade, with the square and narrow rooms forming the arms of a U behind. The present example, with the long rooms parallel to the main axis of the hall, the square rooms at the corners, and the *camerini* flanking the vestibule, is a straightforward replication of the arrangement that first appeared at Villa Poiana (cat. no. 58, figs. 35, 36), and in a more elaborated form at Palazzo Porto (*cf.* cat. no. 66 *verso,* and *Quattro Libri* II:iii:8). It is extremely close to the plan followed in the Villa Pisani at Montagnana (*cf.* cat. no. 98, fig. 67): so much so, that the little fireplaces on the vestibule walls of the *camerini,* only sketched here, show up in the finished project (and the executed building) in the same spots; and the engaged half-columns of this drawing's portico facade

(toward the garden?) reappear in the actual villa on the facade of the great square hall (toward the street).

Both this project and the realized structure at Montagnana are sober, severely conceived examplars of a rigorously purified style, so strict in its composition and details as to justify the identification of an "archaeological revival" in several related projects of these years around 1550. Cat. nos. 92 and 94, for example, show baseless Doric columns (which were built at Montagnana), the latter drawing also with a "thermal window" derived from the Roman baths. Cat. no. 95 is Palladio's attempt to draft an archaeological reconstruction as a project for a modern house, and cat. nos. 72 *verso*–73 extend this idea also to villa designs. The final Palazzo Chiericati facade (cat. no. 93) presents a revived antique stoa as a civic colonnade, and the facade of the Malcontenta is partly based on a specific antique monument (cat. no. 106 and fig. 74). The portico facade of the present plan as well, with its tall pedimented temple-front raised on a high podium approached by a great axial stair, has always been compared with obvious antique prototypes such as the Mausoleum of Romulus (cat. no. 23), which it very closely resembles; other parallels probably also first drafted in the early 1550s occur in cat. nos. 82–85.

98. PLAN PROJECT FOR VILLA PISANI, MONTAGNANA

1550–51

RIBA: Palladio XVI/21.

37.4 × 26.9 cm (single sheet); watermark, angel in circle with star; countermark, A P in upper right corner; laid lines 28 mm. apart (Briquet 647); Talman 54 mark on *verso.*

Red-umber ink and deep umber-gray wash, with pencil underdrawing and additions.

Zorzi 1965, p. 188, fig. 159 (as for Palazzo Porto); Mostra 1973, p. 148 (Burns—as for Palazzo Barbaran); Puppi 1973, fig. 347 (as for Palazzo Porto).

Royal Institute of British Architects, London.

The destination of this extremely fine and careful plan has consistently been assumed to have been a Vicentine palace project; but it is almost certainly a proposal for the suburban palace that Francesco Pisani built on a large garden site just outside the eastern gate of Montagnana, in 1553 (fig. 67). The only changes are a slight diminution of all the measurements, a somewhat more complicated ceiling in the "Hall of the Four Columns" (with a transverse barrel vault intersected by three lower ones), and a compression of the oval stair systems into the spaces flanking the garden loggia, behind the square rooms. The loggia is thus reduced to a Doric porch of four columns with an Ionic one above it, the two thereby becoming precise replicas of the superimposed loggias on the internal (rear) facade of Palazzo Chiericati, whose construction began in 1550–51 (the latter's vaulted stair landings are also identical to those in this

drawing). The Montagnana stair systems in their executed form (with the innermost former windows of the square rooms, on the drawing, converted into doors giving interior access to the flights) find precise prototypes in those at Piombino, built in 1551–52. Thus Francesco Pisani's success in purchasing the last plot of land he needed for this site, in December of 1552 (documents in a private archive in the Veneto, being published by Carolyn Kolb Lewis), accords perfectly with the dating of the most diagnostic elements in the final *Quattro Libri* design, and the documented construction of the house in 1553.

But this project drawing, for all its closeness to the executed fabric, is strangely backward-looking in certain motifs. The twin stairs are almost copied from those on the plan in cat. no. 64, apparently of about 1549; the juxtaposition of a four-column rear loggia and an associated spiral stair system is prefigured in fig. 42 in the same entry; and several parallels for the palace block, garden loggia and flanking stairs are shown on cat. no. 66 *verso.* All these are projects for Palazzo Porto, though the present sheet certainly is not: it has a small but steep stair outside the garden gate, as if for access to water; and in fact a stream occurs at this point both in Francesco Pisani's documents and on the existing site in Montagnana. The parallels with the Vicentine palace are extremely interesting, however, when we recall that Palazzo Porto was inscribed with two completion dates in 1552, the year of Villa Pisani's commencement. Perhaps more than we have suspected of Giuseppe Porto's palace was designed at the very last minute, and what ideas could not be incorporated there, were transferred directly to Montagnana. But we should also remember that Montagnana's executed baseless Doric columns, as well as certain aspects of its *Quattro Libri* design bring it close to the "Greek house" project of c. 1547–48 (cat. nos. 94–95). The latter's design (like the present plan) may thus have been prepared considerably earlier for Francesco Pisani's use on some enclosed urban site—before he acquired his preferred terrain at Montagnana in 1552, and the present drawing was slightly modified for execution in 1553.

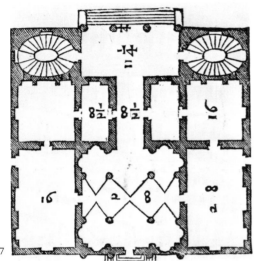

Figure 67

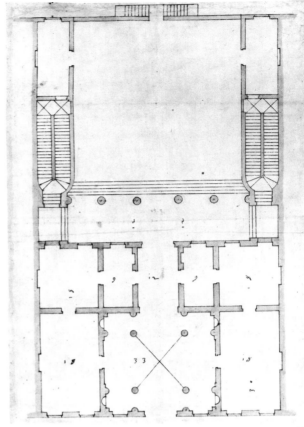

98

---

99. THREE PLAN PROJECTS FOR PALAZZO BARBARAN, VICENZA

1550 (Plans A and B)–1551 (Plan C)

RIBA: Palladio XVI/14-A, B, and C.

Three sheets, now separated by recent restoration.

Drawing A: 29.7 × 21.4 cm.; countermark A, lower right; laid lines 32 mm. apart; Talman 150 mark on *verso;* reddish siena ink with sepia-beige wash; inscribed with measures in Vicentine feet, and scale of 10 feet = 26 mm. (⅞ of a Vicentine inch).

Drawing B: 30.1 × 21.2 cm.; watermark, anchor in circle with star; laid lines 33 mm. apart (*cf.* Mošin 778); Talman 150 mark on *verso;* red siena ink with pale sepia-beige wash; inscribed with measures in Vicentine feet, and scale of 30 feet = 78 mm. (2⅜ Vicentine inches).

Drawing C: 29.8 × 20.6 cm.; watermark, angel in circle with star, with B beneath; laid lines 26 mm. apart (Briquet 669: Vicenza 1542); Talman 150 mark on *verso;* dark umber ink and cool umbergray wash, with some pencil; inscribed with measures in Vicentine feet, and scale of 20 feet = 52 mm. (1¾ Vicentine inches).

Forssman 1965, pp. 97–98, fig. 45 (Drawing A), p. 98, fig. 46 (Drawing B), p. 98, fig. 47 (Drawing C); Zorzi 1965, p. 188, fig. 313; Burns 1973, p. 178; Mostra 1973, p. 148, fig. 156 (Burns); Puppi 1973, p. 395, fig. 557; Arts Council 1975, p. 220, no. 387 (Burns).

Royal Institute of British Architects, London.

Palladio's famous and beautiful palace for Montano Barbaran, at the corner of Contrà Porti and Via Riali in Vicenza, is a late work of 1570–75. The architect describes in the *Quattro Libri* of 1570 how its design had been changed at the moment of his sending the book to press, because of the patron's acquisition of an adjacent lot: he shows a half-elevation for the expanded facade (II:iii:23), with an apology that there had not been time before publication to cut a new block that would show the enlarged plan. But on the preceding page he reproduced his previous plan, for the earlier project involving the smaller site (fig. 70); and that illustration is identical to the drawing of Plan C in the present group. Commentators have all tended to date this pre-existing project to the very eve of the revision for the larger site, but close parallels between these drawings and works around 1550 document it instead to a period some twenty years earlier.

Plan A repeats the very long groin-vaulted hall of the largest Palazzo Porto project, from about 1549 (cat. no. 64), placing it also beside an identical oval stair with semicircular landings, and including the same small service flights tucked in behind the corners of its entrance passage. It also shows an erased apse at the far end of this atrium, derived from the entrance halls of the Theatre of Marcellus

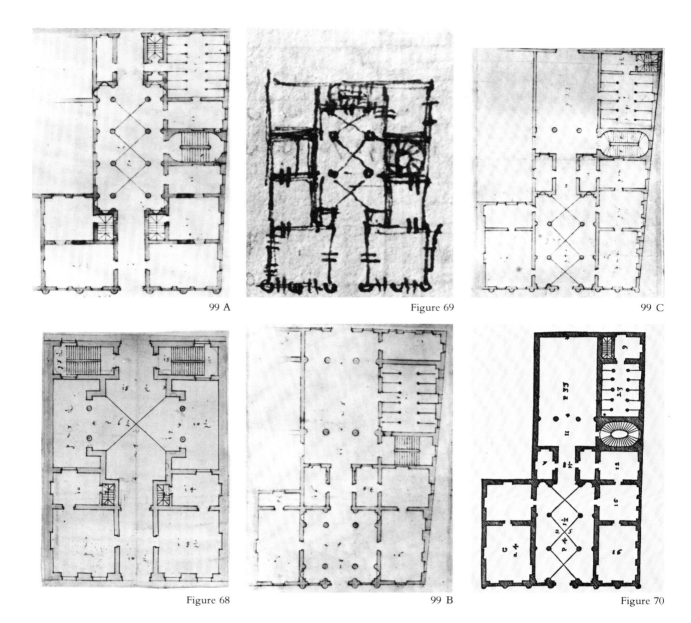

99 A

Figure 69

99 C

Figure 68

99 B

Figure 70

(cat. no. 59). Close parallels for its narrow vestibule between large facade rooms, followed by smaller chambers alongside the service stairs at the corners of the hall, are provided by the finished drawings on RIBA XVI/19-C (fig. 68), as well as a quick sketch on RIBA XI/22 *verso* (fig. 69, and cat. no. 102). Both may well be connected with the planning of Palazzo Porto (*cf*. cat. no. 66); the former also prefigures in twin examples the large oblong stairwell with rectangular landings that identically appears on our present Plan B.

That intermediate design in the trilogy for Palazzo Barbaran is very close to the Villa Pisani project of exactly the same years (cat. no. 98). The facade of Plan B shows the same four engaged columns, composing a pedimented frontispiece, as on the final *Quattro Libri* design for Montagnana (fig. 67); both this motif and the pattern of the three-room suite are borrowed from the "archaeological

villa" project (cat. no. 97), also of about 1550. The incorporation of a large stairwell directly behind the corner room of this suite, adjoining a four-column rear loggia, is exactly paralleled in the executed treatise designs of the Villa Pisani. So is Plan B's "Hall of the Four Columns": Palladio's omission of crossed lines to represent the standard groin vault must indicate his intention of giving it the intersecting barrel vaults that were executed at Montagnana.

Plan C adroitly combines the two preceding schemes, and was drawn a bit later (as demonstrated by the change to segmental landings on the spiral stair, executed at Piombino in 1551); it adds an initial *p* to the measurements, which is a useful chronological indicator for other drawings. The magnificent atrium with its triple groin vault, and these same facade rooms flanking it, appear in the palace as built. The structure is scheduled for restoration by the Palladian Center as its permanent headquarters.

168

100. SKETCH PROJECTS FOR PALACE FACADES, AND FOR THE VILLA BARBARO NYMPHAEUM, MASER

1554

RIBA: Palladio X/15 *recto.*

43.2 × 28.7 cm. (single sheet of beige paper); watermark, anchor in circle with star (*cf.* Mošin 786); Talman 49 mark on *verso.*

Reddish siena ink, with pencil formation upper right. *Verso,* SKETCHES OF PLAN, ELEVATIONS, AND DETAILS OF IMPERIAL FORA (PERHAPS OF VESPASIAN AND NERVA?), ROME; inscribed with descriptions and measures in feet; Zorzi 1957, p. 155, fig. 10; Zorzi 1959, p. 88, fig. 207; Spielmann 1966, p. 153, no. 103 (all as *recto,* and with various identifications).

Zorzi 1954, p. 105, fig. 1; Pane 1961, p. 110, fig. 135:39; Zorzi 1965, pp. 90–91, fig. 66; D'Ossat 1966, p. 37, fig. 43 (detail); Barbieri 1968, p. 59, fig. 100; Mostra 1973, p. 145, fig. 151 (Burns); Puppi 1973, pp. 281, 286, fig. 17; Tafuri 1973, p. 164, fig. 117; Arts Council 1975, p. 239, no. 426 (Burns); Berger 1978, pp. 165–166, fig. 23 (detail).

Royal Institute of British Architects, London.

Burns has convincingly identified the two upper left-hand facades on this sheet as Palladio's visual memoranda of successive stages in the completion of the Palazzo Municipale at Brescia. Lodovico Beretta was selected as architect by the Council of that city on 4 December 1550, and commissioned to draw up final plans for the building's superstructure (its lower story had been built to a model by Tomaso Formenton in the 1490s). Since Palladio is documented to have visited Brescia between 9 September and 15 November 1550, it is very likely that the large elevation quickly sketched at the center of this sheet reflects drawings that he would have made during that autumn to record Beretta's preliminary project. On 3 June 1554 Jacopo Sansovino summarized in a report the results of a consultative visit he had just made to Brescia, and Burns is probably correct in seeing the topmost small sketch on this sheet as a record of Sansovino's recommended design (we should remember that Palladio is documented to have been in Venice and thus easily in contact with Sansovino, during the following month of July: *cf.* cat. no. 73).

The sketches on the *verso* of this sheet offer an independent confirmation of the date, referring as they do to Palladio's trip to Rome in the latter half of that year, in the company of his friendliest Venetian patrons (see Introduction). As we have seen, Daniele Barbaro may well have been among these, and certain drawings made on the journey apparently record his and Palladio's discussion about the Maser nymphaeum (cat. no. 87). I have suggested elsewhere (1977, 1980) that the top right-hand sketch on this sheet probably relates also to that commission, and its execution in 1554–58. The two elaborate palace facades below it may very well be connected with Palladio's sketch plan for a palace on an irregular Venetian site, probably drawn in the spring of this same year (on RIBA XVI/9-B *verso*—*cf.* cat. no. 71). The lower left facade seems to be an alternate for the top story at Brescia, and the left hand is probably Palladio's, holding the sheet.

---

101. FACADE PROJECT FOR A VENETIAN PALACE

1554

Vicenza: 1950 inv. D-27.

43.7 × 58.2 cm. (single sheet); no watermark visible; no collector's mark.

Siena ink, with light gold-beige wash.

Magrini 1845, p. 301; Loukomski 1927, p. 39, pl. 34; Venturi 1940, XI:iii:460–461, fig. 423; Pée 1939/1941, pp. 167–168, n. 12; Pane 1961, p. 311, fig. 347:76; Zorzi 1965, pp. 282–287, fig. 350; Zorzi 1966, p. 153, fig. 168; Ackerman 1966/1977, p. 114, fig. 62; Zorzi 1967, p. 171, fig. 123; Forssman 1972, p. 90, fig. 47; Wilinski 1974–1976, pp. 107–108, fig. 24; Mostra 1973, p. 154 (Burns); Puppi 1973, p. 389, fig. 547; Arts Council 1975, pp. 212–213, no. and fig. 379 (Burns); Burns 1979, p. 18.

Museo Civico, Vicenza.

This extraordinarily beautiful sheet is one of the most wonderfully evocative among Palladio's works, for it is the sole drawing that survives to indicate how he might have responded to the challenge of the most prestigious domestic commission a North Italian architect could obtain: the design of a great palace facade on the Grand Canal in Venice, a *locus* suggested by its water portals and triple-lighted central halls. Such a destination for this sheet has occasionally been doubted, since there are no comparable drawings or buildings by Palladio. But as a kind of reverse proof, the plates in the *Quattro Libri* for two palaces on Venetian sites (II:xvii:71, 72) represent, in relation to it, the same tendency toward miniaturizing a former colossal order, as is demonstrated by the division of the single engaged columns on the first Palazzo Barbaran facade, into the half-size superimposed orders on the second (*Quattro Libri* II:iii:22–23). Indeed the simplified woodcut of the earlier Barbaran facade is in effect a slightly wider precursor of the upper part of our elevation, and its date of 1550/51 (cat. no. 99) helps to establish a chronology for the composition.

The drawing which most effectively documents the genesis of our design is a superb free sketch for the Palazzo Porto facade (fig. 71), which exists as an unpublished and undiscussed vignette on the margin of RIBA XV/1 (fig. 42). That large sheet, as mentioned in cat. nos. 64 and 98, has its closest external parallels in the plans of Palazzo Barbaran and Villa Pisani at Montagnana; it certainly dates before 1552, when Montagnana was begun and Palazzo Porto finished. It prefigures every important element of our Venetian facade: a heavily rusticated basement, incorporating a large portal with rough keystones, tall lateral apertures, and smaller mezzanine windows; an identical

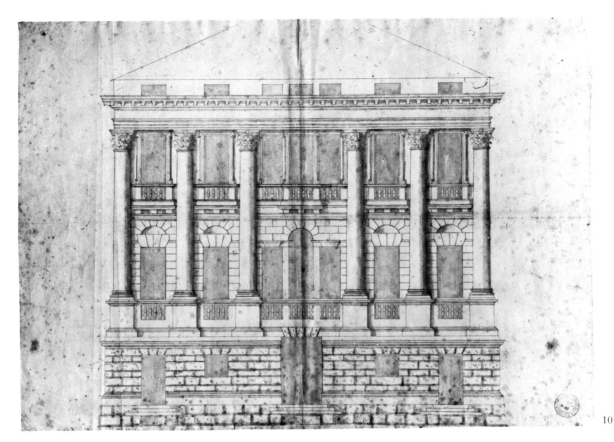

101

Figure 71

Figure 72

171

zone of high pedestals with broadly projecting base moldings, incorporating balustrades in front of long windows on the *piano nobile;* and, most telling of all, a colossal order of engaged columns framing not only these windows, but also an upper range with further balustraded balconies, as a second *piano nobile.*

Almost all these same elements were executed on the facade of Palazzo Valmarana in Vicenza (fig. 72), whose construction was delayed by the death of Palladio's devoted supporter Gian Alvise Valmarana in 1556, but which was certainly designed before that event: it adds a confirming detail, in the drafted fictive rustication around the lower windows. This motif is paralleled even more exactly in the form on our drawing by the inscribed stucco patterns over the windows at Malcontenta (c. 1550–53) and Piombino (built 1551–53); these three unique executed examples of the device thus suggest a range of c. 1553–c. 1555 for the Venetian design. In fact, we can assign it with considerable certainty to the median date of 1554, by a comparison with the two facades of similar proportions and motifs on the preceding sheet of sketches made in that year (cat. no. 100), and by a recollection of Palladio's many contacts with his Venetian patrons at that moment (*cf.* also cat. nos. 70–73, and 87). Among these a particular importance for the present context is suggested by Palladio's letter to the ambassador of Urbino, on whose draft he sketches the plan for a large Venetian palace (*cf.* cat. no. 71: RIBA XVI/9-B *verso*). Burns, finally, has connected with this design a very light pencil sketch on the *verso* of RIBA VIII/23 (cat. no. 15), which shows a small *serliana* and one superimposed window, in a narrow bay between colossal columns (1979, p. 18). Its entablature and attic as well probably relate to our finished facade design; and we might especially remember that it was just such half-used sheets as this—its *recto* shows the amphitheatre at Pola—which Palladio seems habitually to have carried in his traveling portfolio, particularly when visiting Venice to discuss these very antiquities with Daniele Barbaro (*cf.* cat. nos. 72–73 and 90). None of Palladio's projects for a Venetian palace was built, and this design finds its nearest realization in the posthumous Palazzo Porto-Breganze on the Piazzo Castello in Vicenza, whose partial two-bay fragment was executed by Vincenzo Scamozzi.

CHAPTER EIGHT

Ancient and Modern Civic Monuments:

Temples and tombs in the Classical style

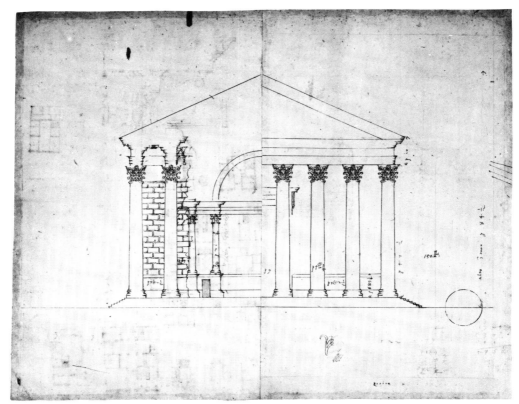

102 *recto*

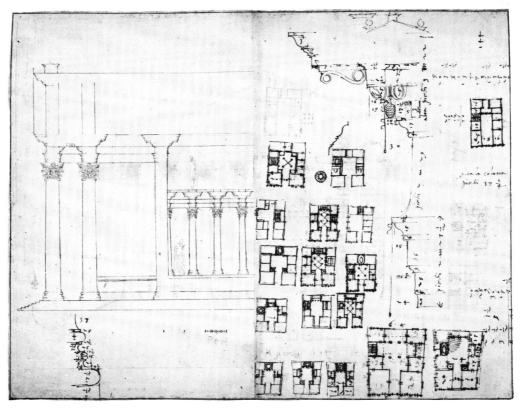

102 *verso*

174

102. HALF ELEVATION, HALF SECTIONS, AND DETAILS OF TEMPLE OF MARS ULTOR, ROME; TWENTY PLAN SKETCHES FOR PALACE PROJECTS

1547

RIBA: Palladio XI/22 *recto* and *verso*.

31.6 × 39.1 cm. (two sheets pasted at center, presumably by Burlington; left piece, 31.6 × 20.2 cm.; right piece, 31.4 × 19.5 cm.); watermark on left piece (with transverse section and plans), small anchor in circle with star; Talman 150 marks adjacent to elevation on *recto,* and to architrave of entablature on *verso.*

Recto, siena ink and beige-gray wash, with pencil additions; inscribed with measures in feet, and scale of 10 feet = 22.5 mm. *Verso,* left piece (section), very light umber ink, with pencil underdrawings and additions; base moldings, red siena ink, inscribed with scale of 36 feet = 47 mm.; right piece (entablature), dark reddish-brown siena ink; plans, very dark red siena ink, and heavy black umber ink, with pencil underdrawing and additions; inscribed with measures in feet.

Zorzi 1954, p. 120, fig. 22 *(verso);* Zorzi 1959, p. 79, fig. 177 *recto* and *verso);* Forssman 1965, p. 62, fig. 29 *(verso);* Zorzi 1965, p. 44. fig. 32 *(verso);* Spielmann 1966, p. 143, no. 43 *(recto* and *verso),* fig. 23 *(recto);* Burns 1973, p. 178, fig. 129 *(verso,* detail); Puppi 1973, pp. 292 *(verso),* 294 *(verso)* 302 *(verso),* fig. 16 *(verso,* detail); Arts Council 1975, p. 221, no. 389 (Burns).

Royal Institute of British Architects, London.

Palladio devoted no less than eight pages in the final book of the *Quattro Libri* to the great temple of Mars the Avenger in the Forum of Augustus, a dedication which that victorious prince had vowed at the Battle of Philippi, and which was dedicated forty years later in 2 B.C. (Boëthius/Ward-Perkins 1970, pp. 190–192). The half transverse section and half facade elevation on the *recto* of this sheet form the basis of the treatise woodcut with a small view through the whole forum (IV:vii:16), and also of a very large double-page spread on pp. 18–19. The left side of the *verso* provides the design for a fine full-page longitudinal section through the porch and front of the cella (p. 17), and for the rich interior base moldings on p. 22. The entablature on the right side of our *verso,* finally, is the source for a superb half-plate detail on p. 20, where it is augmented by a beautiful olive-leaf Corinthian capital, and the decorated ceiling of the colonnade.

Quite surprisingly (for we must assume Palladio to have needed these methodical drawings for his extended treatment of the monument in the *Quattro Libri*), the right *verso* was almost completely covered—even before pasting up, as we know from losses along its edge—with twenty quick sketches of ideas for organizing the plan of an urban palace block. It is possible that at least two sites are involved, for the upper fifteen plans are rectangular, while the lower five are slightly trapezoidal. The planimetric ideas are closely related to the development of the earlier project for Palazzo Barbaran, here dated to c. 1550–51 (cat. no. 99: detail of Plan 6 on this sheet in fig. 69). It seems clear, however, that these spontaneous and inventive sketches substantially predate the formally drafted plans, and that this sheet provided a repertory or anthology from which Palladio selected their forms. Since others among these designs reflect the planning process of Palazzo Porto (*cf.* cat. nos. 64–66, esp. fig. 43), we may thus confidently date the sheet to Palladio's Roman sojourn in 1547, upon his return from which the final designs of Palazzo Porto must have been begun almost at once.

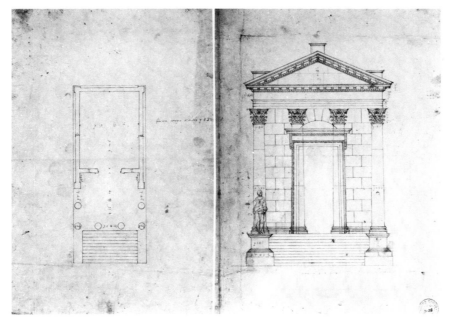

103

103. PLAN AND ELEVATION OF THE TEMPLE OF AUGUSTUS, POLA

c. 1551/52

Vicenza: 1950 inv. D-28.

42.5 × 56.9 cm. (single sheet of heavy paper, folded at center); watermark, anchor in circle with star; no collector's mark.

Siena ink over heavily inscribed lines, with pencil underdrawing; inscribed in transitional handwriting with measures in feet, and with scale of 24 feet = 43 mm. (1½ Venetian inches).

Zorzi 1959, p. 81, fig. 186; Spielmann 1966, p. 151, no. 88, fig. 45.

Museo Civico, Vicenza.

By incorporating unusual amounts of space between its images, and adding an inscription, Palladio in this strong yet delicate drawing attractively suggests one of the curious characteristics of the temple at Pola—namely, its replica-

tion, to create a pair of small temples that formerly framed a much larger one. This example (which is still well preserved today) is inscribed to Rome and Augustus, and dates from A.D. 1 or 2; its twin may have been dedicated to Neptune (Robertson 1929/1959, p. 340). Its drafted images reappear almost exactly, again across a centerfold, in the *Quattro Libri* (IV:xxvii:108–109); the text also describes the town's many other antiquities (*cf.* cat. no. 17). As we have seen, Palladio recalled Pola's richly decorated small temples when sketching an ideal reconstruction of the forum at Halicarnassus (cat. no. 71, fig. 47), which serves to date our present drawing well before 1554. The elevation of its pediment is already sketched on the preceding sheet (cat. no. 102 *verso*, upper right), its labels are written in a hand that can be dated from c. 1551, and its masonry pattern and door frame (seen through two "transparent" columns) appear at Piombino in 1551–53. Its drafting in c. 1551/52 is therefore most convincing.

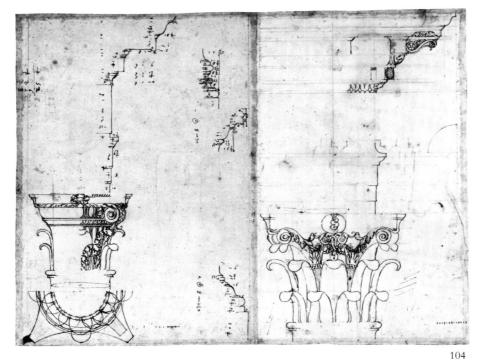

104

Figure 73

176

104. STUDIES OF CAPITALS AND ENTABLATURES OF TEMPLE OF DIANA AT NÎMES, AND TEMPLE OF THE DIOSCURI AT NAPLES

Late 1560s

RIBA: Palladio XIII/18 recto.

28.3 × 37.0 cm. (two sheets of different paper, joined presumably by Burlington: left piece, thinner and deeply yellowed, 28.3 × 19.9 cm.; watermark, Paschal lamb with banner in double oval with Maltese cross [Briquet 51:Vicenza 1551 ff.]; Talman 150 mark on *verso*. Right piece, 28.2 × c. 17.5 cm.; watermark, running angel and star without circle [*cf.* Briquet 633]; Talman 150 mark on *verso*).

Deep umber-brown ink with hint of red, on both pieces; both with pencil underdrawing (very pronounced in layout lines on right), inscriptions, and borders; left piece inscribed with measures in feet, and with scale of 1 foot = 39 mm. (1⅓ Vicentine inches). Right piece drawn with scale of 1 foot = 22.5 mm. (¾ of a Vicentine inch); *verso,* SKETCHES FOR AN ALTAR CHAPEL, extremely dark siena ink (illustrated and discussed at cat. no. 115).

Zorzi 1959, p. 84, fig. 198 (both pieces); Strandberg 1961, pp. 31–40 (Dioscuri drawing at Stockholm); Spielmann 1966, p. 150, no. 81 (right piece), p. 151, no. 90 (left piece); Mostra 1973, p. 22 (right piece), pp. 22–23 (left piece—both Forssman); Arts Council 1975, p. 147, no. 259 (*verso*—Burns).

Royal Institute of British Architects, London.

These drawings—which, though unrelated, nevertheless make an attractive composition in Burlington's montage—were prepared as models for plates in the *Quattro Libri:* the fine Composite capital and entablature from Nîmes are reproduced in this form on IV:xix:123, and the Corinthian order from Naples on IV:xxiii:97. Palladio's images of the "Maison Carrée" and Diana temple at Nîmes came neither from on-site sketches nor the drawings of another architect, but from a printed source. In 1559/60 Jean Poldo d'Albenas published at Lyons his beautiful *Discours historial de l'antique et illustre Cité de Nismes, avec les portraitz des plus antiques et insignes bastimens du dit lieu, réduits a leur vraye mesure et proportions.* Palladio simply republished the two temples from its pages, converting perspective views into orthogonal projections. Forssman has even suggested that his woodcut technician may have been capable of most of this conversion by himself, so that Palladio may not have needed to redraw each plate. The question of a journey to Nîmes thus remains open: Palladio says in the second sentence of the *Quattro Libri* that besides studying books he had "furthermore traveled often to Rome, and to other places in Italy and abroad," to examine and measure the antiquities themselves; but the only foreign site we can be sure he visited was Pola. Still, he had to buy his copy of Poldo d'Albenas somewhere; and it may be that if he found one on a quick trip to Nîmes (as for example in an extension of his visit to Turin in 1566) he would have realized that he need not redraw its monuments himself.

The striking sketch for the Naples capital, its magnificent prototype on a recently discovered drawing in Stockholm (fig. 73), and the text of its *Quattro Libri* publication combine to show Palladio not only as a supremely sensitive artist, but as a fine architectural historian. The Naples temple (whose portico stood intact until the earthquake of 1688) was dedicated as Palladio remarks to Castor and Pollux, the twin sons of Jove. At their temple in the Roman Forum—a very ancient foundation, rebuilt from 7 B.C. to A.D. 6—an inspired Augustan architect conceived a subtle but extraordinarily beautiful allusion to the inseparable devotion of the Twins, by entwining the two foliate spirals at the tops of their capitals. This splendid example of architectural iconography became deservedly celebrated, and has been emulated by masters ranging from the Augustan architect-sculptor at Baalbek in Lebanon, through James Gibbs at St. Martin's-in-the-Fields and the Cambridge Senate House, to Hornblower & Marshall's Natural History Museum for the Smithsonian Institution in Washington. Palladio fully recognized the novelty of the motif, and on the basis of this Naples example he wrote a profoundly significant manifesto in praise of freedom in architectural design. "From this," he said, "as well as from many other instances scattered through this book, one understands that Architects are not forbidden to depart sometimes from standard forms—so long as their variations constitute graceful inventions, that are true to nature" (*QL,* IV:xxiii:95).

Tradition held that the Temple of the Dioscuri was associated at Naples with a second, round temple; we might remember once more Palladio's sketches of "due Tempii, uno Ritondo e l'altro Quadrangulare," as he describes them here, for his ideal reconstruction after Vitruvius of another city set steeply above a port, at Halicarnassus (cat. no. 71, fig. 47). But he comments in his Naples text that no trace could be found there of any rotunda, and that in his opinion even the rectangular structure behind the Dioscuri portico was modern (in which he was correct). He made a handsome drawing of the temple porch, on the *recto* of the Stockholm sheet whose *verso* shows a detail of one of its splendid capitals (fig. 73). Both images are instructive, for the *verso* repeats the forms and techniques of such drawings as cat. nos. 34 and 35, in still finer, more confident, and more three-dimensional syle. The *recto* also recalls cat. no. 34 as a direct prototype, but in a more delicate and more harmonious idiom. Its inscriptions are in the form we have identified as dating from the early 1550s (*cf.* cat. nos. 99 and 103), while its drawings of the pediment relief and acroterial figures are clearly to be ascribed to Bernardino India, whose collaboration with Palladio began in 1552 (cat. no. 70). I would thus date Palladio's journey to Naples during his Central Italian sojourn of 1547, and his Stockholm capital drawing to very shortly afterward; the temple elevation with India's contributions on the other side of that sheet would then be best dated to c. 1551–52, though indeed the figural elements could have been added at almost any moment in the 1550s or 1560s.

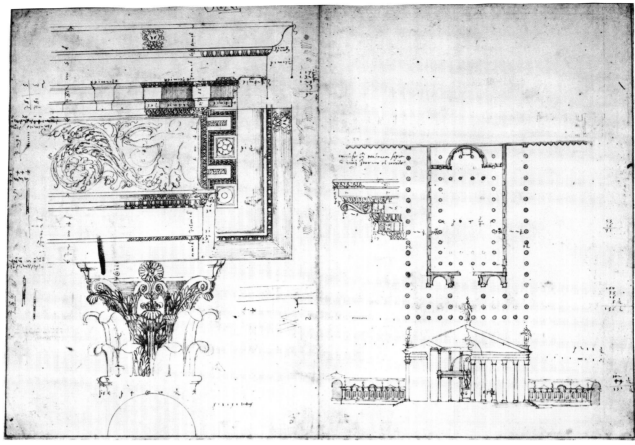

105. PLAN, ELEVATIONS, SECTIONS, AND DETAILS OF THE TEMPLE OF SERAPIS, ROME

1554

RIBA: Palladio XI/23 *recto* and *verso*.

30.1 × 42.2 cm. (single sheet); watermark, anchor in circle with star; countermark, V (upper left); laid lines 29 mm. apart (Mošin 1172); Talman 150 mark on *verso*.

Light red siena ink, with some darker umber ink on right *recto*, and cool blue-gray wash, with pencil and umber crayon additions; inscribed with description and measures in feet, and various scales: on left *recto*, 2 feet = 24.5 mm. (1 antique inch); on right *recto*, same (reduced), plus 40 feet = 37 mm. (1¼ Vicentine inches), and 70 feet = 36 mm.

Zorzi 1959, p. 75, fig. 153 (*recto*), fig. 156 (*verso*); Spielmann 1966, p. 146, no. 58, fig. 31 (*recto*), no. 60 (*verso*); Boëthius/Ward-Perkins 1970, pp. 274–275.

Royal Institute of British Architects, London.

This superb sheet exhibits a sequence of Palladio's most beautiful drawings after antiquity. In them he clearly shows himself to have been inspired by "what must have been, in my opinion, the largest and richest Temple to have been built in Rome" (*Quattro Libri* IV:xiii:41), that is Caracalla's Temple of Serapis on the Quirinal, of about A.D. 215. Modern opinion concurs with Palladio's judgment on both counts: at a height of 58 feet, its columns may have been the tallest erected anywhere in the Roman world (the celebrated ones at Baalbek being only 54½ feet high); and its gargantuan facade, in which twelve of these colossi were aligned under a gigantic pediment, was unique in the architecture of the Empire (Boëthius/Ward-Perkins 1970, p. 274; Ashby 1902, p. 37, fig. 64, for a prototype reconstruction in the Codex Coner). As we have already noted (cat. no. 78) the ornament of this prodigy presents the unusual revival of an "eastern" type from Greece and Asia Minor, earlier manifested most splendidly at Rome

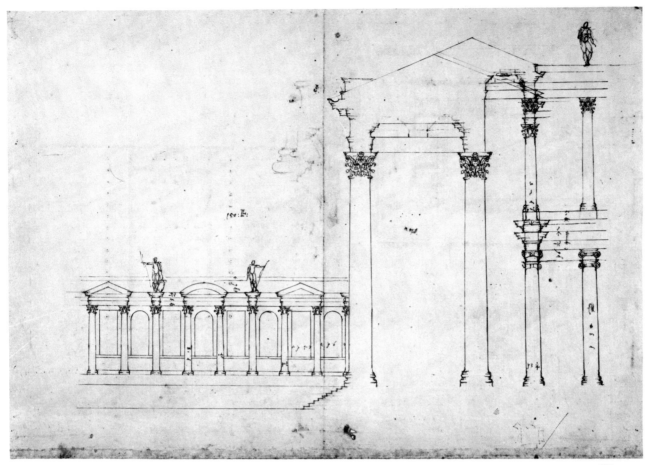

in the temple of its principal champion, Hadrian. It appealed enormously to Palladio, and these drawings of the Hadrianeum (cat. no. 78 right) and the Serapium are among his finest responses to the architectural glories of antiquity.

He had decided that this monarch among temples might appropriately have been dedicated to Jove, and publishes its images as such in his *Quattro Libri:* our left *recto* appears on his p. 47, the right *recto* on p. 42 (for the plan) and 44–45 (for the much expanded elevation/section, on a double-page spread). The *verso* of this sheet presents one such expansion, used for the enlarged section on p. 45: in the background both of it and the small version on the lower right center of the *recto* we catch glimpses of the alternately niched and pedimented precinct wall, which Palladio shows most fully on p. 43 in his treatise. Especially in its treatment at the bottom of this *recto,* with larger openings giving onto hillside chambers (one of which even

has a cusped pediment), this element forms a direct prototype for the garden hemicycle at Maser. That "nymphaeum" and its fountain grotto were built as a direct result of Palladio's trip to Rome in 1554, and thus provide a date for our sheet that is convincingly borne out by its drafting style and inscriptions. Palladio thought it likely that this temple would have had a great open interior court, which he shows ringed with superimposed colonnades, Corinthian over Ionic. As he had just executed exact prototypes for these at Piombino (1551–53) and was still involved (perhaps as late as 1556) with identical ones at Udine, the date of 1554 is doubly confirmed.

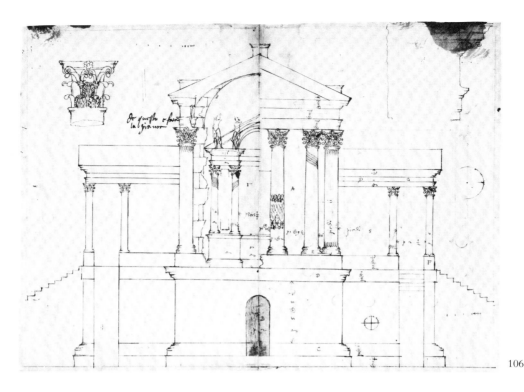

106

106. ELEVATION/SECTION OF THE TEMPIETTO AT THE SPRINGS OF THE CLITUMNUS, NEAR TREVI

c. 1565

RIBA: Palladio XI/15 *recto*.

27.9 × 37.4 cm. (single sheet, with repair strip pasted along separated centerfold on *verso;* stained with ink on upper margin); watermark, small anchor with single stem in circle with star; Talman 150 marks on both halves of *verso*.

Umber ink and dull gray-umber wash, over incised lines and pencil underdrawing; inscribed in transitional hand with measures in feet, and scales (at top left) of 5 feet = 44.5 mm. (1½ Vicentine inches), and (at bottom right) of 4 units = 25.5 mm. (1 Roman inch); later inscribed in mature hand with instruction to assistant. *Verso,* PLAN, ELEVATION AND SKETCH FOR PRECINCT OF TEMPLE OF ANTONINUS AND FAUSTINA, ROME; russet siena ink, inscribed with measures and scale in feet; Zorzi 1959, p. 75, fig. 159; Spielmann 1966, p. 145, no. 53, fig. 27.

Zorzi 1956, pp. 63–64, fig. 21; Zorzi 1959, p. 81, fig. 185; Forssman 1965, p. 114, fig. 52; Spielmann 1966, p. 150, no. 83, fig. 42; Semenzato 1968, p. 38 n. 9, fig. v; Zorzi 1969, p. 125, fig. 213; Gioseffi 1973, p. 57, fig. 17; Mostra 1973, p. 21 (Forssman); Puppi 1973, p. 323.

Royal Institute of British Architects, London.

After a somewhat severely classicizing interlude, corresponding roughly with the decade from the mid-1550s to the mid-1560s, Palladio's architectural and graphic modes began around the latter date to turn toward his magnificently rich and robust late style, still perhaps insufficiently studied as a distinct phenomenon. This drawing is one of the milestones of the change, for it represents Palladio at a moment of advanced maturity (he was approaching his sixtieth year) turning back to a highly decorated gem of

Figure 74

"Antique Baroque" architecture that had already strongly influenced his "first decorated style" (cat. no. 22). In those same years around 1550 it had also strongly influenced certain of his domestic designs, such as Malcontenta's podium and portico (fig. 74), and Piombino's wings; after 1565 it was to have an even greater influence on his church facades. Even in the chaste black-and-white abstraction of its publication on a double-page spread in the *Quattro Libri* (IV:xxv:100–101)—which allows us to date the sheet, through its preparation as a model for the woodcut—we find clearly reflected Palladio's fascination with the exuberance of its ornament. From it, indeed, he drew a moral in his caption about the propriety of decorative detail, which he felt should be as rich as possible in small structures, in order to augment their variety and beauty; but very sparing in great works such as amphitheatres, in order to express economy and solidity.

107

108

107. PALLADIO SHOP: PROJECT FOR FACADE DECORATION OF THE SCUOLA GRANDE DELLA MISERICORDIA, VENICE

1570s

Vicenza: 1950 inv. D-18.

76.5 × 58.1 cm. (two main sheets of different paper, pasted with smaller patches, presumably by Palladio: top piece, 41.9 × 58.0 cm.; bottom piece c. 35 × 58.1 cm.; no watermark or collector's mark visible on either; outer corners beveled.

Siena drafting ink and dark siena-brown wash, on top piece; siena drafting ink and much lighter beige wash, on bottom piece; drawn with scale of 5 feet = 38.5 mm. (1⅓ Venetian inches).

Magrini 1845, pp. 301–303; Loukomski 1927, pp. 37–39, p. vii; Venturi 1940, XI:iii:116–117; Pane 1961, pp. 311–312, fig. 348:78; Mariacher 1962, pp. 106–107, fig. 81; Zorzi 1965, p. 134, fig. 101; Zorzi 1967, pp. 172–174, figs. 208–209; Tafuri 1969, p. 13 (esp. n. 29), fig. 15 (as Sansovino's design of 1532); Burns 1973, p. 180, figs. 109, 122; Mostra 1973, pp. 152–153, fig. 163 (Burns); Puppi 1973, p. 395, no. 111, fig. 559; Tafuri 1973, pp. 153–154, fig. 109; Wilinski 1974–1976, p. 112, fig. 30; Arts Council 1975, pp. 154–155, no. 275 (Burns); Howard 1975, pp. 108–110, fig. 77.

Museo Civico, Vicenza.

In 1570 Jacopo Sansovino died with one of his most celebrated Venetian masterworks still unfinished: and to this day the great Scuola della Misericordia lacks a stone facade, although its rough brick front was certainly prepared to receive one. This famous drawing has long been recognized as a design very likely to reflect closely Sansovino's original intentions, which are documented by the elaborate brick substructure. Various explanations for its production in Palladio's shop have been adduced, most of them favoring a redrafting of a lost prototype by Sansovino. But then in 1969 Tafuri launched the suggestion that this *was* a Sansovino drawing—or one very close to him—recording his principal project of 1532 (which is only known to have proposed a facade embellished with columns). Burns argued strenuously against this idea in 1973, citing many Palladian motifs in the design, and finding in fact few if any detailed traces of Sansovino's style. It should be seen, he concluded, as "Palladio's achievement of a highly successful synthesis, in which he merged his own personal style with an imposed Sansovinesque composition, that was predetermined by the existing structure" (Mostra, p. 153). This is unquestionably the proper view, and the traditional date soon after Sansovino's death (when Palladio had moved to Venice to supervise his churches and work on the Ducal Palace) is doubtless also correct. Documents connected with the Scuola do not give Palladio's name, and the source of his commission for this drawing is unknown. It seems to have been produced against a deadline, for although its architectural drafting is uniformly well executed in a single hand, the sheet was cut (or later assembled) through the middle, in order to assign its figural completion to two quite different artists, evidently in the interests of speed. I do not recognize the author of the decorations in the upper zone, though he is evidently the same draftsman who executed the embellishments on cat. no. 109. The collaborating artist of the lower drawing, however, is certainly Bernardino India, as its comparison with his secure *Holy Family* drawing of the 1570s makes clear (Arts Council 1975, p. 99, no. and fig. 183). Reassembled as a compelling image of civic grandeur, the drawing is indeed one of the central masterpieces of Palladio's spectacular late style.

---

108. BERNARDINO INDIA: COPY OF PALLADIO'S PROJECT FOR DECORATION OF THE UPPER FACADE OF THE SCUOLA DELLA MISERICORDIA, VENICE

1570s

RIBA: Burlington-Devonshire VIII/12.

39.7 × 56.1 cm. (single sheet); watermark, coronet with star (*cf.* Briquet 4834/4835); no collector's mark (Burlington purchase, 1719).

Pinkish siena ink, and light peach-colored siena washes, over incised lines and pencil underdrawing (as on axes of columns); black stains or discolorations.

Smithsonian 1966, no. 6, and frontispiece (Harris—as Palladio); Zorzi 1967, p. 174, fig. 210 (as copy, not supervised by Palladio); Puppi 1973, p. 395 (as shop, with figures by India or Zelotti); Rearick 1980 (letter to author, 10 December 1980).

Royal Institute of British Architects, London.

This wonderful drawing—a copy after the upper sheet in cat. no. 107, or its prototype—is certainly by India, who in this case drew the complete architectural structure as well as the figures. The latter occasionally improve on their models, though the architectural drafting is much less assured (especially, for example, in the fluting of the columns). Why India should have copied the upper drawing from the preceding sheet, when he had probably already executed the figures on the lower one, is unclear. Perhaps he hoped to unite them, as one consistent image of his work; or perhaps the present drawing was produced on commission, for a patron who had seen the Palladian version in cat. no. 107, and wanted a record of it. It is, if anything, even more consistent and persuasive as a brilliantly integrated exemplar of the grand style: it perpetrates an almost High Renaissance mode of exuberant classicism into the last quarter of the 16th century.

109

109. ENTRANCE FACADE OF LATER PROJECT FOR THE RIALTO BRIDGE, VENICE

c. 1565

Vicenza: 1950 inv. D-20.

50.7 × 42.7 cm. (single sheet with beveled corners); no watermark visible; no collector's mark.

Siena ink, light gold and dark siena washes; drawn with scale of 5 (presumably Venetian) feet = 25.5 mm. (1 Roman inch).

Loukomski 1927, p. 38, pl. VIa; Venturi 1940, pp. 470–473, fig. 437; Zorzi 1965, p. 174, fig. 141; Gioseffi 1973, p. 50, fig. 28; Mostra 1973, p. 153 (Burns); Arts Council 1975, p. 126, no. 223 (Burns).

Museo Civico, Vicenza.

This design is a later parallel to Palladio's early project for a Rialto Bridge facade, in cat. no. 70, to which the reader is referred. The two proposals are almost identical in size, and are drawn to the same scale; both have a large central stair between two tall podiums (although the latter elements are much developed, in the present sheet, at the expense of the steps); they have similar orders of engaged columns set against piers and arches, comparable entablatures broken forward of the main wall, attics of the same height with near-identical piers, and figural sculptures along their skylines. But their plans are quite different: the 1554 drawing (cat. no. 70) shows a wide outer pavilion, which would have given access to an enclosed court standing quite far out in front of the bridge (on the pattern of a 1554 plan project, in the Vicenza drawing D-25 *verso*);

the present design is very close to the one Palladio published in the *Quattro Libri* (III:xiii:26–27—fig. 86 at cat. no. 123), with the entrance pavilion set directly against the head of the bridge. It shows the three thoroughfares over the water, as does the published plan. Each of these was to be flanked by small shops, represented here by the wall segments at the end of each file, fronted by niches with over-life-size figures. In the executed bridge—built by Antonio Da Ponte in 1588–91, to a much simpler design—the three walkways remain; but the single rows of shops between them (though potentially double-sided) are in practice open only toward the central passageway.

The great novelty and impressiveness of this design derive from its developed sense of three-dimensional massing. In the service of this primary interest is a strong supporting emphasis on three-dimensional sculpture, and taken together they represent a highly unusual and precocious approach to composition. One great plane of elaborate sculptural decoration is established at the outer perimeter, but (as we see most clearly in the huge podium zone) it is immediately broken forward by a bold projection in front of the lateral portals, probably deep enough to provide access to them by means of a terrace. Then the central sections move sharply forward twice more, accompanied by progressively projecting pedestals, orders, and attics. Complicated counter-rhythms are set up in opposing recessions of parts of the entablature; although the whole remains a little awkward, it is in many ways an astonishing prefiguration of the compositional systems of the early Baroque.

110

110. STUDIES FOR THE FACADE OF SAN FRANCESCO DELLA VIGNA, VENICE

c. 1565

RIBA: Palladio XIV/10.

31.4 × 41.3 cm. (single sheet, with small holes from corroded ink spots); watermark, an orb with star; countermark, Ꝟ E, upper right; laid lines 27 mm. apart (variant of Briquet 3085); no collector's mark (Burlington purchase, 1719).

Umber ink over incised lines.

Forssman 1965, pp. 113–114, fig. 51; Barbieri 1966, pp. 340–341; Spielmann 1966, p. 152, no. 95; Forssman 1967, p. 254, fig. 169 (left half of sheet); Zorzi 1967, p. 7, fig. 6; Timofiewitsch 1969, p. 42, fig. xiv; Gioseffi 1973, p. 52, fig. 30; Mostra 1973, p. 146 (Burns); Puppi 1973, pp. 347, 384, fig. 469; Arts Council 1975, p. 135, no. 244 (Burns).

Royal Institute of British Architects, London.

This highly important drawing was earlier associated with Palladio's planning of S. Giorgio Maggiore (cat. no. 113), but it has more convincingly been recognized as a preliminary study for the facade that Palladio added about 1565–70 to Sansovino's church of San Francesco della Vigna (fig. 75). Burns (1975) questioned this destination on the grounds of incised scale lines (not marked with ink, and hence invisible save in a raking light on the original) which he thought might indicate dimensions for the project that would be too small for San Francesco. But in fact these prove the accuracy of that identification, since the demarcations are not measures but modules (and were left uninked for that very reason: they were a guide to Palladio's own composition, not a key to builders). My values for them differ slightly from those given by Burns, but produce round numbers in an exact ratio of 2:3 with Sansovino's existing fabric—that is a facade 60 modules wide over an intended interior width of 90 Venetian feet, 40 modules high to the point at the center of the attic corresponding to an intended interior height of 60 feet, and so on. Wittkower showed long ago (1949/1971, pp. 96, 106) that Palladio indeed would have been obliged to compose this facade on a modular system, since Sansovino had been constrained to use one on the interior, with the above dimensions worked into a whole series of interrelated harmonic values. His advisors had even decreed that "the front is desired to be in the form of a square, corresponding to the interior. From it one should be able to grasp the form of the building and all its proportions, so that both inside and outside all should be proportionate" (Wittkower 1949/1971, p. 157: misprint of *"nullo"* in Moschini [1815, I:i:61], Wittkower, and Zorzi [1966:35] corrected by Puppi [1973:347] to proper reading of *"nello* modo quadro"). And Palladio does in this drawing show the great central section of the nave facade as a square of 33 modules, both in width and in height to the bottom of the projecting cornice. He may have been particularly interested in the relationship of 1 module on this drawing to 1½ feet on an actual scale, that is in their correspondence through "the ratio of 2:3, which constitutes the diapente, one of the celebrated harmonies"; for that reminder of one of San Francesco's ideal concordances occurs in the same memorandum about its recommended measures (Wittkower 1949/1971, p. 156).

But he eventually revised both the module and the

184

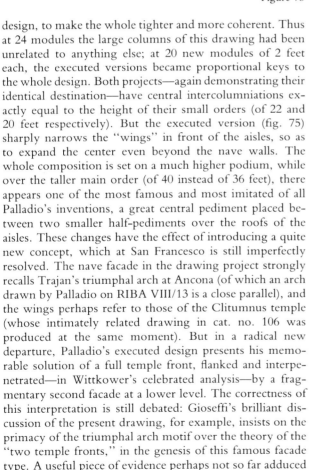

Figure 75

Figure 76

design, to make the whole tighter and more coherent. Thus at 24 modules the large columns of this drawing had been unrelated to anything else; at 20 new modules of 2 feet each, the executed versions became proportional keys to the whole design. Both projects—again demonstrating their identical destination—have central intercolumniations exactly equal to the height of their small orders (of 22 and 20 feet respectively). But the executed version (fig. 75) sharply narrows the "wings" in front of the aisles, so as to expand the center even beyond the nave walls. The whole composition is set on a much higher podium, while over the taller main order (of 40 instead of 36 feet), there appears one of the most famous and most imitated of all Palladio's inventions, a great central pediment placed between two smaller half-pediments over the roofs of the aisles. These changes have the effect of introducing a quite new concept, which at San Francesco is still imperfectly resolved. The nave facade in the drawing project strongly recalls Trajan's triumphal arch at Ancona (of which an arch drawn by Palladio on RIBA VIII/13 is a close parallel), and the wings perhaps refer to those of the Clitumnus temple (whose intimately related drawing in cat. no. 106 was produced at the same moment). But in a radical new departure, Palladio's executed design presents his memorable solution of a full temple front, flanked and interpenetrated—in Wittkower's celebrated analysis—by a fragmentary second facade at a lower level. The correctness of this interpretation is still debated: Gioseffi's brilliant discussion of the present drawing, for example, insists on the primacy of the triumphal arch motif over the theory of the "two temple fronts," in the genesis of this famous facade type. A useful piece of evidence perhaps not so far adduced is the elegantly spare and persuasive facade design of the

Basilica Nova of Maxentius, on fol. 54 *recto* of the Mellon sketchbook (fig. 76: cat. nos. 25 and 113). Its pre-Palladian reconstruction shows superimposed pediments that would actually be interlocking, were it not that the lower, outer element is brought up to the front plane as the dominant image. Palladio resolves this tension in his *Quattro Libri* plate of the Basilica's facade (IV:vi:13), by keeping both pediments on the same plane, where they flow together without a break. But his design with the colossal columns inspired by arches and temples was to prove his best, and it is worth noting one more stage in his development of that configuration.

In January 1558 contracts were drawn up for the execution of Palladio's facade for the Venetian cathedral church of S. Pietro in Castello. Its patron died in 1559, apparently before much could be done, and the facade executed by Francesco Smeraldi in 1594–96 was only a weak pastiche of Palladio's motifs. But the contract mentions six large columns, and we may be able to visualize their effect from what is probably the very similar central section of the Rialto Bridge project on the preceding sheet (cat. no. 109). Many other aspects of that drawing (also evidently inspired by the arch at Ancona) are so closely related as to provide a firm date around 1565 for the present project as well. San Francesco's alleged commencement in 1562 (a date invented by Tassini in the 19th century) has no basis in fact: Vasari saw only its pedestals in place in 1566. One other drawing that might have been connected with it (on the basis of its parallels with cat. no. 109) is described by Magrini (1845, p. 305); although now lost, it sounds very much like some of Palladio's S. Petronio drawings (*cf.* cat. no. 118), and may have represented an important stage in the development of his church facade types.

111

111. PROPOSALS FOR THE GRIMANI TOMBS AT S. FRANCESCO DELLA VIGNA, VENICE

1564

Vicenza: 1950 inv. D-17.

48 × 38.7 mm. (single sheet); no watermark visible; no collector's mark.

Siena and umber inks, very light gold and light siena washes.

Magrini 1845, p. 303; Loukomski 1927, p. 38, pl. VIb; Zorzi 1963, pp. 96–105, fig. 109; Zorzi 1967, pp. 54–55, fig. 101; Mostra 1973, p. 152 (Burns); Puppi 1973, p. 425, fig. 605; Arts Council 1975, pp. 135–136, no. and fig. 245 (MacTavish); Rearick 1980 (letter to author 10 December 1980).

Museo Civico, Vicenza.

The destination of this magnificent drawing impinges on one of the thorniest problems in Venetian 16th-century patronage. Its history has yet to be written, and can only be sketched here in broad terms: it deals with the missing monuments of the Grimani family.

On 7 May 1523 Doge Antonio Grimani died; to this day he has no monument, although his family was one of the richest and most artistically active in Venice. Three months later the son who was the greatest of the family's princely patrons, Cardinal Domenico Grimani, Patriarch of Aquileia from 1498 to 1517, died at Rome. Sansovino was working on Domenico's tomb at the moment of the Sack of Rome in 1527, but because of this disaster nothing came of the Roman project and the Cardinal's body was eventually transferred to Venice (Lotto 1962, p. 48; Paschini 1943, pp. 116, 120). His nephews Marin and Vettor Grimani, in accordance with their uncle's wishes, ordered a tomb to be built for their Ducal grandfather at the church of his patron saint, S. Antonio di Castello—which had already been embellished with a facade and another tomb by their elder uncle Pietro (Martinioni 1663, pp. 29, 32). Once more Sansovino (by now state architect at Venice) provided the design, and Deborah Howard has found documents of 1530–42 implying the construction of this monument (1975, p. 173 n. 41). But the Ducal tomb, if in fact it ever existed, seems instantly to have vanished: Venice's most definitive guidebook in 1663 could only note that the Doge had been "interred alongside a wall" in the chancel at S. Antonio; the great historian Emmanuele Cicogna could only find over the Doge's grave at S. Antonio a modest plaque, tardily installed during the reign of the second Doge Grimani in 1595–1605 (1824, I:169–173, no. 18); and in April of 1542 we find the Doge's grandsons arranging to build the same tomb in a different church.

The new arrangements being undertaken by Cardinal Domenico's nephews were quite extraordinary. In April Vettor and Marin Grimani obtained from the monks of San Francesco della Vigna their private title to the entire facade of that church, with permission to develop it as the setting for a great funerary monument to Doge Antonio (Lewis 1972, p. 29; Howard 1975, p. 69). The transaction mentions an "existing model"—undoubtedly one of the two found among Vettor Grimani's effects at his death (Lewis 1972, pp. 25–26; and 1979, pp. 40–41); and Vettor's close association with and support of Sansovino insures that both designs were Jacopo's.

At this time the Grimani brothers were preoccupied not only with their grandfather's tomb, but also with one for their uncle, Cardinal Domenico, whose body had been repatriated to Venice. It is therefore hardly surprising that we find Vettor Grimani on 9 June 1542 also obtaining as his personal property the whole *interior* facade wall of San Francesco, with the right to use it in perpetuity for the construction of tomb monuments for himself and other members of his family. And indeed we find Marin Grimani making arrangements for just such a monument to Cardinal Domenico on 6 December 1544 (Paschini 1960, p. 71). But Marin died at Orvieto two years later, and—having become a Cardinal himself, as well as being Patriarch of Aquileia once in 1517–29, and again in 1533–45—his body too was shipped home to Venice. Meanwhile Marin's and Vettor's brother Marco, Papal admiral and ambassador, and Patriarch of Aquileia 1529–1533, had died at Rome in the summer of 1544, and his body had likewise been sent home to Venice (*ibid.*, p. 64).

Vettor Grimani thus found himself at the end of 1546 in the exceedingly curious position of having available the bodies of four princely relations, to whom it was his duty to create fitting memorials. In the Venetian world of the mid-16th century, where a family's status was very largely measured by the public honor accorded such conspicuous exemplars of dynastic *virtù,* this was an opportunity beyond the fondest dreams of ambition. And yet nothing came of

it: Vettor (who had hoped to become Doge himself) died in 1558, and was modestly buried—quite against his wishes—in the undecorated family vault at S. Antonio. The survivor who committed this outrage was his youngest brother Giovanni, the last of the Grimani Patriarchs of Aquileia. No sooner had he interred his Procuratorial brother at S. Antonio than he seized Vettor's tomb chapel at S. Francesco, and commissioned Battista Franco to decorate it for himself (*cf.* cat. no. 87). Upon the latter's death he called Federico Zuccaro from Rome, who finished painting the chapel in 1562–64; whereupon the Patriarch (a close friend of Daniele Barbaro) did at least commission this drawing for the inner facade wall from Palladio and Zuccaro, as David MacTavish brilliantly deduced in 1975 (Arts Council, p. 136). As a variant on what must have been Vettor Grimani's preceding design by Sansovino, it fills the spaces of the former windows with three imposing sarcophagi, clearly intended for the two Cardinals at the sides, and Doge Antonio, who is represented by Venice Enthroned at the top (rather than the hapless Vettor—and instead of Marco, as suggested by Sansovino, Magrini and MacTavish).

It will be noted that this wonderful design exactly reproduces many of the forms of Palladio's drawing on the preceding sheet (cat. no. 110) for the external facade—where we can at least hope that the four consoles represent Giovanni Grimani's intention to install memorial busts of his relations. Since Vasari saw the facade rising in 1566, both sheets must date from very shortly before, which accords conveniently with Zuccaro's successful completion of the Grimani chapel in 1564 (Rearick 1958–59, p. 137). But once more we encounter the ghostly tendency of the Grimani monuments to disappear. All three editions of Francesco Sansovino's authoritative and definitive guide to Venice state that the three tombs *were* built on this wall, and could be seen in 1581, 1604, and 1663. But no trace of them exists, or—in my opinion—ever existed, apart from the one spectacular memorial of this sheet, which, like Shakespeare's "powerful rime," may outlive the "marble [or] the gilded monuments of princes." Only Magrini seems to have grasped the truth about this splendid vision, perhaps because he had access to more information about the Grimani tombs than we do. He refers as a matter of common knowledge to provisional *wooden* sarcophagi of the Cardinals Domenico and Marin Grimani, set up on the inner facade wall of S. Francesco; and he comments bitingly on Giovanni Grimani's eventual interment of his greater relatives at the sides of the Grimani chapel, at whose center he had prepared his own resplendent memorial. This, sadly enough, must be the case; and the wooden tombs must be the monuments which even Francesco Sansovino had evidently hoped so much would one day become the sublime memorial sketched on this sheet, or on his father's prototypes for its design. That this Palladio/Zuccaro project was very well known can be demonstrated from Girolamo Campagna's reproduction of most of its forms in his monument of 1601–04 for the second Doge Grimani, in S. Giuseppe di Castello (Timofiewitsch 1972, pp. 268–273, figs. 79–83).

112. PROJECT FOR A FUNERARY CHAPEL, PERHAPS FOR S. GIORGIO MAGGIORE, VENICE

1564/65

Drawings Collection, Budapest Museum of Fine Arts: inv. no. 1989.

47.8 × 33.9 cm. (single sheet); no watermark visible; marks of collectors Giorgio Vasari (inscription and border), Pierre-Jules Mariette (inscription, Lugt 1852), Counts Esterházy (Lugt 1965), and Országos Képtár (Lugt 2000).

Siena ink with beige-gray wash, over incised lines, with some pencil underdrawing; inscribed by Palladio with measures in Florentine (?) *braccia,* of which a scale of 3 = 49 mm. (1⅔ Vicentine inches); mount inscribed "ANDREA. PALLADIO. / ARCHITETTOR. VICE.^{no} / le figure son di Paolo Veronese."; and "fuit Georgii Vasari, nunc P.J. Mariette, 1741."

Kurz 1937, p. 42, fig. 45; Tietze/Tietze Conrat 1944, p. 341, no. 2050; Zorzi 1963, pp. 96–105, fig. 113; Fenyö 1965, p. 33, no. and fig. 31; Zorzi 1965, p. 134, fig. 103; Fenyö 1966, p. 85, fig. 53; Zorzi 1967, pp. 174–176, fig. 211; Puppi 1973, pp. 348–349, fig. 476; Wilinski 1974–1976, pp. 147–148, fig. 53; Verona 1980, pp. 166–167, no. and fig. VII, 7 (Burns); Rearick 1980 (letter to author, 10 December 1980, suggesting Benedetto Caliari as figure artist).

Szépművészeti Múzeum, Budapest.

This very beautiful drawing has proved difficult to connect with any known location, but it clearly dates from around 1564, through its precise analogies with the Grimani tomb drawing of that year for S. Francesco (cat. no. 111), and the Rialto Bridge project of c. 1565 (cat. no. 109). The date is confirmed through its acquisition by Vasari: during the summer of 1564 the great Florentine artist-biographer had requested his agent Cosimo Bartoli to send him representative drawings by Venetian artists, which he was using to prepare the second edition of his *Lives* (Rearick 1958–59, pp. 132–133). Even if Vasari did not acquire the drawing during this first campaign of collecting sheets by Venetian artists, two years later he actually met Palladio, in the course of a journey through Northern Italy to collect more material for the revision of his book. Few commentators, however, have noticed how brief this encounter must have been. Between documented dates of 9 May 1566 in Milan and 27 May in Ferrara, Vasari visited at least Verona, Vicenza and Padua, and spent the days of 20–25 May in Venice. He thus had time, on average, for only parts of two days in each of the mainland towns between Lombardy and the lagoons. It is in fact quite clear from the nature of his comments on Palladio's work that Andrea simply gave him a draft of the *Secondo Libro,* from the treatise then in preparation, as Vasari passed quickly through Vicenza around the middle of May. This very fact strongly implies that the meeting had been prearranged (one cannot imagine Palladio giving up a draft for the *Quattro Libri* on the spur of the moment): so that *if* Vasari eventually sent it back, and *if* it is the famous manuscript preserved at the Museo Correr in Venice (Ms. Cicogna 3617—Zorzi 1959, p. 147 ff.), then we would have a firm date for it that would shortly precede 15 May 1566. In any event the Cicogna manuscript was certainly finished, and in Palladio's hands, when he added to it a pencil notation of Francesco Pisani's death (which occurred on 8 November 1567—ASV, atti G.M. Corradini). The Budapest drawing is thus likely to have been given to Vasari either through correspondence, in the late summer of 1564; or (together with a draft for the second book of the *Quattro Libri*) through a scheduled meeting in Vicenza in mid-May, 1566; or at the latest through correspondence soon after this, when Vasari might have returned the borrowed treatise fragment to Palladio.

For Palladio's measures to be inscribed in *braccia* (rather too prominently, as an afterthought) is therefore less diagnostic of a special Central Italian commission, than it is suggestive of his conversion of an existing sheet, in order to give Vasari a design that would be more comprehensible in Florence. In this regard the drawing's almost exact equivalence with the executed altar chapels of S. Giorgio Maggiore (planned in 1565) offers the possibility, at least, of its original destination there. Among a host of comparable motifs shared by the drawing and S. Giorgio, some of the closest parallels are with the lavabo tabernacles in the antechamber to the refectory. It may thus be possible to envisage a Palladian commission for a similar space, that would accommodate double doors, in which a new monument would have been needed to replace one of the old ones demolished with the former church. The new Michiel monument, placed in another antechamber just south of the church transept, commemorates a Doge and is therefore ineligible; but the Civran monument (later built by Longhena just beyond the north transept) is already an interesting possibility. The only clues we have for identifying the design are the subject's evident middle age and military prowess; on both these counts, and recalling the drawing's precise replication of the graphic techniques of the Grimani tomb design (cat. no. 111), we might remember that Marco Grimani—who was omitted in that commemoration—had died before or near his fiftieth year, as Pope Paul III's Admiral in charge of the Papal Fleet.

ANDREA PALLADIO
ARCHITETTOR VICE.no
le figure son di Paolo Veronese.
fuit Georgii Vasari nunc P.J. Mariette

112

113

113. STUDY FOR THE FACADE OF S. GIORGIO MAGGIORE, VENICE

1565

RIBA: Palladio XIV/12—right.

29.3 × 20.0 cm. (single sheet now detached from the unrelated XIV/12—Left); countermark, A [B?]; laid lines 29 mm. apart; no collector's mark.

Light siena ink, drawn with scale of 12 feet = 39 mm. (1⅓ Vicentine inches); *i* in later hand with heavier ink at top right; pencil sums on *verso*.

Wittkower 1949/1971, pp. 94–95, fig. 33b; Zorzi 1959, p. 79, fig. 175; Forssman 1965, pp. 113–114, fig. 50; Barbieri 1966, pp. 341–344; Spielmann 1966, p. 152, no. 93, fig. 50; Zorzi 1967, p. 7, fig. 5; Isermeyer 1972, p. 112, fig. 62; Mostra 1973, p. 146 (Burns); Puppi 1973, pp. 349, 369, 384, fig. 510; Arts Council 1975, pp. 142–143, no. and fig. 254 (Burns); Frommel 1977, p. 111, fig. 34.

Royal Institute of British Architects, London.

With an importance disproportionate to its size, this drawing marks a pivotal point in Palladio's career, and prefigures his masterful late works in ecclesiastical architecture (cat. nos. 114, 115, 118). Its testimony is fundamental to an understanding of Palladio's planning process, as he developed his design for a new church at the Benedictine monastery on the island of S. Giorgio, directly opposite the entrance to the Grand Canal and the city center of Venice. We know that a Master Gabriel—with Palladio's help—built a large model of the church in November/December 1565, for which he borrowed many drawings (doubtless including this one or one like it); during the week of 20 May 1566 the model was shown to Vasari, who admired it enthusiastically. A very similar plan was kept at the monastery, and is now in the State Archive at Venice (Misc. Mappe 857—illustrated here in fig. 77). It shows the great central four-column temple front on this drawing to have been a free-standing portico projecting

190

from the facade, as Wittkower suspected, and Barbieri reaffirmed; both the plan and elevation have recently been the subject of a brilliant analysis by which Frommel has elucidated Palladio's successive stages of design (*cf.* esp. his reconstruction of a preliminary plan, documented by the sketches at the upper left of this sheet). Since the final plan can be dated through its images of the monastery to the very end of Palladio's life (1576/79), it has the further great advantage of showing that he never changed his mind about the importance of a facade with a free-standing portico, whose columns would rise from ground level (*Quattro Libri* IV:v:9).

These considerations sharply undermine the attempts of several commentators to defend the design of the executed facade with its very tall central pedestals (fig. 78) as a Palladian invention (*cf.* most recently Arts Council 1975). penetrating discussion of the proposals for its authorship, proved beyond any reasonable doubt that it represents an "updating" of the original Palladian idea, by (or at least according to the architectural principles of) Vincenzo Scamozzi, as the greatest Venetian architect of the day. Isermeyer demonstrated (1969, pp. 475–476) that the oculus designed by Palladio in August 1571 (still visible as the frame of a painting on the inner facade wall, but intended

to be open, as depicted in pre-1607 views) would intersect the present facade by cutting the entablature of the main pediment. From this it is clear that the model for the facade which the executing masons agreed to follow was a different one than Palladio had intended; as we have seen, his ideas about the facade never changed throughout the remaining decade of his life. Thus we can understand that his oculus would have opened onto a portico, through a space independent of the outer architrave: Zorzi opportunely includes among his illustrations of S. Giorgio (though without comment on this subject) a *Quattro Libri* section through the Serapis temple portico (IV:xii:46; *cf.* cat. no. 105), showing a barrel vault at exactly this point—within which an oculus with a consonant curve would stand athwart the level of the architrave. We may assume this solution—as well as the cost of the portico—to have displeased the Benedictines, who would thus (at a distance of twenty-five years after Palladio's death) have asked a good architect—such as Scamozzi—to modify Palladio's design into a "portico in relief" applied directly to the facade, on the pattern of S. Francesco (cat. no. 110). Even the language of the facade contract, with its *"modello fatto,"* implying a "model newly made," strongly suggests a recent and revised design.

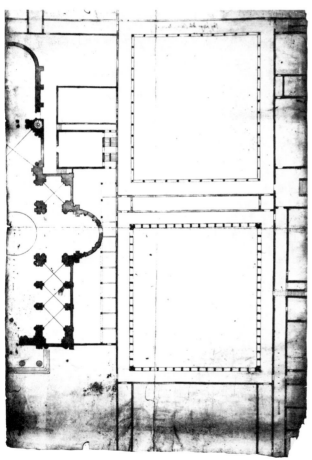

Figure 77

Figure 78

191

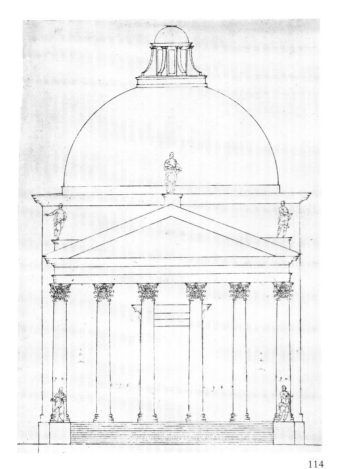

114

Figure 79

114. FACADE PROJECT FOR A VOTIVE CHURCH AT VENICE

December 1576/January 1577

RIBA: Palladio XIV/15.

40.6 × 27.6 cm. (single sheet); watermark, anchor with single stem in circle with star; laid lines 29 mm. apart (Mošin 1381); no collector's mark (Burlington purchase, 1719).

Umber ink, with pencil underdrawing, over incised lines; inscribed with measures in feet.

Timofiewitsch 1959–1960, pp. 79–87, fig. 108; Pane 1961, p. 304, fig. 341:62; Wittkower 1963, p. 62, fig. 13; Wittkower 1963/1974, p. 12, fig. 4; Zorzi 1965, p. 134, fig. 99; Gloton 1966, p. 89, fig. 92; Zorzi 1967, pp. 167–168, fig. 200; Isermeyer 1969, p. 476 n. 2; Mostra 1973, p. 146 (Burns); Puppi 1973, pp. 396, 432, 434, fig. 618; Arts Council 1975, pp. 146–147, no. 258(c) (Burns); Foscari 1975, pp. 44–56, fig. 3; Ackerman 1977, p. 23, fig. 8.

Royal Institute of British Architects, London.

In 1575–77 Venice experienced one of two disastrous outbreaks of plague which were to strike the city in modern times (the second would occur in 1630–31). Although the government used every means to control the contagion (*Venezia e la peste,* 1979), about one third of the population was lost, and ultimately there was nothing left but to pray.

On 4 September 1576 the Senate and Ducal Council pledged to dedicate a new church to the Redeemer, and promised that on every anniversary of the day on which the city might be delivered, the Doge and his full Council would make a solemn procession to it, in order to offer perpetual thanks. (The procession is indeed still made to Palladio's great church of the Redentore [fig. 79], across a bridge of boats every third Sunday in July, as Venice's major religious festival.)

A commission was appointed to choose a site for the new church, to be associated with a monastery or convent for its proper custody and officiation (18 September 1576). On 17 November 1576 two sites were formally proposed, one at the outlying Convent of S. Croce, the other in a stonemason's yard (of which Canaletto has left us a picture) at S. Vitale on the Grand Canal. Because the latter plot was restricted in depth, and because we know Palladio's long-standing patron Marc'Antonio Barbaro to have preferred it, Pane suggested in 1961 that the project on this and the following two sheets, for a great domed, centralized structure, could well have been inspired by that site: Barbaro in fact made an oration in favor of a centralized plan, but the proposal was defeated (Zorzi 1967, p. 133, doc. 7).

115. PLAN PROJECT FOR A VOTIVE CHURCH AT VENICE (I)

December 1576/January 1577

RIBA: Palladio XIV/13.

41.5 × 28.5 (single sheet); no watermark visible; laid lines 29 mm. apart; no collector's mark (Burlington purchase, 1719).

Dark siena ink with purplish umber-gray wash; inscribed with measures in feet, and scale of 20 feet = 56.5 mm. (2 Venetian inches); inscribed in another hand "coro."

Wittkower 1949/1971, p. 100, fig. 40a; Wittkower 1959, p. 65, fig. 52; Timofiewitsch 1959–1960, pp. 79–87, fig. 106; Pane 1961, p. 304, fig. 341:59; D'Ossat 1966, p. 38, fig. 57; Ackerman 1966/1977, p. 138, fig. 78; Zorzi 1967, pp. 167–168, fig. 199; Tafuri 1968, p. 71, fig. 47; Isermeyer 1969, p. 476 n. 2; Isermeyer 1972, p. 132, fig. 59; Mostra 1973, p. 146 (Burns); Puppi 1973, pp. 396, 434, fig. 616; Wilinski 1974–1976, pp. 145–146, fig. 52; Arts Council 1975, pp. 146–147, no. 258 (a) (Burns); Foscari 1975, pp. 44–56, fig. 1; Ackerman 1977, p. 23, fig. 9; Venice 1980, p. 270 (Foscari, in no. 442).

Royal Institute of British Architects, London.

Despite Marc'Antonio Barbaro's orations before the Venetian Senate in favor of building the Republic's new votive church on the Grand Canal site at S. Vitale and in accordance with Palladio's centralized plan, that body instead decided on the present site at the Capuchin monastery on the island of the Giudecca, and on a longitudinal plan that Palladio had prepared as an alternative. The present project (cat. nos. 114–116) was drawn for the Giudecca site before the longitudinal plan had carried the day: hence it gives a width of 80 feet (including its flanking alleys) between the lines of the pre-existing buildings on either side, as prescribed in the Senate's first resolution.

Marc'Antonio, not to be deprived of his wish to see the plan realized, commissioned Palladio privately to redraft it for him at half size, as a villa chapel for his estate at Maser, where Palladio had built a magnificent country palace for Marc'Antonio and his brother Daniele twenty-five years before (cat. no. 90). The moment at which the Maser chapel was begun has not yet been determined, but its frieze is inscribed with the date of 1580, and Palladio is reliably held to have died at the villa, surrounded by drawings (including the present ones) which he was presumably using to design it (or direct its early construction), on 19 August 1580. In a Papal bull of 7 November 1585 (see cat. no. 23) the chapel is described as newly and beautifully built, though not quite finished; but this refers to its state only at the unknown earlier moment at which Marc'Antonio's petition for perpetual title to the church was sent to the Papal Curia. A letter of 15 April 1584 by Lodovico Roncone, published in Gian Domenico Scamozzi's edition of Serlio, already refers to the chapel as built and decorated. It was attested on 25 June 1588 to be fully appointed, and Don Umberto Basso has shown that this document refers to (and is signed by the sculptors of) its stucco decorations, although its testimony seems to have eluded art-historical notice: its masters were Gian Antonio de Salo, and Piero di Benevegnudo, both active together in Venice as collaborators of Vittoria (Basso 1968, pp. 107–114; 1976, pp. 30–36).

The Barbaro tempietto is not the parish church of the village of Maser, although a long tradition has it thus (e.g. Arts Council 1975): rather, it is a private chapel attached in perpetuity to the ownership of a country estate, by the authority of the Sistine bull. The confusion arose because it had been suggested in Marc'Antonio's papal petition that the tempietto might in fact replace the older village church of SS. Paolo e Andrea, and this hope was echoed in an episcopal visitation of 1593, as well as in an earlier comment by the stuccoists: indeed, statues of the local saints Paul and Andrew had been installed on either side of its principal altar before 1588, and probably by 1584 (Basso 1968, pp. 111–112; 1976, p. 34). But Agnoletti (1898:II:500) recounts that the Bishop of Treviso in 1588 had opposed the generous terms of the Papal bull, only to be overridden by the Venetian Senate, which upheld Marc'Antonio Barbaro; relations between the patron and the diocese understandably cooled, the larger structure dedicated to S. Paolo continued as the parish church (as it still functions today), and future Bishops of Treviso did not resume their visitations at the Barbaro chapel until 1640 (Basso 1968, p. 112; 1976, p. 34).

In a deft and suggestive study of the iconography of the Maser tempietto, Wolfgang Lotz in 1977 interpreted its plan (fig. 81)—whose porch, domed rotunda, and sacristies derive very directly from those of the unused Venetian project—as a fusion of the interpenetrating centralized designs of a circle and a Greek cross, possibly representing a Palladian metaphor (following the Quattro Libri IV:ii:6) of the mystic unity of Father and Son. This very revealing observation can be strengthened by the discovery, on the back of a recently uncovered London sheet (RIBA XIII/18 verso: cf. cat. no. 104), of two small plan sketches which are unquestionably preparatory studies for the Barbaro tempietto (fig. 80). They show Lotz's deep recession of altar chapels, with the flat side walls that appear in Palladio's church designs only at Maser; both the outer and inner decorated walls are articulated exactly as in the executed building, save that the latter introduces a consistent row of four equal pilasters (instead of lateral pilasters with two slightly taller central colonnettes) as frames to the three niches for figural sculptures, in the altar tabernacles. Pane (1961, pp. 303–4) and Cevese (in Mostra 1973, p. 94) had both already noticed that this weak revision must be due to the stuccoists: we now, in these last sketches, have an indication of Palladio's original intentions for their form. Indeed these little graphic notes on the back of the Dioscuri capital may well be the last surviving autograph drawings of his life. They were, however, left behind in the Vicenza studio (as demonstrated through Jones's acquisition of them there, attested by Talman's mark), and thus had been superseded by the moment of Palladio's final journey to Maser with the completed plan, in which he had made a decision to support the dome on cylindrical walls instead of square ones with pendentives. On this crucial point the plan sketch of the extended lateral "arm" shows a direct development from the side chapels of our exhibited Venetian plan, and (as Puppi suggested would be necessary, 1973, p. 433) proves that very considerable redrafting was indeed required before Palladio could produce, from the prototype of that project, the design of his new tempietto at Maser. Palladio's small sketches of 1579–80 thus provide the missing link which ties his large, slightly bland votive church project precisely and sequentially to his bold, dramatic, and extraordinarily inventive plan of the Maser tempietto.

The fact that this tighter design is also more comprehensive and coherent than has yet been recognized can now be affirmed, through the evidence of the Venetian plan, by means of a final consideration of the tempietto's iconographic program. The original Venetian church was decreed as the memorial of a sacred vow, made in supplication for the deliverance from the plague, to *"la Divina Maestà"*; it was to be dedicated to the Redeemer, the Savior of mankind; and the vow itself was solemnly offered on the Feast of the Nativity of the Virgin Mary, 8 September 1576 (Zorzi 1967, pp. 130–131, docs. 1–2). The Maser chapel was designed, as Palladio makes clear in his related discussion, as an emblematic manifestation of "the Unity and infinity" of the Divine Majesty of God; its major altar has always been presided over by a central sculpture of the Redeemer (sometimes called the Savior); a central sculpture of the Virgin Mary has always stood on its lateral altar to the south, which was dedicated to the Nativity; while its northern altar, as a final demonstration of this absolute identity of program, was provided—until a replacement was introduced in 1861—with a central sculpture of the plague saint *par excellence,* St. Sebastian tied to the tree (though this was once, by a notoriously poor critic, misinterpreted as Christ bound to the column: Basso 1968, pp. 115–117; 1976, pp. 36–39). Such an uncompromising replication of the precise iconographic program for which Palladio's Venetian project *"in forma rotonda"* had been conceived, allows us to understand the half-size replication of it in the form of a private chapel, by the same patron and the same architect, with the same general and detailed dedications, as an utterly convincing and coherent transfer in which only its site and size have been changed. These last characteristics, however, clinch the relationship. The tempietto, on the private property of the Barbaro villa, although adroitly situated to command a long view from the village, has always been manifestly much too small and too distant to function as the community's parish church. Marc'Antonio's petition of the early 1580s, Sixtus' bull of 1585, the sculptors' reference in 1588, and the rector's hopeful expectancy in 1593, form an isolated initial decade of optimistic and unrealistic references to the tempietto as a potential church of S. Paolo. From the latter moment until the present it has always been called, much more accurately and indicatively, "the chapel of the Redentore" (Basso 1968, p. 187, doc. 21); and thus I believe that it was

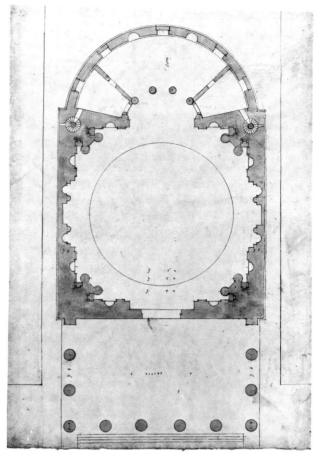

115

never truly intended to serve any public function at all. St. Paul's martyrdom was indeed stuccoed in its pediment, but Palladio explains that this kind of homage to place and cult is a necessary concession and stimulus to local piety (IV:i:5). Saints Paul and Andrew do flank the Redeemer, over the main altar, but the same considerations of local protocol apply, for they are the village saints. Moreover, Marc'Antonio's own patrons Mark and Anthony flank the Virgin Mary; his parents' name saints, Francis and Helen, flank Sebastian; and, most movingly and suggestively of all, Palladio's name saint, Andrea, stands on the right of the Redeemer himself. Marc'Antonio Barbaro's intensely private and personal thank-offering for his own deliverance from the plague thus perpetually stands at Maser, in fulfilment of who knows what personal vow; and his friend Palladio is commemorated there as well, through both the inscription and the image of his patron saint.

194

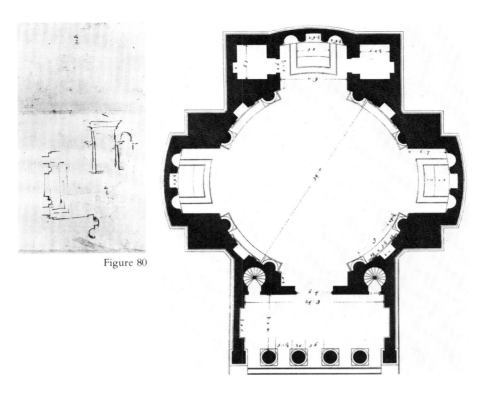

Figure 80

Figure 81

---

116. LONGITUDINAL SECTION OF PROJECT FOR A VOTIVE CHURCH AT VENICE

December 1576/January 1577

RIBA: Palladio XIV/14.

41.2 × 52.4 cm. (single sheet); watermark, anchor in circle with star; no collector's mark, save *"75"* (cancelling *"74"*) in late gray ink on *verso* (Burlington purchase, 1719).

Umber ink; figures in small rectangular panels also umber ink, and also by Palladio; other figures in siena ink, by another hand (Francesco Zamberlan ?); inscribed with measures in feet, and with scale of 10 feet = 32 mm.; inscribed in another hand, *"fianco del portico / altare / fianco / coro."*

Timofiewitsch 1959–1960, pp. 79–87, fig. 107; Pane 1961, p. 304, fig. 341:61; Zorzi 1965, p. 134, fig. 100; Zorzi 1967, pp. 167–168, fig. 201; Isermeyer 1969, p. 476 n. 2; Isermeyer 1972, p. 132, fig. 58: Mostra 1973, p. 146 (Burns); Puppi 1973, pp. 261, 396, 434, fig. 617; Wilinski 1974–76, pp. 145–146, fig. 51; Arts Council 1975, pp. 146–147, no. 258 (b) (Burns—repeating incorrect measures from Mostra 1973); Foscari 1975, pp. 44–56, fig. 2; Paris 1975, p. 40 (note and illustration); Venice 1980, p. 270 (Foscari, in no. 442).

Royal Institute of British Architects, London.

A comparison of this handsome project drawing for Palladio's and Marc'Antonio Barbaro's Venetian votive church *"in forma rotonda"* (*cf.* cat. nos. 114–115) with the little Palladian chapel at the convent of the Zitelle (fig. 82 and cat. no. 117) demonstrates once more the germinal character of this three-part design. The project's facade and domed silhouette (cat. no. 114) directly influenced the final votive church of the Redentore (fig. 79); that first drawing of the project sequence splendidly reiterated Palladio's expectations for a portico facade at S. Giorgio Maggiore (*cf.* cat. no. 113, which it very strongly resembles), and provided a direct prototype for the closely related designs that he recommended at S. Petronio (cat. no. 118), and built at Maser (cat. no. 115). The second drawing with the project's plan, in that latter sheet, not only can be shown through a very late intermediary sketch (fig. 80) to have been the direct source for the Maser tempietto (fig. 81), but provided as well the configuration of the Zitelle chapel (fig. 82), and the apsidal column screen of the Redentore. And this third drawing with the project section, finally, provides most of the elements for the Barbaro chapel walls (the Maser elevation sketch in fig. 80 represents for example a simplification and strengthening of its lateral altar design), as well as almost the whole central section of the Zitelle (fig. 82; see cat. no. 117). Thus major aspects of designs as diverse as S. Petronio (1579), the Barbaro tempietto (1580–84) and the Zitelle (1581–86), as well as the great Redentore itself (1577–91), all derive from this fertile and suggestive project for the Venetian votive church, that Palladio conceived and drafted in two winter months of 1576–77.

195

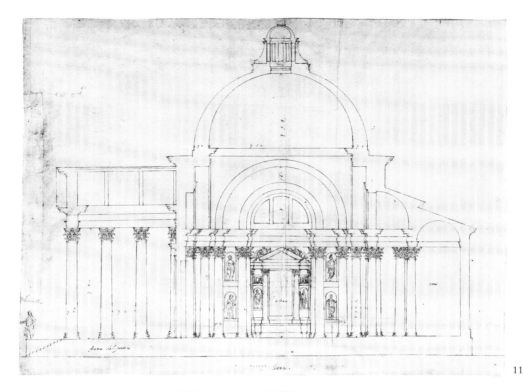

116

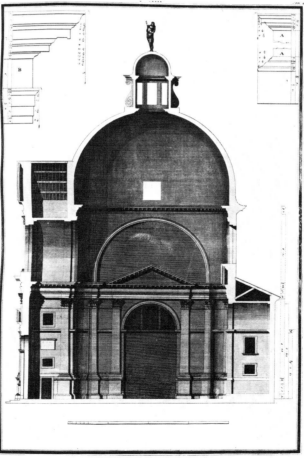

Figure 82

196

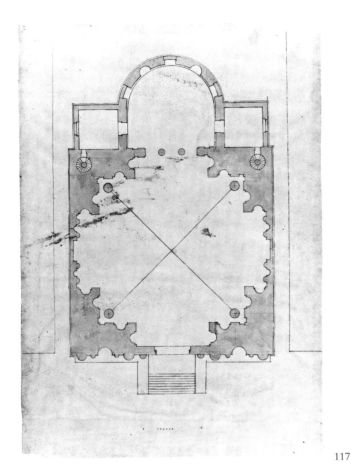

117

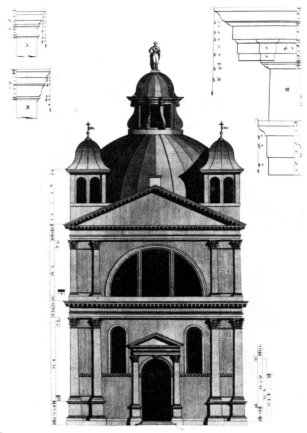

Figure 83

117. SIMPLIFIED PLAN PROJECT FOR A VOTIVE CHURCH AT VENICE (II)

December 1576/January 1577

RIBA: Palladio XIV/16.

41.2 × 28.5 cm. (single sheet); watermark, anchor in circle with star; no collector's mark (Burlington purchase, 1719).

Russet umber ink, and light purplish-gray wash, on pencil underdrawing; drawn with scale of 20 feet = 56.5 mm. (2 Venetian inches); stained with later smudges of siena ink.

Wittkower 1949/1971, p. 100, fig. 40b; Timofiewitsch 1959–1960, p. 86 n. 3; Pane 1961, p. 304, fig. 341:60; D'Ossat 1966, p. 46, fig. 55; Zorzi 1967, pp. 167–168, fig. 202; Tafuri 1968, p. 71, fig. 46; Isermeyer 1969, p. 476 n. 2; Mostra 1973, pp. 146–147 (Burns); Puppi 1973, pp. 396, 434, fig. 615; Arts Council 1975, pp. 146–147, no. 258(d) (Burns); Foscari 1975, pp. 44–56, fig. 4.

Royal Institute of British Architects, London.

This secondary project represents an intermediate stage between Palladio's great visionary votive church proposal (cat. nos. 114, 115, 116) and a more modest and practical development from it, exactly in the same sense as his little secondary sketch on RIBA XIII/18 *verso* was an intermediate step toward the final Maser chapel plan. That transitional sketch, in fig. 80, is also very significantly similar in plan and detail to the design of the lateral chapels on this sheet, which can thus be regarded as one of the direct prototypes

for the Greek cross plan at the Barbaro chapel (fig. 81) The closeness of the Maser sketch to this sheet confirms a somewhat earlier date than 1580 for the planning of the Barbaro tempietto, since the 80-foot width of this project anchors it firmly to the two months before the Venetian Senate's crucial vote on the form of the Redentore (cat. nos. 114, 115). Immediately after that decision in favor of Palladio's larger longitudinal plan, the width of the votive church's site was expanded to 100 feet (17 February 1577: Zorzi 1967, p. 113, doc. 9), and Palladio laid aside for other uses all four of these drawings projected for the 80-foot site.

Our present plan might suggest that Palladio had heard by 1577 about some possible interest, on the part of the poor nuns at the Zitelle, in a more modest version of his great centralized project(s) for the votive church nearby. Or possibly Marc' Antonio Barbaro, the special advocate of the *"forma rotonda,"* even thought at one point of proposing the convent of the Zitelle as a site for the Redentore itself, during these months in which a centralized form for the great votive church was still potentially open. As it happens, we know almost nothing about either the patronage or the date of the severely simple little chapel that was built at the Zitelle, nor even anything beyond the evidence of style (and a twenty-five year later guidebook ascription—Stringa 1604, p. 192) to associate its design with Palladio.

197

Antonio Foscari, in a careful review of this scanty evidence (1975, pp. 52–55), has suggested that a document of 25 June 1582 referring to work that "had been begun" (as we learn, on 19 March 1583, "in the years just past": Puppi 1973, pp. 431–432) could be taken to imply—if we do assume a lifetime intervention by Palladio himself—that the conventual buildings must have been complete by the late 1570s, in order to allow time for the earlier nunnery to be demolished, and its site prepared (as we know to have happened) as the space for a chapel, which thus Palladio might have studied before drafting a design. But in fact no solid evidence supports either this extrinsic back-dating, or the intrinsic stylistic assumption that Palladio might have been directly involved. The Zitelle chapel cannot reasonably be claimed—from the documentation so far discovered—to have been begun before 1581; and even the most optimistic reading of its forms suggests only that pre-existing Palladian plans, such as the one here exhibited, might have been still further simplified and adapted to the modest means of its religious community. Just enough such parallels exist, in fact (as for example in the section already noticed, in both of these larger plans, or in the simplified derivation of the facade from a model such as this drawing) to support the idea that it was not only timbers for scaffolding which the sponsors of the Redentore donated to the neighboring nuns of the Zitelle (in June of 1582), but—at some moment just earlier—perhaps Palladian drawings as well.

---

118. FINAL FACADE PROJECT FOR THE CHURCH OF SAN PETRONIO, BOLOGNA

12th to 27th January 1579

Worcester College Library, from Inigo Jones album no. I/68, now designated H.T. 68 (supplementary series).

49.8 × 36.6 cm. (single sheet); watermark, coronet topped by fleur-de-lis (close variant of Briquet 4844: Lucca 1580); circled identification number 47H in pencil on *recto* (Gotch no. I/47 H).

Two tones of umber ink, over incised lines.

Harris 1971, pp. 34–37, fig. 42; Mostra 1973, p. 149 (Burns); Puppi 1973, p. 406, fig. 578; Arts Council 1975, pp. 243–244, no. and fig. 431 (Burns); Harris and Tait 1979, p. 54. no. 127.

The Provost and Fellows of Worcester College, Oxford.

The present exhibition celebrates the tenth anniversary of John Harris's discovery of this sublime drawing, one of Palladio's greatest masterpieces of both draftsmanship and invention, as well as his latest fully autograph finished drawing to survive. It had lain unrecognized at Oxford since the early 18th century, as a bequest to Worcester College in 1734 by Dr. George Clarke—who presumably acquired it as a Vicenza studio sheet with the Jones collection, directly from Inigo's heirs, John and William Webb. In an extraordinary quirk of fate, an embellished contemporary copy of it had just come on the London market a few years earlier (cat. no. 119), and James Ackerman's careful study of that derivative sheet had enabled him to recognize it as reflecting "Palladio's lost portico project for San Petronio in Bologna" (1967). Harris, in making his discovery at Worcester, was thus enabled by Ackerman's very recent analysis to recognize the new sheet as being unquestionably the lost original design, and announced it as such in 1971.

The circumstances of Palladio's commission have been clearly reviewed by both these scholars, as well as by Panofsky (1930/1955, pp. 196–203), Wittkower (1974, pp. 75–76) and Burns; it is only necessary to comment here that the Worcester design represents the second and more radical of Palladio's completely independent ideas for the huge unfinished facade of Bologna's great medieval church. After a preliminary consultation of 1572 in which he had quickly sketched a quite handsome proposal for retaining the existing Gothic basement and adding a Renaissance design above it, Palladio had heard nothing more from Bologna until the last weeks of 1577. At this point news reached him that the five-year-old design had been considerably criticized, and Palladio replied on 11 January 1578 defending it, but adding at the end a new concept (presumably in response to a Bolognese proposal) that "done with sound design [a portico] would give the work grandeur and commodity, and I like the idea" (Ackerman 1967-II, p. 110). During a second visit between March and October of 1578, however, Palladio presented his first wholly personal and quite revolutionary design (the "project G," in the archive at San Petronio), which would have demolished all medieval traces and created a huge "relief facade," on the models of his Venetian churches (*e.g.,* cat. no. 113). As we noted briefly in the discussion of Palladio's first executed Venetian facade at S. Francesco della Vigna (cat. no. 110), his still earlier but unexecuted (and now lost) project of 1558 for S. Pietro di Castello is described as requiring six large columns and pedestals, plus windows: it may thus have looked very much like Palladio's first truly original design for Bologna (a kind of expanded version of his S. Pietro/S. Francesco scheme) on Project G-Left. On the other half of the same project (G-Right) he brought the interpenetrating large and small orders both down to a much lower common base line, in a closer reflection of his mature preferences, especially as we see them in his design's generic prototype at S. Giorgio (cat. no. 113). But the very mention of that supremely simple and harmonious design with its great free-standing portico—an invention that Palladio had again recommended, with such monumental effect, in his first Venetian votive church project of exactly these same months (cat. nos. 114–116)—reminds us that his last years were particularly devoted to encouraging such designs, and that his very last work, at the Maser chapel, presents the most beautiful of them, finally, in executed form.

118

Therefore it will not surprise us that at a very late moment in his correspondence with the officers of S. Petronio, on 12 January 1579, Palladio writes that he has almost convinced himself of the superiority of a full free-standing portico, and has begun to make drawings of such a design. Just over two weeks later he dispatched a long explanatory letter with this design, or more probably one virtually identical with it, retaining this as a studio copy (thus providing for its acquisition by Jones). Indeed the spacing of the columns is very slightly modified in the memorandum, and thus presumably on the drawing sent, which does not survive at S. Petronio. Otherwise this design matches precisely all the detailed points in Palladio's covering letter, and presents one of the grandest and noblest of all his inventions. At an immense scale, closely comparable to that of the Pantheon itself, he proposes a vast free-standing portico whose plan and elevation would closely follow that hallowed Hadrianic prototype, but with solid end walls fronted with square piers, between which a magnificent file of round columns would be contained. The scheme, except for its colossal size, is exactly followed in the portico of the Maser tempietto of the following year, so that the development of the S. Petronio design in January of 1579 helps us to fix a date for the Barbaro project. Palladio continued to hope that his great portico would be built in Bologna, but S. Petronio's facade stands undecorated to this day.

119

119. CAMILLO AZZONE (?): EMBELLISHED VERSION OF PALLADIO'S FACADE PROJECT FOR SAN PETRONIO, BOLOGNA

1579

57.0 × 38.0 cm. (single sheet); no watermark visible; no collector's mark.

Siena ink and sepia washes; inscribed (in Azzone's hand ?) with measures in feet.

Wienreb 1963, p. 60, no. 97; Ackerman 1967-II, pp. 110–115, fig. 3; Harris 1971, p. 37, fig. 41; Puppi 1973, p. 406; Wittkower 1974, pp. 75–76, fig. 109; Arts Council 1975, p. 244 (Burns, in no. 431).

From the collection of Phyllis Lambert, on loan to the Centre Canadien d'Architecture/Canadian Centre for Architecture.

Ackerman suggested in 1967 (II, p. 114) that this elaborated version of the then lost Palladio portico project for S. Petronio (cat. no. 118) was probably the "copy" documented to have been made in 1579 by one Camillo Azzone (apparently a local Bolognese artist, though otherwise unknown) for dispatch to Rome. This must indeed be the case, and—now that we can compare it with Palladio's original—we may appreciate at once why Pope Gregory XIII is said to have exclaimed upon seeing it that "under no circumstances whatsoever should that portico be built." Poor Palladio, to be represented to His Holiness by such a conflation! As Carolyn Kolb convincingly suggested shortly after this drawing was found (Ackerman, p. 114), it can best be understood as reflecting the skeleton of the Palladian original (*cf.* now cat. no. 118), but overlaying it with a whole repertory of motifs derived from the *Quattro Libri* and other sources: as she pointed out, the most telling of these is its reproduction of the central pavilion of the published project for the Rialto Bridge (III:xiii:26–27, fig. 86). Azzone's use of shading, however, does very helpfully prove that Palladio's corner piers were flat-faced, so that it thus performs an important documentary function.

120

Figure 84

120. NORTH ITALIAN (?) ARTIST: ELEVATION OF AN ALTAR TABERNACLE

c. 1615 or later (perhaps submitted to Palladio's Church of the Redentore in 1679?)

Ashmolean Museum: Ruskin School deposit, 1974.

76.1 × 47.6 cm. (overall dimensions of large principal sheet plus small added flap: main sheet 72.6 cm. high, flap adds 3.5 cm. at top); no watermark visible; various unrelated inscriptions on *verso* of flap, but no collector's mark (Ruskin purchase).

Umber ink, with several colors of wash, from light sepia to very dark umber-brown; heavy incised lines; considerable pencil underdrawing; pricked for transfer; inscribed lower left, in 17th-century hand, *"Desegno Di Andrea Paladio"*; also on *verso, "Del Paladio"* and *"Andᵃ Paladio."*

Image unpublished; *cf.* Arts Council 1975, pp. 147–148, no. 262 (Burns—as circle of Palladio [?] c. 1580).

Ruskin School of Drawing and Fine Art, University of Oxford

Despite Burn's methodical defense of what he thought might be an "early attribution," this is not a drawing from the 16th century nor even from the first years of the 17th, and not from the circle of any recognizable artist (Scamozzi,

Vittoria, Campagna *et al.*) who could be construed in any way as a member or associate of "Palladio's circle"; I doubt very much that it is even from the Veneto. It is included here in order to recommend its more appropriate assignment to some other artistic milieu, and to solicit wider help (since it is indeed an interesting drawing, and its image, as far as I know, has never been published) in the task of making a more accurate attribution. For it is a good deal easier to suggest what this curious image is not than to decide what it may be.

In the first place, it is definitely a project for a large tabernacle to adorn an altar, of the type called a *tabernacolo alla romana:* in Rome itself a prime example that is important because of its date, size, lavishness, and highly prominent position is the one on the central altar of the Chapel of Sixtus V at S. Maria Maggiore, executed by Lodovico Scalzo to the designs of Giambattista Ricci in 1590. We would naturally expect a gap of almost a full generation before the type might become popular in the Veneto, and sure enough (to take a representative example, again large, lavish, prominent and well dated), the one by Girolamo Campagna on the high altar of S. Lorenzo in Venice was made in 1615–17 (Timofiewitsch 1972, pp. 297–299, fig.

201

116). This is one of the touchstones that disproves an early date in Venice for our drawing; for the S. Lorenzo tabernacle—one of the richest that I know in the Veneto, and roughly comparable to ours in apparent size and type—is rectilinear, dry, and brittle in the typical way of Venetian late academic classicism, and is poles apart from our drawing in terms of style. The other most interesting Venetian representative that I can remember is the one from S. Lucia, again attributed to Campagna, which stood from 1864 to 1938 on the high altar of S. Francesco della Vigna. The next important Venetian examples are those by Sardi—S. Pantaleone, 1668, and by Longhena—S. Zanipolo 1652, Scalzi 1654, and Tolentini 1661; all look perhaps a bit later than ours. Perhaps the best comparison is the Late Baroque tabernacle of almost identical silhouette (and some quite similar details) by Giuseppe Mazza and Tommaso Ruer of 1679–80 on the high altar of Palladio's Church of the Redentore: if the Ruskin drawing was submitted as a competition design for that project, both the added figure of the Redeemer and the added inscriptions might explain why a foreign drawing should have become associated with a Palladian context.

An even more clear stylistic incongruity is manifested in Vicenza itself, where—most conveniently—we can actually compare our drawing with a very early surviving and documented tabernacle from the Cathedral (fig. 84). This is a fifteen-foot version crafted in fine cabinetwork with precious woods, gilt, terracotta, and paintings, that was made for the Altar of the Holy Sacrament in 1605–7. It once had a reasonable and indicative traditional attribution to Scamozzi, thus paralleling our case most interestingly—save that here the name matched the style, which the name on the Ruskin drawing does not. But now the documents for it are well published (*Oggetti Sacri* 1980, pp. 61–65, no. 93 [Barbieri], and pp. 65–67 [Dalla Via], with full bibliography), and it can be shown to have been designed by a priestly amateur of architecture named Giacomo Montecchio, who indeed frequented the Scamozzian camp. It is exactly what one would expect to find in Vicenza twenty-five years after Palladio's death. It could not be more radically different from the Ruskin drawing, yet it very strikingly recalls Palladio's own documented creation (well before 1575) of an ebony medals cabinet in the form of an Arch of Constantine (cat. no. 57), which probably looked a great deal like it; the tabernacle's lower central zone might even be plausibly derived from the Palladian prototype.

If Venetian dominions in general and Vicenza in particular must be excluded (at least in the span of 1580–1620, which would subsume all the artists who might have had any first-hand experience of Palladio) as representing a possible locus for the production of this sheet, where then does it belong? Rome itself would be one possibility, and indeed the careful "aedicular" composition of the central pedimented bays might reflect early Roman Baroque precedent; even the competition for the facade of St. Peter's may be recalled in the design. Florence is probably not so likely: Giovanni de' Medici's tabernacle design for the Cappella dei Principi at S. Lorenzo (of. c. 1603–4?) is much less Michelangelesque than this in its decorative elements, and more reminiscent of his own collaborator, Buontalenti (Biblioteca Nazionale di Firenze, Cod. Pal. 3B.1.7.c.68). A drawing of 1619 for the funeral apparatus of a patroness of the Jesuit Order in Naples has a somewhat similar ornamental vocabulary, but a quite different design (Vallery-Radot 1960, p. 435, no. 139, fig. xxxiv). The best proposal may be Milan: there is a stilted look of Lombard classicism to the whole, which is combined with reasonably up-to-date motifs of ornament; the very unusual main pediments, for example, recur almost exactly on a Milan Cathedral facade drawing of the early 17th century, probably by Lelio Buzzi or Lorenzo Binago (Wittkower 1974, p. 43, fig. 58). The peculiar "wings" on our design, in fact, may relate it even more specifically to the lateral extensions on the Milan Cathedral project designs—as possibly the "aedicular" arrangement of the unusually narrow window bays may as well. Once more we have the problem of the migration of motifs: the Ruskin design seems to me to be unthinkable before the prototype of Maderno's S. Susanna, and yet one may find that calculating the time-lag for such Roman developments to reach Milanese artists of the second rank may prove very difficult.★ The figure style, as manifested so richly in the decoration of the sheet, may provide a possibility of dating the work through comparisons with known drawings of similar subjects. Above all, I think, the possibility of the Redentore tabernacle commission in 1679 should be kept strongly in mind.

★ Peter Cannon-Brookes has suggested in correspondence that the drawing may be related to the work of Giuseppe Bernascone, il Mancino, who was active from 1604 in designing the chapels on the Sacro Monte at Varese, for which our sheet might even be construed as a preliminary design for Chapel V.

CHAPTER NINE

The Legacy of Palladio

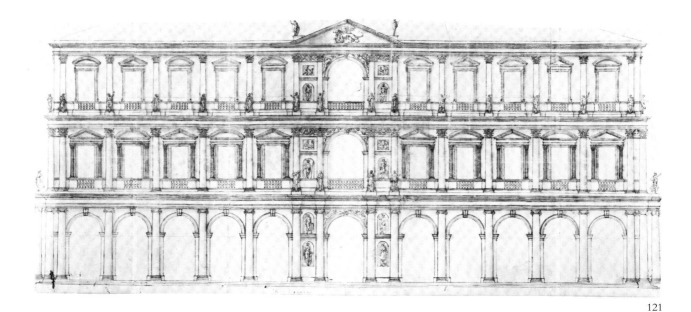

121. FACADE PROJECT FOR THE DUCAL PALACE, VENICE

January–February 1578

Devonshire Collections: Chatsworth SOS/B.

47.9 × 107.2 cm. (three sheets of stained and foxed paper, pasted by Palladio: center sheet, 47.8 × 71.9 cm.; watermark, large coronet with star (*cf.* Briquet 4834), no countermark; left piece, 47.1 × c. 18.5 cm., no watermark visible; right piece, 46.5 × 18.2 cm., no watermark visible); no collector's marks.

Dark brownish siena ink, and light gold-sepia wash, over incised lines; drawn with scale of 10 feet = 56.5 mm. (2 Venetian inches).

Gualdo 1749 and 1959, quoted in Introduction above; Temanza 1778, p. 501; Magrini 1845, p. 312; Harris 1971, p. 34 n. 3; Arts Council 1975, pp. 155, 158–160, no. and fig. 279 (Burns—as "hitherto unpublished and unnoticed"); Venice 1980, p. 102, no. 74 (Olivato).

The Trustees of the Chatsworth Settlement.

"In the collection of original drawings by the celebrated architect Andrea Palladio, that are held by His Grace the Duke of Devonshire in his villa at Chiswick near London . . . there is as well a magnificent and large design hung in a glazed frame, which is very delicately executed in line and wash, and represents the facade of a splendid palace of three stories. It is decorated with orders of columns on each floor, and presents a grand and impressive architectural composition" (Donaldson and Poynter, transl. in Magrini 1845, pp. 309–312, and here retranslated). This as yet unremarked evidence of the special status enjoyed by this great drawing, evidently from the time of its acquisition and installation by Lord Burlington at Chiswick, explains why John Harris should have found it (after the migration of the unbound Burlington drawings to Chatsworth) still hanging prominently—as it does today—at the great Cavendish county seat in Derbyshire: "also at Chatsworth, a single unpublished [*sic*] design for a Venetian public building" (1971, p. 34 n. 3).

Harris's tentative attribution was to Scamozzi, and indeed there is clearly present in the execution a certain "hardness" (Burns, p. 71) that one usually associates with Vincenzo. In fact, the drawing in many ways reminds us of Scamozzi's own design (chosen 10 April 1582) for the Procuratie Nuove in Piazza San Marco.

But Howard Burns in 1975 recognized and published the Chatsworth sheet as Palladio's project for reconstructing the Palazzo Ducale after the fire of 20 December 1577—a design that had previously only been mentioned in passing by Gualdo and Temanza, and implied in a contemporary manuscript account by the chronicler Francesco Molin (Burns transl., p. 158): "the opinions of the best architects in the city were taken, and they all came to the conclusion that the walls had remained sound . . . only Palladio, the celebrated and famous architect, concluded that . . . the facade towards San Giorgio should be destroyed and demolished, and the whole building substantially renewed; and this opinion of his was fomented by Marc'Antonio Barbaro, Procurator of S. Marco, a most able and prominent orator, to such an extent that although it appeared very extravagant to the whole Senate, all the same arguing with all his ability he kept the proposal alive for many days." For exactly sixty days, that is (thus creating time for Palladio to draft this superb vision), until on 21 February 1578 the Senate voted overwhelmingly to restore the Palace as nearly as possible to its former state.

Burns has thoroughly analyzed the design both with regard to Palladio's hopes and the Palace's requirements; his dimensions, however, can be augmented by the following notes, taken from the drawing itself at Chatsworth. Palladio makes the height of the arcade 20 feet, and the ground floor (to the first cornice) 28 feet; the second floor is 25 feet and the third 22½, for a total height of 75½ feet. The existing Palace is quoted by Burns as 74 feet high, with a length on the S. Giorgio side of 219½ feet (but his contemporary plan should be checked against a modern survey). Palladio proposes a slightly reduced length of 183 feet wall to wall, which expands to 189 feet if we include the outer columns (or 191½ feet counting their bases and steps).

So far no one has said much about the place of this design in the international history of architecture, a context in which it deserves at least a brief assessment. On the whole, the couple of generations between Michelangelo's Capitoline Palaces and Carlo Maderno's beginnings of Palazzo Barberini (a revolution completed and extended globally by Borromini and Bernini) were perilous ones for large palace architecture, and most European princes prudently forebore to build during this period; we have already noted the Escorial as its most innovative achievement (cat. no. 90), and that is a measure of the problem. When Pope Sixtus V began his phenomenal rebuilding of Rome in 1585 he could find no more exciting architect than Domenico Fontana, whose Lateran Palace is universally decried for its monotonous banality (someday it may be discovered to have a kind of quiet monumentality, but the star of this style has not yet risen). In such a context, Palladio's design is lively and even festive: its forms are simple and strong, and they achieve a requisite grandeur by their arrangement of architectural masses in bold relief, with almost no dependence on the decoration of figural sculpture. The three stories are in fact quite tall, and a further guarantee against their orders looking frail or repetitive is that they are composed of very large shafts running down through the balconies, thus achieving a much greater size and mass than they would have had if propped up on pedestals as small colonnettes. This last was the solution that Scamozzi chose, in adding what otherwise amounts to the top floor of this design to the two floors of Sansovino's Library that stands opposite, in creating his timid and unoriginal Procuratie of 1582. A further measure of the European situation is that Scamozzi's resulting design—at least as it was simplified and strengthened by Longhena, who extended it around two sides of the Piazza San Marco—has been universally praised. As a powerfully persuasive image only weakly reflected by Scamozzi, and as an exuberant Venetian alternative to Domenico Fontana, it can hardly be doubted that Palladio's Ducal Palace design (if Marc'Antonio Barbaro had carried the day) would have produced the finest great European palace between Michelangelo and Bernini.

---

122. CRISTOFORO SORTE: CONTRACT DESIGN FOR THE CEILING OF THE SENATE CHAMBER IN THE DUCAL PALACE, VENICE

Attested 27 July 1578

Victoria and Albert Museum E.509—1937.

45.9 × 86.4 cm. (single sheet [?] of badly rubbed, stained, and torn paper, laid down on opaque backing); no watermark visible; no collector's mark.

Umber ink with yellow-ochre wash, squared for transfer; inscribed, left to right and top to bottom, *"longo Piedi 15½ / largo Piedi 11½"; "longa Piedi dieci / largo Piedi 7½"; "longo Piedi 12 / largo Piedi 7½"; "longo Piedi 25 onc. 6 in luse / largo Piedi 18 in luse"; "longo Piedi 20 / largo Piedi 11½"; "longo Piedi 9 / largo Piedi 6 onc. 4"*; also inscribed in different hands, *"1578 a[di 2]7 lulio / Io Andra faencimo mi obligo a fare il sufitatto justa la schritura dacordo et ī il presente disegno cōn le saghome che saranno dato dal mz christofaro Sorti et i duj protti / io franᶜᵒ inttagrador da san moizé / Azeruro quantto e sopra [s]critto."*

Wolters 1961, pp. 137–144, fig. 1; Schulz 1962, pp. 195–202; Schulz 1968, p. 44, pp. 111–114, no. 43, fig. 87; Wolters 1968-I, pp. 68–69, fig. 87; Wolters 1968-II, pp. 275–276, fig. 237; Arts Council 1975, pp. 160–161, no. and fig. 280 (Burns); Venice 1980, p. 88, no. 54 (Rinaldi).

Victoria and Albert Museum, London.

This extraordinary sheet—a unique survival of its class, since no other preparatory drawing for a Venetian ceiling framework is known to exist—can now be intimately associated with Palladio's rediscovered project to rebuild the Palazzo Ducale in classical style (cat. no. 121), and this affords a new understanding of his role in the redecoration of this great seat of the Venetian government.

On 11 May 1574 a fire in the Doge's private apartments spread to the major reception and council rooms on the main upper floor of the east wing, requiring their complete rebuilding. The resulting works, which define the appearance of the Senate, College, Anticollege, and their lobby "of the Four Doors" as we see these rooms today, were not quite finished (for example, the Senate still lacked its decorated ceiling) when a second and even more disastrous fire broke out on 20 December 1577 (cat. no. 121). This conflagration destroyed the interiors of both the Gothic wings across the courtyard, leaving the waterfront and Piazzetta facades precariously standing; and this provided the opportunity for Palladio to recommend a complete rebuilding, in which he had the strong support of his prominent Senatorial patron Marc'Antonio Barbaro. Although their proposal was voted down, one result of the immediately increased activity of restoration was that the versatile artist Cristoforo Sorte was called back from retirement in Verona, and assigned the role of drafting ceiling designs for both the almost reconstructed Senate, and the newly burned Great Council hall. His drawing for the Senate ceiling, here exhibited, was prepared in the first six months of 1578; on 27 July (it is just possible to read the date under magnification) it received attestations by the master carvers who were contracting to build it: Andrea of Faenza and Francesco Bello. A certain Master Girolamo was hired soon after, to execute Sorte's associated designs for the wall decoration; but he was an intractable type who embroiled Cristoforo in extended disputes, which the supervising magistrates eventually settled in Sorte's favor, and at the expense of a cabal including Master Girolamo and the nominal Supervisor of Works, Antonio da Ponte.

122

Figure 85

This commission and its history suggest several new conclusions with regard to the notoriously vexing problem of discovering attributions for the various elements of the Ducal Palace reconstructions. Several of its designs merit a closer investigation of the possibility of Palladio's involvement, for they are not only impressive in themselves, but important for the understanding of wider issues—most significantly, in fact, for the development of Venetian Renaissance ceiling design.

Palladio had known Sorte since at least 1561/62, when they made a survey together for Leonardo Mocenigo at Marocco (Arts Council 1975, p. 222), and 1563, when Sorte surveyed another Palladian site at Cicogna (*ibid.*, p. 177). That it was Andrea himself who called Sorte in to assist at the Ducal Palace (thus implying a highly important role for Palladio in supervising the whole reconstruction) is strongly suggested by several factors. In the contractual annotations on this drawing, Sorte is not in fact named as the designer of the ceiling (though Francesco Sansovino accords him this honor in 1581), but simply as the first of three draftsmen from whom Masters Andrea and Francesco will be getting their working drawings of full-size details—the other sources being "the two Supervisors." A convincing body of evidence attests that the *"Proto"* who principally supervised the Palace's rebuilding in 1578–85 was Francesco Zamberlan (Puppi 1973, p. 424, confirming Zorzi 1965, pp. 158–162); and Francesco was the closest assistant, amounting to a "disciple," of Palladio's last years (*ibid.*, p. 99 n. 60, p. 161 n. 46). Palladio was certainly very active at the Palazzo Ducale in 1578, where in fact he was

being powerfully supported by Marc'Antonio Barbaro, as we know now from contemporary sources such as Francesco Molin and Paolo Gualdo, as well as from the Chatsworth drawing (cat. no. 121). Barbaro served as one of the Commissioners for the Restoration of the Palace from February of 1576, and was thereby one of the supervising magistrates who arbitrated in Sorte's favor even after Palladio's death (but evidently in his behalf), at the expense of Antonio da Ponte. Several lines of evidence thus converge to identify "the two *Protos*" who stood behind Sorte's drawing as none other than the faithful Zamberlan, as the active younger engineer who was supervising the daily work of rebuilding, and the great Palladio, the inventive genius who as Zamberlan's master was overseeing the whole operation, and coordinating the activities of trusted associates such as Sorte in the realization of its many components.

That the situation can hardly have been otherwise is further attested by a mass of documentation for the period following the first fire. This has previously been regarded with suspicion by critics committed to a "pure" Palladio, with whose supposedly chaste and abstracted style the Palace's exuberant richness would ill consort. But since we have now seen, in cat. nos. 87 and 89, that Palladio's great talent as an interior designer (one, moreover, of occasionally rather florid taste) extended consistently over his thirty most productive years from 1549, we have no more reason to doubt the overwhelming testimony of the Palazzo Ducale documents. There even exists a precise visual prototype for the kind of works they describe, in Palladio's two big autograph drawings (with figures by Zamberlan) now at Brescia: the second (Zorzi 1965, fig. 78) shows a sculpturally lavish interior decoration, though the fact seems to have been almost consciously suppressed in the Palladian literature.

At the Ducal Palace in Venice Zorzi understood the truth, though he was sometimes too enthusiastic in expressing it (1965, pp. 137–151). He made it clear that the great introductory Sala delle Quattro Porte (whose spectacular ceiling of 1576–77 Francesco Sansovino specifically gives to Palladio, as the keynote to everything that follows) in fact derived all its major elements—most especially the four great doors themselves—from Palladian designs. Through this point, at least, he has been generally (though reluctantly) followed, with predictable quibbles about Andrea's degree of responsibility for the ceiling. But in fact it essentially replicates a magnificent Palladian prototype, at Palazzo Della Torre in Verona (Zorzi 1965, fig. 233), to whose Ducal Palace version Bombarda added some particularly fine stuccoes in Vittoria's—and Palladio's—favorite style. The wonderful ceiling of the Anticollege was similarly claimed as a Palladian design by a highly reliable early source, Girolamo Gualdo Jr., who can now be more confidently trusted on this point; it was executed by Marco del Moro in 1576–77. As early as 22 December 1574 Palladio was supervising execution of the marble chimneypiece in this reception room (though Scamozzi later claimed its crowning plaster decorations), and another in the College or Ducal council chamber beyond it; the door between them is generally acknowledged as one of Andrea's most compelling masterpieces. The counselors' stalls and Ducal throne in the College are essentially documented to Palladio, and may be his earliest works in the Palace, being designed before the end of 1574 and built in 1575, the principal masters being Andrea of Faenza and Francesco Bello. These experienced Palladian collaborators also carved the similar benches in the adjoining Senate, and we have

seen that they contracted in 1578 to execute Sorte's drawing for its ceiling (fig. 85)—which in this total context I would thus be inclined to call Palladio's idea, worked out in broad terms in relation to his other Palace ceilings, but creatively interpreted by Sorte.

Such a view of Palladio's role in the development of these great masterpieces is implicit in Schulz's classic account of their evolution (1968). A standard type exists by mid-century, with clear architectonic relationships between the compartments and with the wall. A new influence appears in the framework for Veronese's sublime ceiling pictures in the College, from which Antonio da Ponte's name must be removed: Temanza hypothesized his association in the 18th century (ibid., p. 105), but Zorzi's review of his career and activity at the Ducal Palace invalidated the suggestion (1965, pp. 138–139), and the reading proposed here of the evidence provided by the Sorte drawing makes it still more implausible. But one month before he was provided with Fabiano paper apparently for drafting the College ceiling, Palladio was working on an exactly comparable design, also with Veronese, at Udine; in the same ten-day span in which Paolo got his first advance for its pictures, Palladio received a payment for works produced, and two days later the wood-carvers began their work; the best of them was given a cash prize, eighteen months later, on the same day as Palladio received a large payment as well. The innovative aspects of this ceiling show up in Palladio's designs at Palazzo Chiericati; Schulz specifically cites Palazzo Thiene and Palazzo Barbaran as prototypes of the next stage, exemplified by Sorte, in which curling strapwork interconnects all the compartments. The one common factor that links all these designs is the inventive personality of Andrea Palladio. Once we develop a comprehensive enough view to avoid fearing that a "Platonic" Palladio would be compromised by these works, they may be seen as one of the most impressive aspects of his genius.

---

123. VINCENZO SCAMOZZI: LATERAL ELEVATION AND SECTION OF PROJECT FOR THE RIALTO BRIDGE, VENICE

December 1587/January 1588

RIBA: Burlington-Devonshire VIII/10.

46.3 × 73.8 cm. (single sheet, with some spotting and corrosion on left); watermark, wheel with six spokes surmounted by cross (simpler variant of Briquet 13324); collector's mark lower right, D surmounted by coronet (Lugt 718: Dukes of Devonshire).

Siena ink, with slight traces of pencil, over incised lines; inscribed lower right, "Vicenzo Scamozzi Ar" (cut at right edge).

Zorzi 1954–1955, pp. 138–208; Zorzi 1967, pp. 230–231, fig. 246; Arts Council 1975, pp. 126–128, no. and fig. 224 (Burns); Venice 1980, p. 127, no. 112 (Maschio).

Royal Institute of British Architects, London.

No collection of Venetian 16th-century architectural projects would be complete without a drawing for the famous stone bridge over the Grand Canal at Rialto. This carefully drafted design is signed by the young Scamozzi (1552–1616), and was evidently presented to the supervising magistrates of the enterprise immediately after his memorandum of 31 December 1587, in which he strongly recommended a three-arch plan (we see its essential structure in the outline at the bottom). It was unfavorably commented upon by a competitor for the commission, Guglielmo de Grandi, in a report of January 1588 (Zorzi 1967, p. 230). After extensive discussion, a single-arch plan was chosen, and Antonio da Ponte was appointed in February 1588 to direct its execution. Just whose design was selected is unclear, for several of the competitors rapidly produced appropriate revisions, as it became apparent in early January that the three-arch type would

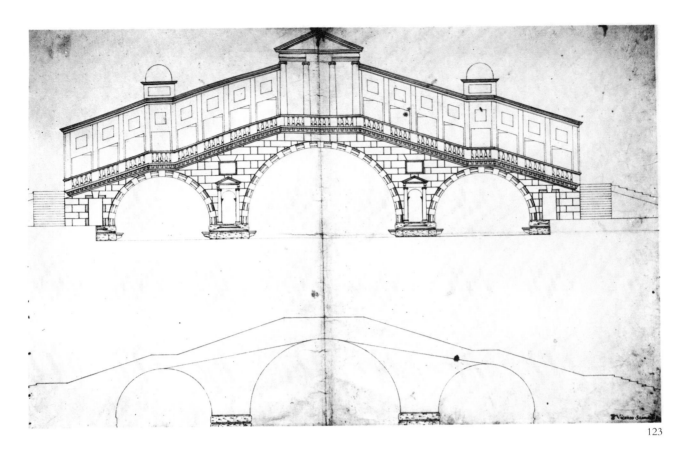

123

probably be rejected: Da Ponte presented his much more economical single-arch proposal on 15 January, while De Grandi and Scamozzi were both paid for further drawings of their projects in late February and early March. Scamozzi had the strongest backing, for not only did he manage to have both his designs published in rhyming broadsides with woodcut illustrations (*ibid.*, figs. 248 [= the three-arch RIBA design exhibited here] and 249), but he obtained the support of Marc'Antonio Barbaro—the most important magistrate for the project—in precipitating an intrigue in August 1588 to have Da Ponte ousted, and himself appointed *Proto*. This attempt failed, but the resulting bridge (completed in 1591) looks extraordinarily like the broadside illustration of Scamozzi's single-arch project, and he subsequently claimed credit for its design (1615, II:330). There may thus have been accomplished a characteristically Venetian compromise, whereby Da Ponte was retained as the official engineer, but Scamozzi's design essentially adopted through Barbaro's support. The documenting woodcuts are both influenced by the executed structure, however, as this sole surviving drawing demonstrates (the roofs and shop doors, in its printed reproduction, are changed to match those that were built). These may reflect changes of detail introduced by Da Ponte for the purpose of compromise, or—especially in the case of the single-arch design—they may simply represent a jealous plagiarism by Scamozzi. He was fully capable of such behavior: this drawing and indeed his whole oeuvre borrows heavily from Palladio

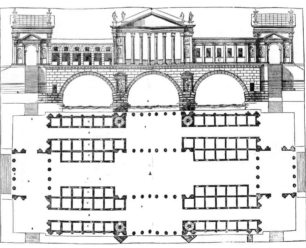

Figure 86

(*cf.* fig. 86), but Scamozzi was so obsessed by the "injustice" of the older master's greater reputation that he never once mentions Andrea in his own long treatise (1615). The fairest assessment, especially in view of Antonio da Ponte's modest architectural abilities (cat. no. 122), is probably that both woodcuts do reproduce original Scamozzi designs (following the clear evidence of this sheet) and that the bridge as built does closely reflect his invention—in part based, characteristically, on prototypes by Palladio.

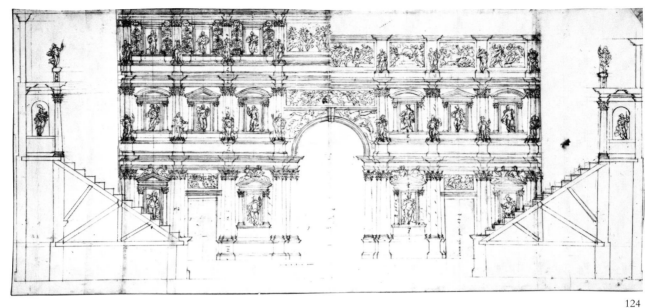

124. INTERIOR FACADE PROJECTS FOR STAGE OF THE TEATRO OLIMPICO, VICENZA

1580

RIBA: Palladio XIII/5.

41.7 × 89.9 cm. (three sheets pasted in Palladio's shop: center sheet, 41.7 × 58.8 cm.; watermark, anchor with thin stem in circle with lozenge-armed cross (Mošin 2446); left piece, 41.8 × c. 16 cm; countermark, B—B with trefoil flower; right piece, 41.8 × c. 16 cm.; no watermark or countermark); Talman 49 mark on *verso* (bleached).

Bright orange-red siena ink, and pale beige-gray wash, with extensive underdrawing in umber crayon and pencil; inscribed in the hand of Marc'Antonio, Palladio's son, with measures in feet, and scale of 6 ft. = 46 mm. ($1^7/_{12}$ Venetian inches), and also with phrase "*in tuto alta 43½.*"

Grant Keith 1917, pp. 105–111, fig. 107; Dalla Pozza 1942, pp. 217–222, fig. 25; and 1943-I, pp. 197–201, fig. 48 (left half); Magagnato 1951, pp. 209–220; Pane 1961, p. 364, fig. 390:46 (detail); Puppi 1963, p. 44; Ackerman 1966/1977, p. 180, fig. 95; Zorzi 1965, p. 134, figs. 104 a and b; Zorzi 1965-II, pp. 70–97, fig. 1; Barbieri 1967, p. 48 n. 70; Zorzi 1969, p. 286, fig. 468; Puppi 1971, p. 87, fig. 72; Gioseffi 1972, p. 60, fig. 21 (detail); Magagnato 1972, p. 144, fig. 78; Mostra 1973, pp. 145–146, fig. 154 (Burns); Puppi 1973, p. 437, fig. 622; Barbieri 1974, p. 310, fig. 162; Arts Council 1975, p. 46, no. and fig. 77 (Burns); Paris 1975, p. 39 (fig. and illustr.); Vicenza 1980, pp. 180–181 (Puppi).

Royal Institute of British Architects, London.

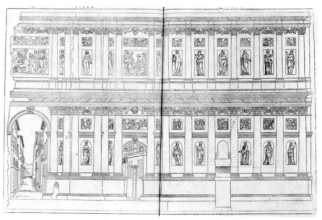

Figure 87

Figure 88

A wonderfully evocative recreation of a whole Roman theatre (even if at reduced scale, and in wood and plaster) was Palladio's last great homage to antiquity and to Vitruvius: permission to build it was granted by the Vicenza council in February 1580, and this drawing thus dates from the last six months of Palladio's life. Burns has shown that it was drafted, to Palladio's design, by his son Marc'Antonio (Arts Council 1975, p. 46). It is one of the only project drawings by the master which is demonstrably not an autograph, a fact certainly to be explained by its late date. We can compare it with Palladio's own almost contemporary sketch for the Maser chapel (fig. 80), to see why he would prefer for such a grand and important design as this to be drafted by a younger, but intimately supervised, associate. The fact that his choice fell upon Marc'Antonio helps to clarify the necessary removal of Francesco Zamberlan from his late collaborators in architectural drafting. Zorzi perceptively assigned a role to Francesco in assisting Palladio with the addition of figures to some of his late sheets (1965, p. 99 n. 60, and p. 161 n. 46), but he seems certainly to have erred in assuming that Zamberlan ever drafted their architectural structure (1965, p. 134). This misconception has been uncritically accepted, even in the case of autograph sheets ranging from the S. Petronio drawings (Barbieri 1967, though justly questioned by Puppi 1973, p. 405) to the great masterpiece of the Palazzo Ducale project (Venice 1980, p. 102, Olivato). It deserves to be laid to rest, through the reaffirmation that Palladio himself produced a series of beautiful drawings almost to the end

of his life—*e.g.* the votive church sheets (cat. nos. 114–117) in January 1577; the Chatsworth Ducal Palace (cat. no. 121), in January 1578; and above all the Worcester facade for S. Petronio (cat. no. 118), in January 1579.

Palladio and Marc'Antonio present in this drawing, whose style is very close to the Chatsworth palace project, the final proposals for the Olimpico stage: that on the right was chosen (fig. 88). It derives very precisely from Palladio's great project of the early 1550s for such a stage reconstruction, published in a magnificent illustration in Barbaro's *Vitruvius* (fig. 87). That design clearly prescribes the insertions of illusionistic sceneries in the arches, though probably only in painted form (following antique models, which Palladio knew from texts). After the main structure of the Teatro Olimpico had been completed in 1584, Scamozzi added actual avenues to achieve such illusionistic perspectives behind the stage, for the opening performance of Sophocles' *Oedipus Rex* (cat. no. 125); they have remained in place ever since (fig. 88).

---

125. VINCENZO SCAMOZZI: FINAL PROJECT FOR PERSPECTIVE AVENUE OF THE TEATRO OLIMPICO, VICENZA

1584/85

Devonshire Collections, Chatsworth: Drawings Vol. IX, "Designs and Sketches by Inigo Jones," fol. 71, no. 108.

29.2 × 41.3 cm. (single sheet); watermark, orb surmounted by star (?) with smaller circle below; no collector's mark visible.

Light umber ink, over heavy lines ruled in pencil, with numbers and some underdrawing; drawn with dimishing scale of Vicentine feet; inscribed with labels, *"Strada / tempio tondo / edificio Cittadiniero / edificio nobile / cittadiniero"* and below with names and heights of parts for each facade.

Grant Keith 1917, p. 111; Loukomski 1940, p. 67, fig. 6; Puppi 1963, pp. 51–55; Zorzi 1965-II, pp. 70–97, fig. 12; Puppi 1966, pp. 26–32; Zorzi 1969, pp. 294–303, fig. 502; Puppi 1971-II, p. 90; Gallo 1973, pp. xxxii–xxxiii, 27, fig. 1; Puppi 1973, p. 439, fig. 628; Vicenza 1980, pp. 182–183, 194–195 (Puppi, in no. 213).

The Trustees of the Chatsworth Settlement.

When Palladio died in the late summer of 1580 the outer walls of the Teatro Olimpico were still rising: on 7 November the main part of the building was almost ready to be roofed. A year later, as discussions continued about the selection of an appropriate inaugural performance, the Academicians decided that more room would be required for the proper development of constructed perspectives behind the stage (*cf.* figs. 87–88), for which Palladio had provided a preliminary drawing on 15 February 1580. The requisite land was granted in response to their petition of 19 January 1582, and the outer structure was finished in 1583.

In the spring of the same year a fateful decision was made to open the new theatre with the great Sophoclean tragedy of *Oedipus the King,* and a highly prestigious director from Ferrara, Angelo Ingenieri, was engaged. He advised the Academicians in December 1583 that the stage scenery should be made to resemble as closely as possible Sophocles' setting of "Thebes, the city of Boeotia, and seat of empire." During 1584 it was decided to follow this suggestion by extending seven radiating avenues behind the stage (whose front had been finished earlier that year), in a classical reference to the seven gates of Thebes, and to embellish their perspectives with the architectural facades of an ideal cityscape. In May 1584 a committee was selected to make arrangements with artists for accomplishing these works, and in an undated letter sent from Venice toward the end of the year (Zorzi 1969, p. 298), Scamozzi declares that he has many things in mind for "this illustrious scenery," but will come to Vicenza to discuss them in person rather than try to write them down. By 14 November 1584 he may have produced not only his preliminary sketches now in the Uffizi (nos. 195A–198A; Puppi 1971, figs. 73–76), but perhaps also this extremely beautiful sheet at Chatsworth, with substantial revisions to his first design (reproduced side by side in Zorzi 1965-II, figs. 11-12, and 1969, figs. 501–502): on that date the backstage perspectives were put "off limits" so that the carpenters could work uninterruptedly. The theatre opened with what must have been a dazzling première, on the Sunday before Mardi Gras, 3 March 1585; and the seven "Theban" avenues, in fact looking more like a Scamozzian dream of an ideal Vicenza than an evocation of the mythic city of Cadmus, have remained to this day (fig. 89)

211

125

Despite Zorzi's ingenious attempts to claim them for Palladio, the drawings for these delightful little perspective avenues are guaranteed to Scamozzi by close parallels in a signed project of 10 May 1588 for his own theatre at Sabbioneta, also in the Uffizi (Zorzi 1969, fig. 507). They represent in a sense the perfect Mannerist conceit, in being extravagant, toy-like, and impossible to use; but they add the intention of recreating a paradigm of ancient Greece to Palladio's Vitruvian reconstruction of an accurate *Romanità,* and thereby make the Teatro Olimpico one of the most precise surviving images of the Renaissance's self-conscious recreation of classical antiquity.

Figure 89

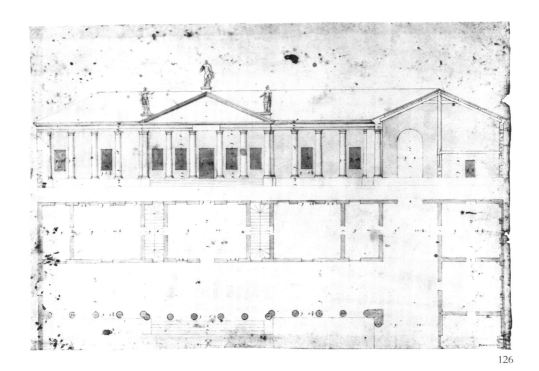

126

126. VINCENZO SCAMOZZI: PROJECT FOR SERVICE WING AT THE VILLA FERRAMOSCA, BARBANO

c. 1575

RIBA: Palladio XIV/5.

33.8 × 47.9 cm. (single sheet); no watermark visible; collector's mark left center edge, *D* surmounted by coronet (Lugt 718: Dukes of Devonshire).

Umber ink and sepia-gray wash; inscribed with measures in feet; later inscribed in different hands, on *recto* (bottom right, in pencil), *"Scamozzi";* on *verso* (in pencil), *"Hettor feramosca";* (in ink) *"Varij disegni fatti in gioventù dal Scamozzi"* (the last words cut, at bottom edge).

Burger 1909, pp. 32–37, fig. 9:1 (as Palladio); Zorzi 1954-I, p. 72, no. 16, fig. 18 (as Palladio); Barbieri 1962, pp. 24–25 n. 48; Zorzi 1969, pp. 49–50, fig. 62; Puppi 1973, p. 285, fig. 357; Burns 1979, pp. 15–16 (as Gian Domenico Scamozzi).

Royal Institute of British Architects, London.

Figure 90

Howard Burns and I noticed independently that this interesting design, so long a mystery among the Palladian sheets in London, was actually a project for completing the courtyard of the villa of Girolamo Ferramosca at Barbano, which still stands (though without this third wing) on the main road between Vicenza and Padua. It is inscribed with the date 1568, and has a main block (which would be just off this plan at the bottom right) with lower flanking wings, of which the projected left-hand one shows here in plan and section along the right edge. The main *corps* is extended by a service wing on its right (northeast) side, corresponding to the one being proposed here to enclose the forecourt on the left, and thus create a symmetrical U-shaped complex (Cevese 1971, pp. 415–418, plan). The project is inscribed on the *verso* with the name of Girolamo's

heir, Hector Ferramosca, and thus clinches the destination documented by its configuration and dimensions.

But what of its artist? Burns has called it a drawing by Gian Domenico Scamozzi, the father of the more famous Vincenzo, since a prefatory letter in a 1584 edition of Serlio (which publishes a Serlian index by Gian Domenico) clearly ascribes a Villa Ferramosca at Barbano to him. In my view, though, that structure is none other than the problematical "archaizing loggia" on the northwest side of the building group, and neither it nor Gian Domenico Scamozzi has anything to do with the structures—either built or projected—around this adjoining eastern court. Indeed, I think the whole idea of Gian Domenico as an architect is probably a mistake: although Lodovico Roncone's eulogistic letter in the Serlio compendium of 1584 suggests that Gian

Domenico was able to perform as an independent designer, in the documents he is called a carpenter—albeit one who pored over Serlio. And the Ferramosca loggia in fact projects the image of a Serlian enthusiast, an amateur of architecture, who makes a low, spreading, unfocused design, innocent of moldings, and haphazard in proportions. While it *looks* archaic, actually the style (or lack of it) is quite typical of 16th-century buildings by provincial hands.

The modish facade on the opposite side, however, together with this design, are both sharply unlike the loggia; and (as Burns has commented) they are remarkably indebted to Palladio (a lifelong tendency of Vincenzo's). They are "schoolboy classic," with thin, self-conscious academic moldings, repetitive symmetries, and one quite interesting motif: the clustered shafts of their central pavilions' corner piers, borrowed from Palladio's facade of Palazzo Chiericati. Indeed the only material change from that prototype, in the part of the villa design on this sheet, is that the frieze is omitted and there is one more bay at each end. The tablet in the central entablature is a "signature motif" of Vincenzo's (*cf.* cat. no. 123).

The *verso,* indeed, clearly labels this sheet and the designs formerly grouped with it, as "Various drawings made in his youth by Scamozzi." The uninflected surname, and the reference to a Scamozzi who was youthful in the late third quarter of the century, both unquestionably refer to Vincenzo (1552–1616) rather than to his father Gian Domenico (c. 1526–1582). A document drawn up at Dr. Girolamo Ferramosca's town house in Vicenza, on 6 January 1575, attests to the young artist's cordial relationship with the elder patron, while one of 10 June 1580 shows him already frequenting the home of the latter's son, Hector. In 1575, when Vincenzo's association with the Ferramosca family is first documented, he was twenty-three years old; this drawing would thus be quite an early sheet, and it is certainly an important one. If the main block of the Barbano villa was really executed in 1568, it may well have been supervised by Gian Domenico; but in my view this drawing strongly suggests that its real inventor was the youthful Vincenzo. If the inscription does not give a retrospective date, then he designed it at sixteen, some eight years before his earliest securely dated masterpiece, the "Rocca" at Lonigo for Vettor Pisani (who died in July of 1576).

127. MARC'ANTONIO PALLADIO: STUDIES FOR A GARDEN WALL AND GATE

c. 1560?

RIBA: Palladio XIII/3.

41.7 × 29.1 cm. (single sheet of spotted, stained, and discolored paper); watermark, crossbow (with traces of illegible countermark lower left); collector's mark (by Burlington) on *verso,* "Door·24·" (his purchase, 1719).

Dark siena ink, and heavy umber and gray-brown washes, over pencil underdrawing: inscriptions concerned with this image are (from top to bottom): *"dado rugola / "[= dado] a bugne / piedi 5 quarti uno* [twice] / *piedi 12½ / [pie]di—7 di luse / p 2 / piedi [2]½ onc. 3"* and other measures in inches; various additional unrelated inscriptions. *Verso,* PRELIMINARY SKETCH FOR THIS DESIGN; light pencil, with inscriptions in feet; additional sketches of a related portal, molding profiles, and detail of an ornamental grill, in umber ink, with smudges of wash.

Loukomski 1938, p. 26, fig. on p. 25; Pane 1961, pp. 228–229, fig. 242:11; Zorzi 1969, p. 50, no. 18, fig. 64; Mostra 1973, p. 145, fig. 153 (Burns); Puppi 1973, p. 341; Arts Council 1975, p. 204, no. 368 (Fairbairn).

Royal Institute of British Architects, London.

Loukomski was evidently an early admirer of this drawing, which is certainly one of the most appealing in the Palladian corpus: he awarded it a full-page plate in the first illustrated study to be devoted to "The Drawings of Palladio" (1938). Fiocco ridiculed his choice, in "offering as typical [of the master] an oafish drawing of a portal with a fretted wall, just because it recalls those of the Villa Badoer" (1949). But the drawing—while admittedly not by Palladio (Fairbairn attributes it to his nephew, who had

127

the same name as one of his sons; *cf.* cat. no. 124)—is not only very handsome, in its robust and confident use of Palladian motifs, but possibly even interesting as a document of their development. Rather than the walls and gate at the front of the Villa Badoer at Fratta (which have a different relationship, though the piers may have been redesigned when they were raised because of the change in street level), or more plausibly the well-preserved Palladian gate at its back (which has a different design), the London drawing seems instead to refer to the damaged back gate of the Villa Pisani at Bagnolo, as Puppi has astutely suggested. The piers of that strongly rusticated

portal (which survive to the impost at the springing of the arch: Zorzi 1969, fig. 77) are the only elements in Palladio's oeuvre that repeat the powerfully projecting engaged columns of this design; taken together with our drawing, they are closely reflected in the well-preserved portal of the nearby plantation center (*ibid.*, fig. 79: cat. no. 47), which can be dated about 1559–62. Our sheet may therefore reflect a stage in Palladio's handling of the rusticated Tuscan order around 1560, and suggest that Andrea may have used his studio assistants (as indicated by this work sheet with a practice drawing) to produce the renderings of these ornamental details.

---

128. FRANCESCO MUTTONI: ELEVATION/PLAN OF PALLADIO'S FACADE FOR PALAZZO SCHIO, VICENZA

1708

CISA: Cappelletti Collection, Codex Twisden, fol. 11 *recto*.

37.5 × 26.1 cm. (right half of full sheet measuring 37.5 × 52.1 cm., stitched as second sheet of six enclosed between 19th century paper boards: left half of this sheet has PLAN, SECTION, AND ELEVATIONS OF PALLADIO'S PALAZZO PORTO-BREGANZE, VICENZA as fol. 2 *verso*); no watermark visible; collector's inscription on inside cover, "Cappelletti già numero 422."

Siena ink and two tones of gray wash, over traces of pencil underdrawing; inscriptions in siena and umber inks, within drafted border: "Figura 9.ma / Metta della Picola Casa Schij à S. Marco. di Paladio. Di questa, e costrutto li Due Soli ordini Rustico, e Corintio, vi Manca il 3.º A, e per questa Causa, fù tagliata la Cornice alle lettere B, C." Drawn with scale of 30 feet = 89 mm. (3 Vicentine inches), and north—T[ramontana]/south—M[ezzodi] orientation. For left half of sheet with Palazzo Porto-Breganze see Puppi 1973, pp. 395–396, fig. 560; Puppi 1980, p. 242 (with transcription); and Vicenza 1980, p. 78, no. 68, fig. on p. 71 (Camerlengo).

Zorzi 1965, p. 292, fig. 364; Mostra 1973, p. 182, no. 35 (Puppi); Puppi 1972–1973, pp. 248–249, 296–298, esp. 297 n. 114; Puppi 1973, pp. 375–376, fig. 523; Lewis 1976, p. 144; Barbieri 1980, pp. 221–222; Puppi 1980, pp. 236–242 (with transcription, p. 242, of entire codex); Vicenza 1980, pp. 75, 78, no. 68, fig. on p. 72 (Camerlengo).

Raccolta Palladiana Cappelletti, Centro Internazionale di Studi di Architettura "Andrea Palladio," Vicenza.

By a margin of almost three-quarters of a century (that is before Bertotti-Scamozzi published it in 1776), the earliest attribution of this small but highly important late work to Palladio occurs here, on the page of a manuscript compendium of antique and Palladian architecture by Francesco Muttoni. I suggested some years ago the identity of the Grand Tourist for whom he produced this "souvenir" of classical architecture in Rome and Vicenza, namely Sir Thomas Twisden (c. 1670–1728), third Baronet, of Bradbourne near East Malling in Kent. Muttoni inscribed the title page of this little guide to good architecture to Sir Thomas (with his name rendered phonetically as *Signor*

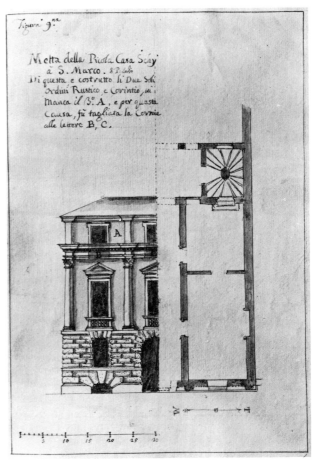

128

Kavaliere Tomaso Twixden Inglese), and commented that they had made their visits of inspection together, to Palladian sites in and around Vicenza. Since the central sheet of the album is dated *"Adi 23. Aprile 1708 in Roma"* and describes an excavation of the so-called "Palace of Nero," and since the obtaining of permission to excavate for antiquities had been a goal of English *milords* on the

Grand Tour at least since the example set by the Earl of Arundel and Inigo Jones a century earlier (Summerson 1966, p. 35), we can be confident that Muttoni is here recording exactly such a relationship with Twisden. This fact likewise dates the Vicenza drawings, for the resources of even the wealthiest *dilettanti* rarely allowed them to travel in Italy for more than a year; and Sir Thomas seems to have been a more modest personality by far than the princely Lord Arundel.

Francesco Muttoni (1669–1747) is now becoming much better known; a variety of recent studies have been summarized in Puppi 1980, with a full publication of the present codex (as well as the newly discovered birth date given here). As Puppi and I have both suggested in discussing Muttoni's drawings (*cf.* cat. no. 129), his Late Baroque view of Palladio is very valuable indeed, especially as a corrective to the classicizing "purism" of successive commentators.

---

129. FRANCESCO MUTTONI: ELEVATION OF SCAMOZZI'S PALAZZO THIENE-BONIN, VICENZA

1730s

Library of Congress Rare Book Division, NA 2633. M8 (folio), fol. 15 *recto*.

36.5 × 26.5 cm. (single sheet, pasted along inner edge to support strip, and stitched into album of 26 sheets); no watermark visible; collector's marks (inside album cover), printed bookplate of Lorenzo Urbani; penciled price of L. 200; pencil acquisition number 200580/13.

Siena ink, with sepia and blue-gray wash, on pencil underdrawing; drawn with inscribed scale of 40 feet = 119 mm. (4 Vicentine inches); inscribed also in ink with number, "*Tav. XXVIII*" (over erasure of former *V*), and letters "*T / V / Y / Z*"; further inscribed in pencil (on labeled pasted at top), "*5 Prospetto del Palazzo predetto, alla parte di OSTRO.*" *Verso,* inscribed in ink, "*a[di] 14 Genaro 1739/40 acordata l'incisione di questo foglio al Sig.° Giorgio Fosati p Filippi 6 val L66 come nel Proc. A. C.ᶜ 22 Ter. et copia B·C·8·Terga. / Fran.ᶜᵒ Mutoni Aff.*"

Image unpublished: *cf.* Lewis 1976, p. 134.

The Library of Congress, Washington, D.C.

The excellent architect and even better architectural historian Francesco Muttoni, before his death in 1747, had been able to consign to his Venetian publisher, Angiolo Pasinelli, eight volumes of what may probably be called the most important work on Palladio between the *Quattro Libri* and our own day, that is his great *Architettura di Andrea Palladio vicentino . . . accresciuta di moltissime Fabbriche inedite* (1740–48), whose history was thought to have ended with a posthumous ninth volume, brought out in 1760 by his engraver and publishing colleague, Giorgio Fossati. But Muttoni had announced, both in his advertising Prospectus of 1739 (whose map of Palladian sites in the Veneto was intended for his final volume, and is reproduced here on page two) as well as in a 1743 preface to his fourth volume published in 1746, that a forthcoming tenth volume would include notes and measured drawings of certain still partially buried Roman antiquities (which were the same ones he had drawn in the Twisden album: Puppi 1980), plus some Palladian and modern works including his own church at Leffe near Bergamo. Thus it was possible, in announcing the discovery of the corresponding Palladian and modern plates in this hitherto unknown album in Washington, to demonstrate that they and the Codex Twisden (cat. no.

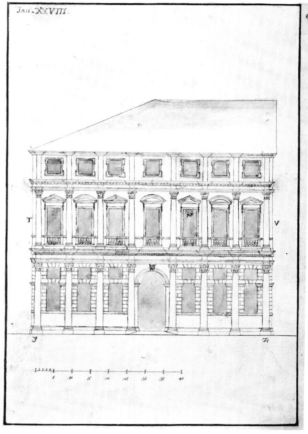

129

128) taken together constitute the two major components of Muttoni's projected tenth volume for his *Architettura* (Lewis 1976). In the present exhibition they are brought together for the first time with representative sheets (cat. nos. 60, 130) from a third group that has been published in the meantime, comprising twelve Muttoni drawings at Chatsworth (Barbieri 1980). Several more such sheets are known to exist, but are unlocated (e.g. Puppi 1973, fig. 612); they and the Chatsworth leaves may not (or may not all) have been intended for the *Tenth Book;* but we probably have represented, in these three recent publications of new Muttoni materials, almost all the projected contents of the final volume of his *Architettura di Andrea Palladio.*

That great work, because of its small edition and high cost, has remained very rare, and its fame has been largely eclipsed by a more popularly successful work, very comparable in type and contents, which Ottavio Bertotti-Scamozzi published in Vicenza in 1776–83. Indeed, Bertotti's *Fabbriche e Disegni di Andrea Palladio* can be seen in some sense as a kind of mass-market revision of its fundamental predecessor in Muttoni's *Architettura*. Muttoni and Fossati, at great expense, arranged for the measuring, drawing, and engraving of a great many Palladian fabrics not included in the *Quattro Libri* (the Venetian churches are an outstanding example), and many other works besides; Muttoni had acquired a substantial number of Palladio's own drawings (including those now in Vicenza), and had studied others; and he had been indefatigable in examining the buildings themselves. His work is thus the fundamental bedrock of critical and visual evidence on which most Palladian scholarship and publication rests, with the obvious additions of new visual and documentary material that have been added to the subject since his time. Some of these new results were contributed by Bertotti-Scamozzi; but on the whole he could re-engrave Muttoni's plates, and the resulting savings gave his work the edge that carried it into wide popularity and subsequent editions, whereas Muttoni's remained largely inaccessible, through its own criteria of completeness and especially of beauty.

Muttoni's conclusions, however, deserve to be taken seriously and studied carefully (especially now that a splendid modern reprint of the published work is available: Muttoni 1740–48/1973, and the unpublished materials are almost all accessible as well). This problematical palace for Francesco Thiene, as an example, was accurately judged by Puppi to be "preponderantly and decisively the responsibility of Scamozzi" (1973, p. 403); Muttoni—who was its first and perhaps best-informed commentator—calls it definitely (and in the context of an inclusive study of Palladio) "an unpublished work by Vincenzo Scamozzi." In considering the stiff and accurate classicism of its execution (whose dates are 1572/77–1586/93), we can hardly doubt that Palazzo Thiene-Bonin's earliest and most recent students are mutually correct. And now Muttoni, who should emerge from the greatly renewed interest in his work and writings as one of the Veneto's most interesting architects, as well as one of Palladio's most sensitive historians, gives us an added measure of assurance that Scamozzi must have invented (or very heavily revised) its designs as well.

---

130. FRANCESCO MUTTONI: ELEVATION AND PLAN PROJECT FOR PALAZZETTO MAIOLI, VICENZA

Dated 1706

Devonshire Collections: Chatsworth F.4

27.4 × 27.7 cm. (single sheet); watermark, three diminishing crescents in line (*cf.* Heawood 863/873); no collector's mark; inventory number F.4, top left.

Umber ink, on pencil underdrawing; labeled, inscribed with measures in feet, and with scale of 48 Vicentine feet = 79 mm. (2⅔ Vicentine inches); further inscribed with page number ("68"), with cardinal directions, and with list of specifications for the building. *Verso* inscribed with page number ("67"), and with label: *"1706—Casino d'idea in Picolo / Per il S.ͭ Gio.̈ Batt.ͭ Maioli appreso la / Porto del Castello in Vicnz.̈"*

Barbieri 1980, pp. 222–226, fig. 7 (as an unidentified villa).

The Trustees of the Chatsworth Settlement.

This is probably the best sheet with which to represent Francesco Muttoni as a Neo-Palladian architect (especially since it comes from the very little-known *dossier* of his drawings at Chatsworth), that is in the second of his important roles, in addition to his fundamental activity as the first really thorough Palladian historian. Its one very recent publication omitted the note giving its identity—by which some trace of it can probably still be found, around Piazza Castello, or at least in the archives, at Vicenza. And most significantly for our present purposes, because of Muttoni's importance as a connoisseur and collector of Palladio's drawings, it may be capable of telling us a good deal about Muttoni's distant, but revered, master.

For this design of Muttoni's of a casino at the Porto Castello is evidently based on (or directly inspired by) a drawing such as the RIBA sheet (Palladio XIV/8) in fig. 91. The same tall rusticated basement is surmounted by the same Corinthian order, concentrated in a slightly projecting central pavilion that carries a low pediment. In both cases one bay on either side of this frontispiece completes the facade, and within the central element a large arched portal on the ground floor is surmounted by a strongly emphasized central window above.

But the curious thing about the RIBA sheet is that several modern commentators have assumed it to be an English drawing, in fact a preliminary study by Inigo Jones for his great masterpiece of the Queen's House at Greenwich (Whinney 1970, pp. 33–35; Harris 1971, p. 34 n. 6). This, in my view, it almost certainly is not: I doubt very strongly indeed that Jones had anything to do with it, save (as usual) for collecting it, and—quite possibly—sketching the very Jonesian cartouche into the pediment, which is the element that seems first to have led Jones's commentators to claim the whole design as his. I cannot find any trace of Jones's hand in any other part of the sheet; and, to look back once more at Muttoni, the local Vicentine interest in this type of facade seems to me to argue for its production at the fountainhead.

But when? Is the problematical RIBA drawing a work contemporaneous with Muttoni, in 1706? Or with Jones, who spent considerable time in Vicenza in 1613 and 1614? Or is it in fact a drawing from the circle of Palladio himself, or a member of his shop? I tend to favor the third and earliest possibility. That the sheet is Muttonian (or Late

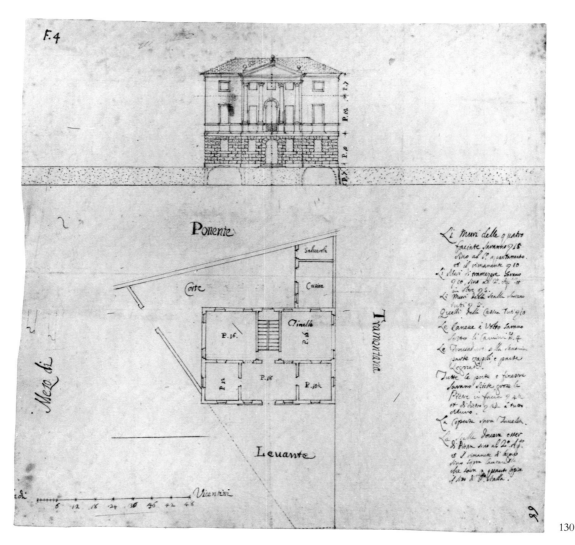

130

Baroque at all) can probably be ruled out by its style, not only graphic but architectonic: Muttoni's taller, tighter, more elegantly attenuated version of a similar facade demonstrates the distance of the London sheet from such an evidently 18th-century interpretation.

That the design might come from the world of Inigo Jones is less easy to dismiss. Jones's longest residence in the Veneto dates from a mere thirty years after Palladio's death; and his early sojourn very probably brings us back to within only a little more than fifteen years after the master's demise. A drawing produced by a Palladian son or nephew who had got a bit rusty might, just possibly, look quite a lot like this. I think it is perhaps wisest to ask, cautiously, for the more careful campaigns of technical investigation that are suggested in the Introduction, before trying to pronounce a verdict. By then, too, we may know more about the dates of the Devonshire "old master" drawings stamps, one of which appears on this sheet. Such a longer view should help us analyze more clearly the drawing's evident relation to Palladio's Palazzo Capra (*QL* II:iii:21), and allow us a better perspective from which to judge the period of its production.

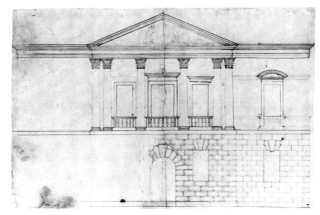

Figure 91

218

Bibliography

Ackerman, James S.: "Palladio's Lost Portico Project for San Petronio in Bologna," *Essays in the History of Architecture presented to Rudolf Wittkower,* London, 1967, pp. 110–115(II).

Ackerman, James S.: *Palladio's Villas,* Locust Valley, New York, 1967.

Ackerman, James S.: *The Architect and Society—Palladio,* Harmondsworth, etc., 1966 (first edition), 1977 (second edition).

Agnoletti, Carlo: *Treviso e le sue pieve* (2 volumes), Treviso, 1897–98.

Allsopp, Bruce, editor: *Inigo Jones on Palladio* (2 volumes), Newcastle-upon-Tyne, 1970.

Arts Council of Great Britain: *Andrea Palladio 1508–1580; the portico and the farmyard:* catalogue by Howard Burns, in collaboration with Lynda Fairbairn and Bruce Boucher, London, 1975.

Ashby, Thomas: "Sixteenth-century drawings of Roman buildings attributed to Andreas Coner," *Papers of the British School at Rome* 2 (1904), pp. 1–96, plus 165 plates of facsimile.

ASV: Archivio di Stato di Venezia; Avogaria de Comun, *Nascite* [Births], *Necrologii* [Deaths], *Segretarie alle voci* [Nominations in the Great Council]; all in Venice, State Archive.

Auden, W. H., and Elizabeth Mayer, translators: *J. W. Goethe, Italian Journey (1786–1788),* London, 1962.

Azzi Visentini, Margherita: *Il palladianesimo in America e l'architettura della villa,* Milan, 1976.

Barbaro, Daniele: *I dieci libri dell' architettura di M. Vitruvio,* Venice, 1556.

Barbieri, Franco: "Francesco Zamberlan architetto de 'La Rotonda'," in *La rotonda di Rovigo,* Venice, 1967, pp. 37–72.

Barbieri, Franco: "I disegni di Francesco Muttoni a Chatsworth," *Arte Lombarda* 55/57 (1980), pp. 219–235.

Barbieri, Franco: "Il Palazzo Chiericati," in *Il Museo Civico di Vicenza* (first volume), Vicenza, 1962, pp. 9–62.

Barbieri, Franco: "Il Teatro Olimpico," *Bollettino del CISA* 16 (1974), pp. 309–322.

Barbieri, Franco: *La Basilica palladiana* [*Corpus Palladianum,* III], Vicenza and University Park, 1968 (Italian edition), 1970 (English edition).

Barbieri, Franco: " 'Le chiese e i ponti di Andrea Palladio' di Giangiorgio Zorzi," *Bollettino del CISA* 8 (1966), pp. 337–355.

Barbieri, Franco: "Palladio come stimolo nell'architettura neoclassica," *Bollettino del CISA* 13 (1971), pp. 43–54.

Barbieri, Franco: "Palladio in villa negli anni quaranta," *Arte Veneta* 24 (1970), pp. 63–80.

Barbieri, Franco: " 'Palladios Lehrgebäude' di Erik Forssman," *Bollettino del CISA* 6 (1964), pp. 323–333.

Bartsch, Adam von: *Le peintre graveur,* Vienna, 1802–21 (first edition); Leipzig 1854–76; Würzburg, 1920–22; etc.

Bassi, Elena: *Palazzi di Venezia; Admiranda Urbis Venetae,* Venice, 1976.

Basso, don Umberto: *Cronaca di Maser,* Montebelluna, 1968.

Basso, don Umberto: *La villa e il tempietto dei Barbaro a Maser di Andrea Palladio,* Montebelluna, 1976.

Benetti, Aldo: *Borgoricco e la via Cornara in età romana,* Verona, 1974.

Berger, Ursel: "Die Villa Thiene in Quinto," *Arte Veneta* 31 (1977), pp. 80–94.

Berger, Ursel: *Palladios Frühwerk* [*Dissertationen zur Kunstgeschichte,* 5], Cologne/Vienna, 1978.

Bertotti-Scamozzi, Ottavio: *Le fabbriche e i disegni di Andrea Palladio* (4 volumes), Vicenza, 1776–83 (first edition), 1796 (second edition).

Bieganski, Piotr: "La struttura architettonica di alcune ville di Palladio," *Bollettino del CISA* 10 (1968), pp. 15–30.

Botter, Mario: *La Villa Giustinian di Roncade* [*Piccole monografie delle ville venete,* I], Treviso, 1955.

Boëthius, Axel, and J. B. Ward-Perkins: *Etruscan and Roman Architecture* [*The Pelican History of Art*], Harmondsworth, etc., 1970.

Briquet, Charles Moïse: *Les filigranes; dictionnaire historique des marques du papier* (4 volumes), Geneva, 1907 (first edition), Leipzig, 1923 (second edition), Amsterdam, 1968 (jubilee edition, edited by Allan Stevenson).

Brizio, Anna Maria: "Il barocco come continuità del Palladio; il barocco come contestazione al Palladio," *Bollettino del CISA* 12 (1970), pp. 63–73.

Bruschi, Arnaldo: *Bramante,* London, 1973, 1977.

Bruschi, Arnaldo: *Bramante architetto,* Bari, 1969.

Burger, Fritz: "Der Kodex Burlington," *Repertorium für Kunstwissenschaft* 32:4 (1909), pp. 327–330 (II).

Burger, Fritz: *Die Villen des Andrea Palladio,* Leipzig, 1909.

Burlington; Richard Boyle, fourth Earl of Burlington and Cork: *Fabbriche antiche disegnate da Andrea Palladio vicentino,* London, 1730.

Burns, Howard: "I disegni del Palladio," *Bollettino del CISA* 15 (1973), pp. 169–191.

Burns, Howard: "I disegni del Palladio," *Bollettino del CISA* 21 (1979), in press: citations from typescript (18 pp.).

Canova, Antonio, and Giovanni Mantese: *I castelli medioevali del vicentino,* Vicenza, 1979.

Cevese, Renato: *I modelli della mostra del Palladio,* Milan/Venice, 1976.

Cevese, Renato: " 'Le opere pubbliche e i palazzi privati di Andrea Palladio' di Gian Giorgio Zorzi," *Bollettino del CISA* 6 (1964), pp. 334–359.

Cevese, Renato: "Replica alla lettera di Gian Giorgio Zorzi," *Bollettino del CISA* 7 (1965), pp. 340–347.

Cevese, Renato: *Ville della provincia di Vicenza* [*Ville italiane; Veneto,* 2] (2 volumes), Milan, 1971 (first edition), 1980 (second edition).

Chastel, André: "Palladio et l'escalier," *Bollettino del CISA* 7 (1965), pp. 11–22.

Cicogna, Emmanuele Antonio: *Delle inscrizioni veneziane,* Venice, 1824–53 (first edition); Bologna, 1969 (reprint).

Colvin, Howard Montagu: *A biographical dictionary of English architects, 1600–1840,* London, 1978 (second edition).

Crema, Luigi: "L'architettura romana nel Veneto e nell'Istria," *Bollettino del CISA* 8 (1966), pp. 167–178.

Dalla Pozza, Antonio M.: "Palladiana III, IV, V, VI," *Odeo Olimpico* [*Memorie dell'Accademia Olimpica di Vicenza*], 2 (1942), pp. 123–260.

Dalla Pozza, Antonio M.: "Palladiana VII," *Odeo Olimpico* 3 (1943), pp. 231–259.

Dalla Pozza, Antonio M.: "Palladiana VIII, IX," *Odeo Olimpico* 4 (1943–63), pp. 99–131.

Dalla Pozza, Antonio M.: "Palladiana X, XI, XII," *Odeo Olimpico* 5 (1964–65), pp. 203–238.

Dalla Pozza, Antonio M.: *Palladio,* Vicenza, 1943 (II).

D'Ossat, Guglielmo De Angelis: "Bramante e Palladio," *Bollettino del CISA* 8 (1966), pp. 34–42.

D'Ossat, Guglielmo De Angelis: "Palladio e l'antichità," *Bollettino del CISA* 15 (1973), pp. 29–42.

Fancelli, Paolo: *Palladio e Praeneste; archeologia, modelli, progettazione* [*Studi di storia dell'arte,* 2], Rome, 1974.

Fenyö, Iván: *Disegni veneti del Museo di Budapest,* Venice, 1965.

Fenyö, Iván: *North Italian Drawings from the Collection of the Budapest Museum of Fine Arts,* New York, 1966.

Fiocco, Giuseppe: "L'esposizione dei disegni di Andrea Palladio a Vicenza," *Arte Veneta* 3 (1949), pp. 184–187.

Förster, Otto Helmut: *Bramante,* Munich/Vienna, 1956.

Forssman, Erik: *Il palazzo Da Porto Festa di Vicenza* [*Corpus Palladianum,* VIII], Vicenza and University Park, 1973 (Italian edition), 1979 (English edition).

Forssman, Erik: "La concezione del palazzo palladiano," *Bollettino del CISA* 14 (1972), pp. 83–104.

Forssman, Erik: "Palladio e Vitruvio," *Bollettino del CISA* 4 (1962), pp. 31–42.

Forssman, Erik: *Palladios Lehrgebäude,* Stockholm, etc., 1965.

Forster, Kurt W., and Richard J. Tuttle: "Giulio Romano e le prime opere vicentine del Palladio," *Bollettino del CISA* 15 (1973), pp. 107–119.

Foscari, Antonio: "Per Palladio; note sul Redentore a S. Vidal e sulle Zitelle," *Antichità Viva* 14:3 (1975), pp. 44–56.

Frommel, Christoph Luitpold: "Palladio e la chiesa di S. Pietro a Roma," *Bollettino del CISA* 19 (1977), pp. 107–124.

Frommel, Christoph Luitpold: *Der Römische Palastbau der Hochrenaissance* (3 volumes), Tübingen, 1973.

Gallo, Alberto: *La prima rappresentazione al Teatro Olimpico,* Milan, 1973.

Gallo, Rodolfo: "Andrea Palladio e Venezia," *Rivista di Venezia* I (1955), pp. 23–48.

Gardani, Dante Luigi: *La chiesa di S. Maria della Presentazione (delle Zitelle) in Venezia,* Venice, 1961.

Gazzola, Piero: *Michele Sanmicheli; catalogo della mostra,* Venice, 1960.

Geymüller, Heinrich Adolf von: *Raffaello Sanzio studiato come architetto,* Milan, 1884.

Gioseffi, Decio: "Il disegno come fase progettuale dell'attività palladiana," *Bollettino del CISA* 14 (1972), pp. 45–62.

Gioseffi, Decio: "Palladio e l'antico," *Bollettino del CISA* 15 (1973), pp. 43–66.

Gombrich, [Sir] Ernst: "Zum Werke Giulio Romanos," *Jahrbuch der Kunsthistorischen Sammlungen in Wien* 8 (1934) pp. 79 *ff.,* and 9 (1935), pp. 121 *ff.*

Grant Keith, William: "A theatre project by Inigo Jones," *Burlington Magazine* 31 (1917), pp. 61–70, 105–111.

Grant Keith, William: "Inigo Jones as a collector," *Journal of the Royal Institute of British Architects* 33 (19 December 1925), pp. 94–108.

Gualdo, Paolo: "Vita di Andrea Palladio" (edited by Giovanni Montenari, in the second edition of his work,) *Del Teatro Olimpico di Andrea Palladio in Vicenza,* Padua, 1749.

Gualdo, Paolo: "Vita di Andrea Palladio" (edited by Gian Giorgio Zorzi), *Saggi e Memorie di Storia dell'Arte* 2 (1958–59), pp. 91–104.

Harris, John: *Inigo Jones and John Webb* [*Catalogue of the Drawings Collection of the Royal Institute of British Architects,* VII], Farnborough, 1972.

Harris, John: "Three unrecorded Palladio designs from Inigo Jones's collection," *Burlington Magazine* 113 (1971), pp. 34–37.

Harris, John, and A. A. Tait: *Catalogue of the Drawings by Inigo Jones, John Webb and Isaac de Caus at Worcester College Oxford,* Oxford, 1979.

Heawood, Edward: *Watermarks, mainly of the 17th and 18th centuries* [*Collection of Works and Documents Illustrating the History of Paper,* I], Hilversum, 1950 (with corrected reprint, 1957).

Heydenreich, Ludwig H. and Wolfgang Lotz: *Architecture in Italy, 1400 to 1600* [*The Pelican History of Art*] (translated by Mary Hottinger), Harmondsworth, etc., 1974.

Heydenreich, Ludwig H.: "La villa: genesi e sviluppi fino al Palladio," *Bollettino del CISA* 11 (1969), pp. 11–22.

Hofer, Paul: *Palladios Erstling; die Villa Godi Valmarana in Lonedo bei Vicenza* [*Palladio-Studien,* 1], Basel, etc., 1969.

Hofmann, Theobald: *Raffael in seiner Bedeutung als Architekt,* Zittau, 1900–11 (first edition), Leipzig 1914 (second edition).

Howard, Deborah: "Four centuries of literature on Palladio," *Journal of the Society of Architectural Historians* 39:3 (1980), pp. 224–241.

Howard, Deborah: *Jacopo Sansovino; Architecture and Patronage in Renaissance Venice,* New Haven, etc. 1975.

Huse, Norbert: "Palladio und die Villa Barbaro in Maser," *Arte Veneta* 28 (1974), pp. 106–122.

Isermeyer, Christian Adolf: " 'Die Sakrale Architektur Palladios' di Wladimir Timofiewitsch," *Bollettino del CISA* 11 (1969), pp. 472–476.

Isermeyer, Christian Adolf: "La concezione degli edifici sacri palladiani," *Bollettino del CISA* 14 (1972), pp. 105–135.

Krautheimer, Richard: *Early Christian and Byzantine Architecture* [*The Pelican History of Art*], Harmondsworth, etc., 1965.

Krencker, Daniel M., and E. Krüger, H. Lehmann, and H. Wachtler: *Die Trierer Kaiserthermen*, Augsburg, 1929.

Kubelik, Martin: *Die Villa im Veneto* (2 volumes), Munich, 1977.

Kurz, Otto: "Giorgio Vasari's Libro de' Disegni," *Old Master Drawings* 12 (June/December 1937), pp. 1–15, 32–44.

Lewis, Carolyn Kolb: *The Villa Giustinian at Roncade* [*Outstanding Dissertations in the Fine Arts*], New York, etc., 1977.

Lewis, Douglas: "A new book of drawings by Francesco Muttoni," *Arte Veneta* 30 (1976), pp. 132–146.

Lewis, Douglas: "Disegni autografi del Palladio non pubblicati; le piante per Caldogno e Maser, 1548–1549," *Bollettino del CISA* 15 (1973), pp. 369–379.

Lewis, Douglas: "Il significato della decorazione plastica e pittorica a Maser," *Bollettino del CISA* 22 (1980), in press.

Lewis, Douglas: "Introduction to the Patronage of Palladio's Works in Domestic Architecture," text of lecture for 16 May 1972 meeting of the Washington Renaissance Colloquium, the Folger Institute of Renaissance and 18th Century Studies, Washington, D.C.; typescript in library of the National Gallery of Art.

Lewis, Douglas: "Palladio, Andrea," *The Encyclopedia Americana,* volume 21 (1979), pp. 207–208.

Lewis, Douglas: "Sansovino and Venetian Architecture," *Burlington Magazine* 121 (1979), pp. 38–41 (II).

Lewis, Douglas: "Un disegno autografo del Sanmicheli e la notizia del committente del Sansovino per S. Francesco della Vigna," *Bollettino dei Musei Civici Veneziani* 17: 3/4 (1972), pp. 7–36(II).

Lotto, Lorenzo: *Lettere inedite* (edited by Luigi Chiodi) [*Monumenta Bergomensia,* VIII], Bergamo, 1962.

Lotz, Wolfgang: "Il tempietto di Maser," *Bollettino del CISA* 19 (1977), pp. 125–134.

Lotz, Wolfgang: "Osservazioni intorno ai disegni palladiani," *Bollettino del CISA* 4 (1962), pp. 61–68.

Lotz, Wolfgang: "Palladio e Sansovino," *Bollettino del CISA* 9 (1967), pp. 13–23.

Loukomski, Georges K.: *Andrea Palladio* [*Les Grands Architectes*], Paris, 1927.

Loukomski, Giorgio K.: "Disegni dello Scamozzi a Londra," *Palladio* 4:2 (1940), pp. 65–74.

Loukomski, Giorgio K.: "I disegni del Palladio a Londra," *Palladio* 2 (1938), pp. 15–26.

Lugt, Frits: *Les marques de collections de dessins & d'estampes,* Amsterdam, 1921; *Supplément,* The Hague, 1956.

Magagnato, Licisco: "La concezione del teatro palladiano," *Bollettino del CISA* 14 (1972), pp. 137–147.

Magagnato, Licisco: "The genesis of the Teatro Olimpico," *Journal of the Warburg and Courtauld Institutes* 14:3–4 (1951), pp. 209–220.

Magrini, Antonio: *Il palazzo del Museo Civico in Vicenza,* Vicenza, 1855.

Magrini, Antonio: *Memorie intorno la vita e le opere di Andrea Palladio,* Padua, 1845.

Mantese, Giovanni: "La famiglia Thiene e la riforma protestante a Vicenza," *Odeo Olimpico* 8 (1969–70), pp. 81–186.

Marconi, Pirro: *Verona romana,* Bergamo, 1937.

Mariacher, Giovanni: *Il Sansovino,* Verona, 1962.

Marzari, Giacomo: *La historia di Vicenza,* Venice, 1591 (first edition); Vicenza, 1604 (second edition).

Moschini, Giannantonio: *Guida per la città di Venezia* (2 volumes), Venice, 1815 [S. Francesco memorandum vol. I., pp. 56–61, n. 3].

Mošin, Vladimir: *Anchor Watermarks* [*Collection of Works and Documents Illustrating the History of Paper,* XIII], Amsterdam, 1973.

Mostra del Palladio; Vicenza, Basilica palladiana (exhibition directed, and catalogue edited by Renato Cevese), Milan/Venice, 1973.

Morsolin, Bernardo: *Giangiorgio Trissino; o monografia di un* [*gentilhuomo*] *letterato nel secolo XVI,* Vicenza, 1878 (first edition); Florence, 1894 (second edition with expanded title).

[Muttoni, Francesco:] *Architettura di Andrea Palladio vicentino . . . accresciuta di moltissime fabbriche inedite,* Venice, 1740–48 (volumes 1–8); continued (volume 9) by Giorgio Fossati, Venice, 1760; reissued (volumes 1–8) by L'Editrice "La Roccia," Trento, 1973.

Nachod, Hans: "A recently discovered architectural sketchbook," *Rare Books; Notes on the History of Old Books and Manuscripts* 8:1 (1955), pp. 1–11.

Nichols, Frederick Doveton: *Palladio in America* (exhibition catalogue, with Walter Muir Whitehill), Milan, 1976, pp. 99–128.

Oggetti sacri del secolo XVI nella diocesi di Vicenza (exhibition directed, and catalogue edited by Tullio Motterle), Vicenza, 1980.

Olivato, Loredana: "Due codici veneti cinquecenteschi d'architettura," *Arte Veneta* 32 (1978), pp. 153–160.

Palladio, Andrea: *L'antichità di Roma / Descritione de le chiese,* Rome/Venice, 1554.

Palladio, Andrea: *I Commentari di C. Giulio Cesare,* Venice, 1574/1575.

Palladio, Andrea: *I Quattro Libri dell'Architettura,* Venice, 1570 (first edition), etc.

Pane, Roberto: *Andrea Palladio,* Turin 1948 (first edition), 1961 (second edition).

Panofsky, Erwin: "The first page of Giorgio Vasari's 'Libro' " *Städel-Jahrbuch* 6 (1930), pp. 25–72 (in German); *Meaning in the Visual Arts,* Garden City, 1955, pp. 169–235 (English translation).

Paris, Expositions de "Palladio, sa vie, son oeuvre," et de "L'influence de Palladio en France": André Chastel, *et al.,* "Spécial Palladio," *Les Monuments Historique de la France* 2 (1975), pp. 34–41 ("Les dessins de Palladio").

Paschini, Pio: *Domenico Grimani cardinale di S. Marco,* Rome, 1943.

Paschini, Pio: *Il cardinale Marino Grimani ed i prelati della sua famiglia,* Rome, 1960.

Pée, Herbert: *Die Palastbauten des Andrea Palladio,* Würzburg, 1939 (first edition), 1941 (second edition).

Penrose, Francis C.: "Address," *Journal of the Royal Institute of British Architects* (3rd series), 2:6 (17 January 1895), pp. 166–167 ("Drawings by the Old Masters in Architecture").

Phelps, Albert C.: "A leaf from the note-book of Antonio San Gallo the Younger," *Art Bulletin* 16:1 (1934), pp. 19–22.

Popham, Arthur Ewart: *Catalogue of the drawings of Parmigianino* (3 volumes), New Haven, 1971.

Puppi, Lionello: "Alle origini del neopalladianesimo; il contributo comasco di Francesco Muttoni," *Arte Lombarda* 55/57 (1980), pp. 236–242.

Puppi, Lionello: *Andrea Palladio; l'opera completa,* Milan, 1973 (first edition, in 2 volumes); 1975 (second edition, in one volume); New York, 1975 (English translation by Pearl Sanders).

Puppi, Lionello: "Gli spettacoli all'Olimpico di Vicenza dal 1585 all'inizio del '600," *Studi sul teatro veneto fra Rinascimento ed età barocca*, Florence, 1971 (II).

Puppi, Lionello: *Il Teatro Olimpico*, Vicenza, 1963.

Puppi, Lionello: "La 'Morosina' d'Altavilla," *Rivista dell'Istituto Nazionale di Archeologia e Storia dell'Arte* 19–20 (1972–73), pp. 296 ff.

Puppi, Lionello: *La Villa Badoer di Fratta Polesine* [*Corpus Palladianum*, VII], Vicenza and University Park, 1972 (Italian edition), 1975 (English edition).

Puppi, Lionello: "Prospettive dell'Olimpico," *Arte Lombarda* 11:1 (1966), pp. 26–32.

Puppi, Lionello: *Scrittori vicentini d'architettura del secolo XVI*, Vicenza, 1973 (II).

Puppi, Lionello: "The villa garden of the Veneto from the 15th to the 18th century," *The Italian Garden* [*Dumbarton Oaks Colloquium on the History of Landscape Architecture*, I], Washington, 1972, pp. 81–114.

Puppi, Lionello: "Un letterato in villa: Giangiorgio Trissino a Cricoli," *Arte Veneta* 25 (1971), pp. 72–91.

Rearick, W. Roger: "Battista Franco and the Grimani Chapel," *Saggi e Memorie di Storia dell'Arte* 2 (1958–59), pp. 105–139.

Rigoni, Erice: *L'arte rinascimentale in Padova; studi e documenti*, Padua, 1970.

Robertson, D. S.: *A Handbook of Greek and Roman Architecture*, Cambridge, 1929 (first edition), 1959 (second edition, reprinted).

Rosci, Marco: *Il tratato di architettura di Sebastiano Serlio* (publishing—in a second volume—the Munich manuscript of Book VI), Milan, 1966.

Rosenfeld, Myra Nan: see Sebastiano Serlio, edition of Columbia University manuscript of Book VI, 1978.

Sansovino, Francesco: *Venetia città nobilissima et singolare; con le aggiunte di Giustiniano Martinioni*, Venice, 1663 (third edition of 1581 original); Venice, 1968 (amplified reissue, edited by Lino Moretti; see Stringa).

Scamozzi, Vincenzo: *L'idea dell' architettura universale*, Venice, 1615.

Schulz, Juergen: "Cristoforo Sorte and the Ducal Palace of Venice," *Mitteilungen des Kunsthistorischen Institutes in Florenz* 10:3 (1962), pp. 193–208.

Schulz, Juergen: *Venetian Painted Ceilings of the Renaissance*, Berkeley, etc. 1968.

Schweikhart, Gunther: *Le antichità di Verona di Giovanni Caroto*, Verona, 1977.

Semenzato, Camillo: *La Rotonda* [*Corpus Palladianum*, I], Vicenza and University Park, 1968 (Italian edition), 1968 (English edition).

Serlio, Sebastiano: *Il settimo libro d'architettura nel qual si tratta di molti accidenti*, [Book VII], Frankfort, 1575.

Serlio, Sebastiano: *Il terzo libro nel quale si figurano e descrivano le antiquita di Roma* [*Book III*], Venice, 1540.

Serlio, Sebastiano: *On Domestic Architecture* (reduced facsimile of Columbia University manuscript of Book VI, edited by Myra Nan Rosenfeld), New York, 1968.

Serlio, Sebastiano: *Regole generale di architetura* [Book IV], Venice, 1537.

Serlio, Sebastiano: *Tutte l'opere d'architettura . . . et un'indice . . . da M. Gio. Domenico Scamozzi*, Venice, 1584 (first complete compendium edition); Bologna, 1978 (reprint, edited by Fulvio Irace).

Sgarbi, Vittorio: *Palladio e la Maniera; i pittori vicentini del Cinquecento e i collaboratori del Palladio, 1530–1630*, Venice, 1980.

Smithsonian Institution: *Italian Architectural Drawings Lent by the Royal Institute of British Architects, London* (catalogue by John Harris), Washington, 1966.

Spielmann, Heinz: *Andrea Palladio und die Antike*, Munich, etc., 1966.

Stella, Aldo: *Dall'anabattismo al socinianesimo nel Cinquecento veneto; ricerche storiche*, Padua, 1967.

Strandberg, Runar: "Il tempio dei Dioscuri a Napoli," *Palladio* 11 (1961), pp. 31–40.

Stringa, Giovanni: *Venetia città nobilissima et singolare . . . da M. Francesco Sansovino; et hora . . . ampliata*, Venice, 1604 (second edition of original of 1581; see Sansovino).

Summerson, [Sir] John: *The Architect and Society—Inigo Jones*, Harmondsworth, etc., 1966.

Tafuri, Manfredo: *Jacopo Sansovino e l'architettura del '500 a Venezia*, Padua, 1969.

Tafuri, Manfredo: "Sansovino 'versus' Palladio," *Bollettino del CISA* 15 (1973), pp. 149–165.

Tafuri, Manfredo: "Teatro e città nell'architettura palladiana," *Bollettino del CISA* 10 (1968), pp. 65–78.

Tait, A. A.: "Inigo Jones—architectural historian," *Burlington Magazine* 112 (1970), pp. 234–235.

Tassini, Giuseppe: *Curiosità veneziane*, Venice, 1863 (first edition); Venice, 1970 (seventh edition, revised by Lino Moretti).

Temanza, Tommaso: *Vite dei più celebri architetti e scultori veneziani*, Venice, 1778 (first edition); Milan, 1966 (amplified re-issue, edited by Liliana Grassi).

Tietze, Hans, and Erica Tietze-Conrat: *The drawings of the Venetian painters in the 15th and 16th centuries*, New York, 1944 (first edition), 1970 (reprint, edited by David Rosand).

Timofiewitsch, Wladimir: "Ein unbekannter Kirchenentwurf Palladios," *Arte Veneta* 13–14 (1959–60), pp. 79–87.

Timofiewitsch, Wladimir: *Girolamo Campagna; Studien zur venezianischen Plastik um das Jahr 1600*, Munich, 1972.

Timofiewitsch, Wladimir: *La chiesa del Redentore* [*Corpus Palladianum*, III], Vicenza and University Park, 1969 (Italian edition), 1971 (English edition).

Tomasini, Francesco: *Theatro genealogico delle famiglie nobili di Vicenza*, Venice, 1677 (first edition); Bologna, 1976 (reissue).

Traversari, Gustavo: *L'arco dei Sergi*, Padua, 1971.

Vallery-Radot, Jean: *Le recueil de plans d'édifices de la compagnie de Jésus conservé à la Bibliothèque Nationale de Paris*, Rome, 1960.

Valmarana, Mario: "Il palladianesimo negli Stati Uniti d'America," *Palladio; la sua eredità nel mondo*, Venice, 1980, pp. 261–281.

Vasari, Giorgio: *Le vite de' più eccellenti pittori, scultori ed architettori*, Florence, 1568 (edited by Gaetano Milanesi, Florence, 1881: vol. VII, pp. 527–531, for Palladio).

Venditti, Aldo: *La Loggia del Capitaniato* [*Corpus Palladianum*, IV], Vicenza and University Park, 1969 (Italian edition), 1971 (English edition).

Venezia e la peste, 1348–1797 (exhibitions directed by Franco Miracco, catalogue edited by Orazio Pugliese), Venice, 1979 (first edition), 1980 (second edition).

Venice, Palazzo Ducale: *Architettura e Utopia nella Venezia del Cinquecento* (exhibition directed, and catalogue edited by Lionello Puppi), Milan, 1980.

Venturi, Adolfo: *Storia dell'arte italiana;* volume XI, *Architettura del Cinquecento* (parte III), Milan, 1940 (first edition); Nendeln, 1967 (reprint).

Verona, Palazzo della Gran Guardia: *Palladio e Verona* (exhibition directed by Licisco Magagnato, catalogue edited by Paola Marini), Venice, 1980.

Vicenza, Palazzo Leoni-Montenari: *Andrea Palladio; il testo, l'immagine, la città* (exhibition directed by Guglielmo Cappelletti and Lionello Puppi; catalogue edited by the latter), Vicenza, 1980.

Vitruvius: *The Ten Books on Architecture* (translated by Morris Hicky Morgan), Cambridge 1914 (first edition); New York, 1960 (reissue).

von Blanckenhagen, Peter: *Flavische Architektur,* Berlin, 1940.

Weinreb, Ben: *Catalogue no. 2,* London, 1963.

Whinney, Margaret: "An unknown design for a villa by Inigo Jones," *The Country Seat; Studies . . . presented to Sir John Summerson,* London, 1970, pp. 33–35.

Wilinski, Stanislaw: "Studi palladiani," *Odeo Olimpico* 11–12 (1974–76), pp. 67–152.

Wilkinson, Catherine: "The Escorial and the invention of the imperial staircase," *Art Bulletin* 57 (1975), pp. 65–90.

Wittkower, Rudolf: *Architectural Principles in the Age of Humanism,* London, 1949 (first edition), London, 1952 (second edition), London, 1962 (third, revised edition), New York, 1971 (third edition, corrected and adjusted).

Wittkower, Rudolf: *Gothic vs. Classic; Architectural Projects in Seventeenth-Century Italy,* New York, 1974 (II).

Wittkower, Rudolf: *Palladio and English Palladianism,* London, 1974.

Wittkower, Rudolf: "Pseudo-Palladian Elements in English Neo-classicism," *England and the Mediterranean Tradition,* London, 1945 (first edition); *Palladio and English Palladianism,* London, 1974, pp. 153–174 (second edition).

Wittkower, Rudolf: "Sviluppo stilistico dell' architettura palladiana," *Bollettino del CISA* I (1959), pp. 61–65.

Wittkower, Rudolf: "The 'Menicantonio' Sketchbook in the Paul Mellon Collection," *Idea and Image,* London, 1978, pp. 90–107.

Wolters, Wolfgang: "La decorazione plastica delle volte e dei soffitti a Venezia e nel Veneto nel secolo XVI," *Bollettino del CISA* 10 (1968), pp. 268–278 (II).

Wolters, Wolfgang: *Plastische Deckendekorationen des Cinquecento in Venedig und im Veneto,* Berlin, 1968.

Wolters, Wolfgang: "Zu einem wenig bekannten Entwurf des Cristofero Sorte," *Mitteilungen des Kunsthistorischen Institutes in Florenz* 10:2 (1961), pp. 137–144.

Zorzi, Gian Giorgio: "Alcuni disegni di Gio. Maria Falconetto," *Palladio* (new series) 5: 1–2 (1955), pp. 29–55.

Zorzi, Gian Giorgio: "Altri disegni di vari artisti riguardanti monumenti antichi," *Palladio* (new series) 6: 1–2 (1956), pp. 54–67.

Zorzi, Gian Giorgio: "Antichi monumenti veronesi nei disegni palladiani di Londra," *Palladio* (new series), 1:1 (1951), pp. 1–20.

Zorzi, Gian Giorgio: *Contributo alla storia dell' arte vicentina nei secoli XV e XVI;* Venice, 1916 (*parte prima*); 1925 (*parte seconda: Architetti, ingegneri, muratori, scultori, tagliapietre*); 1937 (*parte terza: Il preclassicismo e i prepalladiani*).

Zorzi, Gian Giorgio: "Disegni palladiani delle antichità," *Saggi e Memorie di Storia dell'Arte* I (1957), pp. 63–79.

Zorzi, Gian Giorgio: *I disegni delle antichità di Andrea Palladio,* Venice, 1959.

Zorzi, Gian Giorgio: "Il mausoleo del Divo Romolo nei disegni e nelle invenzioni di Andrea Palladio," *Quaderni dell'Istituto di Storia dell'Architettura* 6–8 (1961), pp. 179–184.

Zorzi, Gian Giorgio: "Il tempio della Fortuna Primigenia di Palestrina nei disegni di Andrea Palladio," *Palladio* (new series), 1:4 (1951), pp. 145–152.

Zorzi, Gian Giorgio: "La 'Villa di Mecenate' e il tempio di Ercole Vincitore a Tivoli nei disegni di Andrea Palladio," *Palladio* (new series) 7:4 (1957), pp. 149–171.

Zorzi, Gian Giorgio: *Le chiese e i ponti di Andrea Palladio,* Venice, 1967.

Zorzi, Gian Giorgio: *Le opere pubbliche e i palazzi privati di Andrea Palladio,* Venice, 1965.

Zorzi, Gian Giorgio: "Le prospettive del Teatro Olimpico," *Arte Lombarda* 10:2 (1965), pp. 70–97 (II).

Zorzi, Gian Giorgio: *Le ville e i teatri di Andrea Palladio,* Venice, 1969.

Zorzi, Gian Giorgio: "Progetti giovanili di Andrea Palladio per palazzi e case in Venezia e in terraferma," *Palladio* (new series) 4:3 (1954), pp. 105–121 (II).

Zorzi, Gian Giorgio: "Progetti giovanili di Andrea Palladio per villini e case di campagna," *Palladio* (new series) 4: 1–2 (1954), pp. 59–76.

Zorzi, Gian Giorgio: "Quattro monumenti sepolcrali disegnati da Andrea Palladio," *Arte Veneta* 17 (1963), pp. 96–105.

Zorzi, Gian Giorgio: "Rivendicazione di alcuni scritti giovanili di Vincenzo Scamozzi", *Atti dell'Istituto veneto di scienze, lettere, e arti* 113:2 (1954–55), pp. 169 *ff.*

Zorzi, Gian Giorgio: "Una restituzione palladiana—il palazzo Civena di Vicenza," *Arte Veneta* 3 (1949), pp. 99–103.

PHOTO CREDITS